# The Architecture of Cognition

John R. Anderson

LAWRENCE ERLBAUM ASSOCIATES, PUBLISHERS
Mahwah, New Jersey

Originally published 1983.

Copyright © 1996 by Lawrence Erlbaum Associates, Inc.
All rights reserved. No part of this book may be reproduced
in any form, by photostat, microform, retrieval system, or any
other means, without the prior written permission of
the publisher.

Lawrence Erlbaum Associates, Inc., Publishers
10 Industrial Avenue
Mahwah, New Jersey  07430

**Library of Congress Cataloging-in-Publication Data**

Anderson, John Robert 1947-
  The architecture of cognition.
    p.   cm.
  Includes bibliographical references and index.
  ISBN 0-8058-2233-X (pbk. : alk. paper)
  1. Cognition--Data processing.  2. Human information
processing.  3. Digital computer simulation.  I. Title.
  BF311.A5894  1983       153          82-21385

Books published by Lawrence Erlbaum Associates are printed
on acid-free paper, and their bindings are chosen
for strength and durability.

Printed in the United States of America

10 9 8 7 6 5 4 3 2 1

To Russ and J.J.,
from whom I have learned much
about the evolution and development
of cognition

# Preface

In the mid 1960s, when I was an undergraduate, three of the active areas of research in psychology were learning theory, psycholinguistics, and cognitive psychology. At that time there was no coherent connection among the three, but the question of how language could be acquired and integrated with the rest of cognition seemed interesting. However, there was no obvious way to tackle the question because the field just did not have the relevant concepts. There were the options of pursuing a graduate career in learning theory, cognitive psychology, or psycholinguistics. I chose cognitive psychology and I believe I chose wisely (or luckily).

When I went to Stanford in 1968, Gordon Bower assigned me a hot issue of the time: to understand the categorical structure in free recall. As we analyzed free recall it became clear that we needed a complete model of the structure of human memory, with a particular focus on meaningful structure. Bower and I worked on this for a number of years, first developing the model FRAN (Anderson, 1972), then HAM (Anderson and Bower, 1973). Through this work we came to appreciate the essential role of computer simulation in developing complex models of cognition. HAM, the major product of that effort, was a complete model of the structures and processes of human memory, having as its central construct a propositional network representation. It successfully addressed a great deal of the memory literature, including a fair number of experiments on sentence memory that we performed explicitly to test it.

Critical to predicting a particular experimental phenomenon was deciding how to represent the experimental material in our system. Usually our intuitions about representation did lead to correct predictions, but that was not a very satisfactory basis for prediction. The memory system had to be understood as a component of a more general cognitive system. The reason for choosing a particular representation lay in the properties of the general system. For instance, choice of a representation for a sentence depended on the operation of a natural-language parser, which, unlike the facts represented in HAM, is a skill. There is a fundamental distinction between declarative knowledge, which refers to facts we know, and procedural knowledge, which refers to skills we know how to perform. HAM, a theory of the declarative system, was incomplete because the representation chosen in the declarative system depended on operations of components of the procedural system such as the parser.

The first step to developing a more complete theory was identifying an appropriate formalism to model procedural knowledge. My first effort was to use the augmented transition networks (ATNs), which had seemed so appropriate for natural-language processing. A theory of language acquisition was developed in that framework. However, ATNs proved to be at once too restrictive as computational formalisms and too powerful as models of human cognition. These difficulties led me to consider the production-system models Allen Newell had been promoting, which had some similarities to ATNs. I have to admit that at first, when I focused on surface features, production systems seemed unattractive. But as I dug deeper, I became more and more convinced that they contained key insights into the nature of human procedural knowledge.

The ACT system, the product of my three years at Michigan, 1973–1976, and described in Anderson (1976), was a synthesis of the HAM memory system and production-system architecture. In this system a production system was used for the first time as an interpreter of a propositional network. ACT also borrowed the spreading activation concept from other researchers, such as Collins and Quillian. Its production system operated on a working memory defined by the active portion of its long-term memory network. In a computer simulation version of ACT, called ACTE, it was possible to "program" production sets that modeled various tasks. Much of my 1976 book describes such production sets that modeled various small tasks.

However, although ACTE answered the question of where propositional representations came from—they came from the actions of productions—now the natural question was, where do productions come from? This led to the issue of a learning theory for production systems. Paul Kline, Charles Beasley, and

I then developed ACTF, the first production system to contain an extensive theory of production acquisition. A viable version of ACTF was running in 1977.

After moving to Carnegie-Mellon in 1978, I spent the next four years trying to "tune" the ACT system and make it address language acquisition. My attempts produced some major reorganizations in the theory, including changes in the spreading activation mechanisms, a theory of production pattern matching, augmentations to the architecture to handle goals, and additions to the production-learning mechanisms, all of which are described in this book. Paul Kline and David Neves collaborated in the early part of this effort. In the later years I was guided by the A.C.T. research group, which has included Frank Boyle, Gary Bradshaw, Renee Elio, Rob Farrell, Bill Jones, Matt Lewis, Peter Pirolli, Ron Sauers, Miriam Schustack, and Jeff Shrager. I was able to finally apply ACT to language acquisition. The new version of ACT is called ACT* (to be read ACT-star). The theory has evolved from the original concern with categorical free recall to address an ever-widening set of questions. Each theory along the way raised questions that the next one answered. Finally, the widening circles have expanded to encompass my original interest in learning theory, psycholinguistics, and cognitive psychology. While it is undoubtedly not the final theory, it achieves a goal set fifteen years earlier.

ACT* is a theory of *cognitive architecture*—that is, a theory of the basic principles of operation built into the cognitive system. ACT stands for Adaptive Control of Thought. It is worth reviewing what this title means and why it is apt. First, this theory concerns higher-level cognition or thought. A major presupposition in this book is that higher-level cognition constitutes a unitary human system. A central issue in higher-level cognition is control—what gives thought its direction, and what controls the transition from thought to thought. As will become apparent, production systems are directed at this central issue. A major concern for me has been to understand the principles behind the control of thought in a way that exposes the adaptive function of these principles. Ultimately, understanding adaptive function brings us to issues of human evolution, which are largely excluded from this book (but see Anderson, 1982c).

It needs to be emphasized that production systems address the issue of control of cognition in a precise way that is relatively unusual in cognitive psychology. Other types of theoretical analyses may produce precise models of specific tasks, but how the system sets itself to do a particular task in a particular way is left to intuition. In a production system the choice of what to do next is made in the choice of what production to execute next. Central to this choice are the conflict resolution strategies (see Chapter 4). Thus production systems have finally succeeded in banishing the homunculus from psychology.

In writing this book I have been helped by a great many people who provided comments on drafts. Gary Bradshaw, Bill Chase, Renee Elio, Ira Fischler, Susan Fiske, Jim Greeno, Keith Holyoak, Bill Jones, Paul Kline, Steve Kosslyn, Matt Lewis, Brian MacWhinney, Michael McCloskey, Allen Newell, Jane Perlmutter, Rolf Pfeifer, Steven Pinker, Peter Pirolli, Zenon Pylyshyn, Roger Ratcliff, Lance Rips, Paul Rosenbloom, Miriam Schustack, and Jeff Shrager have commented on one or more of these chapters. Robert Frederking, Jay McClelland, Ed Smith, and two anonymous reviewers have read the manuscript in its entirety. Eric Wanner has been an exceptional editor—reading and commenting on the entire book. Lynne Reder has gone through this book with me, word by word and idea by idea, exposing weaknesses and providing a number of the ideas developed here. The A.C.T. research group, as well as my "Thinking" classes, have gone over these ideas many times with me.

Many people have worked hard to get the programs and experiments running. My graduate students, Gary Bradshaw, Renee Elio, Bill Jones, Matt Lewis, Peter Pirolli, and Miriam Schustack, have been valuable collaborators. Takashi Iwasawa and Gordon Pamm wrote countless experiment-running programs and data analyses; Barbara Riehle and Rane Winslow greatly assisted in testing subjects; and Takashi Iwasawa and Frank Boyle did much work on the geometry project. Two outstanding undergraduates, Rob Farrell and Ron Sauers, have been responsible for the GRAPES simulation of the acquisition of LISP programming skills. Among her many other duties, Rane Winslow had primary responsibility for preparing and coordinating this manuscript, and I am deeply grateful to her for all of her resourcefulness and hard work. Monica Wallace was responsible for the last months of shepherding the book into publication.

Finally, I want to thank those government agencies who have done so much to support my research. Research grants from NIE and NIMH were critical in the development of ACTE and ACTF, and a current grant from the Information Sciences branch of NSF (IST-80-15357) has supported the geometry project. My simulation work has taken place on the SUMEX facility at Stanford, supported by grant P41RR-00785-08 from NIH; on Carnegie-Mellon's computer facilities, supported by contract F33615-81-K-1539 from ARPA; and on our Psychology VAX, purchased through grant BNS-80-13051 from NSF. My language acquisition research is supported by a contract from ONR. I would like to express special appreciation to the Personnel and Training Research Program of ONR (Marshall Farr, Henry Halff) and to the Memory and Cognition Program at NSF (Joe Young). These two groups have been long-standing supporters of the ACT research and have provided the stable funding that a project of this scale needs; the current sources of support are N00014-81-C-0335 from ONR and BNS-82-08189 from NSF. Marshall Farr, Henry Halff, and Joe Young have also provided valuable input to the research.

# Contents

# 1 | Production Systems and ACT

## A Unitary Theory of Mind and Production Systems

THEORISTS ARE STRONGLY influenced by their various preconceptions. The most deeply rooted preconception guiding my theorizing is a belief in the unity of human cognition, that is, that all the higher cognitive processes, such as memory, language, problem solving, imagery, deduction, and induction, are different manifestations of the same underlying system. This is not to deny that there are many powerful, special-purpose "peripheral" systems for processing perceptual information and coordinating motor performance. However, behind these lies a common cognitive system for higher-level processing. Moreover, the essence of what it is to be human lies in the principles of this core, higher-level system. We may not differ from the many mammalian species to which we are related in our peripheral perceptual and motor processes, but we assuredly do differ in our complex thought patterns and our intelligence.

The view that the mind is unitary is certainly not universally held; it may not even be a majority opinion. To quote the most noted proponent of the alternative view:

We may usefully think of the language faculty, the number faculty, and others as "mental organs," analogous to the heart or the visual system or the system of motor coordination and planning. There appears to be no clear demarcation line between physical organs, perceptual and motor systems, and cognitive faculties in the respects in question. In short, there seems little reason to insist that the brain is unique in the biological world, in that it is unstructured and undifferentiated, developing on the basis of uniform principles of growth or learning—say those of some

1

learning theory, or of some yet-to-be conceived general-purpose learning strategy—that are common to all domains. (Chomsky, 1980, p. 3)

This faculty approach holds that distinct cognitive principles underlie the operation of distinct cognitive functions. The unitary approach holds that all higher-level cognitive functions can be explained by one set of principles. In some ways the faculty approach seems just plain common sense. Many cognitive theories, extending back at least to the phrenology of Gall (see Boring, 1950, for a discussion of this and the more "reputable" faculty theories) have held this view. Its truth might almost seem a tautology: clearly we perform different intellectual functions, so it might seem that we must have different faculties for these functions. The faculty proposals that have been advanced have always gotten into difficulties in their specifics, but it never has been clear whether there is anything fundamentally wrong with the faculty approach.

The early proposals for unitary systems (for example, stimulus-response, or S-R, theories) were also shown to be basically inadequate. However, the unitary theory found an important metaphor in the modern general-purpose computer and, perhaps more significantly, in symbolic programming languages, which showed how a single set of principles could span a broad range of computational tasks. It also became clear that the set of computational functions was unlimited, meaning that general processing principles were essential to span broad ranges of tasks. It made no sense to create a special system for each conceivable function.

A number of candidates for a general system have been offered, including general problem solvers (Fikes and Nilsson, 1971; Newell and Simon, 1972; Sacerdoti, 1977), general inference systems (Green and Raphael, 1969; McDermott and Doyle, 1980; Robinson, 1967), and general schema systems (Bobrow and Winograd, 1977; Minsky, 1975; Rumelhart and Ortony, 1976; Schank and Abelson, 1977). My research has been predicated on the hypothesis that production systems provide the right kind of general computational architecture for achieving a unitary mental system. The particular line of production system theories I have developed all go under the name ACT. This book will describe a special ACT instantiation called ACT* (to be read ACT-star). As will become clear, ACT* is not just a random member of the ACT series. It is the product I have been working toward for the past seven years. In ACT* the same core system if given one set of experiences develops a linguistic facility, if given another set of experiences develops a geometry facility, and if given another set of experiences develops a programming facility. Therefore ACT* is very much a unitary theory of mind.

### ARGUMENTS FOR A UNITARY THEORY OF MIND

One thing that distinguishes us from other creatures is our ability to acquire complex skills. All distinctively human activities—such as mathematics, language, chess, computer programming, sculpture—are acquired skills. There may be a significant innate component to their successful acquisition, but with the possible exception of language it is totally implausible to suggest that we have evolved special faculties or "organs" for mathematics, chess, computer programming, or sculpture. People become expert at activities for which there was no possibility of anticipation in our evolutionary history, and the essence of the human genius is just this plasticity. It is unnecessary to propose special organs for special abilities when we can fashion articulate abilities where there is no possibility of a prior organ. If all these abilities are fashioned from the same initial system (which hardly need be a tabula rasa), then in an important sense the adult human mind is a unitary construction.

Language is an important special case that might be the exception to the rule. It is not totally implausible to propose that it has had a long evolutionary history in which various language-specific adaptations have occurred. However, it seems more plausible that the language-specific adaptations are few and minor, that the language faculty is really the whole cognitive system. In our evolution we may have developed or enhanced certain features to facilitate language, but once developed, these features were not confined to language and are now used in nonlinguistic activities. Thus the mind is a general pool of basic structures and processes, which has been added to under evolutionary pressure to facilitate language. The additions have been used in skills, for example, computer programming, that were not anticipated in the original evolutionary developments. Part of the evidence for this view are the remarkable communalities between language and other skills, which will be discussed later in this book.

There is a tendency to regard the existence of "language areas" and other localizations of function in the brain as strong evidence for faculties. However, there is nothing necessary about this inference, as shown by a computer analogy: two programs can occupy different areas of computer memory, much as two different cognitive abilities might lie in two separate regions of the brain. However, the two programs may have identical principles. For instance, I can have one ACT simulation doing language and another doing geometry. Thus, there need be no connection between distinct physical location and distinct cognitive principles. The real issue concerns the uniqueness of the structure and processes underlying cognitive functions, not their physical location.[1]

Another major reason for not believing in an organ for language or for other cognitive activities is that the boundaries between these organs cannot be drawn a priori. It is pretty clear where the activity of the lung leaves off and that of the circulatory system takes over, but this cannot really be said for cognitive faculties. The lung and the heart are both involved in an activity such as running, but it is possible to identify their distinctive contributions. It has been proposed that there is a language faculty, a number faculty, a deduction faculty, and a problem-solving faculty, but if there are such faculties, their activities are terribly intertwined in a task like computer programming. When we look at an expert programmer creating a program, we cannot separate the contributions of the various faculties. Indeed, if we applied any reasonable criterion for individuating faculties, we would have to conclude that computer programming was a separate faculty. This is because some of the core principles for this skill organization, such as strategies for creating recursive programs, apply across the entire range of programming behaviors and are seldom if ever evoked elsewhere. Since it is nonsense to suggest a programming faculty, we should be more skeptical of other proposed faculties.

An expert's execution of a skill is special in that a strong task-specific cognitive organization has developed through extensive experience. This is not the case with the novice, but analysis of novice behavior gives no more comfort to the faculty approach. The remarkable feature of novices is that they are able to put together so many different facets of knowledge to solve a task. A novice programmer brings together recent facts learned about programming and the programming language, facts from mathematics, real-world experiences as analogies, general problem-solving skills, deductive strategies, linguistic analyses —all to solve the problem. The novice's attempts at synthesizing this knowledge can be terribly off target, but this is only for lack of the right knowledge, not because of a fundamental incompatibility of the knowledge categories. What is remarkable is the ease with which novices switch among categories and the sheer impossibility of identifying where one faculty might begin and another end. Compartmentalization is similarly impossible in the case of language use (see Schank and Birnbaum, in press).

In summary then, there are three lines of evidence for the unitary approach. One is the short evolutionary history of many of the higher human intellectual functions, such as those concerned with mathematical problem solving. The second is that humans display great plasticity in acquiring functions for which there was no possibility of evolutionary anticipation. The third is that the various cognitive activities have many features in common.

I would like to head off two possible misinterpretations of my position. First, the unitary position is not incompatible with the fact that there are distinct systems for vision, audition, walking, and so on. My claim is only that higher-level cognition involves a unitary system. Of course, the exact boundaries of higher-level cognition are a little uncertain, but its contents are not trivial; language, mathematics, reasoning, memory, and problem solving should certainly be included. Second, the unitary position should not be confused with the belief that the human mind is simple and can be explained by just one or two principles. An appropriate analogy would be to a programming language like INTERLISP (Teitleman, 1976), which is far from simple and which supports a great variety of data structures and functions. However, it is *general-purpose*, that is, one can use the same data structures and processes in programs for language and for problem solving. Individual programs can be created that do language and problem solving as special cases. In analogy to INTERLISP, I claim that a single set of principles underlies all of cognition and that there are no principled differences or separations of faculties. It is in this sense that the theory is unitary.

## Production Systems: History and Status

Production system theories have gradually increased in prominence in psychology over the past decade. Their basic claim is that underlying human cognition is a set of condition-action pairs called productions. The condition specifies some data patterns, and if elements matching these patterns are in working memory, then the production can apply. The action specifies what to do in that state. The basic action is to add new data elements to working memory. Informally stated, a typical production rule might be:

IF person 1 is the father of person 2
and person 2 is the father of person 3
THEN person 1 is the grandfather of person 3.

This production would apply if *Fred is the father of Bill* and *Bill is the father of Tom* were active in working memory. It would make the inference *Fred is the grandfather of Tom* and deposit this fact in working memory.

Production systems can be traced back to the proposals of Post (1943), but Post production systems bear little resemblance to current production systems except that the current condition-action pairs can be viewed as derived from the rewrite rules of Post's formalism. Production system theories are similar to stimulus-response theories in many ways but with important differences that remove the computational inadequacies of S-R theories. Most notably, the production is very much like the stimulus-response bond (Anderson, 1976; Newell and Simon, 1972). One might conceive of production systems as "cognitive" S-R theories, despite the contradiction in the connotations of these terms.

Modern production systems began with Newell's work at Carnegie-Mellon in the early sixties and Waterman's later dissertation work (1970) at Stanford. Right from the start production systems had an ambiguous status, being in part programming languages for computer science and in part psychological theories. A series of publications in the early seventies (Hunt and Poltrack, 1974; Newell, 1972, 1973; Newell and Simon, 1972) brought production systems to the awareness of psychologists.

The concept of a production system is vague, and it is hard to determine where its boundaries end and where other computer science formalisms or psychological theories begin. In computer science a more general category, sometimes called *pattern-directed systems* (see Waterman and Hayes-Roth, 1978), includes deduction systems like MYCIN (Shortliffe, 1976) and other types of architectures, such as schema systems and linguistic rewrite systems. As in production systems, control is in response to the appearance of data, but behavior does not necessarily involve adding elements to working memory. For instance, a major category of action in MYCIN was to update the probabilities of various medical diagnoses.

Production systems are not strictly a Carnegie-Mellon phenomenon, although the concentration there is undeniable (a recent report of a subset of the CMU research is contained in Klahr, Langley, and Neches, 1983). Besides my own work, which started elsewhere, the ideas have been used by Bower (1977), Brown and Van Lehn (1980), Collins (1977), Greeno (1976), Jeffries, Turner, Polson, and Atwood (1981), Kieras and Bovair (1981), Lewis (1978), and Ohlsson (1977). Although the idea is gradually gaining popularity, it is by no means a dominant construct in cognitive psychology, partly because of the technical difficulty both in creating production systems and in understanding someone else's production system. This is the price paid for the precision with which production systems model information processing; no other psychological theories have been as precise and detailed in their modeling of cognitive tasks.[2] As with any emerging scientific formalism, there is a lot to learn about the human engineering of the formalism and about communicating to the scientific community the essential results of work with that formalism. Over the past few years there has been progress in this direction.

### An Example of a Production System

An example of a production system that performs a specific task will be useful as a concrete referent for interpreting more abstract points that will be made later.

#### TRACING THE BEHAVIOR

An example set of productions for performing addition is given in Table 1.1. This example assumes that the subject has memorized the addition table. The conditions of these productions are given by the IF part and their actions by the THEN part.[3] Figure 1.1 illustrates the flow of control among the productions in that set. Application of these productions is controlled by the setting of goals; Figure 1.1 basically shows which productions respond to which goals and which productions set which goals. It is easiest to understand such a production system by tracing its application to an example problem such as the following addition problem:

614
438
683

Production P1, the first to apply, would set as a subgoal to iterate through the columns. Production P2 then changes the sub-

**Table 1.1**   *A production system for performing addition*

P1      IF the goal is to do an addition problem
        THEN the subgoal is to iterate through the columns of the
             problem.

P2      IF the goal is to iterate through the columns of an addition
             problem
        and the rightmost column has not been processed
        THEN the subgoal is to iterate through the rows of that right-
             most column
        and set the running total to 0.

P3      IF the goal is to iterate through the columns of an addition
             problem
        and a column has just been processed
        and another column is to the left of this column
        THEN the subgoal is to iterate through the rows of this column
             to the left
        and set the running total to the carry.

P4      IF the goal is to iterate through the columns of an addition
             problem
        and the last column has been processed
        and there is a carry
        THEN write out the carry
        and POP the goal.

P5      IF the goal is to iterate through the columns of an addition
             problem
        and the last column has been processed
        and there is no carry
        THEN POP the goal.

P6      IF the goal is to iterate through the rows of a column
        and the top row has not been processed
        THEN the subgoal is to add the digit of the top row to the
             running total.

P7      IF the goal is to iterate through the rows of a column
        and a row has just been processed
        and another row is below it
        THEN the subgoal is to add the digit of the lower row to the
             running total.

P8      IF the goal is to iterate through the rows of a column
        and the last row has been processed
        and the running total is a digit
        THEN write the digit
        and delete the carry
        and mark the column as processed
        and POP the goal.

Table 1.1   *(continued)*

---

P9       IF the goal is to iterate through the rows of a column
          and the last row has been processed
          and the running total is of the form "string digit"
       THEN write the digit
          and set carry to the string
          and mark the column as processed
          and POP the goal.

P10      IF the goal is to add a digit to another digit
          and a sum is the sum of the two digits
       THEN the result is the sum
          and mark the digit as processed
          and POP the goal.

P11      IF the goal is to add a digit to a number
          and the number is of the form "string digit"
          and a sum is the sum of the two digits
          and the sum is less than 10
       THEN the result is "string sum"
          and mark the digit as processed
          and POP the goal.

P12      IF the goal is to add a digit to a number
          and the number is of the form "string digit"
          and a sum is the sum of the two digits
          and the sum is of the form "1 digit*"
          and another number sum* is the sum of 1 plus string
       THEN the result is "sum* digit*"
          and mark the digit as processed
          and POP the goal.

---

goal to adding the digits of the rightmost column and sets the running total to 0. Then production P6 sets the new subgoal to adding the top digit of the row (4) to the running total. In terms of Figure 1.1, this sequence of three productions has moved the system down from the top goal of doing the problem to the bottom goal of performing a basic addition operation. The system has four goals stacked, with attention focused on the bottom goal.

At this point production P10 applies, which calculates 4 as the new value of the running total. In doing this it retrieves from the addition table the fact that $4 + 0 = 4$. Production P10 also pops the goal of adding the digit to the running total. Popping a goal means shifting attention from the current goal to the one above it in the hierarchy. In this situation, attention will return to iterating through the rows of the column. Then P7 ap-

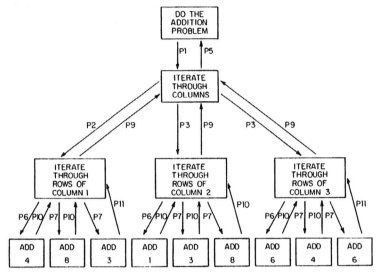

**Figure 1.1**   *A representation of the flow of control in Table 1.1 among the various goals. The boxes correspond to goal states and the arrows to productions that can change these states. The goal at the origin of the production corresponds to the goal that elicits the production, and the goal at the terminus of the arrow corresponds to the goal that is set after the application of the production. Control starts with the top goal.*

plies, which sets the new subgoal of adding 8 to the running total. P10 applies again to change the running total to 12, then P7 applies to create the subgoal of adding 3 to the running total, then P11 calculates the new running total as 15. At this point the system is back to the goal of iterating through the rows and has processed the bottom row of the column. Then production P9 applies, which writes out the 5 in 15, sets the carry to the 1, and pops back to the goal of iterating through the columns. At this point the production system has processed one column of the problem. I will not continue to trace the application of this production set to the problem. Note that productions P2–P5 form a subroutine for iterating through the columns, productions P6–P9 an embedded subroutine for processing a column, and productions P10–P12 form an embedded subroutine for adding a digit to the running total.

SIGNIFICANT FEATURES

Productions form the system's *procedural* component. For a production to apply, the clauses specified in its condition must be matched against the information active in working memory. This information is part of the system's *declarative* component. Not everything the system knows is in working memory; information must be retrieved from long-term memory (the system's main declarative component) and deposited in working memory. The example above required the retrieval of addition facts like 4 + 8 = 12.

Both the condition and the action of each production consist of a set of clauses (basically each line of a production corresponds to a clause). The set of clauses in the condition specifies a total pattern that must be matched for the production to apply. That is, there must be a separate data clause in working memory matching each condition clause. The action clauses specify separate actions to be taken. Most actions add to the contents of working memory, but some cause external behavior. The actions are executed in sequence.

Productions contain variable slots, which can take on different values in different situations. The use of these variables is often implicit, as in Table 1.1, but in some cases it is important to acknowledge the variables that are being assumed. As an illustration, if production P9 from Table 1.1 were written to expose its variable structure, it would have the form shown below, in which the terms prefixed by LV are local variables.[4]

    IF the goal is to iterate through the rows of LVcolumn
        and LVrow is the last row of LVcolumn
        and LVrow has been processed
        and the running total is of the form "LVstring LVdigit"
    THEN write LVdigit
        and set carry to LVstring
        and mark LVcolumn as processed
        and POP the goal.

Local variables can be reassigned to new values each time the production applies. For instance, the terms LVcolumn, LVrow, LVstring, and LVdigit will match whatever elements lead to a complete match of the condition to working memory. Suppose, for instance, that the following elements were in working memory:

The goal is to iterate through the rows of column 2
Row 3 is the last row of column 2
Row 3 has been processed
Running total is of the form "2 4"

The four clauses in the production's condition would match this working-memory information, and the following variable bindings would be created:

LVcolumn = column 2
LVrow = row 3
LVstring = 2
LVdigit = 4

Local variables assume values within a production to match the condition and execute the action. After the production applies, variables are free to be rebound in another application.

PSYCHOLOGICAL COMMENT ON THE EXAMPLE

This example was meant mainly to illustrate the computational character of production systems. However, it should be emphasized that a set of conditional, goal-factored rules such as these can provide a fairly accurate model of arithmetic behavior (Brown and Van Lehn, 1980). That is, such rules can be considered the *units* of the skill. Brown and Van Lehn discuss how various errors or "bugs" in children's subtraction can be explained by the deletion of individual rules.

## Frameworks, Theories, and Models

To understand how ACT relates to other ideas in the field, it is useful to make distinctions among the terms *framework, theory*, and *model*. A framework is a general pool of constructs for understanding a domain, but it is not tightly enough organized to constitute a predictive theory. However, it is possible to sample from this pool, tie the constructs together with additional details, and come up with a predictive theory. One might regard "information-processing psychology" as such a framework, although it is an especially loose one. Production systems are a more specific framework within the information-processing framework. There is a general ACT framework that is a further specialization, within which specific ACT theories have been created.

One cannot evaluate a framework according to the standard verificational logic associated with scientific theories. That is, the production system framework makes no unique empirical prediction that distinguishes it from, say, a schema system framework. Rather, one judges a framework in terms of the success, or fruitfulness, of the theories it generates. If the theories lead to many accurate accounts of interesting phenomena, the framework is regarded as fruitful.

A theory is a precise deductive system that is more general than a model. Specific production systems such as Newell's (1973) system and the 1976 ACT (Anderson, 1976) system, are theories. A model is the application of a theory to a specific phenomenon, for instance, performance of a mental arithmetic task. Thus, the production set in Table 1.1 constitutes a modest model.

Production systems are particularly general in that they claim to be *computationally universal*—capable of modeling all cognitive activity.[5] One consequence of computational universality is that a production system can accomplish the same task in a number of different ways.[6] This is a point in favor of production system theory, because we know that people are capable of performing a single task in various ways. If the task is complex, different people will do it differently, and the same person will even behave differently on different occasions. However, because of their plasticity, production systems do not make unique predictions about how a task will be performed. Instead, the predictions are largely implicational: if a subject performs a task in such-and-such a way, then such-and-such behavior will be observed.

Although subjects can perform tasks in many ways, one or a few methods are usually preferred. It is reasonable to ask why a person performs a task in the way he or she does. To answer this question one needs a learning theory to specify that given a particular prior experience, the person will develop a certain production set that in a certain context will lead him to behave in a certain way, which will yield particular phenomena. Chapters 6 and 7 are concerned with such a learning theory for ACT.

### The Neoclassical Production System

As noted earlier, the general category of production systems is a framework for theories. By now there are many theories to instantiate that framework. Newell's theories and ideas constitute a major subframework. Two major efforts have been made to establish his ideas as running computer systems: PSG (Newell and McDermott, 1975) and, more recently, OPS (Forgy and McDermott, 1977; Rychener and Newell, 1978). However, neither implementation is identical to Newell's basic ideas. His most recent statement about production system architecture (Newell, 1980) is different in many ways from either. Also, these implementations have features that are not relevant to the psychological status of the theory. Lenat and Harris (1978) have called the Newell system "neoclassical" architecture, and I will continue with that term. Other production systems, including

ACT, can all be seen as baroque variations on the neoclassical architecture in that they attempt to *add* to it to remedy perceived defects.

The neoclassical system places a heavy emphasis on simplicity. It is an attempt to make do with the bare minimum: production rules, a single uniform working memory, simple rules of conflict resolution, and not much else. The motivation for simplicity derives in part from the standard scientific desire for parsimony, but it also derives from the desire to facilitate the development of psychological mechanisms for production learning, which must be capable of producing the full space of productions that are used. If that space is simply structured, it is thought to be easier to define learning mechanisms capable of producing the required productions.

The neoclassical system emphasizes modular productions, in which each production is independent of the others and capable of being added, deleted, or separately modified. This means that production learning can proceed one production at a time without concern for interactions among the productions in a set.

## WORKING MEMORY AND PRODUCTION MEMORY

Working memory in the neoclassical system consists of a number of slots, each of which holds one clause or element. An element is a list or relational structure built out of relations and arguments; $(8 + 3 = 11)$ could be an element. Working memory, which can hold a limited number of elements, orders them according to recency. As new elements enter, old ones are pushed out. This conception shows the strong influence of the buffer model of Atkinson and Shiffrin (1968). The original limit on working memory was taken to be on the order of seven elements, reflecting the results of memory span tests. However, it often proves difficult to simulate behavior given this limit, and informal proposals have been made to increase it to twenty or more elements. In nonpsychological engineering applications of the OPS system (McDermott, 1981), the limit on working memory is simply eliminated.

Another feature of the neoclassical architecture is that the only long-term memory is production memory. There is not a separate declarative memory to encode facts like "George Washington was the first president of the United States" or the addition facts used in the simulation in Table 1.1. This is a major point where ACT differs from the neoclassical system. Newell would achieve the effect of a separate declarative memory by having one or more productions fire to deposit declarative information into working memory. For instance, a production responsible for retrieving this information might look like:

IF George Washington is mentioned
THEN note that he was the first president of the United States.

## PARALLELISM, SERIALITY, AND CONFLICT RESOLUTION

In the earlier neoclassical architecture (but not in Newell, 1980), multiple productions may have their conditions matched, but only a single production can apply at a time. A set of *conflict resolution principles* determines which production will apply. The original conflict resolution principle in PSG involved a simple ordering of productions, with the highest-ordered production applying. The ordering was simply specified by the person who wrote the productions with the goal of making them function correctly. The conflict resolution principles in the OPS system, which seem more plausible, involve a combination of refractoriness, recency, specificity, and production ordering. Refractoriness prevents a production from repeating if it matches the same data structure, thus preventing most accidental looping. Recency, probably the most powerful principle, selects the production that matches the data element most recently added to working memory. If two or more productions match the same most recent element, then a test is performed to see which has the second most recent element, and so on. Should a tie remain after all the elements have been matched, the specificity principle is applied. Essentially this principle says that the production with more condition elements is preferred. If there still are competing productions (and this is very seldom the case), then the conflict is resolved by an ordering of the productions.

Because only a single production can apply during any cycle of the system, it is difficult to model the parallelism in human cognition. We can be simultaneously perceiving objects, driving a car, generating a sentence, and processing a conversation. Underlying a process like language comprehension are a large number of parallel, interacting processes such as perception, syntactic parsing, semantic interpretation, and inference (Anderson, Kline, and Lewis, 1977). In addition to the behavioral evidence for parallelism, it is clear that our neural hardware supports it. It is argued (J. A. Anderson, 1973) that the brain is not at all a serial computer because individual operations take relatively long times (10 msec or more) to perform. However, the brain achieves computational power by doing many operations in parallel. The neoclassical theory depends heavily on parallel processing in its pattern matching, but parallelism must go beyond pattern matching.

Newell (1980) proposed a variant of production system architecture called HPSA77, which involved a major departure from the previous serial conception. He proposed it as an analysis of how the HARPY speech recognition system (Lowerre, 1976) could be achieved in a production system framework. HPSA77 is probably the best current instantiation of Newell's beliefs about production system architecture. He distinguished between productions that did not involve variables and those that did. He proposed that productions without variables could apply in parallel without restriction and that productions with variables had a limited serial restriction. His basic claim was that there was a variable-using mechanism that could handle the variables in only one instantiation of a production at a time. All limitations on parallelism came from this limitation; if the production involved no variables, there was no limitation; if it did involve variables, the production would have to "wait its turn" to use the variable mechanism.

Learning

Although many of its design decisions were motivated by learning considerations, the neoclassical system has not had a strong position on how learning proceeds. What has been implemented basically follows the ideas of Waterman (1974, 1975), who proposed that productions could deposit in working memory specifications as to the condition and action of a new production. Then a special BUILD operator would be called to create the production according to these specifications. The following production might cause new productions to be built to encode arithmetic facts:

IF the addition table reads "LVA + LVB = LVC"
THEN tag [the goal is to add LVA and LVB] as condition
    and tag [the answer is LVC] as action
    and BUILD.

If this production read "3 + 2 = 5" from the addition table, it would deposit in working memory the following clauses:

(CONDITION [the goal is to add 3 and 2])
(ACTION [the answer is 5]).

The BUILD operator finds all clauses in working memory tagged with CONDITION and all clauses tagged with ACTION. It makes the first set of clauses the condition and the second set the action. In the simple case above, the BUILD operator would produce:

IF the goal is to add 3 and 2
THEN the answer is 5.

Now whenever the goal is set to add 3 and 2, this production is there to execute and deposit the answer 5 in working memory.

The BUILD operator has enabled a lot of research on production learning, as has a similar *designation* process in ACT (see Anderson, Kline, and Beasley, 1980). However, production learning should be more automatic and less the result of deliberate strategy than it is with BUILD. As will be discussed at length in Chapter 6, deliberate production building has dangerous consequences and implies psychologically unrealistic skill acquisition capabilities. With the development of the chunking theory (Newell and Rosenbloom, 1981; Rosenbloom and Newell, 1983), the neoclassical architecture has the beginning of a theory of automatic production learning.

PERFORMANCE ASSUMPTIONS

In contrast to the uncertainty with respect to production learning, the theory of how existing production sets are executed is quite clear, and it addresses both errors and processing time. Errors in performance are due to failures of working memory; for instance, if a carry flag is lost from working memory, an error will be made in solving an addition problem. The time taken to execute a behavior is a linear function of the number of productions that apply and the number of actions in each production. Notably, processing time is not a function of the complexity of production conditions, even though most of the time involved in computer implementation is in matching the conditions. This reflects a belief in a very powerful parallel pattern-matching architecture.

## The ACT Production System

AN OVERVIEW

The system described in Anderson (1976) was ACTE. Subsequently we developed the ACTF system, which was described to some extent in Anderson, Kline, and Beasley (1977, 1980).

ACTF differed from ACTE in some details of the performance system, and principally in that it had a theory of production acquisition. Both systems were developed as simulation programs that embodied all the assumptions of the then-current theory. These simulations had the character of programming languages in which various ACT models could be implemented. The experience with ACTE and ACTF over the past several years has provided a basis for major reformulations of many aspects of the original theory to improve its psychological accuracy. Each reformulated aspect has been implemented and tested as a simulation program. Simulating the various aspects (in computer cycles) has become quite expensive as we have moved to assumptions that are less efficient in the computer simulation, although not necessarily in the operations of the human brain. Because of the computational cost, we have not created a general simulation that embodies all these assumptions at once.

One might think that by logical progression this system should be called ACTG. However, we call it ACT* to reflect the belief that it is the final major reformulation within the ACT framework. In previous ACT theories the performance subtheories were not fully integrated with the learning subtheories, but this gap is now closed. The assumptions of ACT* have also been revised to remedy the known difficulties of the earlier theories. The only part I feel is tentative concerns certain assumptions about the pattern matcher. These assumptions will be flagged when the pattern matcher is discussed in Chapter 4.

The previous paragraph implies that I expect ACT* to be wrong. This expectation is based not on any weaknesses in the theory, but on the nature of progress in science, which comes from formulating theories that account for a wide range of known phenomena and then finding out what is wrong with these theories. I regard a progression like the one from HAM (Anderson and Bower, 1973) through ACTE (Anderson, 1976) to ACT* as an example of reasonable scientific progress.

In my 1976 book on ACTE, I compared it to the HAM theory: "In completing the HAM book we had the feeling that we had more or less defined the HAM theory once and for all and that the major task ahead of us was to test its empirical consequences. I feel less certain that ACT has achieved its final shape as a theory. There remains much exploration to be done as to the potential of the theory and variations on it, largely because ACT is a theory of much broader generality than HAM and consequently has more potential to explore. In this book I have caught the ACT theory in a stage of development and presented that [p. 3]." I now believe that ACT has reached the stage of development that HAM did. Except for further work on the pattern matcher, my plan for future research is to try to apply this theory wide and far, to eventually gather enough evidence to permanently break the theory[7] and to develop a better one. In its present stage of maturity the theory can be broadly applied, and such broad application has a good chance of uncovering fundamental flaws.

## THE GENERAL ACT FRAMEWORK

Since ACT* is substantially revised over the earlier theories, one might wonder why I consider it as part of the ACT framework. To answer this question, we must look at the general framework of which all these theories are instantiations, as illustrated in Figure 1.2. An ACT production system consists of three memories: *working, declarative,* and *production.* Working memory contains the information that the system can currently access, consisting of information retrieved from long-term declarative memory as well as temporary structures deposited by encoding processes and the action of productions. Basically,

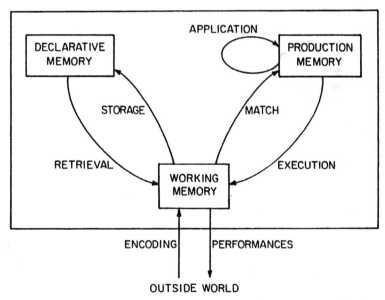

**Figure 1.2**    *A general framework for the ACT production system, identifying the major structural components and their interlinking processes.*

working memory refers to declarative knowledge, permanent or temporary, that is in an active state.

Most of the processes shown in Figure 1.2 involve working memory. *Encoding* processes deposit information about the outside world into working memory; *performance* processes convert commands in working memory into behavior. These two processes are not central to the ACT theory, unlike the other processes illustrated. The *storage* process can create permanent records in declarative memory of the contents of working memory and can increase the strength of existing records in declarative memory. The *retrieval* process retrieves information from declarative memory. In the *match* process, data in working memory are put into correspondence with the conditions of productions. The *execution* process deposits the actions of matched productions into working memory. The whole process of production matching followed by execution is referred to as *production application*. Note that the arrow called *application* cycles back into the production memory box, reflecting the fact that new productions are learned from studying the history of application of existing productions. Thus, in a basic sense, ACT's theory of procedural learning is one of learning by doing.

By itself, this general framework does not constitute a theory. A predictive theory must specify the following matters:

1. The representational properties of the knowledge structures that reside in working memory and their functional consequences.
2. The nature of the storage process.
3. The nature of the retrieval process.
4. The nature of production application, which breaks down to:
   a. The mechanism of pattern matching.
   b. The process that deposits the results of production actions in working memory.
   c. The learning mechanisms by which production application affects production memory.

ACT* differs from ACTE in its instantiation of each of these points except 2 and 4b, where the two theories basically agree.

### The Assumptions of ACT*

Table 1.2 lists the fourteen basic assumptions of ACT* (what is listed as assumption 7 is not an additional assumption), and

Table 1.3 gives, for comparison, the twelve assumptions of ACTE. These lists include both the general architectural assumptions on which the theories agree and the more specific assumptions on which they tend to disagree. Details still need to be worked out about how these assumptions apply in various situations, and this is done in part in later chapters. Here I will go through the assumptions one by one, explain the meaning of each, and indicate some of their motivations.

The first assumption, 0, is a technical one. In ACTE, theoretical development was close to its computer simulation implementation, in which we were forced to generate the behavior in discrete time steps. Therefore, all the theoretical development was done in terms of discrete time intervals, although it does seem implausible that the many parallel processes in human cognition should march forward lockstep in such intervals. This was made part of the ACTE system only as an approximation. ACT* is more removed from any simulation embodiment, and we were motivated to work toward a theory in which time was continuous. All the basic assumptions in ACT*, then, will be cast in terms of continuous time.

*The basic architectural assumption.* Fundamental to all ACT theories has been the distinction between declarative and procedural knowledge, and this is a major difference between ACT and the neoclassical system. ACT has a number of advantages over the neoclassical architecture because of the decoupling of declarative memory from procedural memory. First, in conflict resolution the process of retrieving data from declarative memory does not have to compete with the productions that perform the task. The example production discussed earlier illustrates how the neoclassical system uses productions to retrieve declarative information. Such memory-retrieval productions must compete with those that perform the task, and the competition is aggravated because conflict resolution in the neoclassical system tended to allow only a single production to apply. The problem would not be as severe if the amount of task-relevant information were small, but the results on associative priming (see Chapter 3) have shown us that the amount of information brought into working memory, at least temporarily, is very large. Thus far there has been no attempt in the neoclassical system to integrate this broad-band, diffuse associative retrieval with the productions required to perform a task. I doubt that it can be done in a way that is consistent with the temporal properties of human information processing.

Another difficulty in the neoclassical approach concerns the

**Table 1.2**  *Assumptions of ACT\**

0.  *Technical time assumption.* Time is continuous.
1.  *Basic architectural assumption.* There is a production system component that operates on the declarative knowledge representation.
2.  *Declarative representation.* Declarative knowledge can be decomposed into a tangled hierarchy of cognitive units. Each cognitive unit consists of a set of no more than five elements in a specified relation.
3.  *Activation of declarative memory.* At any time $t$, any cognitive unit or element $i$ has a nonnegative level of activation $a_i(t)$ associated with it.
4.  *Strength in declarative memory.* Each memory node $i$ (cognitive unit or element) has a strength $s_i$. The relative strength $r_{ij}$ of a link between node $i$ and node $j$ is defined as $s_j / \Sigma_K s_K$ where the summation is over nodes connected to $i$.
5.  *Spread of activation.* The change in activation at a node $i$ is described by the following differential equation

$$\frac{da_i(t)}{dt} = Bn_i(t) - p^* a_i(t)$$

    where $n_i(t)$ is the input to the node at time $t$ and is defined as

$$n_i(t) = c_i(t) + \sum_j r_{ji}\, a_j(t)$$

    where $r_{ji}$ is the relative strength of connection from node $j$ to $i$ and $c_i(t)$ is zero unless $i$ is a source node. If $i$ is a source node, $c_i(t)$ is a function of the strength of $i$.
6.  *Maintenance of activation.* Each element that enters into working memory is a source of activation for $\Delta t$ time units. There is a single goal element which can serve as a permanent source of activation.
7.  *Decay of activation.* ACT\*'s assumptions about decay are already implied in 5 and 6.
8.  *Structure of productions.* All productions are condition-action pairs. The condition specifies a conjunction of features that must be true of declarative memory. The action specifies a set of temporary structures to be added to memory.
9.  *Storage of temporary structures.* When a temporary cognitive unit is created and there is not a permanent copy of it, there is probability $p$ that a permanent copy will be created. If there is a permanent copy, its strength will be increased one unit.
10.  *Strength of productions.* Each production has a strength associated with it. That strength increases one unit with every successful application of the production.

Table 1.2 (continued)

11. Production selection. When the condition of a production achieves a satisfactory match to a set of declarative structures, the production is selected to apply. The pattern matcher is represented as a data-flow network of pattern tests. The rate at which these tests are performed is a function of level of activation of the pattern node that performs the tests. The level of activation of that node is a positive function of the strength of the node, the level of activation of the data structures being matched, and the degree of match to these structures. It is a negative function of the level of activation of competing patterns matching to the same data.

12. Goal-directed processing. Productions can specify a goal in their condition. If their goal specification matches the current goal, these productions are given special precedence over productions that do not.

13. Production compilation. New productions can be created from the trace of production application. Composition collapses a sequence of productions into a new one. Proceduralization builds new productions that eliminate the long-term memory retrievals of old ones.

14. Production tuning. New productions can be created by generalizing or discriminating the conditions of existing productions. Generalization works from pairs of more specific productions to create more general ones. Discrimination works from feedback about erroneous production application to create more specific productions that avoid the mistakes.

difference in the time taken to store declarative versus procedural information. A fact may be committed to memory after a few seconds of study. In contrast, it appears that new procedures can be created only after much practice (see Chapter 6). It is difficult to explain this huge discrepancy if both types of knowledge are encoded in the same way.

*Declarative representation.* Knowledge comes in chunks or *cognitive units* as they are called in ACT*. Cognitive units can be such things as propositions (for example, (hate, Bill, Fred)), strings (one, two, three), or spatial images (a triangle above a square). In each case a cognitive unit encodes a set of elements in a particular relationship. Chunks contain no more than five elements.[8] More complex structures can be created by hierarchical structures, such as a sentence's phrase structure or a proposition embedded in another. In such cases one cognitive unit appears as an element of another. These are familiar ideas in cognitive psychology, and stated at this level, there is much evidence for cognitive units (Anderson and Bower, 1973; Bad-

**Table 1.3** *Assumptions of ACTE*

0. *Technical time assumption.* Time is discrete.
1. *Basic architectural assumption.* There is a production system component which operates on the declarative knowledge representation.
2. *Declarative representation.* Declarative memory is represented as a propositional network of nodes and links.
3. *Activation of declarative memory.* At any time $t$, any memory node or memory link is either in the active state or not. If a link is active, the two nodes it connects are active, but if the two nodes are active the link need not be active.
4. *Strength in declarative memory.* Each link emanating from a node has a strength associated with it.
5. *Spread of activation.* Let $x$ be an active node and let $l$ be a non-active link from $x$ to $y$. Let $s$ be the strength of $l$ and let $S$ be the total strength of all nodes attached to $x$. There is a probability $1 - e^{-s/aS}$ that activation will spread from $x$ to activate $l$ and $y$ (if $y$ is not already active) in the next unit of time. The parameter $a$ is a time-scale parameter reflecting rate of spread of activation.
6. *Maintenance of activation.* A maximum of 10 nodes may be designated as part of the Active List (ALIST). Nodes in ALIST are not deactivated during dampening. The ALIST serves much the same function as a short-term memory. Items can be removed from ALIST only by displacement on a first-in, first-out basis.
7. *Decay of activation.* After $D$ units of time, activation will be dampened throughout the network. This means that all links and all nodes not on the ALIST are deactivated. Some such dampening process is required to prevent activation from growing continuously to the point where all of memory becomes active.
8. *Structure of productions.* All productions are condition-action pairs. The condition specifies a conjunction of features that must be true of declarative memory. The action specifies a set of temporary structures to be added to memory.
9. *Storage of temporary structures.* When a temporary link is created and there is not a permanent copy of it, there is probability $p$ that a permanent copy will be created. If there is a permanent copy, its strength will be increased by one unit.
10. *Strength of productions.* Each production has a strength associated with it. That strength increases one unit with every successful application of the production.
11. *Production selection.* The process by which productions are chosen is a two-stage affair. There is an initial selection phase. All the productions are tested against memory to see which might be applicable. This initial selection takes no time but also involves only a partial test of the productions. The productions which pass this screening are then tested to see if their conditions are totally satisfied in long-term memory. The speed at which the test is performed varies directly with $s$, the strength of the production, and with $n$, the number of productions simultaneously being tested. The probability of completing this test in any unit of time is $1 - e^{-s/bn}$.

deley, Thomson, and Buchanan, 1975; Broadbent, 1975; Mandler, 1967; Miller, 1956; Simon, 1974). The interconnections of these structures and elements can define a network structure like that in Figure 1.3, referred to as a *tangled hierarchy*, which is pieced together from cognitive units joining sets of elements. The resulting network can be relatively complex because of the various ways cognitive units can be combined. For instance, a unit can serve as an element in another unit, and the units can be joined when the same element occurs in several of them. It is useful to think of the knowledge structure so formed as a simple network in which all elements or units are *nodes* and the connections among them are *links*. This network structure will prove useful in understanding spreading activation, for instance.

The representational system in ACT* differs from ACTE in two ways. First, the cognitive units are not conceived as being built from more primitive links, which is significant with respect to activation and storage. In ACTE, individual links were activated and stored; in ACT* whole units have this property. Chapter 2 reviews the evidence for taking this larger-grained view of the contents of declarative memory.

Second, ACT* allows for multiple types of cognitive units, whereas in ACTE there was only the proposition. In Chapter 2 I argue for three types: temporal strings, spatial images, and ab-

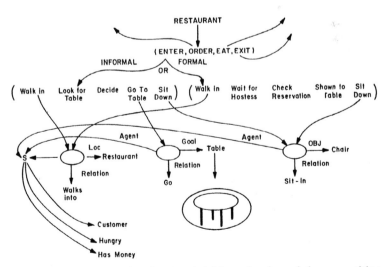

**Figure 1.3** *An example of a tangled hierarchy formed from cognitive units. See Chapter 2 for discussion of the conventions.*

stract propositions. These types differ in their representational assumptions and hence they are called *representational* types. More generally, I claim that the cognitive system has evolved many different representational types, each intended to facilitate a certain type of computation. An analogy with computer science is the existence of data types such as arrays and lists, which serve different functions.

In allowing multiple representational types, ACT* also contrasts with the neoclassical architecture, in which the only type is the list structure. Chapter 2 reviews the numerous arguments for the ACT* multitype system instead of a single-type system. For instance, an interesting argument is one of adaptive value. One wants to perform very different operations on different types of knowledge—for example, judgments of order, finding the direction to a goal, making an inference (note that these different operations are not confined to a particular faculty). These operations require the system to do distinct types of computation on different knowledge structures. It is interesting that in most efficient computer implementations distinct representations (data structures) and processes are used to handle order information, spatial information, and symbolic information. It has gotten to the point where distinct hardware (for example, LISP machines) is being created. Thus we see that computers have developed distinct data types in response to some of the same pressures to produce intelligent behavior that humans have felt during their evolution. This is evidence, of a sort, that humans would have evolved the capacity to process different data types.

*Activation.* All the ACT theories have an activation process that defines a working memory; productions can match only the knowledge that is currently active. A major difference between ACT* and ACTE is that activation is a continuously varying property of nodes in ACT*, whereas it is an all-or-none property in ACTE. A structure's level of activation controls the rate at which it is matched and its probability of successful matching. Thus if two structures might be matched to the same pattern, ACT* will prefer the more active one, which is important in situations such as resolving ambiguity of meaning. Consider the sentence, *The robber took the money from the bank.* There are two senses of *bank*, both of which would be active in ACT*, but the monetary institution sense would be more active because of activation spread from *"robber"* and *"money"* and thus this sense would be selected. Swinney (1979) documents evidence that both senses of the word are activated initially, then the

more active, contextually primed sense is selected. We were unable to model such selection in the all-or-none activation system of ACTE (Anderson, Kline, and Lewis, 1977) because both
senses would be active, and there would be no basis for selection.

Activation serves the function in ACT of an associative relevancy heuristic. That is, activation measures how closely associated a piece of information is to information currently used,
and it is a heuristic assumption that associated information is
most likely to be needed to guide processing. To simply have
two levels of activation (*on* and *off*) severely limits the value of
activation as a relevancy heuristic. The value is maximized
when activation can take on a continuous range of levels. There
are neurophysiological arguments for a continuously varying
level of activation. At some level of abstraction it is reasonable
to identify activation with rate of neural firing (although nodes
probably do not correspond to simple neurons; see Hinton and
Anderson, 1981). Since the rate of neural firing varies continuously, it follows that activation should do so also.

*Strength in declarative memory.* Each node in declarative memory has an associated strength, which is basically a function of
the frequency of use of that cognitive unit or element. The exact
factors that seem to be implicated in strength accumulation will
be discussed in Chapter 5. With the concept of node strength, it
is possible to define the relative strength of association between
nodes. If we are considering the connection from node $i$ to node
$j$, its relative strength is defined as $r_{ij} = s_j / \Sigma_k s_k$ where $s_j$ is the
strength of node $j$ and the summation is over all the nodes, in-
cluding $j$, that are connected to $i$. These relative strengths are
important in the spread of activation (Assumption 5), because
more activation flows down stronger paths.

In ACTE the strength of links was the primitive concept, and
there was no separate notion of node strength. Link strength
was treated separately because links were formed indepen-
dently of the propositions they defined. Thus different links
could have different strengths depending on how frequently
they were used. With the introduction of all-or-none storage of
cognitive units, this reason for an independent link strength
evaporates. On the other hand, there is evidence that the
strength of a node determines how much activation it can emit
(as reviewed in Chapter 5). Thus there has been a switch from
treating link strength as primitive in ACTE to treating node
strength as primitive in ACT*. However, the derived concept of
relative link strength serves the same function in ACT* as the

more primitive construct in ACTE; it determines how much activation goes down a path.

*Spread of activation.* The basic equation in Assumption 5 in Table 1.2 for spread of activation is continuous both in time and in quantity of activation. This is in keeping with the character of the ACT* theory. The momentary change in activation, according to the differential equation, is a function of the input to a node and a spontaneous rate of decay at that node. The parameter $B$ governs how rapidly activation accumulates from the input converging on the node, and the parameter $p^*$ governs how rapidly the activation of the node decays. The input to that node is a possible source activation plus the sum of activation from associated nodes weighted by relative strengths. Source nodes provide the "springs" from which activation flows throughout the network. Note that the amount of activation provided by a source node is a function of the strength of the node.

ACTE's spreading activation process was different from ACT*'s in two ways. First, as already mentioned, in ACTE activation was an all-or-none property of nodes rather than a continuous property. Second, in ACTE the time necessary for spread of activation determined the temporal properties of information-processing; in ACT* the important variable is time for pattern matching. As will be discussed in Chapter 3, the parameters we assume for the differential equation in Assumption 5 imply that activation spreads rapidly from the source nodes, and asymptotic levels of activation are rapidly achieved throughout the long-term structure. Chapter 3 also will review the current evidence indicating that activation effects can be rapidly felt throughout the network. What takes time is the processing of information, once activated. ACT* proposes that level of activation controls the rate of pattern matching required for production application.

*Maintenance of activation.* Activation is spread from various *source nodes*, each of which supports a particular pattern of activation over the declarative network. The total activation pattern is the sum of the patterns supported by the individual source nodes. When a node ceases to be a source, its pattern of activation quickly decays.

Nodes can become source nodes in a number of ways. They can be created by the perception of objects in the environment, and any elements deposited in working memory by a production's action become transient source nodes. These stay active for a Δ*t* period of time and then cease to be sources. If the source node is an environmental encoding of an object and the node turns off, a new source node can be recreated to replace it if the object is still in the focus of perception. Thus the external environment effectively serves as a means for maintaining activation in the network. However, if the source node is the product of an internal computation (that is, an action of a production), its activation will begin to decay as soon as it turns off. A special goal element permits one internal source that is not so transient, and this enables the system to maintain focus on a current goal.

This system of maintaining activation makes for a much more viable and psychologically realistic model of working memory than was implied by the slot model of the neoclassical architecture or the ALIST construct of ACTE. In the neoclassical architecture it proves difficult to hold the requisite information for many tasks in a small number of working memory slots.[9] The total working memory capacity in ACT*, although transient, is much larger. Also the ACT* analysis explains why memory span varies with the material and why this variation appears to be related to the rate of rehearsal (Baddeley, Thomson, and Buchanan, 1975). The neoclassical architecture, with its fixed number of slots, would have difficulty in explaining this variation. The neoclassical architecture would similarly be committed to the prediction that the capacity of working memory would not increase with familiarity in the domain. On the other hand, if we assumed that more familiar concepts could spread more activation, we would predict greater working memory capacity for concepts of greater familiarity. There is considerable controversy about the basis for increased performance with practice, but Chapter 5 presents the evidence that increased capacity of working memory is a component of the improvement.

*Decay of activation.* Unlike ACTE, ACT* does not require a separate dampening process to turn off activation in the network. The dampening process in ACTE was an awkward discrete simulation of loss of activation from the network. In ACT* the continuous equation in Assumption 5 and the analysis of source nodes in Assumption 6 imply a complete model of how activation disappears from the network. When a source node turns off, its pattern of activation rapidly decays from the network. Rapid decay is implied by the same differential equation that implies rapid asymptotic patterns of action.

*Structure of productions.* ACT* maintains the same basic assumptions as ACTE about production structure. In detail, ACT*'s productions are somewhat simplified, omitting such things as control nodes and global variables.

*Storage of temporary structures.* Temporary structures can enter working memory from one of two sources; the encoding process can place descriptions of the environment in working memory, and the action of productions can create structures to record the results of internal computations. If a temporary cognitive unit is created in working memory, there is a probability *p* that a copy of it will be created in declarative long-term memory. If a copy is created, it will have one unit strength. If a cognitive unit is created in working memory and a copy already exists in long-term memory, its long-term strength will increase by one unit.

ACTE's assumptions are identical to these except that in ACTE the storage processes were defined on individual associative links, with a large number of links making up a proposition. In ACT* the storage processes do not operate on single associative links; rather, they operate on whole cognitive units—string, image, and proposition units. As noted earlier, these units cannot have more than five elements, so there are limits to how much can be encoded in a single storage act.

*Strength of productions.* As in ACTE, productions in ACT* accrue strength with successful practice. Stronger productions have their conditions matched more rapidly.

*Production selection by pattern matching.* Pattern matching is the mechanism that decides which productions will apply. A fundamental claim of the production system architecture is that pattern matching underlies all varieties of cognition, providing its data-driven quality. While pattern matching is not restricted to perception, it is easiest to illustrate in that context. One can model perceptual recognition by productions in which the conditions to be matched have descriptions of the patterns, and the production actions involve labeling the perceived object. Figure 1.4 illustrates part of a hypothetical pattern network for recognizing three letters, F, A, and O, composed of simple vertical and horizontal bars (McClelland and Rumelhart, 1981). It is assumed that each top node in Figure 1.4 is a production that recognizes a letter. The production nodes are decomposed into nodes representing subpatterns, which are decomposed into nodes that correspond to individual letter strokes. Only the top nodes in the network correspond to productions; the subpattern nodes are shared by multiple productions. The individual letter strokes correspond to clauses of a production condi-

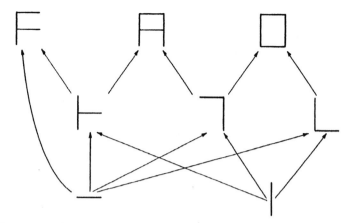

**Figure 1.4** *A simple data-flow network for discussion of pattern-matching.*

tion. Thus, corresponding to the A might be a production of the form

> IF a position contains two vertical bars, V1 and V2,
> and two horizontal bars, H1 and H2,
> and the top of V1 is connected to the left of H1
> and the top of V2 is connected to the right of H2
> and the middle of V1 is connected to the left of H2
> and the middle of V2 is connected to the right of H2
> THEN the object is an A.

Note that this pattern says nothing directly about the features which, if present, indicate that the element is not an A (for example, a bottom horizontal bar). Other patterns that include these features that must be absent in an A will inhibit the A pattern. Thus these features have their influence implicitly through inhibition. Pattern matching is achieved by combining tests up from the bottom of such a network. Tests are performed to determine what elements in working memory match the primitive features at the bottom nodes. Supernodes combine the test results to determine if they are compatible. For instance, the ⊢ pattern is a supernode that tests if the left point of the horizontal bar corresponds to the midpoint of the vertical bar. Thus the data flows up from the bottom of the network until compatible instantiations of the top node are found. The individual nodes in the network are computing in parallel so all patterns are being matched simultaneously. This system design was strongly influenced by the data-flow pattern matching proposed by Forgy (1979).

Because the process of performing tests at a node takes considerable time, evidence for a match at a node will gradually build up or decrease with time. The node's level of activation, which reflects the system's current confidence that the node will result in a match, determines the speed of pattern matching. The level of activation of the bottom terminal nodes is determined by the activation of the data structures to which they are attached. The level of activation of higher nodes is determined by how closely they match, how closely their subpatterns and superpatterns match, and how closely alternative patterns match. There is a set of excitatory and inhibitory influences among the pattern nodes somewhat similar to the scheme proposed by McClelland and Rumelhart (1981) and Rumelhart and McClelland (1982). Subpatterns of a node send positive activation to the node. This positive activation is referred to as *bottom-up excitatory influence*. Thus activation of the ⊢ pattern in Figure 1.4 increases activation of the F pattern. Alternate interpretations (in this case, A and H) of the same subpatterns compete by means of *lateral inhibitory influences*. Finally, patterns support the activation of their subpatterns by *top-down excitatory influences*. So a highly active A will tend to support activation of the ⊢ node. These computations on activation are designed to achieve the *data refractoriness* principle, the idea that each data structure will be matched to a single pattern. This phenomenon is ubiquitous in perception (the mother-in-law and wife picture can be seen only one way at a time), and similar phenomena also exist at higher levels of cognition (a person who shoots himself is not perceived as a murderer).

Much of the actual pattern matching is achieved by the lateral inhibition process forcing a choice among different interpretations of the same subpattern. A fundamental difference between declarative and procedural memory is that there is not a similar inhibitory process in spread of activation through declarative memory. Activation of a data structure in declarative memory provides only positive evidence for the usefulness of associated data structures.

The pattern-matching process permits productions to apply even if their conditions are not completely matched. If a production's condition is the best interpretation of the available data and enough pieces of the pattern are available to get the pattern above threshold, that production will apply. In permitting such partial matching, ACT* differs strikingly from ACTE.

Many errors in performance of a skill (see Norman, 1981) can be explained by such partial matching. For instance, use of a related but incorrect word in speaking is attributed to an incomplete specification of the desired word in working memory that matches best the pattern of a wrong word. The partial matching process also explains the *word superiority* effect (Reicher, 1969; Wheeler, 1970; for a recent discussion see McClelland and Rumelhart, 1981). Top-down influences from the word pattern can facilitate identification of the partial letter pattern.

ACT* is unique among production systems in its emphasis on pattern matching process. This emphasis is consistent with the experiences in implementing production systems. Even the most efficient pattern matchers take 95 percent of the computer cycles spent on running production systems. The fact that pattern matching is so expensive in all known implementations is suggestive evidence that it should be the major temporal bottleneck in human cognition, as it is in the ACT* theory.

*Goal-directed processing.* The use of goal structures in ACT*'s execution of actions is a significant improvement over ACTE or the neoclassical architecture. ACT*'s productions can create and transform a hierarchical goal structure that reflects the current plan of action. Such a hierarchical goal structure is illustrated in the example of Figure 1.1 and Table 1.1. ACT* focuses attention on a goal by making it a strong source of activation. It can shift focus of attention within this goal structure. For instance, when a goal is achieved it is popped, and attention is shifted to the next goal. This goal structure solves the focus-of-attention problem much more effectively than the control nodes of ACTE and the neoclassical systems. Its use accounts for the ubiquitous hierarchical structure of human behavior (see Chapter 4), and the focus of attention it produces explains the strong seriality in the overall flow of human cognition. The goal structure is a principled construction with a clear semantics. That is, subgoals are asserted as necessary and sufficient conditions for achieving the goal. The semantics of these goal structures is built into the production system processes that use them. The use of goal structures greatly facilitates the process of acquiring new productions (see Chapter 6).

Cognitive processing is serial in many respects because only one goal can be attended to at a time. The current goal becomes a powerful source of activation, so pattern-matching resources are biased to match structures involving that goal. Consequently, productions that refer to a goal must match that goal element to get an overall match. Also, productions that refer to a goal are more likely to match and to match more rapidly than those that do not refer to a goal. This explains why focusing attention on an unfamiliar pattern will facilitate matching it, as observed by LaBerge (1973). This will also cause capacity to be shifted from matching other patterns, producing the cost-benefit tradeoff observed by Posner and Snyder (1975). These points will be expanded in Chapters 3 and 4.

*Production compilation.* Because ACT* has a set of mechanisms to account for acquisition of productions, it can deal with the major source of underdeterminacy that plagued earlier systems like ACTE. This underdeterminacy derives from the fact that there are many possible production sets for performing a particular task, and the choice of one rather than another may appear arbitrary. As noted earlier, a principled explanation for the choice of a particular production set lies in the learning mechanisms that give rise to it. In practice, it may be difficult to derive the subject's current production set, because it may be difficult to identify all the relevant aspects of the learning history. However, in principle it is always possible to make such derivations, and in practice a learning theory does add constraint to the postulation of production sets.

According to ACT*, all knowledge initially comes in declarative form and must be interpreted by general procedures. However, by performing a task, *proceduralization* gradually replaces the interpretive application with productions that perform the behavior directly. For example, rather than verbally rehearsing the side-angle-side rule in geometry and figuring out how it applies to a problem, a student eventually has a production that directly recognizes the application of side-angle-side. This proceduralization process is complemented by a *composition* process that can combine a sequence of productions into a single production. Proceduralization and composition, which together are called *knowledge compilation,* create task-specific productions through practice. Knowledge compilation is the means by which new productions enter the system. They are acquired gradually and with caution because productions do control behavior rather directly. Gradual creation of a set of task-specific productions makes it more likely that errors will be detected in the learning process before the system has totally relinquished control to the new production set. This process corresponds to the automatization noted in many domains (for example, Shiffrin and Schneider, 1977).

*Production tuning.* Once a production set has been created, it can be tuned for a domain. Productions accumulate strength according to their history of success. Generalization and discrimination processes search for problem features that are predictive of the success of a particular method. Composition continues to collapse frequently repeated sequences of productions into single productions. These various learning processes produce the gradual, continued improvement in skill performance that has been noted by many researchers (see Fitts, 1964). Chapter 6 will discuss the wide range of skill improvement, and Chapter 7 will show how tuning accounts for many of the phenomena observed in first-language acquisition.

The procedural learning mechanisms, which are gradual and inductive, contrast sharply with the abrupt and direct learning that is characteristic of the declarative domain. This contrast is the best evidence for the declarative-procedural distinction, which is basic to the ACT architecture.

RULES AND NEURAL PLAUSIBILITY

It is worth noting that ACT* is a rule-based system (the productions being the rules), but one in which we are concerned with how these rules are implemented in a psychologically and a neurally plausible manner. Recently, it has been argued (see Hinton and Anderson, 1981; and especially Anderson and Hinton, 1981) that there are no rules in the brain, only a system of parallel interactions among connected neurons involving excitation and inhibition. It is argued that the apparent rulelike quality of human behavior is an illusion, that humans do not truly possess rules any more than a bouncing ball possesses rules that guide its behavior.

ACT* makes the point that there need be no contradiction between a rule-based system and the kind of neural system that was found plausible by Anderson and Hinton (1981). According to the ACT* framework these researchers have simply confused the levels of description. They have focused on the neural interactions that implement the rules and have not acknowledged the rules—a case of not seeing the forest for the trees. Again, a computer metaphor may help make this point: A program in a high-level language is compiled in machine code, but the fact that machine code executes the program should not obscure the fact that it derived from the higher-level language. Just as both higher-level and lower-level computer languages exist, so do both cognitive rules and neurons.

One might counter that the human "machine code" does not correspond to any higher-level rules, that the human system programs itself directly in terms of machine code, but this seems highly implausible. Intelligent behavior requires an integration of units that probably could not be achieved if the system were organized at such a myopic level. It is telling that most of the interesting applications of neural models have been to peripheral processes like word recognition (for example, McClelland and Rumelhart, 1981) which require little higher-level integration. When we look at complex cognitive processes we see a seriality and a structure unlike anything that has been achieved in a neural model before ACT* used rules to structure the networks. Even these modest "ruleless" neural networks have to be carefully structured by the theorist (an implicit reservoir of rules) rather than grown according to general principles. The examples of successful modification of neural nets are even more modest (but see Hinton and Anderson, 1981, for a few examples). When we look at learning in ACT* (Chapters 6 and 7) we will see that rule organization plays an absolutely critical role in structuring the acquisition of complex cognitive skills. It is unlikely that we can have an accurate psychological theory without rules, any more than we can have an accurate psychological theory without a plausible neural implementation.

### Production Systems versus Schema Systems

If we grant that some single, general, computationally universal system underlies human cognition, then the question arises, why are production systems the right kind? It is well known that generality and computational universality can be achieved in very different architectures. The most commonly offered alternatives to production systems are the various schema architectures (for example, Bobrow and Winograd, 1977; Minsky, 1975; Rumelhart and Ortony, 1976; Schank and Abelson, 1977). Like production systems, schema systems are frameworks that can be instantiated by specific theories. The final choice between the two frameworks will be based on their fruitfulness—that is, on how well the specific theories predict data. None of the schema theories have had their psychological interpretations specified as completely or with as much detail as ACT*, and this is an obstacle to careful comparison. In the absence of specific schema theories comparable to ACT*, one is left to evaluate general features of the two frameworks. It may well be that some schema theories, now or forthcoming, will not correspond to the characterization given here. If so, it will be interesting to see whether they can avoid the problems and still maintain an architecture that is fundamentally different from that of production systems.

SPECIFICATION OF THE SCHEMA FRAMEWORK

The two major components of the schema framework are a working memory and a schema memory. The major control cycle of the system involves matching schemata to the contents of working memory. Thus recognition is the basic force. Information enters working memory from the environment but also by the action of schemata. Specifically, if a schema is partially matched by the information in working memory it will create further information to complete the match. For instance, we see the front part of a cube, which enters working memory, and then our cube schema fills in the rear part of the cube. While there may be other processes for creating schemata, it is frequently proposed that an instantiated schema in working memory can be deposited in schema memory and then serve as a new more specific schema. An object is recognized the second time by having its schema match the representation in working memory. Another proposal (Rumelhart and Norman, 1981) is that a second schema can be created as an analogical modification of the first.

Schemata are organized hierarchically according to a part structure. One schema can occur as part of another, as a window schema is part of a wall schema. In matching the whole schema it may be necessary to invoke matching the part schema, and matching the part schema may invoke matching the whole. Also important is a generalization hierarchy. In recognizing a Labrador retriever, for instance, we may call on information stored in a dog schema or an animal schema.

With a little more technical fleshing out, this schema structure would lead to a computationally universal system, so it is certainly capable of producing humanlike cognition. Moreover, a number of empirical phenomena are suggestive, to say the least, of schema operation. However, whether we should consider this structure as the basic human cognitive architecture is a separate issue.

One serious question about schema theories is how one gets any action from them. A frequent proposal (Abelson, 1981; Rumelhart and Ortony, 1976) is that in matching a schema to a situation and in adding missing pieces, one can add instructions to act. So in recognizing a situation as a buying schema and recognizing oneself as the buyer, one fills in that one is to provide money to the seller and then one acts accordingly. Note that the same schema, if matched to a situation in which one was the seller, would generate different behavior.

## IMPLEMENTING SCHEMATA IN PRODUCTION SYSTEMS

It is possible to have much of the computational character of a schema system in a production system. For instance, the processes that match production conditions, especially in a partial-match system like ACT*, provide many of the features associated with schema instantiation. Indeed, much of the literature on prototype formation (such as Franks and Bransford, 1971; Hayes-Roth and Hayes-Roth, 1977; Medin and Schaffer, 1978) associated with schema theory can be explained by the ACT learning processes defined on the patterns contained in production conditions (Anderson, Kline, and Beasley, 1979; Elio and Anderson, 1981). However, the pattern-matching processes in production systems are not nearly so powerful or unbounded as schema systems. For example, it is not possible to dynamically invoke a second production in service of matching the condition of a first one. The amount of computation that goes into matching any one production is bounded by the size of its condition. In a schema system, on the other hand, in trying to recognize a street scene one can evoke a truck schema, which can evoke a car schema that will evoke a wheel schema, which can evoke a tire schema, which can evoke a rubber schema, and so on.

On the other hand, because it is computationally universal, ACT* can simulate the operation of any schema by the operation of some production set. For instance, consider the use of schemata to elaborate stories, as is done by script theory (Schank and Abelson, 1977). As shown in the appendix to Chapter 5, this situation can be modeled by having a set of productions apply to a declarative representation of the schemata. A sequence of productions applies in which each production either puts a small piece of the schema into correspondence with a story or uses a small piece of the schema to elaborate on the story. While the end products in the ACT case and the schema case are identical, the performance details are presumably not the same. In the ACT case, time to make the correspondence should be basically linear with the complexity of the schema, and errors should increase as more partial products are kept in memory. Schema theories are rather thin in their performance assumptions, but there is no reason to expect the same predictions to hold.

## CRITICISMS OF SCHEMA THEORY

A major problem with schema theory is that it blurs the procedural-declarative distinction and leaves unexplained all the contrasts between procedural and declarative knowledge. It also leaves unexplained the automatization phenomena (see Chapter 6) associated with the transition from a declarative base for performance of a skill to a procedural base. For example, in becoming proficient in a foreign language we move from using the rules of the language in a slow and conscious manner to applying them without any awareness of the rules.

There are good reasons for wanting to have both declarative and procedural knowledge structures. Declarative knowledge is flexible and can be accessed in many ways. Schemata are more declarative in character and have similar flexibility. Procedural knowledge is rigid but efficient. The condition-action asymmetry of production systems is committed to the idea that efficiency can be achieved by capitalizing on the structure and direction of information flow. One can only go from the instantiation of the condition to the execution of action, not from the action to the condition. This contrasts with schemata such as the buyer-seller schema, where it is possible to instantiate any part and execute any other part. The asymmetry of productions underlies the phenomenon that knowledge available in one situation may not be available in another. Schemata, with their equality of access for all components, cannot produce this. Also, in many cases the symmetry of schemata can lead to potential problems. For instance, from the fact that the light is green one wants to infer that one can walk. One does not want to infer that the light is green from the fact that one is walking. No successful general-purpose programming language has yet been created that did not have an asymmetric conditionality built in as a basic property. We should expect no less from the human mind.

A second major problem with schemata, reflected in the criticisms in Anderson (1976), is that the units of knowledge tend to be too large, thus forcing the system into modes of behavior that are too limited. A hallmark of human intelligence is its ability to combine information in new ways. A production system, having smaller units, permits a richer possibility for recombination. Indeed, Schank's (1980) move from scripts to MOPs, which have a facility for dynamic reconfiguration, reflects recognition of this problem.

The size of schemata also makes it difficult to construct effective theories about their acquisition. Technically, it is difficult to construct learning mechanisms that can deal with the full range of schema complexity. Empirically, it is transparent that learning is gradual and does not proceed in schema-sized jumps. This has led schema theorists (Rumelhart and Norman,

1981) to propose that we never learn new schemata but only modifications of existing ones.

## Parsimony

This completes the initial sketch of the ACT* theory, its motivation, and its differences from other frameworks in cognitive science. Even though many of the details have not been filled in, the total theory is not simple. On the other hand, the theory set forth in Table 1.2 is not complex, given the standards of the biological sciences, past efforts at psychological theories (Hull, 1943), and current efforts in cognitive science (Wexler and Culicover, 1980). I would argue that, if anything, the theory set forth in Table 1.2 is too simple, reflecting its incompleteness.

### LOCAL VERSUS GLOBAL PARSIMONY

Parsimony, although a valid and important principle of science, is often used incorrectly in the study of cognition. We all work on part of the picture, and what is parsimonious for a part may well not be parsimonious for the whole. An example where parsimony for the part fails to reflect parsimony for the whole concerns adult models of cognition. It is often possible to create simple and pristine models for performing a specified task (for example, linear syllogisms) under specified circumstances by a select population of subjects. However, this ignores the possibility that the learning and developmental history that gave rise to these processes was complex, varied, and even contradictory. A plausible (and parsimonious) learning theory, given such a learning history, might not have a parsimonious end product to reflect the adult model. Indeed, as a greater variety of studies comes in, it is becoming apparent that the only reasonable model of adult performance on linear syllogisms will be quite complex (Ohlsson, 1980).

Another relevant case concerns Chomsky's (1980) proposal for various "mental organs." Looking at a restricted aspect of language behavior and in strict obedience to parsimony defined on that aspect, Chomsky has come up with a series of characterizations of the language facility that seem quite unlike other cognitive systems. Therefore he proposes that language must be a special mental organ and that every other mental function has its own "organ" with its own principles of operation. The final product seems nonparsimonious, because parsimony was applied to linguistic analysis without consideration of the rest of the cognitive system.

PARSIMONY AND EVOLUTION

The most important case of local parsimony violating global parsimony concerns cognitive systems from an evolutionary perspective. It is implausible that evolution would have produced the simplest structure for the human mind. That is, parsimonious cognitive models have a danger of forcing nonparsimonious assumptions about their evolution. One might say that evolution abhors a parsimony. Evolution typically produces multiple systems for achieving a function. For instance, multiple sensory systems have evolved to perceive the same world. The current evidence suggests that multiple neural centers extract different but overlapping information from the visual signal. It seems only reasonable to suppose that the mind would evolve multiple overlapping systems to optimize various aspects of mental processing.

This claim is distinct from the assertion that there are different faculties for different functions. Using a computer analogy, the cognitive system is like a rich and complex programming language with many special hardwired features. Different tasks are solved by different configurations of the common set of these features. The faculty approach amounts to claiming that language is coded according to principles of LISP on a LISP machine, that imagery is coded according to principles of PASCAL on a PERQ, mathematics coded according to principles of FORTRAN (if such principles exist) on an IBM machine, and so on. These various modules could interact by some message passing, perhaps in an interlingua, but each would march forward according to its own principles. The objection to the faculty proposal is not its lack of parsimony but rather the difficulty of separating such cognitive functions in practice or of anticipating them in evolution.

I am a recent convert to the realization that parsimony is often misapplied in cognitive science, so I feel compelled to elaborate at length on this point. A standard belief in cognitive science is that adding an extra assumption to a theory should be done only after a decade of evidence, and perhaps not then. Whatever the validity of this attitude for the physical sciences, it makes no sense for the biological sciences, especially in understanding a biological phenomenon as complex as human cognition. Imagine a scientist of a past generation arguing, "I know digestion is performed by the stomach; therefore, I have a strong bias against believing it is performed by the intestine. And if nature should be so perverse as to have the intestine also do digestion, I am almost certain it will be the exact same mechanisms as are involved in the stomach. And if, God forbid, that seems not to be the case, I will search for some level where there is only a uniform set of digestive principles—even if that takes me to a subatomic level."

We can be sure that the human mind is not to be explained by a small set of assumptions. There is no reason to suppose the mind is simpler than the body. Every effort to discern a small set of operating principles for the human mind has fallen on disaster. The issue between the faculty approach and the unitary approach is only secondarily one of complexity. The major issue is whether a complex set of structures and processes spans a broad range of phenomena (a unitary approach) or whether different structures and processes underlie different cognitive functions (the faculty approach). The only choice is between two complex viewpoints.

From a biological point of view, it seems clear that our characterization of mind is going to be at some intermediate level of parsimony. On the one hand, a great deal of information is transmitted by the genetic code. On the other hand, the amount of information in the code is much less than the potential complexity of the body or the brain. There are many ways (such as bilateral symmetry) that the same genetic information is made to do multiple duty. Thus we should expect to see numerous mental principles, but we should also expect to see each principle showing up in many contexts.

### THE DANGER OF IGNORING PARSIMONY

The danger in this freedom from the tyrannical rule of parsimony is that assumptions will be spun out in a totally unprincipled and frivolous way. Although the system is complex, it is equally certain that most principles will have at least a modestly general range of application. If one feels free to propose a new assumption at each turn, there is a real danger that one will miss the fact that the same process underlies two phenomena and so miss the truth about cognition. For this reason, new assumptions should not be added frivolously. I have worked with the following criteria for introducing a new theoretical distinction:

1.  There is a broad range of evidence from numerous empirical domains that points to its existence.

2. There is no obvious way to incorporate these phenomena within existing mechanisms.
3. There is a good argument for the adaptive value of the mechanism.

The first two criteria are standard statements related to considerations of parsimony. However, because of the third I do not feel the need to give the first two as much weight as I did when I formulated the 1976 ACT theory. The consequences of this slight deemphasis on parsimony have hardly been disastrous. Although it is impossible to apply a metric to parsimony, it is clear that ACT* is much less than twice as complex as ACTE, while it accounts for much more than twice as many phenomena.

A good example is the concept of node strength (Assumptions 4 and 5 in Table 1.2). For six years I assumed only link strength for dividing activation. I refused to adopt the concept that different nodes have different capacities for spreading activation, even though in 1976 strong circumstantial evidence pointed to such a concept. Eventually, as partially documented in Chapter 5, the evidence became overwhelming. The current theory has node strength as a primitive concept and link strength as a defined construct, so it is only marginally more complex, but it is much more accurate. In retrospect I think I was being foolishly faithful to parsimony in trying to avoid the assumption of differential node capacity. It makes eminent adaptive sense that more frequently used nodes would have greater capacity for spreading activation. The cognitive system is just concentrating its resources where they will be most used. Some interesting assumptions would be required to explain why we would not have evolved differential capacity for nodes of differential frequency.

If the human mind is to be understood through many principles, one cannot expect ACT* or any other theory at this time to be a complete theory of mind. It takes a good deal of effort to identify and formulate a single principle, and the time put into ACT is hardly sufficient to do more than make a beginning. Hopefully, it will at least provide a framework for discovering new principles. Again, consider an analogy: it is important, perhaps essential, to understand the overall functioning of the circulatory system before trying to understand the principles that govern the behavior of capillaries in providing nutrients to tissues. Similarly, it is useful to have an understanding of the overall cognitive architecture before working out the details of how pattern matching treats temporal strings. This book sets forth the basic ACT* architecture and illustrates its application in various domains. The book might be considered as seven "essays" on certain aspects and applications of the ACT* theory.

# 2 | Knowledge Representation

## The Role of Representation in the ACT* Theory

KNOWLEDGE REPRESENTATION has always been recognized as central to the construction of a theory such as ACT*, and eight years of experience working with the ACT system have certainly confirmed its importance. Our experience with the ACT system had some surprises. First, despite all the wonderful arguments for the sufficiency of propositional representations, they often proved quite cumbersome. In later years, as I became more eclectic, I found that nonpropositional representations could work well in a production system framework. Moreover, when I observed what was good or bad about a representation, I found it was not its form or notation that was important. This was surprising because issues of form and notation had occupied so much of the discussion. Rather, the important issue was what could or could not be done easily with a representation.

It is not that different representations are needed for different applications but rather, for different aspects of the same application. The generation of geometry proofs (Anderson, 1981, 1982; Anderson et al., 1981) is a good example. One needs linear structures to represent the order of statements in a proof; spatial structures to represent the diagram; and propositional structures to represent the logical interpretations of postulates.

In this chapter I propose and describe the tri-code theory of knowledge representation. This theory assumes three codes or representational types: a temporal string, which encodes the order of a set of items; a spatial image, which encodes spatial configuration; and an abstract proposition, which encodes meaning.[1] This proposal for three types of knowledge representation is a major departure from my long-standing position (Anderson and Bower, 1973; Anderson, 1976) that the only type of knowledge representation is propositional. It might also seem contradictory to my more recent claims (Anderson, 1976, 1978, 1979) that it is not possible to discriminate among various representational notations. In Anderson (1982) I discuss at length the connection between the current proposal and past theoretical and metatheoretical discussions in cognitive science. The central issue is the distinction between representations from the point of view of the processes defined on them and representations from the point of view of the notations used to express them. My past claims had been about notation; the current claims are in terms of process. It is impossible to identify whether a particular notation correctly expresses the structure of a representation or whether different knowledge structures are encoded according to different notations (Anderson, 1978, 1982). On the other hand, it is possible to decide that different knowledge structures have different processes defined upon them. The basic assumption is that representations can be defined in terms of the processes that operate on them rather than the notation that expresses them.

This chapter sets forth the representational assumptions that are the foundation for the rest of the book. I will specify the notation to be used, although I make no claim for its uniqueness. Also I will specify how the production system processes operate on the various representational types and present empirical and logical evidence for the existence of such processes. The research in this book is based mostly on propositions, less on strings, and least on images. Therefore, the claims for image representation, especially, are somewhat tentative and incomplete. However, it is important to address this topic because imagery has been so important in discussions of mental representation.

There may well be more than the three representational types proposed here. However, there are severe constraints on the postulation of new representational types. There must be substantial empirical data that cannot be explained by existing types, and there must reasonably have been time in our evolutionary history to create such a representation and an adaptive advantage to doing so. As an example of the second constraint, it would make no sense to propose a separate "algebra code" for parenthetical expressions. The most likely candidate for an additional code is a kinesthetic and/or motor code as suggested by Posner (1967, 1973).

THE BASIC ARGUMENT

Representational types are defined in terms of the processes that operate upon them; Figure 1.2 illustrates the basic processes in ACT*. Five processes interact with the contents of working memory. (My concern in this chapter is with the representations of information in working memory—it is assumed that the long-term knowledge representations mirror these.) The encoding process deposits representations of the environment into working memory. The storage process deposits permanent records of temporary working-memory information into declarative memory. The retrieval process brings these records back into working memory. The match process selects productions to apply according to the contents of working memory. Finally, the execution process creates new working memory structures through production actions. The reason for the different representational types is that these basic processes treat different knowledge structures differently.

Table 2.1   *The properties of the three representations*

| Process | Temporal string | Spatial image | Abstract proposition |
|---|---|---|---|
| ENCODING PROCESS | Preserves temporal sequence | Preserves configural information | Preserves semantic relations |
| STORAGE PROCESS | All or none of phrase units | All or none of image units | All or none of propositions |
| RETRIEVAL PROCESS | All or none of phrase units | All or none of image units | All or none of propositions |
| MATCH PROCESS | | | |
| (A) DEGREE OF MATCH | End-anchored at the beginning | Function of distance and configurations | Function of set overlap |
| (B) SALIENT PROPERTIES | Ordering of any two elements, next element | Distance, direction, and overlap | Degree of connectivity |
| EXECUTION: CONSTRUCTION OF NEW STRUCTURES | Combination of objects into linear strings, insertion | Synthesis of existing images, rotation | Insertion of objects into relational slots, filling in of missing slots |

Table 2.1 provides an organizational structure, crossing the three representational types with the various ACT processes.[2] Each cell lists some of the properties of each process-by-type combination. Neither Table 2.1 nor this chapter lists all the properties of the processes that operate on any representational type. However, enough properties have been enumerated to justify the claim of distinct types. That is, the properties of the processes defined on each of these types are unlike those of the processes defined on any other type. Note, however, that the three data types are not distinguished with respect to the storage and retrieval processes for declarative memory. The final section of this chapter will consider the consequences of not distinguishing among these data types in declarative memory.

The case for distinct representational types will be made with respect to the *kinds* of encoding, match, and execution processes. My argument is not, for instance, that a match process is defined for one representational type and not for others. A production system could not function if that were the case. Rather, the argument is that different match processes are defined for different types. The evidence for this will come from the fact that the match process has different properties when applied to different representational types.

## Temporal Strings

### ENCODING

The encoding process creates strings to record the sequential structure of events. An important use is to encode word or morpheme order in language. It is interesting to ask how stimuli are segmented into event units, but if we assume this segmentation, the encoding processes must preserve the ordinal structure of events.

A significant aspect of the encoding process is that it records *ordinal but not interval* information about the event units, so in an important sense it is an abstraction from the event being encoded. There are numerous situations in which one would want to process ordinal rather than interval information. For instance, the difficulty in converting speech into segmented units (Gill et al., 1978) is testimony that one would not want to represent the interval properties of a speech signal after the units are extracted. Most rules of language interpretation (after phoneme identification) make only minimal reference to exact temporal properties, perhaps because of the difficulty of processing the temporal structure of a sequence. Similarly, inferring the causal structure of an event sequence is critically dependent on the ordinal structure but often is not critically dependent on the interval structure. Events like pauses may be significant, but they become another element, a pause, in the event sequence.[3] Pauses may also be important in determining the hierarchical structure of an ambiguous stimulus (Bower and Springston, 1970).

Further evidence for the belief that temporal strings encode only ordinal information lies in the poor quality of human judgment about absolute time. The current proposal for ordinal encoding corresponds to Ornstein's theory (1969) that perception of time is related to the number of intervening events (or units in a string representation). This is not to say that we cannot perceive or remember interval properties of a time sequence, but that such properties are not directly encoded in the structure of the temporal string. Such information can optionally be encoded as attributes of the ordered elements ("the goal was scored at 2:03 of the second period").[4]

Long sequences of events are not encoded as single-level linear structures but rather as hierarchies of strings within strings. This is frequently referred to as phrase structuring, where a phrase refers to the units in a level of the hierarchy. A phrase contains five or fewer elements. The idea of such hierarchical organization for temporal strings with a limited number of elements at any level has been proposed by many researchers (Broadbent, 1975; Chase and Ericsson, 1981; Johnson, 1970; Lee and Estes, 1981; Wickelgren, 1979). These phrase structures are often indicated by the location of pauses in serial recall.

*Propositional versus string representation.* One of the standard arguments for a propositional system over a multicode system (Pylyshyn, 1973; Anderson and Bower, 1973) has been that the propositional code is sufficient to encode all kinds of information. Much of our research on language processing (Anderson, Kline, and Lewis, 1977) has worked with propositional encodings of sentence word order. Figure 2.1 shows the propositional network representation for *the tall young man*. The reader is undoubtedly struck by the complexity of this representation relative to the simplicity of the string to be represented. It is complex because one has to use conventions that are optimized for representing the complexities of other knowledge structures, and because one cannot capitalize on the peculiar properties of the simple knowledge to be represented. The problem is not just one of awkward notation; there is considerable inefficiency because the processes must also operate on the needless detail.

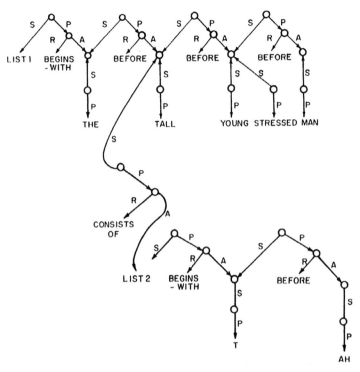

**Figure 2.1**   *A propositional representation of string information, also representing the information that* young *is stressed and that* tall *was pronounced "T + AH." (Adapted from Anderson, 1976.)*

Figure 2.2, showing a possible network notation for the string encoding *the tall young man,* illustrates how other information besides word order would be encoded. It shows that *tall* was pronounced without articulating the *l,* and that *young* was stressed. To represent particular information about these instantiations of the word, one needs a type–token distinction; that is, it is not the word *young* in general that is stressed, but rather this token of it. When one needs to be explicit about the type–token distinction, it is useful to use a network notation. In Figure 2.2, individual nodes represent the word tokens, which point to the words by type links. Also illustrated here are attribute links (to indicate that token 3 is stressed) and a substructure link to indicate the contents of token 2. Thus, in addition to the string structure, there are conventions to represent category information (the types for the tokens), attribute information, and substructure information. Similar category, attri-

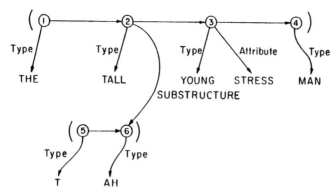

**Figure 2.2**  *A string representation of the information shown in Figure 2.1. This network makes explicit the type-token distinction. Also represented are substructure links giving part information and attribute links giving additional properties of the tokens.*

bute, and substructure embellishments are used for the image and propositional representations.

The network representation in Figure 2.2, with thirteen links, is much more compact than the representation in Figure 2.1, with forty-two links. This notational difference is significant because it implies a corresponding difference in the complexity of the processing. This contrast illustrates the efficiencies to be gained by permitting different representational types.

*Image versus string representations.* If one cannot subsume string information under propositional encodings, a natural tendency is to try to subsume it under spatial information. One might try to reduce temporal strings to one-dimensional spaces. However, they are not spatial structures because they do not encode interval information, and spatial structures do. Comparisons of temporal versus spatial encodings of sequential structure (Anderson, 1976; Healy, 1975, 1977; Hitch, 1974; Mandler and Anderson, 1971) have not generally supported the idea that spatial and temporal encodings are the same. Generally, temporal encodings are superior for storing order information. Significantly, R. Anderson (1976) found that the difference between temporal and spatial encodings is greater for words than for pictures. Healy (1975) found phonemic encoding only for temporal but not for visual presentation. Mandler and Anderson (1971) argue that when temporal and spatial presentations are confounded, subjects set up two independent and additive codes. In sum, it is improbable that a temporal code is just a degenerate case of a spatial code.

## STORAGE AND RETRIEVAL

Temporal strings are stored in long-term memory and are retrieved according to their phrase units. Johnson (1970) has nicely documented the memory consequences of this hierarchical phrase structure. By various spacing techniques, he was able to control the phrase structure of arbitrary strings of letters. He found that there was a high probability of recalling an item if one recalled another item within the same phrase, but across phrase boundaries the conditional recall probabilities were much lower.

The phrase structure units of temporal strings have the memory properties of cognitive units (Anderson, 1980). Cognitive units are encoded all or none into long-term memory and are similarly retrieved; that is, either all the elements of a phrase structure unit will be remembered, or none will be. This would certainly result in the high conditional recall probabilities noted by Johnson. However, this notion predicts an even stronger within-phrase contingency than Johnson found—essentially, recall of one element should imply perfect recall of all other members. In fact, various complications can degrade all-or-none recall to some-or-none recall, as found by Johnson. This will be discussed later in this chapter after I have established further assumptions about representation.

## PATTERN MATCHING: DEGREE OF MATCH

Much of the distinctive character of temporal strings is in the processes that match temporal patterns. In the production system framework this means how production conditions are matched to data in working memory. An interesting situation occurs when the system has to process data that partially match a well-known pattern. There are strong asymmetries in speed and success of recognition. One of the strongest effects is front anchoring; for instance, JVLV is much more likely to call to mind JVLVB than is VLVB. Horowitz, White, and Atwood (1968) confirmed that the beginning of a letter string is a superior cue, and two more recent research endeavors (Anderson, 1982; Angiolillio-Bent and Rips, 1982) have systematically documented that the major factor determining speed of string recognition is a match to the front portion of the string. This research has also provided evidence for end anchoring, but this effect was somewhat weaker in Angiolillio-Bent and Rips and much weaker in Anderson. Interestingly, in more recent unpublished research Angiolillio-Bent has found that the physical spacing of the elements does not matter, only their ordinal structure.

## PATTERN MATCHING: SALIENT PROPERTIES

Some patterns specify what the data structures they match must look like (for example, the pattern *the* can be matched by only one sequence of letters). Sometimes, however, the pattern is only testing for a certain property of the data structure that does not uniquely specify it. To illustrate this distinction, contrast checking the complete spelling of a word with testing if it begins with the correct letter. It is easier to determine that *illustration* begins with *i* than to determine that it is spelled correctly in all places. It might seem only logical that partial information can be matched more rapidly than complete information. However, some partial specifications are harder to verify than full specifications. Consider two examples from spelling: First, it is harder to decide that *linosrtau* contains all the letters in *illustration* than to decide that *illustration* matches the word exactly. Thus, it is harder to verify set information than sequence information, although set information is part of sequence. Second, it is harder to verify that a word is spelled correctly in every second position—for example, *ixlxsxrxtxox*—than that it is spelled correctly in all positions.

A *salient property* is a partial pattern specification that can be matched more rapidly than the full specification. Different data types have different salient properties. One salient property of temporal strings involves judging the order of two elements in a string—for example, is March before June? It is easier to judge this than to retrieve the intervening elements. A second salient property involves judging which elements are adjacent—for example, is Thursday the day before Friday? While these properties can be judged much more rapidly than the full string, it is not the case that either property is judged in constant time. Several important factors affect the speed with which these judgments can be made and further characterize the processing of strings.

*Retrieval of the next element.* There is an analogy between temporal strings and lists used in programming languages like LISP. One feature of lists is calculation of the *next* element. Most lists provide rapid access to the first element; subsequent members are retrieved by chaining through a series of nexts. The same seems to be true of strings. Sternberg (1969) documents that in a short string the time to calculate the next element depends on the position of the item in the list, with later items taking longer. When it comes to longer, hierarchically structured strings, the main factor is position within the subphrase (Klahr, Chase, and Lovelace, in press).

The operation of extracting the next element distinguishes temporal from spatial images. If no direction is specified, the next element in a multidimensional spatial image is not defined. Even with a direction specified, Kosslyn (1980) has shown that the time taken to go between two elements is a function of the physical distance between them and not the number of intervening objects.

*Order judgments.* Frequently one must judge the order of two elements from a string. This is accomplished in a production system by the use of special match predicates for order. For instance, the following production would directly retrieve the answer to the question whether A is before D in the string ABCDEF:

> IF asked "Is LVX before LVY?"
> and LVX is before LVY
> THEN respond yes.

The first clause just matches the question while the second requires direct access to information about order in the memorized string.

A great deal of work has been done on linear orderings (Potts, 1972, 1975; Trabasso and Riley, 1975), suggesting that such order information is quite directly available and that one does not have to chain through the intermediate terms between A and D to determine their order (that is, order judgments are not implemented as a series of nexts). In these experiments subjects learn a linear ordering by studying a set of pair orderings—for instance, A is before B, B is before C, C is before D, D is before E, and E is before F. Even though subjects memorize only the adjacent pairs, judgments are easier to make the farther apart the elements are. This result is generally taken as evidence against a propositional encoding for linear order information. Even when linear order judgments are made over very long strings (Woocher, Glass, and Holyoak, 1978) in which the elements must be chunked into subphrases, with many judgments crossing phrase boundaries, judgment time is still a function of ordinal distance between elements. Woocher, Glass, and Holyoak failed to find that phrase boundaries had any effect on order judgments.

ACT* does not have a psychological mechanism for extracting

linear order information. Although it would be perfectly reasonable to develop such a mechanism, our current purposes are served if we can demonstrate that temporal strings show a distance effect unlike that for other representational types. One might be able to borrow one of the current proposals about how ordering judgments are made (see Holyoak and Patterson, 1981), and embed it within ACT.

It is interesting to consider the results in experiments like those of Hayes (1965) or Hayes-Roth and Hayes-Roth (1975), in which subjects must commit to memory partial orderings rather than simple linear orderings. That is, they have to remember things like A > B, A > C; but B and C are not ordered. In such situations subjects cannot encode the information in a simple linear string; possibly they encode it propositionally. In this case, the opposite distance effects are obtained—the farther apart a pair of items, the longer it takes the subject to judge. Presumably, they have to chain through the propositions about the pairwise orderings that define the partial ordering.

CONSTRUCTION OF NEW STRINGS

Strings are created not only by encoding the order of events in the environment, but also as the outcome of internal computation. We can mentally calculate a string that encodes all the primes under 20: (((1 2 3) (5 7)) ((11 13) (17 19))). Nothing in such a construction operation is unique to strings; similar structure-building operations apply to the other representational types. However, an important property of strings is that an existing one can be modified by inserting or deleting an element. For instance, we can modify the string above by inserting a 0 after the 17.

The insertion operation strengthens the correspondence between temporal strings and computer lists and shows why it is adaptive that strings be ordinal rather than interval structures. An insertion operation is defined only on an ordinal structure, not an interval one. The ability to insert elements into strings is critical in domains as disparate as transforming an English sentence (see Chapter 7) to solving a detective mystery by inserting the critical hypothetical event.

Deletion, the complementary operation to insertion, makes even clearer the distinction between a temporal string and a spatial image. Deleting an event from a string does not create a string with a "hole." It is intriguing to consider the characteristics of strings formed by insertions and deletions. A considerable amount of memory research has been concerned with whether subjects show positive transfer from one list to another list derived from it by deletions and insertions (for reviews see Murdock, 1974; Young, 1968). Unfortunately for our current purposes, that research has confounded detecting such transformations with using them to aid in retention of the list.

### PURPOSE OF TEMPORAL STRINGS

It is noteworthy that many of the unique properties of temporal strings are the same as the properties of lists in a programming language like LISP. Like lists, they encode order rather than interval information, and they can be accessed only from the front. Like lists they are designed to permit insertion, deletion, and access to the next element. However, one property we have considered is unlike most list structures: that the order of two elements can be judged without retrieving the intervening elements. Also unlike lists, temporal strings can be indexed from a member (what list does February occur in?), a property they share with the other representational types. This double linking from structures to elements and from elements to structures is a general property of human knowledge structures.

## Spatial Image Representation

### ENCODING AND NOTATION

Spatial images are structures that preserve the configuration of elements of a spatial array. My current best guess is that a spatial image encodes configural information but not absolute size. The experiment by Kubovy and Podgorny (1981) supports this conjecture. They presented their subjects with a pair of random polygons and had them judge whether the polygons matched in shape. Same-shape polygons could vary in size and in rotation in the plane. The researchers found that rotation had a large effect on judgment but that change in size had no effect at all, just as predicted from the image representation I propose here. That is, the image preserves information about relative position and not about absolute distance or size. Unfortunately, as Kubovy and Podgorny note, size transformation effects have been found by other researchers. The experimental issue is tricky because size effects would be expected to whatever degree subjects were making their judgments about the shape of a figure in terms of its position in a framework that did not increase with the size of the figure. In this case, the overall configuration changes with size; that is, the periphery of the larger figure is relatively closer to the border.

The current proposal, that images preserve orientation and not size, is based on what seems important about a spatial image. People need to recognize a pattern when the size changes (for example, letters in a different size type) and seemingly do so with ease. On the other hand, the identity of an object may change if it is rotated (for example, a Z becomes an N; a square becomes a diamond), and people find it difficult to make matches that must correct for rotation. However, I also must stress that no major claim in this book rests on the proposal that images do not encode absolute size in their structure. Far from that, the tri-code proposal would be strengthened if it could be shown that images do encode absolute size, because this property is not encoded in temporal strings or abstract propositions.

A notation for expressing spatial images is somewhat awkward for scientific discourse, and much of the debate over image representation has really been caused by this awkwardness. Figure 2.3 illustrates a number of ways to represent spatial images. One might use the actual stimulus (a), but this notation is ambiguous about exactly what is stored in the image. Because of working memory limitations, all the details of all three objects in (a) could not be encoded in a single image. If the visual detail is encoded it must be done by means of subimages. In (a) it is not clear whether the detail of the objects is encoded at all, and (b) and (c) illustrate that ambiguity. The letters in each array are tokens for the parts, but in (b) these tokens point to subimages that encode the visual detail, while in (c) there are only categorical descriptors. In (b) each of these subimages would have an encoding of its subparts, but this is not shown. The full encoding in (b), including subimages, allows judgments such as whether the triangle is equilateral. Part (d) gives a more precise encoding of (c), reducing the array to coordinate information. Part (e) is a loose English rendition of the image information. There is not a "correct" notation. One chooses a notation to make salient the information being used by the processes operating on the representation. If one is concerned with the processes that operate on the position of subelements, then (d), where that information is explicit, is preferable to (c), where it is implicit. Whatever the choice of notation, it should not obscure what the image really is: information about the spatial configuration of a set of elements.

Images, like strings or propositions, can encode structure, category, and attribute information. Parts (b) and (c) of the figure illustrate the use of categorical and substructure information, which can be used to embed images within images to ar-

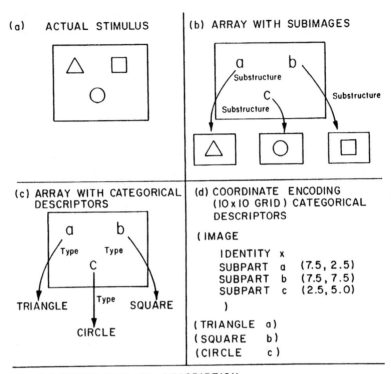

**Figure 2.3**   *Alternate notations for visual images.*

bitrary depth. Thus an important part of this proposal is that images can have a hierarchical character. Attributes of elements in an image include size and color.

*Hierarchical structure.* Spatial images have the same capacity limitations as temporal strings. That is, in a single image unit it is possible to encode the relative positions of only five or fewer objects. However, as part (c) of Figure 2.3 illustrates, it is possible to simply note the position of objects in an image without recording the detail of these objects by subimages.

One consequence of hierarchical organization is that it is possible to have accurate information about the spatial configuration of the objects in a scene with very little information about what the objects look like. This property is an important way in which spatial images differ from true pictures, and it agrees with people's experiences of imagery, such as the vivid image of a zebra whose stripes cannot be counted (Bower, 1972), or Pylyshyn's (1973) room scene in which the lamp can be located but not described. It also is in accord with results such as Navon's (1977), that one can identify the configurational properties of a structure before the components. In Bower's example the zebra might be represented in terms of the relative position of head, legs, body, and perhaps a stripe or two without specifying all the stripes. In Pylyshyn's example the location of the lamp in the room and of other furniture might be represented without specifying their details. In these cases it is possible (optional) that the whole image can point to more detailed information in a subimage, such as the face with stripe information or the lamp. However, as Navon states, it takes longer to retrieve the detail because the subimage must be retrieved from the whole image.

This representation is basically in accord with other hierarchical proposals such as Hinton's (1979), Marr and Nishihara's (1978), and Palmer's (1977). Their proposals pursue technical issues to a level that is not important to the points I make here.

*Comparison with Kosslyn.* Kosslyn (1980) presents criteria for distinguishing between propositional representations and quasi-pictorial representations of images. If measured by Kosslyn's criteria, my proposal here (as well as those of Hinton, Marr and Nishihara, and Palmer) is a hybrid. I propose that like a propositional representation, a spatial image has a clear structure with relations (the spatial configurations) and arguments (the elements). Like a quasi-pictorial representation, it preserves information about shape and has a nonarbitrary relation to the object represented. Unlike a proposition, it has no syntax or truth value. Unlike quasi-pictorial representation, size is not an inherent property.

Kosslyn develops and argues for a quasi-pictorial theory. Given the overall purpose of this chapter and of the book, it would be a digression to get into a point-by-point, experiment-by-experiment accounting of why this hybrid model is to be preferred to a pure propositional or a pure quasi-pictorial. Evidence not discussed here is reviewed in Anderson (1980a), Hinton (1979), and Palmer (1977), among others. In general terms, images have been shown to have both structural (relational) and quantitative (metric) properties. Hybrid proposals try to acknowledge this. In fact, Kosslyn tries to deal with the structural properties of images by proposing auxiliary propositional representations and distinguishing between skeletal and elaborated images. Most important for my purposes here, however, is that this hybrid representation identifies process-properties of images that have no correspondence in the other two representations.

*The Santa study.* A claim of the current theory is that images encode the relative positions of objects in multidimensional space and that strings do not. The study by Santa (1977) nicely illustrates this basic difference. The two conditions of his experiments are illustrated in Figure 2.4. In the geometric condition (*A*), subjects studied a spatial array of three geometric objects, two above and one below, that had a facelike property; without much effort one can see eyes and a mouth. After subjects studied it, this array was removed and subjects were immediately presented with one of a number of test arrays, some of which are illustrated in the figure. The subjects' task was to verify that the test array contained the same elements, though not necessarily in the same spatial configuration, as the study array. They should respond positively to the first two arrays in (*A*) and negatively to the other two. The two positive test arrays provide an interesting contrast. The first is identical to the study array, but in the second the elements are arrayed linearly. (Other positive test arrays, not illustrated, presented the three

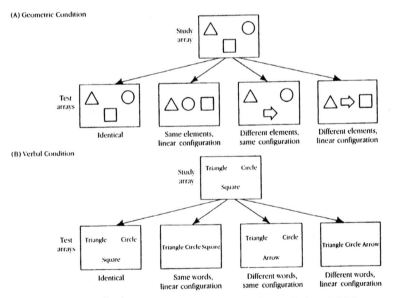

**Figure 2.4** *In Santa's experiment (1977), subjects studied an initial array and then had to decide whether one of a set of test arrays contained the same elements. (Anderson, 1980b; by permission of W. H. Freeman and Co., © 1980.)*

items in different orders.) Santa predicted that subjects would make a positive judgment more quickly in the first case, where the configuration was identical, since, he hypothesized, visual memory would preserve spatial information. The results, displayed in Figure 2.5, confirmed Santa's predictions.

The results from the geometric condition test are more impressive when they are contrasted with those from the verbal condition, illustrated in Figure 2.4(B). The words are arranged in the same configuration as the geometric objects in (A). However, because it involved words, the study stimulus did not suggest a face or have any pictorial properties. Santa speculated that subjects would encode the word array into a string according to normal reading order—that is, left to right and top to bottom: triangle, circle, square. When one of the test stimuli was presented, subjects had to judge whether the words were identical to those in the study stimulus. All the test stimuli involved words, but the possibilities were the same as in the geometric condition test, with two of the positive stimuli being an identical configuration and a linear configuration. Note that the order in the linear array is the same as that in which Santa predicted subjects would encode the study stimulus. Since subjects had encoded the words linearly from the study array, Santa predicted that they would be fastest on a linear test array. As Figure 2.5 illustrates, his predictions were again confirmed. There is a strong interaction between the type of material, geometric versus verbal, and the display condition, identical versus linear.

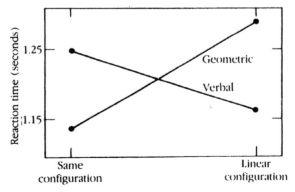

**Figure 2.5** *Reaction times for Santa's experiment, showing interaction between the type of material and the test configuration. (Anderson, 1980b; by permission of W. H. Freeman and Co., © 1980.)*

STORAGE AND RETRIEVAL

According to the theory presented here, image units are stored and retrieved in the same all-or-none manner as string phrases. This means that image recall should produce the same chunking that Johnson (1970) observed in his research. To my knowledge, such research has yet to be done except in studies of the games of chess and go (Chase and Simon, 1973; Reitman, 1976), which have confirmed this prediction.

PATTERN MATCHING: SALIENT PROPERTIES

It has been frequently noted (for example, Kosslyn and Pomerantz, 1977; Paivio, 1977) that spatial images have many salient properties. For instance, just as it was possible to directly test for the order of two objects in a temporal string, so it is possible to directly test an image for the distance between two objects, direction between two objects, and whether they overlap.

An example adapted from Simon (1978) illustrates the salient property of overlap judgment: "Imagine but do not draw a rectangle 2 inches wide and 1 inch high, with a vertical line cutting it into two 1-inch squares. Imagine a diagonal from the upper left-hand corner to the lower right-hand corner of the 2 × 1-inch rectangle. Imagine a second diagonal from the upper right-hand corner to the lower left-hand corner of the right *square*. Do the two diagonals cross?" One's intuition is that the answer to this question is immediately available upon formation of the image.

Another salient property of an image concerns the relative positions of two objects. Maki (1981) and Maki, Maki, and Marsh (1977) have looked at subjects' ability to make north-south or east-west judgments about the positions of cities on a map. It is of interest to compare their results with the results on judgment of linear orderings. As in the research on linear orderings they found the judgments were faster the farther apart the cities were. However, there is an important difference; the hierarchical structure of the picture affects the judgment, so distance effects disappear for pairs of cities on opposite sides of a state boundary (Maki, 1981). Stevens and Coupe (1978) have shown that position judgments can be severely distorted by the hierarchical character of an image representation. They documented the common misconception that Reno is east of San Diego, which derives from the fact that Nevada is east of California and the location of the cities is represented with respect to the location of the states. On the other hand, judgments of linear ordering seem unaffected by attempts to impose a hierarchical structure (Woocher, Glass, and Holyoak, 1978).

### PATTERN MATCHING: DEGREE OF MATCH

The Santa study illustrated that speed of matching is affected by the spatial configuration of a series of objects. It is also affected by the interval properties of the figure. Speed of pattern matching seems to be a continuous function of the degree of distortion between the pattern configuration and the data to be matched. For instance, Posner and Keele (1970) documented that time to recognize a random dot pattern is a function of the distance the dots in the test pattern had been moved from their positions in the prototype. This is unlike what is seen with matching strings or propositions.

Another unique feature of image pattern matching is that a data structure can be matched to a pattern solely on the basis of a match in the configuration of the elements, even if the elements do not at all match the pattern. For instance, without trying, one can see the structure in Figure 2.6 (adapted from Palmer, 1975) as a face. With temporal strings, in contrast, it is unlikely that one string of elements will evoke recognition of a completely different one. Of course, one-dimensional strings without interval structure do not permit the same variety of configurational properties as images and so lack much of the uniqueness of an image configuration.

### IMAGE CONSTRUCTION

New knowledge structures can be created by the action of productions. In the case of a temporal string the possibility for construction was pretty mundane—elements could be ordered

**Figure 2.6** *Fruitface.*

to form a new phrase unit. For images the possibilities are more interesting and provide some of the unique properties of image representation. As with strings, new images can be synthesized by combining old ones—for instance, one can imagine a triangle on top of a square, a friend on an elephant, or a line between two points. In each of these cases, the larger image is constructed by specifying the location of one subimage relative to the other—for example, we might specify that the bottom line of the triangle be identical with the top line of the square. Images so constructed have the same hierarchical character as phrase units constructed from subphrases.

The hierarchical character of a synthesized description may not correspond to the description that would be derived if the object encoded were actually perceived. This is illustrated by the synthesis problems in Figure 2.7, which show the difficulty of identifying the objects formed by synthesis. For instance, (b) is hard to perceive because separate line segments in the parts become single lines in the whole. This informal example agrees with the careful studies of Palmer (1977), who showed that the ease of recognizing synthesized objects depends critically on whether the subunits correspond to those into which the whole object would naturally be segmented. Thus, the image representation system allows different descriptions for the same object.

Image rotation, as studied in experiments such as those of Shepard and Metzler (1977), is a special case of image construction. A new image can be constructed as a small rotation of another. By a series of such rotations a new image can be generated in any orientation. The sort of production that performs rotation would match the to-be-rotated image in its condition and perform the rotation in its action, creating a new image, slightly rotated, in working memory. Iteration of this production would achieve further rotation. The literature implies that images can be rotated only in small increments.

*A production system for mental rotation.* Because of the importance of research on mental rotation in discussions of imagery and because it is frequently thought that production systems and imagery processes are incompatible, it is useful to consider a production system that is actually capable of simulating the Shepard and Metzler (1971) task. This system has the further advantage of showing how different types of representation can be coordinated within one set of productions—indeed, within one production. It will borrow heavily from a proposal of Just and Carpenter (1976) although it is not identical to it.

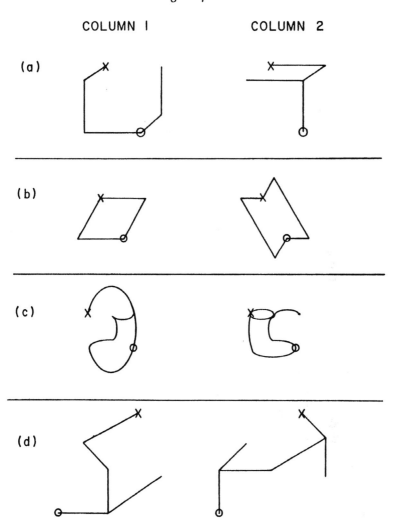

COLUMN 1    COLUMN 2

(a)

(b)

(c)

(d)

**Figure 2.7** *Synthesis problems. Combine the two figures in the two columns so the X's and O's overlap. What is the resulting image?*

One question about the Shepard and Metzler figures is whether they are rotated as single objects or are rotated and moved in pieces, as Just and Carpenter claim. It may well be that inexperienced subjects, like those used by Just and Carpenter, rotate these figures in fragments, whereas experienced subjects, like those used by Shepard and Metzler, rotate whole figures. I, a relative novice at mental rotation, have introspective experiences close to the piecemeal analysis modeled here.

Figure 2.8 is a hierarchical representation of a Shepard and Metzler figure. It is analyzed into two overlapping elbows (subfigures), each of which is analyzed into two overlapping arms (subsubfigures). It is assumed that for rotation the arms need not be broken into individual cubes.

Just and Carpenter identify three substages in matching these figures. The first is to find end parts (arms) of the two figures that correspond. The second is to rotate the end part of one figure into congruence with the end part of the other, beginning the creation of an image that is the rotation of one figure. The third substage completes construction of this image by moving copies of the remaining pieces of the figure to the image and testing for congruence. Just and Carpenter suggest that this third stage can involve rotation or not; the current model assumes no rotation. Just and Carpenter call these stages search, transformation, and confirmation. The current model maintains these distinctions but breaks each stage down into more information-processing detail.

The appendix to this chapter provides a detailed specification of the production system and its application to the problem of taking two figures and trying to create an image of one rotated into congruence with the other. Figure 2.9, a summary illustration of the operation of that production system, shows the two figures, the focus of attention on each figure (the shaded areas), and the contents of the mental image. The simulation starts out (a) by focusing on the two upper arms; in (b) an image of the upper arm of object 2 is created, and by a series of rotations it is brought into congruence with the upper arm of object 1 (c). When an attempt is made to attach the other arm in the upper elbow of object 2, a mismatch is discovered (e), which leads to abandonment of the attempt to make the upper parts of the two objects correspond. In (f) an attempt is made to create a correspondence between the lower elbow of object 2 and the upper elbow of object 1. In (g) an image is created of the lower arm of object 2 and is rotated into congruence with the upper arm of object 1. Then in Figure (h)–(l) the various arm fragments are attached until a complete image is achieved.

This production system predicts that the angle of rotation has two effects. First, the greater the angle of rotation the greater the likelihood of false starts, as illustrated in Figure 9(a)–(e). Second, a number of rotations are required to align the initial segments, (c) and (g). The production system also predicts that the complexity of the image has an effect in terms of the number of separate pieces that need to be imaged (b)–(l). This example

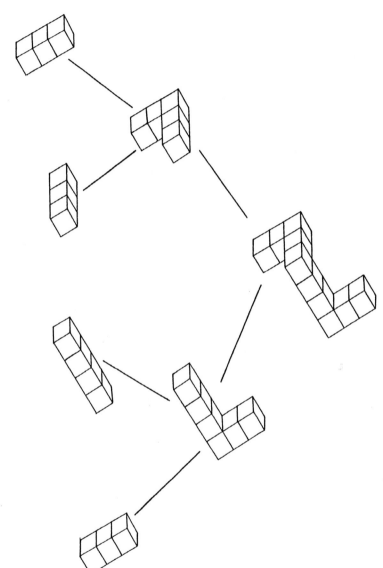

**Figure 2.8** Decomposition of a Shepard and Metzler figure into subfigures and subsubfigures.

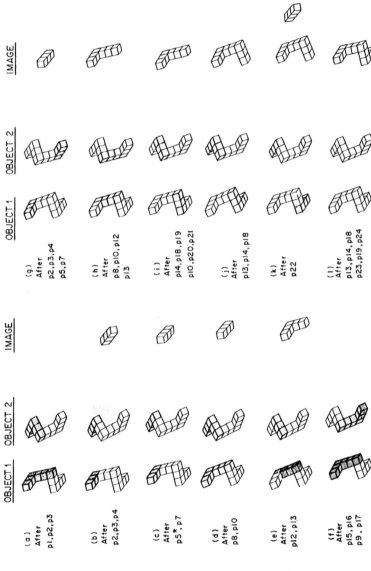

**Figure 2.9** *Various states of working memory during the processing of a pair of Shepard and Metzler figures. The shaded areas of the two objects represent focus of attention.*

illustrates that imagery is compatible with a production system architecture and that the distinct character of imagery corresponds to distinct processes that operate on images in the production system. To the best of my knowledge, the example accurately models the empirical phenomena. It predicts the basic rotation result and is consistent with the qualitative eye movement data of Just and Carpenter (1976).

The theory makes an interesting set of predictions about the relationship between complexity and rate of rotation. Because complexity is correlated with the number of subparts, complexity will have an effect on judgment time. However, the actual rotation operation is performed on only a single part, so there need not be an interaction between complexity and rate of rotation. On the other hand, greater complexity of the stimulus or greater angle of rotation can result in more false starts, where the system starts out with one correspondence and then must try another. In situations where there is not a clear basis for anchoring the correspondences, there would be a multiplicative relationship between complexity and angle of rotation. This is a rather complicated prediction but it is at least consistent with the complicated and superficially contradictory empirical picture about effects of complexity on rate of rotation (Cooper and Podgorny, 1976; Carpenter and Just, 1978; Pylyshyn, 1979; Shwartz, 1980). The eye movement data of Just and Carpenter give strong support to the idea that effects of angle of rotation are due both to rotation of a single part and to false correspondences.

## Abstract Propositional Representation

### ENCODING

The encoding of propositional representations is more abstract than that of temporal strings or spatial images in that the code is independent of the order of information. For instance, the propositional representation (hit John Bill) does not encode the difference between *John hit Bill* and *Bill was hit by John.* What it does encode is that the two *arguments,* John and Bill, are in the abstract *relation* of hitting. In encoding a scene of John hitting Bill, the propositional representation does not code who is on the left and who is on the right. Propositional encodings are abstract also in that they identify certain elements as critical and ignore all others. Thus the encoding of the scene may ignore all physical details, such as John's or Bill's clothing.

One of the principal lines of empirical evidence for propositional representations comes from the various sentence memory studies showing that memory performance is better predicted by semantic variables than by the word structure of the original sentence. This research includes the long tradition of experiments showing that memory for the gist is better than memory for exact wording (Begg, 1971; Bransford and Frank, 1971; Sachs, 1967; Wanner, 1968) and experiments showing that the best prompts for recalling a particular word in a sentence are words that are semantically rather than temporally close (Anderson and Bower, 1973; Lesgold, 1972; Wanner, 1968). Similar demonstrations have been offered with respect to picture memory (Bower, Karlin, and Dueck, 1975; Mandler and Ritchey, 1977), that it is the underlying semantic relations that are predictive of memory. In reaction against this research, some experiments have demonstrated good verbatim memory for sentences (Graesser and Mandler, 1975) or good memory for visual detail that is not semantically important (Kolers, 1978). However, these observations are not troublesome for the multirepresentational position being advanced here, although they can be embarrassing for the pure propositional position that has been advanced. What is important for current purposes is that there are highly reproducible circumstances in which memory is good for the meaning of a stimulus event and not for its physical details. To account for these situations it is necessary to propose a representation that extracts the significant semantic relationships from these stimuli. To account for situations that show good memory for detail, one can use the temporal string or image representation.

Another distinctive feature of abstract propositions is that there are strong constraints among the elements. Thus *hit* takes two arguments, *give* three, and *decide* must have as one of its arguments an embedded proposition. There is nothing like this with strings or images, which encode directly what is in the world, and any combination is logically possible. One element of a string or image does not constrain what the other elements might be. Propositions, on the other hand, represent *relational categorizations* of experience, and the mind has only learned to see certain patterns.[5]

Propositional representations have been particularly important to the development of ACT*. Historically, ACT* emerged from ACTE, which had only propositional representations, and therefore, many of the empirical and theoretical analyses were concerned with these. Although I believe that the ACT architecture applies equally well to all knowledge representations, the majority of the analyses in subsequent chapters work with propositional representations.

As with the other representations, the true significance of the abstract proposition lies in the way it is treated by the production system processes. Unlike the encoding processes for temporal strings or spatial images, the structure of an abstract proposition is not a direct reflection of environmental structure. Rather it reflects an abstraction of an event, and the encoding process itself is something that must be learned. With respect to language, each child must learn the process of comprehension (sometimes innocuously called a "parser") for his native language. Similar extraction processes must be at work in learning to interpret nonlinguistic experiences and to identify the meaningful invariances (innocuously called perceptual learning and concept acquisition). Because the propositional encodings are not direct reflections of external structure but are determined by experience, many of the representations proposed over the years have had a somewhat ad hoc character. Until the abstraction processes underlying the formation of perceptual and linguistic parsers are specified, there will be unwanted degrees of freedom in propositional representations, and they will remain as much a matter of intuition as of principle. The learning theory in Chapters 6 and 7 is a step in the direction of specifying how we learn to transform input into new higher-order representations.

Propositional representations, like strings and images, involve structure, category, and attribute information. Figure 2.10 illustrates how this information would be used to represent *The tall lawyer believed the men were from Mars.* A central node represents the propositional structure, and links emanating from it point to the various elements. The labels identify the semantic relationships. The labeled network notation is appropriate because the links in a net are order-free, just as elements of a proposition are. The reader may recognize such a representation as the structure introduced by Rumelhart, Lindsay, and Norman (1972) in the early days of the LNR model. Many other, more complex network notations exist (Anderson and Bower, 1973; Norman and Rumelhart, 1975; Schank, 1972). Kintsch (1974) introduced a linear notation for network structure that is technically more tractable for large sets of propositions than a network representation like that in Figure 2.10. As with the other representational types, such notational differences are not significant. What is important is the information that the notation encodes and how that information is used. Choice of notation is a matter of convenience.

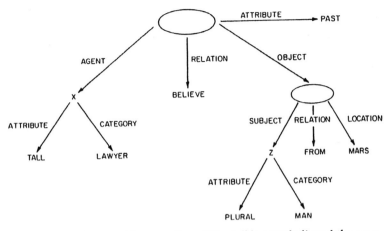

**Figure 2.10**   *A proposition encoding of* The tall lawyer believed the man came from Mars.

ALL-OR-NONE STORAGE AND RETRIEVAL

According to ACT*, a proposition such as *X believed Y*, in Figure 2.10, is encoded and retrieved in an all-or-none manner. There has been a mild debate about this (see Anderson, 1980; Anderson and Bower, 1973; R. C. Anderson, 1974; Goetz, Anderson, and Schallert, 1981), and I have found myself on the other side of the issue—that is, proposing partial memory for propositions. The basic empirical research concerns subjects' memory for sentences in which it seems reasonable to assume that certain phrases convey basic propositions. For instance, *The doctor shot the lawyer* might be said to convey a basic proposition. Subjects cued with part of a proposition, such as *the doctor*, may recall only part of the remainder. Numerous theories have been developed to account for this partial recall (Anderson and Bower, 1973; Jones, 1978). One problem is that the degree of recall is much less than would be expected under some notions of chance. For instance, if we cue with the subject of the sentence, recall of the object is much greater if the verb is recalled than if it is not. Depending on the experiment, object recall is 60–95 percent if the verb is recalled, and 3–15 percent if it is not.

This empirical evidence provides weak evidence at best on all-or-none memory for propositions, and elsewhere (Anderson, 1976, 1980) I have tried to identify the ambiguities. In contrast to the murkiness of the empirical picture, the evidence for an all-or-none system is quite clear from considerations of functional value within a production system. Our experience has been that it is not adaptive to store or retrieve partial propositions because partial information cannot be easily used in further processing, and its retrieval only clutters up working memory, or worse, misleads the information processing. It seems unlikely that an adaptive system would waste capacity on useless partial information. In this case, where the empirical evidence is ambiguous, our general framework can guide a decision.

Arithmetic facts may be the easiest examples for illustrating the impact of partial encoding. If we store the proposition (5 = (plus 3 2)) as (= (plus 3 2)), with the sum omitted in a partial encoding, the fact is of no use in a system. Whether partial encoding leads to disaster rather than just waste depends on one's system assumptions; if propositions encoded facts like (6 = (plus 3 2 1)), imagine what a disaster the partial encoding (6 = (plus 3 2)) would lead to! The crisp semantics associated with arithmetic propositions makes clear the consequences of partial encoding. However, similar problems occur in an inferential system if (Reagan defeated Carter) is encoded as (defeated Carter) or if (Mary give Bill Spot tomorrow) is encoded as (Mary give Bill Spot).

The complaint against the partial encoding scheme is not simply that errors are made because of the failure to encode information. It is transparent that humans do fail to encode information and do make errors as a consequence. It can be argued that failure to encode is actually adaptive in that it prevents the memory system from being cluttered. The occasional failure of memory may be worth the savings in storage and processing. This is a difficult argument to evaluate, but it does make the point that failure to encode may not be maladaptive. However, the result of partial encoding *is* maladaptive; the system still has to store, retrieve, and process the information, so there is no savings in processing or storage. The partial memory that is retrieved is no better than nothing and perhaps is worse. An adaptive system would either jettison such partial encodings if they occurred or at least refuse to retrieve them.

PATTERN MATCHING: SALIENT PROPERTIES

One of the salient properties of a propositional structure is its ability to detect that elements are connected before detecting how. The ability to make connectedness judgments shows up in a wide variety of experimental paradigms, but it would be useful to describe an experiment from my laboratory which had as its goal to simply contrast judgments of connectedness with judgments of form. Subjects studied simple subject-verb-object sentences like *The lawyer hated the doctor* and then saw test sentences that exactly matched (The lawyer hated the doctor), that had subject and object reversed (The doctor hated the lawyer), or that had one word changed (The lawyer hated the sailor, The lawyer kicked the doctor). Two types of judgments were made. In the proposition-matching condition, subjects were asked to recognize if a test sentence conveyed the same meaning as the study sentence. In this condition they should respond positively to the first type of test sentence given above and negatively to the other two types. In the connectedness task, subjects were asked if all three words came from the same sentence. Thus, they should respond positively to the first two types of test sentences and negatively to the third type. All subjects responded more rapidly in the connectedness condition, indicating that access to information about whether concepts are connected is more rapid than is access to how they are connected.

Reder and Anderson (1980) and Reder and Ross (1981) also present evidence that subjects are able to make judgments about thematic relatedness more rapidly than about exact relationships. In those experiments subjects learned a set of thematically related facts about a person—for instance, a set of facts about John at the circus. Subjects could judge that a fact was consistent with what they had studied faster than they could judge whether it had been studied. For instance, they could judge that *John watched the acrobats* was consistent before they could decide whether they had studied that sentence. This paradigm will be considered further in Chapter 5.

In many memory experiments this rapid detection of connectivity can interfere with rejection of a foil. Collins and Quillian (1972) report that subjects find it difficult to reject *Madrid is in Mexico* because of the spurious connection. Glucksberg and McCloskey (1981) report that subjects find it easier to decide they don't know a fact like *John has a rifle* if they have learned nothing connecting *John* and *rifle* than if they have explicitly learned the fact *It is not known whether John has a rifle*. Anderson and Ross (1980) showed that subjects were slower to reject *A cat is a snake* if they had learned some irrelevant connecting fact like *The cat attacked the snake*. King and Anderson (1976) report a similar effect in an experiment in which subjects retrieved experimentally learned facts. These similarity effects will be discussed further in Chapter 3.

## PATTERN MATCHING: DEGREE OF MATCH

There is a natural tendency to think of propositions and word strings as being the same—a single, verbal representation (Begg and Paivio, 1969). However, the strong ordinal metric properties in the pattern matching of word strings is not found with propositions. In particular, as discussed earlier, there is a strong dependence on matching first elements in word strings. The same phenomenon is not found with propositions (Dosher, 1976). In unpublished research in our laboratory we have had subjects memorize in a meaningful way sentences like *The lawyer helped the writer*. They were then presented with a set of words and were asked to recognize the sentence that these words came from. We found they were just as fast to recognize the probe *Writer helped lawyer* as *Lawyer helped writer*. Thus the memory for meaningful information does not show the same order dependence as the memory for meaningless strings of items.

## CONSTRUCTION OF PROPOSITIONS

As with images and strings, propositional structures can be created by combining either primitive elements or elements that are structures. However, the relational structure imposes a unique condition on proposition construction: the relation takes a fixed number of slots, no more and no less. When a relation is constructed but not all the arguments specified, we fill in the missing arguments. Thus if we hear "Fred was stabbed," we cannot help but fill in a dummy agent. The various proposals for propositional systems differ in the richness proposed for default slots and for inference procedures to fill these slots. One feature that often accompanies proposals for "semantic decomposition" (Schank, 1972; Norman and Rumelhart, 1975) is a rich system for inferring the occupants of various slots. However, by their nature all propositional systems require some default system. The notion of a missing slot that must be filled in with a default value is not meaningful for images or strings.

## FUNCTION OF A PROPOSITIONAL CODE

The distinctive properties of propositions derive from their abstract, setlike structure. People learn from experience which aspects or higher-order properties of an event are significant, and to represent these they develop a code, which is more direct and efficient than storing the details. Rather than representing all the pieces of information that enable one to infer that

A has thrown a ball (A raised his hand over his head, A's hand held round object, A's hand thrust forward, A's hand released the ball, the ball moved forward, etc.) or the exact words of the sentence that was parsed into this meaning, the code represents the significant relationship directly. The propositional representation does yield economy of storage in long-term memory, but other advantages are probably more significant. For instance, the representation will occupy less space in working memory and will not burden the pattern matcher with needless detail. Thus, it often will be easier to manipulate (think about) these abstracted structures. Another advantage is that the inferential rules need be stored only for the abstract relation and not separately for all the types of input that can give rise to that relation.

### Storage and Retrieval

In ACT* theory storage and retrieval are identical for the three representational types. A unit (phrase, image, or proposition) is treated as an unanalyzed package. Its internal contents are not inspected by the declarative processes, so these processes have no basis for responding to a phrase differently than to a proposition. It is only when units are operated upon by productions that their contents are exposed and processing differences occur. This is a fundamental difference between declarative memory, which treats all types the same, and production memory, which treats them differently. If ACT* is correct in this hypothesis, traditional memory research (for example, Anderson and Paulson, 1978; Paivio, 1971), which attempted to find evidence for different types, is doomed to failure because it is looking at declarative memory. Traditional research has been used to argue for different types by showing better memory for one type of material, but one can argue that the research is better explained in terms of differential elaboration (Anderson, 1976, 1980; Anderson and Bower, 1973; Anderson and Reder, 1979).

The term *cognitive unit* (Anderson, 1980) is used for structures that have all-or-none storage and retrieval properties. By this definition, all three types are cognitive units. Because of limits on how much can be encoded into a single unit, large knowledge structures must be encoded hierarchically, with smaller cognitive units embedded in larger ones. It has been suggested (Broadbent, 1975) that the limits on unit size are related to the limits on the ability to access related information in working memory. For a unit to be encoded into long-term memory, all of the elements must be in working memory and the system must be able to address each element. Broadbent notes that the number of elements in a chunk corresponds to the number of values one can keep separate on physical dimensions (for instance, the number of light intensities that one can reliably label). He suggests that problems with larger chunks might be "discrimination" problems in identifying the locations of the individual elements in working memory.

One can retrieve elements from a hierarchical structure through a top-down process, by starting with the top structure, unpacking it into its elements, and unpacking these, and so on. Similarly, it is possible to retrieve elements in a bottom-up manner by starting with a bottom node, retrieving its embedding structure, then the structure that embeds it, and so on. These steps can fail either because the unit to be retrieved was not encoded or because it cannot be retrieved.

Figure 2.11 presents a hypothetical hierarchical structure, with twenty-seven terminal elements, in which certain units (marked with an X) are unavailable for recall. Using a top-down search, it would be possible to retrieve A, B, and C from the top structure; C, D, and E from A; 1, 2, and 3 from C; and 4, 5, and 6 from D. The structures from E and B are not available; I, J, and K can be retrieved from C; the structures from I and J are not available, but 25, 26, and 27 are available from K. (This retrieval process can be driven by spreading activation, which will be described in Chapter 3.) Thus, although each individual act of retrieval is all-or-none, only nine terminal elements are retrieved from the twenty-seven-element terminal array. Also

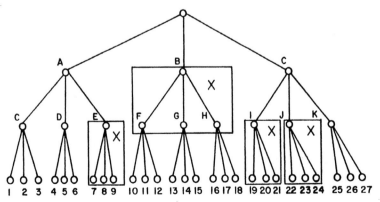

**Figure 2.11** *A hypothetical hierarchical encoding in which the boxed units cannot be retrieved.*

note that if cued with 10, the subject would be able to retrieve the fragment F and hence the elements 11 and 12 but nothing else of the hierarchy.[6] Such hierarchical retrieval would produce the phrase patterns documented for linear strings (Johnson, 1970), propositional structures (Anderson and Bower, 1973), and story structures (Owens, Bower, and Black, 1979; Rumelhart, 1978). To my knowledge no one else has explored this issue with respect to picture memory, but it would be surprising if such hierarchical recall structures were not also found there.

If one could segment a structure to be recalled into its hierarchical units, one should see all-or-none recall for the separate units. The empirical phenomenon is never that clear-cut, partly because subjects do not adopt entirely consistent hierarchical encoding schemes. The hierarchical structure of their scheme might differ slightly from the one assumed by the experimenter. A more important reason for deviation from hierarchical all-or-none recall is that the subject may produce elaborations that deviate from the specified hierarchy. For example, consider a subject's memory for the multiproposition sentence *The rich doctor greeted the sick banker.* A typical propositional analysis (Kintsch, 1974; Goetz, Anderson, and Schallert, 1981) would assign *rich* and *doctor* to one unit, and *sick* and *banker* to another. However, a subject, elaborating mentally on what the sentence means, might introduce direct memory connections between *rich* and *banker* or between *doctor* and *sick.* Then, in recall, he may recall *sick* and *doctor* but not *rich* and *banker,* violating the expected all-or-none pattern. The complications produced by such elaborations are discussed in Anderson (1976).

MIXED HIERARCHIES AND TANGLED HIERARCHIES

To this point the discussion has largely assumed that hierarchies consist of units of the same representational type. However, representations can be mixed, and there is considerable advantage to this flexibility. If one wanted to represent *John chanted "one, two, three,"* it is more economical to represent the object of John's chanting as a string. That is, the string would appear as an element of a proposition. Again, to represent the sequence of events at a ball game, one might want a linear ordering of a sequence of propositions describing the significant events. Strings and images would be mixed to represent a spatial array of nonsense syllables or a sequence of distinct images. One would use a mixture of images and propositions to encode comments about pictures or the position of various semantically significant objects without encoding the visual details of the object.

This discussion of hierarchies has assumed that a particular element or subhierarchy appears in only one hierarchy, but much of the expressive power of the system derives from the fact that hierarchies may share subhierarchies, creating *tangled hierarchies*. For instance, the same image of a person can appear in multiple propositions encoding various facts about him. Anderson and Bower (1973, chap. 9) showed that subjects had considerable facility at sharing a subproposition that participated in multiple embedding propositions. Hierarchies can overlap in their terminal nodes also, as in the case of two propositions connected to the same concept.

Figure 2.12 shows a very tangled hierarchy inspired by the script from Schank and Abelson (1977, pp. 43 and 44). Note that the central structure is a hierarchical string of events with various propositions and images overlaid on it. In general, what Schank and Abelson refer to as a script corresponds to a temporal string structure setting forth a sequence of events.[7] This structure is overlaid with embellishing image, propositional, and string information. In Figure 2.12 a string encodes the main element of the restaurant sequence (enter, order, eat, and exit), another string unpacks the sequence involved in entering, an image unpacks the structure of a table, and so on. Schank's more recent proposal of MOPs (1980) comes closer to the generality of this tangled hierarchy concept.

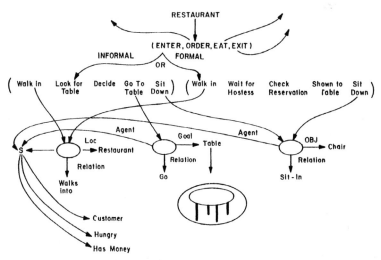

**Figure 2.12** *A tangled hierarchy of multiple representational types.*

## Final Points

Table 2.1 summarized the features that distinguish the three types of representation: they encode different information and have different pattern-matching and construction principles. One might question whether these processes are really distinct. To consider a wild but instructive example, suppose someone proposed the following "propositional" model to account for distance effects in judging relative position in a linear ordering. Each object is given a propositional description that uniquely identifies its position. So the string ABCDEFGH might be encoded as follows: "A's position is 0 followed by 0 followed by 0," "B's position is 0 followed by 0 followed by 1," and so on, with each position encoded in binary by a sequence of three propositions specifying the three digits. To judge the order of two items, a subject would have to retrieve the binary encodings and then scan them left to right until a first mismatching digit was found. Then a judgment could be made. The farther apart the items, the fewer propositions would have to be scanned *on the average* to find a mismatch. One could make numerous challenges to this proposal, but I will focus on one. The time necessary to make linear-order judgments (often less than a second) is less than the times to chain through three propositions in memory (seconds—see the experiment by Shevell and Anderson in Anderson, 1976, p. 366). Thus one cannot get the temporal parameters right for this hypothetical propositional model. This illustrates an important constraint that blocks many creative attempts to reduce one process to another, supposedly more basic process. The times for the basic processes must add up to the time for the reduced process.

Despite the fact that the three representational types clearly have different processes working on them, I have used the same basic network notation for all three with structure, attribute, and category information. The fact that similar notation can be used for distinct types reflects the fact that the notation itself does not contain the significant theoretical claims.

Finally, I should stress that the production system framework makes it easy to communicate among the representational types. The condition and action of a production can specify different types of structures. Also, the condition of a production can match working memory elements of one type, and the action can create working memory elements of another type. For instance, in reading one can imagine matching first the spatial image code, converting this to string code, then converting this to a propositional code.

## Appendix: Production Set for Mental Rotation

Table 2.2 provides a production set that determines if two Shepard and Metzler figures are congruent. This production set is much more general than the Shepard and Metzler task, however; it will decide whether any pair of simultaneously presented connected figures is congruent after rotation. Figure 2.13 illustrates the flow of control produced by the production system among the subgoals of the task. This production set assumes that the subject uses the stimuli as an external memory and is internally building an image in working memory. Figure 2.9, earlier, indicated where attention is focused in external memory and what is currently being held in internal working memory at various points during the correspondence.

**Table 2.2** *A production system for rotating Shepard and Metzler figures*

P1     IF the goal is to compare object 1 to object 2
     THEN set as the subgoal to create an image of object 2 that is
     congruent to object 1.

P2     IF the goal is to create an image of object 2 that is congruent
     to object 1
     and part 1 is a part of object 1
     THEN set as a subgoal to create an image of a part of object 2
     corresponding to part 1.

P3     IF the goal is to create an image of a part of object 2 corresponding to part 1
     and part 2 is an untried part of object 2 in locus A
     and part 1 is in locus A of object 1
     THEN set as a subgoal to create an image of part 2 that is congruent to part 1
     and tag part 2 as tried.

P4     IF the goal is to create an image of object 2 that is congruent
     to object 1
     and object 2 has no subparts
     THEN build an image of object 2
     and set as a subgoal to make the image congruent to
     object 1.

P5     IF the goal is to make image 1 congruent to object 2
     and image 1 and object 2 do not have the same orientation
     and the orientation of object 2 is less than 180° more than
     the orientation of image 1
     THEN rotate image 1 counterclockwise.

**Table 2.2**  *(continued)*

P6      IF the goal is to make image 1 congruent to object 1
        and image 1 and object 1 have the same orientation
        and image 1 and object 1 do not match
   THEN POP with failure.

P7      IF the goal is to make image 1 congruent to object 1
        and image 1 and object 1 match
   THEN POP with success
        and record that image 1 is congruent to object 1.

P8      IF the goal is to create an image of object 2 that is congruent
           to object 1
        and an image is congruent to object 1
   THEN POP with that image as the result.

P9      IF the goal is to create an image of object 2 that is congruent
           to object 1
        and no congruent image was created
   THEN POP with failure.

P10     IF the goal is to create an image of a part of object 2 cor-
           responding to part 1
        and an image is congruent to part 1
   THEN POP with that image as the result.

P11     IF the goal is to create an image of a part of object 1 cor-
           responding to part 1
        and there are no more candidate parts of object 2
   THEN POP with failure.

P12     IF the goal is to create an image of object 2 that is congruent
           to object 1
        and there is an image of part 2 of object 2 that is con-
           gruent to part 1 of object 1
        and part 3 of object 1 is attached to part 1
        and part 4 of object 2 is attached to part 2
   THEN build an image of part 4
        and set as the subgoal to attach to the image of part 2 this
           image of part 4 so that it is congruent to part 3.

P13     IF the goal is to attach image 2 to image 1 so that image 2 is
           congruent to part 3
        and image 1 is an image of part 1
        and image 2 is an image of part 2
        and part 2 is attached to part 1 at locus A
   THEN attach image 2 to image 1 at locus A
        and set as a subgoal to test if image 2 is congruent to
           part 3.

P14     IF the goal is to test if an image is congruent to an object
        and the image and the object match
   THEN POP with success.

**Table 2.2** (*continued*)

P15　IF the goal is to test if an image is congruent to a part
　　　and the image and the object do not match
　　THEN POP with failure.

P16　IF the goal is to attach image 1 to image 2 so that it is congruent to a part
　　　and a subgoal has resulted in failure
　　THEN POP with failure.

P17　IF the goal is to create an image of a part of object 2 corresponding to part 1
　　　and part 2 is an untried part of object 2
　　THEN set as a subgoal to create an image of part 2 that is congruent to part 1
　　　and tag part 2 as tried.

P18　IF the goal is to attach to image 1 image 2 so that it is congruent to part 3
　　　and this has been successfully done
　　THEN POP with the combined image 1 and image 2 as a result.

P19　IF the goal is to create an image of object 1 that is congruent to object 2
　　　and object 2 is not primitive
　　　and a successful image has been synthesized
　　THEN that image is of object 1
　　　and it is congruent to object 2
　　　and POP with that image as the result.

P20　IF the goal is to create an image of object 2 that is congruent to object 1
　　　and an image 1 of part 2 of object 2 has been created
　　　and the image is congruent to part 1 of object 1
　　　and part 1 is attached to part 3
　　　and part 2 is attached to part 4
　　　and part 4 is not primitive
　　THEN set as a subgoal to attach images of primitive parts of part 4 to the image so that they are congruent to part 3.

P21　IF the goal is to attach images of primitive parts of object 2 to image 1 so that they are congruent to object 1
　　　and part 2 is a primitive part of object 2
　　　and part 2 is attached to object 4
　　　and image 1 is an image of object 4
　　　and image 1 is congruent to object 3
　　　and part 1 is attached to object 3
　　　and part 1 is a primitive part of object 1
　　THEN build an image 2 of part 2
　　　and set as the subgoal to attach image 2 to image 1 so that it is congruent to part 1.

**Table 2.2**  (*continued*)

| | |
|---|---|
| P22 | IF the goal is to attach images of primitive parts of object 2 to image 1 so that they are congruent to object 1 and image 2 has been created of part 2 of object 2 and part 2 is attached to part 4 of object 2 and image 2 is congruent to part 1 of object 1 and part 1 is attached to part 3 of object 1 THEN build image 3 of part 4 and set as the subgoal to attach image 3 to image 2 so that it is congruent to part 3. |
| P23 | IF the goal is to attach primitive parts of object 2 to image 1 so that they are congruent to object 2 and all the primitive parts have been attached THEN POP with the result being the synthesized image. |
| P24 | IF the goal is to compare object 1 and object 2 and an image of object 2 has been created congruent to object 1 THEN POP with the conclusion that they are congruent. |

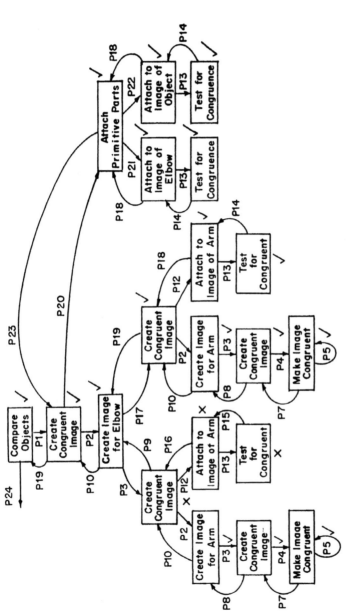

**Figure 2.13** *The flow of control among goals in the production system of Table 2.2. Checks signify successful goals, and X's unsuccessful goals.*

# 3 | Spread of Activation

## Introduction

ONE OF THE KEY FACTORS in human intelligence is the ability to identify and to utilize the knowledge that is relevant to a particular problem. In the ACT theory, spreading activation serves a major role in that facility. Activation controls the rate at which information is processed by the pattern matcher for production conditions. Since information can have an impact on behavior only by being matched in the condition of a production, activation controls the rate of information processing. It is the "energy" that runs the "cognitive machinery." Activation spreads through the declarative network along paths from original sources to associated concepts. A piece of information will become active to the degree that it is related to current sources of activation. Thus, spreading activation identifies and favors the processing of information most related to the immediate context (or sources of activation).

There are numerous reasons for believing in a spreading activation mechanism. One is that it corresponds to our understandings of neurophysiology. The neurons and their connections can be thought of as a network. The rate of firing of a neuron can be thought of as the level of activation. (It is believed [Hinton and Anderson, 1981] that neurons encode information by the rate of firing.) However, there are many ways to make a correspondence between neural constructs and the cognitive constructs of a spreading activation model, and there is no compelling basis for deciding among them. Rather than a node-to-neuron correspondence, it may be more reasonable for nodes to correspond to sets of neurons (Hinton and Anderson, 1981). Nonetheless, the general set of "neurophysiological hunches" that we possess is probably an important consideration in many people's acceptance of spreading activation.

It is hard to pinpoint the intellectual origins of the idea of spreading activation. In part it was anticipated in association-ist models of thought going back to Aristotle (see Anderson and Bower, 1973, for a discussion of the history of associative models). The process of tracing chains of connections can be found in early experimental psychology programs, in Freud's psychodynamics, and in Pavlov's ideas. These models were largely serial, with one thought leading to just one other. On the other hand, the neural network models of the 1940s and 1950s (for example, Hebb, 1949) stressed parallel interactions among many elements.

The work of Quillian (1969) was important to the current resurgence of work on spreading activation, and he is proba-bly responsible for the use of the term. His major contribu-tion was to relate this idea to the growing understanding of symbolic computation and to suggest how it might be used to facilitate the search of semantic networks. Collins and Quillian (1969, 1972) popularized an application of this con-struct to retrieval of categorical facts (for example, *a canary is a bird*), leading to what was once called "the semantic mem-ory paradigm."

Currently, two major research paradigms are important to understanding spreading activation. One is the *priming* para-digm (Meyer and Schvaneveldt, 1971) on the effect that pre-senting an item has on the processing of associated items. For instance, recognition of the word *dog* is facilitated if it is preceded by the word *cat*. These results provide direct evi-dence that processing of items can be primed through asso-ciation. The literature on fact retrieval (Anderson, 1974) stud-ies subjects' ability to retrieve previously studied information (such as whether they recognize *The lawyer is in the bank*). Both literatures will be discussed in detail in later sections of the chapter.

### FUNCTION OF ACTIVATION

Activation measures the likelihood that a particular piece of knowledge will be useful at a particular moment. It is a reason-able heuristic that knowledge associated with what we are pro-cessing is likely to be relevant to that processing. Spreading ac-tivation is a parallel mechanism for spreading measures of associative relevance over the network of knowledge. These measures are used to decide how to allocate resources to later, more time-consuming processes, such as pattern matching, that operate on the knowledge. These later processes will devote more resources to the more active knowledge on the heuristic assumption that this is likely to be the most useful. This was the basis of Quillian's argument for why spreading activation was a good artificial intelligence mechanism. It avoided or reduced the costly knowledge search processes that can be the pitfall of any artificial intelligence project with a large data base. Unfortunately, the process of computing the spread of activation is computationally expensive on standard computers. On serial computers, time to compute spread of activation tends to increase with the square of the number of nodes in the spreading process. Fahlman (1981) has tried to develop parallel machinery that will reduce the computational cost. Until such machinery becomes available, this apparently good idea will not see extensive use in pure artificial intelligence applications (applied knowledge engineering). However, it is reasonable to propose that it is relatively cheap for the brain to spread activation but relatively expensive for it to perform symbolic computation.

Activation does not directly result in behavior. At any point of time a great deal of information may be active, but an active network is like Tolman's rat buried in thought (Guthrie, 1952, p. 143). There must be processes that convert this activation into behavior. A serious gap in much of the theorizing about spreading activation is that these processes have not been specified. A major strength of the ACT production system is that one is forced to specify these interfacing processes. In ACT*, activation has an impact on behavior through the production system's pattern matcher, which must determine whether a set of knowledge structures in the network fits the pattern specified by a production condition. The level of activation of the knowledge structures determines the amount of effort that goes into making the correspondence. If the structure is inactive, no attempt is made to match it. If its activation level is low, the rate of matching may be so slow that the system follows some other course of behavior before the pattern matcher can completely match the structure. If it is sufficiently active to lead to a production execution, the activation level will determine the speed of the pattern matching and hence of the execution.

In the standard terminology of cognitive psychology, spreading activation defines working memory for ACT. Because there are degrees of activation, ACT's concept of working memory is one of degrees. The process of spreading activation amounts to the process of bringing information into working memory, thus making it available.

In this chapter I will first discuss the properties of spreading activation in the ACT theory, explain how spreading activation affects behavior, and present arguments for its general conception. Then I will consider some evidence from the priming and recognition literatures to determine whether ACT is compatible with the results. Finally, I will consider the relation between ACT's spreading activation and traditional concepts of working and short-term memory.

## Mechanisms of Activation

Activation flows from a source and sets up levels of activation throughout the associative network. In ACT*, various nodes can become sources. In this section I will specify how nodes become and stay sources, how activation spreads through the network, and how levels of activation in the network and rate of production firing are related. Because this section uses quite a lot of mathematical notation, Table 3.1 provides a glossary.

### SOURCES OF ACTIVATION

There are three ways in which an element can become a source of activation in working memory. First, an element that encodes an environmental stimulus will become a source. For example, if a word is presented, its memory representation will be activated. Second, when a production executes, its actions build structures that become sources of activation. Third, a production can focus the goal element on a structure in working memory, and the elements of such a focused structure can become sources of activation.

To illustrate the first and second ways, consider someone reading and recognizing the sentence *In the winery the fireman snored.* At a low level of processing, the encodings of individual letter strokes (features) would appear as active entities in working memory. At a second level, letter- and word-recognition productions would recognize patterns of these features as words and deposit in working memory active encodings of their word interpretations (not unlike the word recognition model of McClelland and Rumelhart, 1981, or the model in Chapter 4). At this level a perceptual interpretation of an event is being produced by a production action. After the second level, productions would recognize the sentence encoding and deposit an active representation of the response code in working memory.[1]

**Table 3.1**  *Glossary of notation*

| | |
|---|---|
| $a$ | Level of activation of a node |
| $a_i$ | Level of activation of node $i$ |
| $a_i(t)$ | Level of activation of node $i$ at time $t$ |
| $A$ | Vector giving level of activation of all nodes in network |
| $A(t)$ | Vector giving activation of nodes at time $t$ |
| $A_i(t)$ | Vector giving the activation at time $t$ supported by source $i$ |
| $B$ | Strength of coupling between a node and its input |
| $c^*$ | Amount of source activation |
| $c_i^*$ | Amount of source activation for node $i$ |
| $c_i^*(t)$ | Amount of source activation for node $i$ at time $t$ |
| $C^*$ | Vector giving source activations of all nodes in network |
| $C^*(t)$ | Vector giving source activations of nodes at time $t$ |
| $c$ | Net source activation, defined as $c^*B/p^*$ |
| $c_i$ | Net source activation of node $i$ |
| $C$ | Vector giving net source activation of all nodes in network |
| $\delta t$ | Delay in transmission of activation between nodes |
| $\Delta t$ | Period of time that a node will stay a source without maintenance |
| $n_i(t)$ | Total activation input to node $i$ at time $t$ |
| $N(t)$ | Vector giving input to all nodes at time $t$ |
| $p^*$ | Rate of decay of activation |
| $p$ | Amount of activation maintained in spread, defined as $p = B/p^*$ |
| $r_{ij}$ | Strength of the connection from node $i$ to node $j$ |
| $R$ | Matrix of the connecting strengths between the nodes in the network |
| $s_i(T)$ | Total activation over the nodes in the network maintained by source $i$ after $i$ has been a source for $T$ seconds |

The elements entered into working memory (letter features, words, and so on) all start out as sources of activation. However, unless focused, these elements stay active only $\Delta t$ period of time. Thus a great deal of information can be active at any one time, but only a relatively small amount will be maintained active. This is like the conception of short-term memory sketched out in Shiffrin (1975). Sources of activation are not lost, however, if they are encodings of elements currently being perceived. Even if the node encoding the perceptual object did become inactive, it would be immediately reactivated by reencoding. An element that is made a source by direct perception can become inactive only after it is no longer directly perceived. Also, the current goal element serves as a permanent source of activation.

COGNITIVE UNITS PROVIDE NETWORK CONNECTIONS

As discussed in Chapter 2, declarative memory consists of a network of cognitive units. For instance, two elements like *doctor* and *bank* can be connected just by appearing in the same propositional structure (*The doctor is in the bank*). Figure 3.1 gives an example of a piece of long-term memory in which unit nodes connect element nodes. Two units in temporary active memory encode the presented sentence *Doctor hates the lawyer who is in the bank*. Nodes corresponding to the main concepts are sources of activation. From these sources activation spreads throughout the network. For purposes of understanding spread of activation, we can think of long-term memory as a network of

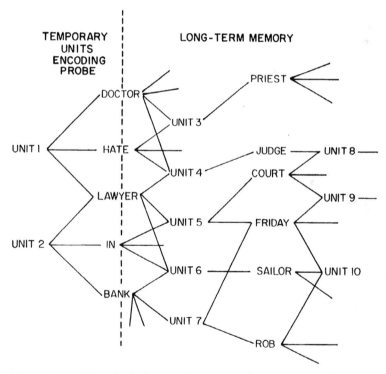

**Figure 3.1**  *A hypothetical network structure. In temporary active memory is encoded* The doctor hates the lawyer who is in the bank. *In long-term memory are illustrated the facts* The doctor hates the priest, The lawyer hates the judge, The lawyer was in the court on Friday, The sailor is in the bank, The bank was robbed on Friday, *and* The sailor was robbed on Friday.

nodes, with no distinction between unit nodes and element nodes.[2]

### SPREAD OF ACTIVATION

The network over which activation spreads can be represented as an $n \times n$ matrix $R$ with entries $r_{ij}$. The value $r_{ij} = 0$ if there is no connection between $i$ and $j$. Otherwise, its value reflects the relative strength of connection from $i$ to $j$. A constraint in the ACT theory is that $\Sigma_i r_{ij} = 1$. This guarantees that the activation from node $i$ is divided among the attached nodes according to their strengths of connection. The level of activation of a node will increase or decrease as the activation coming into it from various sources increases or decreases.

The activation of a node varies continuously with increases or decreases in the input. A bound is placed on the total activation of a node by a decay process. This conception can be captured by the model of a leaky capacitor (Sejnowski, 1981), and the change in activation of node $i$ is described by the differential equation:

$$\frac{da_i(t)}{dt} = Bn_i(t) - p^* a_i(t) \tag{3.1}$$

Here $a_i(t)$ is the activation of node $i$ at time $t$, and $n_i(t)$ is the input to node $i$ at time $t$. This equation indicates that the change in activation level is positively proportional (proportionality given by the strength of the *coupling factor*, $B$) to the amount of input and negatively proportional (proportionality given by the *decay factor*, $p^*$) to the current level of activation. The second factor describes an exponential decay process. The behavior of this equation is fairly easy to understand in the case of constant input $n$. Suppose the initial activation of node $i$ is $a_0$ and there is constant input $n$. Then activation of node $i$ at $t$ is given as:

$$a_i(t) = a_0 + \left(\frac{nB}{p^*} - a_0\right)(1 - e^{p^* t}) \tag{3.2}$$

Thus the activation moves from $a_0$ to $nB/p^*$. It approaches its new value according to an exponentially decelerating function. The new value is proportional to both the input, $n$, and the strength of coupling, $B$, and inversely proportional to the decay factor, $p^*$. The rate of approach is controlled by $p^*$.

The behavior of the system is usually more complicated than

Eq. (3.2) indicates because the input to $i$ varies with time and depends on the reverberation of the activation through the network. However, Eq. (3.2) still serves as a good first approximation for understanding what is happening. That is, the current input is driving the activation toward some resting level, and the rate of approach is exponential.

If a node is not a source node, the input is just the activation received from nodes connected to it. If it is a source node,[3] it receives an additional source activation $c_i^*$. (As will be discussed in Chapter 5, the size of this source activation depends on the strength of node $i$.) The input to node $i$ can be expressed as:

$$n_i(t) = c_i^*(t) + \sum_j r_{ji} a_i(t - \delta t) \qquad (3.3)$$

where $c_i^*(t) = 0$ if $i$ is not a source node at time $t$, and $c_i^*(t) = c_i^*$ if it is. The term in the sum indicates that the activation from a node $j$ is divided among the attached nodes according to the relative strengths $r_{ji}$. The value $\delta t$ appears in Eq. (3.2) to reflect the delay in transmission between node $i$ and node $j$. In a neural model it might reflect the time for information to travel down an axon.

Equations (3.1) to (3.3) may be represented more generally if we consider an $n$-element vector $A(t)$ to represent the activation of the $n$ nodes in the network, another $n$-element vector $I(t)$ to represent the inputs to them, and a third $n$-element vector $C^*(t)$ to reflect the activation from the source nodes. Then Eqs. (3.1) and (3.3) become:

$$\frac{dA(t)}{dt} = BN(t) - p^*A(t) \qquad (3.4)$$

and

$$N(t) = C^*(t) + RA(t - \delta t) \qquad (3.5)$$

where $R$ is the matrix of connection strengths. The general solution for Eq. (3.4) is given as:

$$A(t) = e^{-p^*t}A(0) + \int_{-\infty}^{t} e^{-p^*(t-x)}BN(x)dx \qquad (3.6)$$

There is no general closed-form solution to this equation.

McClelland (1979) dealt with the situation where $\delta t = 0$ and there was no reverberation (that is, activation does not feed back from a node to itself either directly or through intermediate nodes). The first assumption may be approximately true, but the second is invalid in the current context.

In ACT* $\delta t$ is assumed to be small (on the order of a millisecond), and the decay factor $p^*$ is large. In this case the activation level of the network will rapidly achieve asymptotic level. At asymptotic level, $dA(t)/dt = 0$, and we can derive from Eqs. (3.4) and (3.5):[4]

$$A = C + pRA \qquad (3.7)$$

where $C = BC^*/p^*$ and $p = B/p^*$. If $p < 1$, Eq. (3.7) describes a set of simultaneous linear equations with finite, positive solu­tions for all the $a_i$. (If $p > 1$, activation grows without bound and there is no solution for Eq. [3.7].) Thus the activation pattern in the network can be determined by solving this set of equations. The parameter $p$ is the *maintenance factor* that reflects what proportion of a node's activation is maintained in the spread to the neighboring nodes.

In this system each source supports a particular subset of activation over the network. Let $A_i(t)$ be a vector describing the subset of activation supported by source $i$. Then the total activation is just the sum of the subsets supported by all sources $i$, that is

$$A(t) = \sum_i A_i(t) \qquad (3.8)$$

Let $s_i(T)$ denote the sum of activation over all the nodes supported by source $i$ $T$ seconds after $i$ became a source node. $s_i(T)$ represents the activation of $i$ due to its source contribution, plus the activation of its associated nodes due to the source contribution, plus the activation of their associated nodes, and so on. That is, $s_i(T)$ is the sum of the entries in $A_i(t)$. To calculate $s_i(T)$ we need to represent $T$ in terms of the number, $n$, of $\delta t$ time units that have passed: $T = n\delta t$. The activation will have had a chance to spread $n$ units deep in the network by the time $T$. Then,

$$s_i(n\delta t) = c_i \sum_{i=0}^{n} p^i \left[ 1 - \sum_{j=0}^{i-1} \frac{p(i,n)^j \, e^{-p(i,n)}}{j!} \right] \qquad (3.9)$$

where $p(i,n) = p^*(n - i)\, \delta t$. In the limit this has the value:

$$s_i(T) \xrightarrow[T \to \infty]{} c_i/(1 - p) \tag{3.10}$$

Reasonable values for the parameters might be $p^* = 1$, $B = .8$ (and hence $p = .8$), $\delta t = 1$ msec. With such values, the quantity in Eq. (3.9) achieves 73 percent of its asymptotic value in 10 msec, 91 percent in 20 msec, and 99 percent in 40 msec. Thus, to a good approximation one can reason about the impact of the asymptotic activation values without worrying about how asymptote was achieved. Thus Eq. (3.7) is the important one for determining the activation pattern. The appendix to this chapter contains some uses of Eq. (3.7) for deciding about the impact of various network structures on distribution of activation. It shows that level of activation tends to decay exponentially with distance from source.

The rapidity of spread of activation is in keeping with a good number of other experimental results that will be reviewed in this chapter and with the adaptive function of spreading activation. As mentioned earlier, activation is supposed to be a relevancy heuristic for determining the importance of various pieces of information. It guides subsequent processing and makes it more efficient. It would not make much adaptive sense to compute a spreading activation process if that computation took a long time to identify the relevant structures of memory.

SUMMING UP

This section has shown in detail how a spreading activation mechanism, consistent with our knowledge of neural functioning, produces a variation in activation levels. Equation (3.7) describes asymptotic patterns of activation, which, it was shown, are approached so rapidly that one can safely ignore spreading time in reaction time calculations. Thus a coherent rationale has been established for using Eq. (3.7). In some enterprises (see Chapter 5), faced with complex networks, one might want to resort to solving the simultaneous equations in (3.7). However, for the purposes of this chapter, its qualitative implications are sufficient.

The level of activation of a piece of network structure determines how rapidly it is processed by the pattern matcher. Chapter 4 will go into detail about how the pattern matcher performs its tests and how it is controlled by level of activation. For current purposes the following approximation is useful: if the pattern tests to be performed have complexity $K$ and the data has activation $A$, the time to perform the tests will be $K/A$. Thus time is directly proportional to our measure of pattern complexity and inversely proportional to activation. This implies a multiplicative rather than an additive relationship between pattern complexity and level of activation. In this chapter pattern complexity will remain an intuitive concept, but it will be more precisely defined in the next chapter.

## Priming Studies

Priming involves presenting subjects with some information and then testing the effect of the presentation on access to associated information. In the lexical decision task (Becker, 1980; Fischler, 1977; McKoon and Ratcliff, 1979; Meyer and Schvaneveldt, 1971; Neely, 1977), the one most frequently used, it is found that less time is required to decide that an item is a word if it is preceded by an associated word. For instance *butter* is more rapidly judged to be a word when preceded by *bread*. These paradigms strongly demonstrate the importance of associative spread of activation. They are particularly convincing because the priming information is not directly part of the measured task, and subjects are often unaware of the associative relations between the prime and the target. The fact that priming is obtained without awareness is a direct reflection of the automatic and ubiquitous character of associative spread of activation. Beneficial effects of associatively related primes have also been observed in word naming (Warren, 1977), free association (Perlmutter and Anderson, unpublished), item recognition (Ratcliff and McKoon, 1981), sentence completion and sensibility judgments (Reder, in press), and word completion (Schustack, 1981).

While facilitation of the associated word is the dominant result, inhibition is sometimes found for words unrelated to the prime (Neely, 1977; Fischler and Bloom, 1979; Becker, 1980). For instance, judgment of *butter* may be slower when preceded by the unrelated *glove* than when preceded by *xxxxx* if the subject consciously expects the following word to be related—a word such as *hand*, rather than *butter*—after *glove*. If the subject is not aware of the predictive relation between the associative prime and the target, or if the prime-to-target interval is too short to permit an expectation to develop, only positive facilitation is observed. Neely has related this to Posner and Snyder's (1975) distinction between automatic and conscious activation.

A PRODUCTION SYSTEM MODEL

Table 3.2 provides a set of productions that model performance in a lexical decision task, and Figure 3.2 illustrates the flow
of control among them. Central to this analysis is the idea that
the subject enters the experiment with productions, such as P1,
which automatically label stimuli as words. There would be one

**Table 3.2** *Productions for performance in the lexical decision task*

1. **A word-naming production**
   P1    IF the word is spelled F-E-A-T-H-E-R
         THEN assert that the word is similar to FEATHER.

2. **Productions that perform automatic lexical decision**
   P2    IF the goal is to judge if the stimulus is spelled correctly
         and a word is similar to the stimulus
         and the stimulus mismatches the spelling of the word
         THEN say no.

   P3    IF the goal is to judge if the stimulus is spelled correctly
         and a word is similar to the stimulus
         and the stimulus does not mismatch the spelling of the
         word
         THEN say yes.

3. **Productions that perform deliberate lexical decision**
   P4    IF the goal is to judge if the stimulus matches an anticipated
         word
         and a word is anticipated
         and the stimulus does not mismatch the spelling of the
         word
         THEN say yes.

   P5    IF the goal is to judge if the stimulus matches an anticipated
         word
         and a word is anticipated
         and the stimulus mismatches the spelling of the word
         THEN change the goal to judging if the stimulus is correctly
         spelled.

4. **An optional production that capitalizes on nonwords similar to
   the anticipated word**
   P6    IF the goal is to judge if the stimulus matches an anticipated
         word
         and a word is anticipated
         and the stimulus is similar to the word
         and the stimulus mismatches the spelling of the word
         THEN say no.

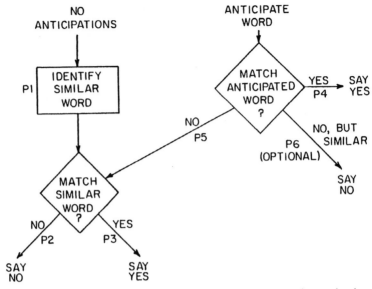

**Figure 3.2**   *A representation of the flow of control among the productions in Table 3.2.*

such production per word. Not only will they label actual words, but they will label near-words like FEATHFR with its closest matching word. The mechanisms of such word identification and partial matching will be described in the next chapter. It is reasonable to suppose that such productions exist, given that throughout our lives we have to recognize briefly presented and imperfectly produced words. The difficulty of proofreading text for spelling errors is also evidence that such partial-matching productions exist.

Since productions like P1 will label partial matches, the subject cannot respond simply upon the firing of P1; the spelling of the similar word must be checked against the stimulus. It has been suggested that the results typically observed in lexical decision tasks depend on the fact that the distractors are similar to words (James, 1975; Neely, 1977). Certainly the subject needs some basis for rejecting distractors, and that basis may well have an impact upon the process for recognizing targets. According to the model presented here, the subject rejects a stimulus as a nonword if it mismatches a hypothesized word and accepts the stimulus if a mismatch cannot be found.

Productions P2 and P3 model performance in those situations where the subject is not consciously anticipating a particular word[5] but is operating with the goal of seeing if the stimulus matches the spelling of the word judged as similar. These productions therefore must wait for a production like P1 to first label the stimulus.[6]

Productions P4 and P5 model performance when the subject is consciously anticipating a word. In this case there is no need to wait for the stimulus to be labeled as similar to a word; it can be matched against the anticipated word. If it matches, the subject can exit with a quick yes. If not, the subject cannot yet say no. He might have expected FEATHER, but was presented with SHOULDER or SHOULDFR, in which case he must return to the goal of judging a similar word. Production P5 switches to the goal of judging the similar word. It is assumed that while P5 was applying, a word-naming production like P1 would also have applied to produce a hypothesis about the identity of the stimulus. Therefore, in Figure 3.2, P5 goes directly to the similarity judging box where P2 and P3 can apply. Note that P2 and P3 have the goal of checking the spelling, while P4 and P5 have the goal of matching an anticipated word. Because the two goals are contradictory, P2 and P3 cannot apply in parallel with P4 and P5, but only after P5.

P6 reflects an optional production for which there is some experimental evidence, as I will discuss. It generates a no if the stimulus does not match but is similar to an anticipated word. In contrast to P5, P6 avoids the need to go onto P2 and P3. Thus, if FEATHER were anticipated, it would generate a quick no to FEATHFR. It would also erroneously generate a quick no to HEATHER. However, no experiment has used words similar but not identical to anticipated words.

THE PATTERN-MATCHING NETWORK

Figure 3.3 provides a schematic illustration of how the pattern matching for productions P2–P5 is implemented. The top half of the figure illustrates the pattern network, and the bottom half a hypothetical state of the declarative network that drives the pattern matcher. Critical to the operation of this system is the subnode A, which detects conflicts between word spelling and the information in the stimulus. When the goal is to judge a similar word, P2 and P3 will be applicable. Note that P2 receives positive input from both A, which detects a spelling mismatch, and from the clause noting the most similar word. P2 thus performs a test to see if there is a misspelling of the similar word. P3 receives a positive input from the similar word node but a *negative* input from the A node. P3 thus checks that there

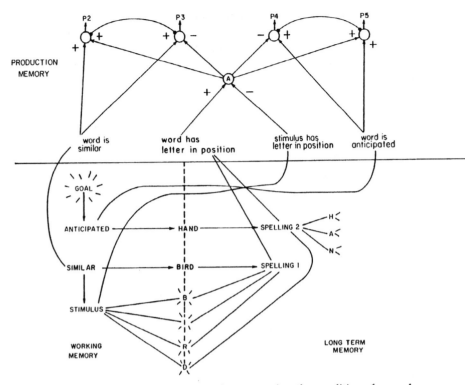

**Figure 3.3**   *The pattern network representing the conditions for productions P2, P3, P4, and P5 in the lexical decision task. Also represented are the temporary structures created to encode the probe, the sources of activation (from which rays emanate), and the connections to long-term memory. For simplicity, the goal elements in P2–P5 are not represented.*

are no misspellings. P2 and P3 are mutually inhibitory, and only one can apply.

Similarly, P4 and P5 are applicable when the goal is to judge an anticipated word. If there is no conflict with the *anticipated* word, P4 will apply to say yes. If there is a conflict with the *anticipated* word, P5 will apply to switch the goal to judge a similar word. As with P2 and P3, P4 and P5 are mutually inhibitory.

The bottom section of Figure 3.3 illustrates the situation in declarative memory. Anticipating a word (for example, *hand*) amounts to keeping active in memory a proposition to that effect ("*hand* is anticipated"), with activation maintained by the goal element. The letters of the stimulus keep the spelling information active. Activation spreads from these temporary memory structures to activate spelling information for various words in long-term memory. In addition to the stimulus and the anticipated word, a third potential source of activation is presentation of an associated priming word, which can activate the target word.

BASIC PREDICTIONS OF THE MODEL

This model explains the basic effects observed in the priming paradigms. First, presenting a word will increase the activation of all related words and their spelling information. This will speed the rate at which P2 can detect a mismatch to a related word and hence the rate at which P3 can decide that there is a match. On the other hand, if the probe is not related, the rate at which P2 and P3 apply will be unaffected by the prime. Thus the model predicts only facilitation and no inhibition in paradigms of automatic priming.

Conscious anticipation of the probe has two advantages; first, the spelling information is more active, and second, there is no need for initial identification by a word-naming production like P1. On the other hand, if the anticipation is not met, there is the cost of switching the goal to judging a similar word. Thus the model predicts both benefit and cost in paradigms of conscious priming.

Table 3.3 is an attempt to analyze the full combinatorial possibilities of the lexical decision task. The subject may or may not have a conscious anticipation and may or may not have automatically primed a set of words. In the case of conscious anticipation or automatic priming, the stimulus may or may not match the items anticipated or primed (a nonword FEATHFR

**Table 3.3**  *Analysis of automatic and conscious priming for words and nonwords: comparisons with control condition*[1]

|  |  | Match anticipation | Not match anticipation | No anticipation |
|---|---|---|---|---|
| MATCH PRIME | Word | $S^+$, $A^+$ | $E^-$, $A^+$ | $A^+$ |
|  | Nonword | $E^-$, $A^+$ | $E^-$, $A^+$ | $A^+$ |
| NOT MATCH PRIME | Word | $S^+$ | $E^-$ | — |
|  | Nonword | $E^-$ | $E^-$ | — |
| NO PRIMING | Word | $S^+$ | $E^-$ | Control |
|  | Nonword | $E^-$ | $E^-$ | Control |

1. $A^+$ is the advantage of automatic activation. $S^+$ is the advantage of conscious anticipation. $E^-$ is the cost if the anticipated word is not presented.

would be considered to match a primed word like FEATHER). Finally, the stimulus may be a word or a nonword. Table 3.3 gives all eighteen possibilities created by these combinations.

The standard control cases are when there is no anticipation or priming; Table 3.3 gives the relevant differences between these controls for word and nonword and the other cases. These predictions are based on the assumption that the subject uses productions P2–P5, as shown in Table 3.2, but not the optional P6. There are three factors: $A^+$ refers to the activation-based advantage of automatic priming; $S^+$ refers to the priming advantage associated with conscious anticipation through activation of spelling information and omission of the similarity judgment production (P1); and $E^-$ refers to the cost of having judgment of the anticipated word followed by the attempt to match some other word. As the table shows, the theory predicts that the effects of automatic and conscious priming are cumulative. Also, no advantage of conscious anticipation is predicted for nonwords.

Neely (1977) came close to including all the possibilities of Table 3.3 in one experiment. He presented subjects with a prime followed at varying delays by a target stimulus. He was able to separate automatic priming from conscious priming by telling subjects to anticipate the name of a building when they saw *body part* as a prime. In this way there would be conscious anticipation of a building but automatic priming of a body part. On some trials Neely surprised subjects by following *body part* with a body-part word such as *leg*. When there was a 700 msec delay between prime and target, the benefit of priming for a body part was less than the cost of the failed anticipation, yielding a net inhibition. However, on such trials there was less inhibition for a surprise body-part word than for a surprise bird word. This is the result predicted if one assumes that the benefits of automatic priming combine with the cost of conscious inhibition. It corresponds to the contrast between the not-match-anticipation, match-prime situation and the not-match-anticipation, not-match-prime control in Table 3.3.

Fischler and Bloom (1979) and Neely (1977) have reported that conscious priming has a beneficial effect on nonword judgments, contradicting the predictions in Table 3.3. There appear to be small decreases in latency for nonwords similar to the primed word. However, there is also a slight increase in the false-alarm rate. According to Table 3.2, conscious priming has no beneficial effects for nonwords because execution of P5, which rejects the word as failing expectations, must be followed by P2, which rejects the match to a similar word. Thus if a subject expects FEATHER and sees SHOULDFR, P5 will reject the match to the expected word and change the goal to judge the spelling of a similar word. If SHOULDER is selected as similar, P2 will reject the match to SHOULDFR and execute *no*. There is no benefit associated with having a nonword similar to a conscious expectation, so a subject will be no faster if FEATHFR is presented when FEATHER is expected. To account for the small benefits observed, one might assume that subjects sometimes use the optional P6 in Table 3.2, which would produce faster performance for similar nonwords.

INTERACTION WITH STIMULUS QUALITY

A critical question is how well ACT can explain the various factors that modulate the degree of priming. For instance, Meyer, Schvaneveldt, and Ruddy (1975) report that the effect of priming is increased in the presence of degraded stimuli. The patterns matched in P2 and P3 are combinations of information about the physical stimulus and about the spelling pattern. The rate of pattern matching will be a function of both sources of activation. Degrading the stimulus will lower the level of activation from the physical stimulus and so increase processing time. It also means that pattern matching is more dependent on activation of the spelling information, so there will be an increased priming effect.

It should be noted here that Meyer and colleagues propose a different interpretation of their results. Using Sternberg's (1969) additive factors logic, they assume from the interaction of stimulus quality and priming that semantic context primes the perceptual processing before information from lexical memory is involved. The ACT analysis is that stimulus quality affects the rate of lexical pattern matching (P2 and P3) by affecting the amount of activation coming from the perceptual encoding. The experiment by Meyer and colleagues offers no basis for separating the two interpretations. However, it should be noted that the ACT explanation predicts the direction of the interaction, not just its existence.

EFFECTS OF SIZE OF EXPECTED SET

In many experiments subjects cannot predict the specific word that will occur. For instance, they might be primed with a category (*dog*) and be led to expect any member of that category. They might prepare for a small number of members in the category (collie, poodle, labrador) and avoid the similarity stage (P2 and P3) if the item is one of these. However, the number of items they can expect is small, corresponding to the limitation on the number of items that can be kept active in working memory. If the set of words that might follow the prime is greater than the number that can be kept active, subjects have only a probability of correctly anticipating the word. Consistent with this, Becker (1980) has shown that the amount of facilitation is a function of the size of the primed set. Fischler and Bloom (1979) have shown that there are positive benefits only for the most probable continuations of a sentence.

Preparing for more than one word would mean holding more than one assertion of the form "*collie* is anticipated" active in working memory. The number of assertions that can be held active should be limited by the capacity to maintain information in an active state. One effect of maintaining more assertions would be to decrease the amount of activation being expended by P5 to test any one anticipated word because activation from the stimulus has to be divided among all the words. Thus it should take longer for P5 to detect a mismatch and to switch to the similarity stage. In this way, ACT can explain the other result observed by Becker: that inhibition was greater when larger sets were expected.

### Time Course of Priming

By looking at the amount of priming at various intervals after a stimulus, it is possible to make inferences about the loss of activation in the semantic network. Meyer, Schvaneveldt, and Ruddy (1972) show that approximately half of the priming benefit remains 4 seconds after the prime. Other studies (for example, Swinney, 1979) have shown rapid decay of priming by the unintended meaning of an ambiguous word, such that in less than a second, no priming remains. From the Meyer et al. study, something like 4 seconds can be taken as a high estimate on the half life of priming, and from the Swinney study, something like 400 msec can be taken as a low estimate. According to ACT theory, these half-life estimates reflect the parameter $\Delta t$, the time a node can stay active without rehearsal. There is some difficulty in assessing when subjects cease to rehearse or focus an item. The higher times in Meyer et al. may reflect maintenance activity by the subject.

A related issue is the time course of the rise of activation. Fischler and Goodman (1978), Ratcliff and McKoon (1981), and Warren (1977) have shown that automatic priming is nearly at maximum less than 200 msec after presentation of the prime.

Schustack (1981) found high degrees of priming even when the onset of the prime followed the onset of the to-be-primed target. This superficially anomalous result can be understood when we realize that processing of the target occurs over a time interval that overlaps with presentation of the prime (Fischler and Goodman, 1978). In any case it is apparent that onset of facilitation is rapid. These studies also provide little or no evidence for a gradual rise in priming as claimed by Wickelgren (1976). That is, the size of the priming effect is nearly maximal close to its onset. The empirical picture is consistent with the ACT analysis in which an asymptotic pattern of activation is rapidly set up in the declarative network, and this pattern determines the rate of pattern matching.

INTERACTION WITH PATTERN MATCHING

The size of the priming effect depends on the difficulty of the pattern matching. Word naming (Warren, 1977) produces smaller priming effects than lexical decision. In a word-naming task one simply has to say the word, without checking it carefully for a subtle misspelling. (Indeed, word naming is basically implemented by P1 in Table 3.2.) Similarly, McKoon and Ratcliff (1979) have found larger priming effects on item recognition than on word–nonword judgments. Recognition judgment requires matching contextual information and so is more demanding of the pattern-matching apparatus. As noted earlier, ACT predicts this relationship between pattern complexity and level of activation.

THE STROOP PHENOMENON

One challenging phenomenon that must be accounted for is the effect of associative priming in the Stroop task (Warren, 1974). The Stroop task involves naming the color of a word. It takes longer to name the color if the word is preceded by an associatively related word. In this task the priming effect is negative. To explain this, it is necessary to assume, as is basic to all analyses of the Stroop task (for a review see Dyer, 1973), that there are competing tendencies to process the color of the word and to name the word. These competing tendencies can be represented in ACT by the following pair of productions:

P7     IF the goal is to say the name of the color
          and LVconcept is the color of LVstimulus
          and LVcode is the articulatory code for LVconcept
   THEN generate LVcode.

P8     IF the goal is to say the name of the word
          and LVconcept is the identity of LVstimulus
          and LVcode is the articulatory code for LVconcept
    THEN generate LVcode.

Consider what happens when *dog* is presented in red. The following information will be active in working memory:

1. The goal is to say the name of the color.
2. Red is the color of the stimulus.
3. "Red" is the response code for red.
4. Dog is the identity of the stimulus.
5. "Dog" is the response code for dog.

Fact 5 is a long-term-memory structure that is made more active through priming of *dog*. There is a correct instantiation of P7 involving facts 1, 2, and 3. However, there is a partial instantiation of P7 involving 1, 2, and 5, and a partial instantiation of P8 involving 1, 4, and 5. The instantiation of P7 is partial because *red* in 2 does not match *dog* in 5 (that they should match is indicated by the same variable LVconcept in the second and third clauses of P7). The instantiation of P8 is partial because *word* in the first clause of P8 mismatches *color* in fact 1. These partial matches will compete with the correct instantiation of P7, and the amount of competition they provide will be increased by the primed activation of fact 5.[7]

This analysis does not identify the Stroop interference as being at the level of either perceptual encoding (Hock and Egeth, 1970) or response competition (Morton, 1969). Rather, it is taking place at the level of matching competing patterns to data in working memory, where the critical piece of data (response-code association as in fact 5 above) is not a perceptual encoding nor a motor response. This corresponds most closely to the "conceptual encoding" analysis of the Stroop task (Seymour, 1977; Stirling, 1979).

This example shows that increased activation does not inevitably lead to better performance. If that activation goes to a production responsible for generating the correct behavior, it will lead to better performance; if it goes to unrelated productions it will have no effect; if it goes to competing productions it will have a detrimental effect.

## The Fact-Retrieval Paradigm

In a typical fact-retrieval situation (Anderson, 1974; Anderson and Bower, 1973; Hayes-Roth, 1977; King and Anderson, 1976; Lewis and Anderson, 1976; Thorndyke and Bower, 1974), a fact is presented that subjects have stored in memory (either a fact about the world, known by all subjects, or a fact learned as part of an experiment). Subjects are simply asked whether or not they recognize the fact, such as *Hank Aaron hits home runs.* They must reject foils like *Hank Aaron comes from India* (Lewis and Anderson, 1976).

The fact retrieval paradigm is a much more direct and deliberate study of retrieval than the typical priming study. It is not at all obvious, a priori, that the two paradigms would tap the same processes, and the relation between the paradigms needs further research. However, the preliminary indication is that the two phenomena do involve the same processes. It is possible to prime the recognition of experimentally studied material (Fischler, Bryant, and Querns, unpublished; McKoon and Ratcliff, 1979). Experimentally acquired associations have been shown to lead to priming of lexical decisions (Fischler, Bryant, and Querns, unpublished; McKoon and Ratcliff, 1979).

A major experimental variable in the study of fact retrieval has been called *fan,* which refers to the number of facts studied about a concept. The more facts are associated with one particular concept, the slower is the recognition of any one of the facts. In the current framework this manipulation is interpreted as affecting the amount of activation that is spread to a particular fact. The assumption is that each concept or node has a limited capacity for spreading activation, and as more paths are attached to it, the amount of activation that can be spread down any path is reduced. There are considerable experimental advantages in being able to more or less directly control the amount of activation spread to a portion of the network.

PRODUCTION IMPLEMENTATION

In Table 3.4 productions P1 through P4 model recognition and rejection of probes in the fact-retrieval experiment described by Anderson (1976, p. 258). Subjects studied location-subject-verb sentences of the form *In the bank the lawyer laughed.* After committing the sentences to memory, subjects were shown four types of probes: (1) three-element targets, which were identical to the sentences studied; (2) three-element

**Table 3.4**    *Productions for performance is a fact-retrieval task*

---

P1    IF the goal is to recognize the sentence
        and the probe is "In the LVlocation the LVperson LVaction"
        and (LVaction LVperson LVlocation) has been studied
    THEN say yes.

P2    IF the goal is to recognize the sentence
        and the probe is "In the LVlocation the LVperson LVaction"
        and (LVaction LVperson LVlocation) has not been studied
    THEN say no.

P3    IF the goal is to recognize the sentence
        and the probe is "The LVperson LVaction"
        and (LVaction LVperson LVlocation) has been studied
    THEN say yes.

P4    IF the goal is to recognize the sentence
        and the probe is "The LVperson LVaction"
        and the probe (LVaction LVperson LVlocation) has not been
        studied
    THEN say no.

---

foils, consisting of a location, subject, and verb that had all
been studied but not in that combination; (3) two-element targets in which, for example, the subject and verb were from the
target sentence; and (4) two-element foils in which the subject
and verb came from different sentences. Response to these four
types of probes is handled by productions P1–P4, respectively,
in Table 3.4.

Production P1 recognizes that the current probe matches a
proposition previously stored in memory. The elements in
quotes refer to the probe, and the elements in parentheses refer
to the proposition in memory. P1 determines whether the
probe and proposition match by checking whether the variables (LVlocation, LVperson, and LVaction) bind to the same
elements in the probe and the proposition. P2 will fire if the
variables do not match in a three-element probe. Productions
P3 and P4 are like P1 and P2 except that they respond to two-
element probes.

PATTERN MATCHING STRUCTURE

Figure 3.4 illustrates schematically the structure of production memory for P1–P4 and their connections to declarative
memory. Each production is represented as consisting of two
clauses,[8] which are represented as separate elements at the bottom of the figure. The elements, called terminal nodes, perform

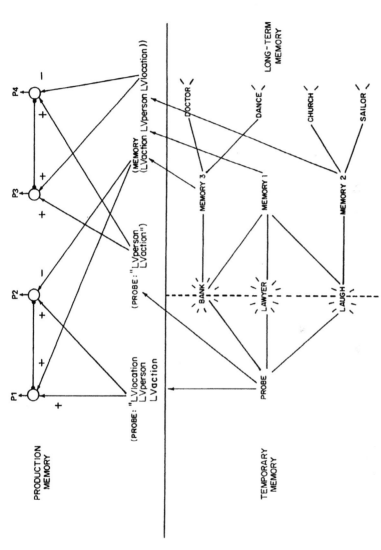

**Figure 3.4** The pattern network representing the conditions for productions P1–P4 in the fact recognition task. Also represented are the active concepts in the probe—bank, lawyer, and laugh—and their connections to long-term memory. Sources of activation are indicated by rays emanating from those nodes.

tests to find clauses in declarative memory that match them. These clauses are combined at higher nodes. The two-input nodes with two positive lines perform tests of the variable identity between the two clauses. So P1 checks that LVlocation, LVperson, and LVaction are the same in probe as in memory structure. A negative two-input node like P2 will fire if there is input on its positive line and no compatible input on its negative line.

In Figure 3.4 declarative memory is partitioned into temporary memory, representing the probe, and long-term memory, encoding the studied facts. The main sources of activation are the individual elements (*bank, lawyer, laugh*), which are encodings of the external probe. From these elements activation spreads to the probe and throughout long-term memory. The probe is connected to two terminal nodes in production memory that test for the two probe patterns (two-element and three-element). The rate at which the nodes perform their tests is determined by the level of activation of the probe structure. Similarly, the propositions in declarative memory are connected to the proposition terminal node in production memory. Again, the rate at which any proposition is processed by the pattern node is a function of the level of activation of that proposition. Also, the rate of pattern testing at the higher nodes in production memory is a function of the level of activation of the data (declarative memory) elements being tested. In the case of the positive P1 and P3, this level will be the sum of the activation of the probe and the memory elements. In the case of negative P2 and P4, this level will be affected only by the probe activation.

The absence test in P2 is implemented by setting up an inhibitory relation between P1 and P2, and similarly, the absence test in P4 is handled by an inhibitory relation between P3 and P4. Strong evidence for P1 will repress P2 and prevent it from firing. If there is not sufficient evidence for P1, P2 will build up evidence for itself and eventually fire. P2 in this model is set to accumulate activation from the proposition twice as fast as P1, so if there is not a good match to P1, P2 will repress it. This inhibitory relationship makes P2 wait to see if P1 will match. The mechanisms of production pattern matching are described in Chapter 4. However, there are three important features to note now about how the pattern matcher treats P1–P4:

1. Pattern matching will take longer with high-fan probes, those whose elements appear in multiple study sentences. The fan from an element reduces the amount of activation that can

go to any propositional trace or to the probe encoding it. Pattern matching for targets is a function of the activation of the propositional trace and the probe.

2. It should take longer to recognize larger probes because more tests must be performed. In this experiment, three-element probes took longer than two-element probes. For ample additional evidence in support of this prediction, see Anderson (1976, chap. 8).

3. Foils that are more similar to studied sentences should be harder to reject. In this experiment "overlap" foils were used that had two of three elements in common with a studied sentence. Subjects found these harder to reject than nonoverlap foils. Again, for many confirmations of this prediction, see Anderson (1976, chap. 8). ACT* predicts that a partial match of the positive production pattern (for example, P1) will inhibit growth of evidence at the negative production pattern (for example, P2). More generally, ACT* predicts difficulty in rejecting partial matches.

REJECTION OF FOILS

An interesting question is, how does a person decide that he does not know something? In these experiments this question is addressed by ACT's model for foil rejection.[9] The most obvious model, which is obviously incorrect, is that subjects exhaustively search their memories about a concept. However, foils are rejected much too quickly for this to be true; typically, the times to reject foils are only slightly longer than the times to accept targets. Anderson (1976) and King and Anderson (1976) proposed what was called the *waiting model,* in which subjects waited some amount of time for the probe to be recognized. If it was not recognized in that time, they would reject it. The assumption was that subjects would adjust their waiting time to reflect factors, like fan, that determine the time taken to recognize targets.

*Implementation of the waiting model.* The current ACT theory provides a more mechanistic instantiation of the waiting model. As indicated in Figure 3.4, a foil is rejected by a production whose condition pattern detects the absence of information in memory. If a production is looking for the presence of subpattern S1 and the absence of pattern S2, two pattern nodes are created. One corresponds to the positive conjunction S1&S2, and the other to S1& ~S2. In Figure 3.4 the S1&S2 conjunctions correspond to productions P1 and P3, and the S1& ~S2 conjunctions to P2 and P4. An inhibitory relation is established between the positive S1&S2 and the negative S1&~S2. Both positive and negative patterns receive activation from S1, but only the positive pattern receives activation from S2.[10] In the figure, the common subpattern S1 refers to the encoding of the probe, and S2 refers to the memory proposition. The S1&~S2 pattern builds up activation either until total activation reaches a threshold or until it is repressed by accruing evidence for the positive S1&S2 pattern.

A long-standing question in the ACT theory is how subjects adjust their waiting time to reflect the fan of elements in a foil. Such an adjustment makes sense, because if they did not wait long enough for high-fan targets, they would be in danger of spuriously rejecting them. However, for a long time there was no plausible mechanism to account for adjusting the waiting time. The obvious idea of counting links out of a node and setting waiting time according to the counted fan is implausible. But the current pattern-matching system provides a mechanism for adjusting waiting time with no added assumptions. Note in Figure 3.4 that the fan of elements will affect not only the activation of the memory elements but also that of the probe encoding. This activation will determine the amount of activation that arrives at the S1&~S2 conjunctions in P2 and P4, and thus fan will cause activation to build more slowly to threshold for the foil-detecting productions. It will also have the desired effect of giving high-fan targets more time to complete pattern matching.

One should not conclude from this discussion that the only way of responding *no* is by this waiting process. As in the Glucksberg and McCloskey (1981) experiment, subjects can retrieve information that allows them to explicitly decide they don't know. They may also retrieve information that implies the probe is false (for example, *Ronald Reagan is a famous liberal senator from Alabama*). However, absence detection by waiting is an important basic mechanism for concluding that one does not know anything about a particular fact.

*Tests of the waiting model.* It is predicted that a foil is harder to reject the more features it shares with a target (leading to activation of S2 and S1&S2 in the above analysis). As reported earlier, Anderson (1976) found that overlap foils including a number of words from the studied sentence took longer to reject than non-overlap foils. The experiment by King and Anderson illustrates another kind of similarity that may slow down foil rejection. We had subjects study sentences such as

The doctor hated the lawyer.
The doctor ignored the model.

This was called a connected set because the two sentences had the same subject. Unconnected sets were created in the same mold but did not have the same subject. The task was to recognize whether verb-object pairs came from the same sentence. So *hated the lawyer* would be a positive probe and *hated the model* a negative probe. Negative probes or foils were always constructed by pairing a verb and an object from different sentences in a set, either connected or unconnected. Subjects showed no difference in speed of recognizing positive probes from connected and unconnected sentence sets, but they were slower and made more errors in rejecting foils from connected than those from unconnected sets. The connected foils were spuriously connected from verb to object through the shared subject, causing a partial match to the positive conjunction (S1&S2) and inhibiting the production that detected the absence (S1& ~ S2).

Anderson and Ross (1980) have performed an extension of this logic to study what is nominally called semantic memory. Subjects studied sentences like *The cat attacked the snake* in the first phase of the experiment, then judged the truth of categorical probes like *A cat is a snake* in the second phase. They were slower and made more errors in these categorical judgments when they had learned an irrelevant sentence, like *The cat attacked the snake*, linking the two categories in the first phase.

Anderson and Ross suggested that similarity effects in semantic memory are to be understood in terms of spurious intersections. These similarity effects in semantic memory are the findings that it is harder to reject a pair of the form *An A is a B* the more similar A and B are. So *A dog is a bird* is harder to reject than *A dog is a rock*. Thinking of the similarity effect in terms of the number of prior connections between the subject and predicate of the sentence makes it possible to understand the experiments (Collins and Quillian, 1972) in which subjects are slow to reject foils when the relationship between subject and predicate is not one of similarity but some other associative relation. Example sentences from Collins and Quillian are *An almond has a fortune* and *Madrid is Mexican*.

Another result that can be understood in this framework has been reported by Glucksberg, Gildea, and Bookin (1982). They found that subjects have considerable difficulty in rejecting as false statements like *Some surgeons are butchers*, which have a high degree of truth metaphorically but a low degree of truth literally. This difficulty can be predicted because of intersections between subject and predicate.

### Effects of the Number of Sources of Activation

In ACT*, activation spreads from multiple sources at once, and activation converging on one node from multiple sources will sum. A typical sentence recognition experiment presents probes with multiple concepts like *The fireman snored in the winery*. *Fireman, snored,* and *winery* all provide indices into memory and hence are sources for activation. The amount of activation converging on the trace connecting these concepts should be the sum of the activation from each concept. Thus, the time taken to recognize the sentence should be affected by the fan of each concept. As reviewed in Anderson (1976), this prediction has been consistently confirmed, despite fairly strong efforts to get the subject to focus on only one of the elements in the sentence.

Another implication of the sum model is that the more concepts provided for recognition, the more activation should accumulate. For instance, the sentence *In the bank the lawyer mocked the doctor* consists of four major concepts—*bank, lawyer, mock,* and *doctor*. If the subject is presented with two, three, or four of these elements and asked if all the words occurred in one sentence, there should be twice as much activation accumulated at the propositional trace with a four-element probe as with a two-element probe.[11] Unfortunately, it does not follow that recognition times will be faster, because the subject must perform more complex pattern tests to determine that more elements are properly configured. The evidence in Anderson (1976) was that the greater complexity of the pattern tests overrode the activation advantage. I have found a similar outcome in simulating pattern matching with networks such as the one in Figure 3.4.

However, a recent unpublished experiment of mine has avoided this confounding. In this experiment subjects did not have to recognize all elements in the sentences. They learned to assign numbers to four-element (location-subject-verb-object) sentences such as *In the bank the lawyer cheated the doctor,* then were presented with probes consisting of all four elements, random subsets of three, or random subsets of two. All the elements came from one sentence, and subjects were asked to retrieve the number of that sentence. The number could always be retrieved from any two words in a probe, so the complexity of the pattern matching did not increase with the number of elements in the probe (although it might take longer to initially encode the stimulus). In each case subjects only had to test if two words came from a sentence. The extra word or two in three- and four-element probes just provided extra sources of activation. In this experiment, subjects took 2.42 seconds to recognize two-element probes, 2.34 seconds to recognize three-element probes, and 2.29 seconds to recognize four-element probes.

Another prediction of this model is that fan effects should be smaller when the probes contain more elements. This is based on the following analysis: Suppose $n$ elements, with fan $f$, are presented. The total activation arriving should be $nA/f$, and recognition time should be a function of the inverse, or $f/nA$. Note that the fan effect is divided by the number of elements.

Another unpublished experiment contrasting recall and recognition provides a test of this prediction. The material learned consisted of subject-verb-object sentences. The objects were always unique (fan 1), but the subject and verb occurred in one, two, or three sentences. In the recognition condition, subjects saw a sentence and had to recognize it. In the recall experiment, they saw subject and verb and had to recall the object. In both cases the pattern-matching operations would have to identify subject, verb, and object, so pattern complexity was held constant. Although the subject and verb might have occurred in multiple sentences, they occurred only once together, so the to-be-recalled object was uniquely specified. Table 3.5 presents the recognition and recall performance as a function of subject and verb fan. In this experiment the two fans were correlated; if the subject fan was $n$, the verb fan was $n$ also. As can be seen, fan had a much greater effect on the recall condition than on recognition.

Table 3.5 also presents the predictions for this experiment based on a simple model that assumes the total activation in the recognition condition was $(2/f + 1)A$, where $f$ = fan, and in the other recall condition was $(2/f)A$. The $2/f$ refers to the summed activation from subject and verb; the 1 in the recognition equation refers to the extra activation from the one-fan object. Reaction time is predicted by an inverse function of activation, and a single intercept was estimated for the recall and recognition conditions. As can be seen, this model does a good job of accounting for the differences in the size of fan effects. In

**Table 3.5** *Observed and predicted reaction times as a function of fan and whether recognition or recall was required*[1]

| Fan | Recognition[2] | Recall[3] |
|-----|----------------|-----------|
| 1 | Obs: 1.35 sec | Obs: 1.54 sec |
|   | Pred: 1.33 sec | Pred: 1.55 sec |
| 2 | Obs: 1.58 sec | Obs: 2.07 sec |
|   | Pred: 1.55 sec | Pred: 2.22 sec |
| 3 | Obs: 1.70 sec | Obs: 2.96 sec |
|   | Pred: 1.68 sec | Pred: 2.89 sec |

1. Obs = observed; Pred = predicted; RT = reaction time. Correlation: $r = .991$; standard error of observed times = .07 sec.
2. Predicting equation: $RT = .88 + 1.34/(2/f + 1)$.
3. Predicting equation: $RT = .88 + 1.34/(2/f)$.

Anderson (1981) a similar but more elaborate model has been applied to predicting the differences in interference (fan) effects obtained in paired-associate recognition versus recall.

JUDGMENTS OF CONNECTEDNESS

As discussed in Chapter 2, subjects can judge whether elements are connected in memory more rapidly than they can judge *how* they are connected (Glucksberg and McCloskey, 1981). Detecting connectivity is a more primitive pattern-matching operation than identifying the type of connection. I speculated in Chapter 2 that detection of connectivity might be a property unique to propositional structures.

Another unpublished study confirms again the salience of connectivity information within propositional structures and also checks for an interaction with fan. After studying true and false sentences of the form *It is true that the doctor hated the lawyer* and *It is false that the sailor stabbed the baker,* subjects were presented with simple subject-verb-object sentences (*The sailor stabbed the baker*). They were asked to make one of three judgments about the sentence—whether it was true, whether it was false, and whether it had been studied (as either a true or false sentence). The last judgment could be made solely on the basis of connectivity, but the other two required a more complex pattern match that would retrieve the studied truth value. Crossed with the type of question was the type of sentence—true, false, or a re-pairing of studied elements—about which the question was asked. The terms could be either one- or two-fan. Thus the design of the experiment was 3 (types of question) × 3 (types of sentence) × 2 (fan).

Table 3.6 presents the results of the experiment classified according to the described factors. Table 3.7 presents the average times and fan effects collapsed over type of question or type of material. Note that subjects were fastest to make studied judgments in which they only had to judge the connectivity of the elements. They were slower on true and false judgments. Significantly, the fan effect is 497 msec for true and false judgments but only 298 msec for studied judgments. Thus fan has less effect on connectivity judgments than on judgments of exact relationship. This is further evidence for the expected interaction between complexity of the pattern test and level of activation. Subjects are also faster to judge re-paired material than other material, but they do not show smaller fan effects. Thus, the effect of question type on fan is not just a matter of longer times showing larger effects.

An interesting series of experiments (Glass and Holyoak, 1979; Meyer, 1970; Rips, 1975) has been done on the relative difficulty of universal statements (*All collies are dogs*) versus particular statements (*Some collies are dogs, Some pets are cats*). When subjects have to judge only particulars or universals, they judge particulars more quickly than universals. On the other hand, when particulars and universals are mixed, subjects are faster to judge universals. This can be explained by assuming that subjects adopt a connectivity strategy in the particular-only blocks. That is, it is possible to discriminate most true particu-

**Table 3.6** *Mean reaction times (sec) and percentages correct (in parentheses) in the truth experiment*

| Question | True? | False? | Studied? |
|---|---|---|---|
| NO-FAN QUESTION | | | |
| True | 1.859 | 2.886 | 1.658 |
| | (.913) | (.841) | (.903) |
| False | 2.612 | 2.741 | 1.804 |
| | (.832) | (.785) | (.903) |
| Re-paired | 1.703 | 2.174 | 1.440 |
| | (.982) | (.931) | (.970) |
| FAN QUESTION | | | |
| True | 2.451 | 3.262 | 1.896 |
| | (.842) | (.822) | (.862) |
| False | 2.863 | 3.429 | 2.171 |
| | (.801) | (.714) | (.829) |
| Re-paired | 2.165 | 2.786 | 1.728 |
| | (.962) | (.881) | (.929) |

**Table 3.7**  *Average reaction times (sec) and fan effects (sec) in Table 3.6*

| Type of question | | Type of material | |
|---|---|---|---|
| AVERAGE RT | | | |
| True? | 2.276 | True | 2.335 |
| False? | 2.880 | False | 2.603 |
| Studied? | 1.783 | Re-paired | 1.999 |
| AVERAGE FAN EFFECTS | | | |
| True? | .435 | True | .402 |
| False? | .559 | False | .435 |
| Studied? | .298 | Re-paired | .454 |

lars (*Some cats are pets*) from false particulars (*Some cats are rocks*) on the basis of connectivity. On the other hand, many false universals have strong connections between subject and predicate—*All cats are pets* and *All dogs are collies*—which rules out the possibility of a connectivity strategy.

### The Nature of Working Memory

Working memory, that subset of knowledge to which we have access at any particular moment, can be identified with the active portion of ACT's memory. According to this analysis it consists both of temporary knowledge structures currently being attended and the active parts of long-term memory. Such a conception of working memory has been offered by a number of researchers, including Shiffrin (1975). Since activation varies continuously, working memory is not an all-or-none concept. Rather, information is part of working memory to various degrees.

MEMORY SPAN

What is the relationship between this conception of an active or working memory and traditional conceptions of short-term memory? The momentary capacity of working memory is much greater than the capacity of short-term memory, which traditionally was placed in the vicinity of seven units based on memory span (Miller, 1956). However, memory span measures the sustained capacity of working memory rather than the amount of information that is momentarily active. There are severe limitations on the amount of information that can be maintained in an active state in the absence of external stimulation. The only element that sustains activation without rehearsal is the goal element. The size of the memory span can be seen to partly reflect the number of elements that can be maintained active by the goal element. Rehearsal strategies can be viewed as an additional mechanism for pumping activation into the network. By rehearsing an item, one makes that item a source of activation for a short time.

Broadbent (1975) has argued that memory span consists of a reliable three or four elements that can always be retrieved and a second set of variable size that has a certain probability of retrieval. That is, subjects can recall three or four elements perfectly but can recall larger spans, in the range of seven to nine elements, only with a probability of around .5. The ACT analysis offered here corresponds to Broadbent's analysis of memory span. The certain three or four elements are those whose activation is maintained from the goal. The other elements correspond to those being maintained probabilistically by rehearsal. According to this view rehearsal is not essential for a minimal short-term memory. Probably the correct reading of the relation between rehearsal and short-term memory is that while rehearsal is often involved and is supportive, minimal sets can be maintained without rehearsal (Reitman, 1971, 1974; Shiffrin, 1973). It is also relevant to note here the evidence linking memory span to the rate of rehearsal (Baddeley, Thomson, and Buchanan, 1975).

THE STERNBERG PARADIGM

The various paradigms for studying memory span have been one methodology for getting at the traditional concept of short-term memory. Another important methodology has been the Sternberg paradigm (Sternberg, 1969). In the Sternberg experiment, time to recognize that an element is a member of a studied set is found to be an approximately linear function (with slope about 35 msec per item) of the size of the set. This is true for sets that can be maintained in working memory. The traditional interpretation of this result is that the subject performs a serial high-speed scan of the contents of short-term memory looking for a match to the probe. J. A. Anderson (1973) has pointed out that it is implausible that a serial comparison process of that speed could be implemented neurally. Rather he argues that the comparisons must be performed in parallel. It is well known (Townsend, 1974) that there exist parallel models which can predict the effects attributed to serial models.

In the ACT framework, these judgments could be implemented by productions of the form:

P5      IF the goal is to recognize if the probe is in LVset
        and LVprobe is presented
        and LVprobe was studied in LVset
    THEN say yes.

P6      IF the goal is to recognize if the probe is in LVset
        and LVprobe is presented
        and LVprobe was not studied in LVset
    THEN say no.

These productions are of the same logic as the fact-recognition productions in Table 3.4. Their rate of application will be a function of the level of activation of the matching structure. The more elements there are in the memory set, the lower will be the activation of any item in that set because it will receive activation from the goal element and less maintenance rehearsal. A rather similar idea was proposed by Baddeley and Ecob (1973). The amount of activation coming to these productions will be a function of the fan of LVset, among other things. The amount of activation from LVset will be $A/n$, where $n$ is the number of elements in the memory set. Then the total activation of the structure being matched to the probe is $A^* + A/n$, where $A^*$ is the activation coming from other sources such as LVprobe.

Under the hypothesis that match time is an inverse function of activation, recognition time will vary as a function of $1/(A^* + A/n)$. This predicts a somewhat negatively accelerated function of $n$, set size; the degree of negative acceleration will be a function of $A^*$. Despite the textbook wisdom about the effect of linear set size, the obtained functions are more often than not negatively accelerated (Briggs, 1974). ACT's waiting process for absence detection also predicts that the time to reject foils approximately parallels the target functions. That is, activation of the first clause in P6 (the goal is to judge if the probe is in LVset) will be a function of the fan from LVset. Note that the ACT model is just one instantiation of the class of parallel models for performing in the Sternberg task (see Ratcliff, 1978; Townsend, 1974).

Variations on this analysis of the Sternberg task were offered in Anderson and Bower (1973) and Anderson (1976). However, at that time they stood as post hoc analyses nearly identical in prediction to the serial account of the phenomenon. There was no independent evidence for this account over the serial one. Some recent experiments by Jones (Jones and Anderson, 1981; Jones, unpublished) have confirmed predictions that discriminate between the two accounts. We compared associatively related memory sets (*plane, mountain, crash, clouds, wind*) with unrelated sets. Because of the associative interrelationships, activation of some members of the set should spread to others. Thus the dissipation in activation with increase in set size should be attenuated. Correspondingly, we did find smaller set size effects with the related memory sets. These experiments provide evidence that a spreading-activation-based conception of the Sternberg paradigm is better than the high-speed memory scan. That is, we have shown that the long-term associative relationships over which the spread occurs can facilitate recognition of an item in short-term memory.[12]

## Appendix: Example Calculations

It is useful to look at a few hypothetical examples of asymptotic activation patterns. Some involve rather simple and unrealistic network structures, but they illustrate some of the properties of the spreading activation mechanisms.

### LINEAR CHAINS

Figure 3.5a represents a simple linear chain that starts with node 0 and extends to nodes 1, 2, 3, and so on, with node $n$ connected to both $n - 1$ and $n + 1$, except for 0, which is connected just to 1. Assume that all links in the chain are of equal strength. Assuming that node 0 becomes a source and that one unit of activation is input at 0, one can derive the asymptotic pattern of activation. Letting $a_i$ refer to the activation of the $i$th node in the chain, $a_i = kr^i$ where $r = (1 - \sqrt{1 - p^2})/p$ and $k = 2/(1 - rp)$. The exception to this rule is the activation for node 0 which has activation level $a_0 = 1/(1 - rp)$. Since $r$ is a fraction, activation level decays away exponentially with distance from source. Assuming $p = .8$, which is a typical value in our simulations, $r = .5$, $k = 3.33$, and $a_0 = 1.67$. Note that although $a_0$ is only given one unit of activation as a source, reverberation increases its level an additional .67 units.

Figure 3.5b illustrates another kind of linear chain, this one centered at node 0 and extending to $-\infty$ and $+\infty$. Again we can solve for asymptotic patterns of activation assuming one unit of input at node 0. Again activation decays exponentially with distance $a_i = kr^i$, and again $r = (1 - \sqrt{1 - p^2})/p$ and $a_0 = 1/(1 - rp)$, but now $k = 1/(1 - rp)$.

Thus activation tends to decay away exponentially with distance from source, and one can safely ignore the effects of distant structure. This is one reason why a network will reach a near-asymptotic pattern of activation rather quickly. That is,

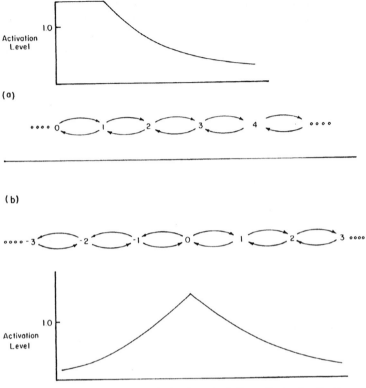

**Figure 3.5**  *Two simple linear chains for calculating effects of activation at distance.*

the distant structure that the activation takes longer to reach has little effect on the final pattern of activation. The data of McKoon and Ratcliff (1980) on linear chains in paragraphs are relevant here. They were able to show that priming decayed approximately exponentially as a function of distance, as predicted by this analysis.

UNANALYZED STRUCTURE

In typical applications one can specify only a small fragment of the semantic network because the full network contains millions of nodes. I will refer to the specified fragment as the *analyzed structure* and the remainder as the *unanalyzed structure*. In an application we assume that some nodes in the analyzed structure are sources of activation, and we calculate the spread among the other nodes. We either ignore the existence of the unanalyzed structure or assume that activation spreads into the unanalyzed structure and never spreads back. It is impossible to fully calculate reverberations into the unanalyzed structure and back. The interesting question is, what are the consequences of failing to consider the unanalyzed structure? Does it change everything in the analyzed structure by a multiplicative scale factor, or does it change the ordinal relations among the activation levels of the analyzed nodes? Is there some way to "correct" for the effect of reverberation through the unanalyzed structure without actually specifying the reverberation?

The effect of the unanalyzed structure will depend on its properties. In one situation, shown in Figure 3.6, it does have minimal impact. One node $X$ from the analyzed structure is represented, with no connections from the unanalyzed structure to the analyzed structure other than directly through $X$.[13] Thus, in a sense, the analyzed structure has captured all the "relevant" connections in memory. Assume that the relative strength of $X$'s connections to the unanalyzed structure is $s$ and hence the relative strength of its connections to the analyzed structure is $1 - s$. We can classify the nodes in the unanalyzed structure according to their minimum link distance from $X$. A node will be in level $i$ if its minimum distance is $i$. Node $X$ will be considered to be level 0. Let $a_i$ be the total of the activation of all nodes in level $i$. By definition a node in level $i$ has connec-

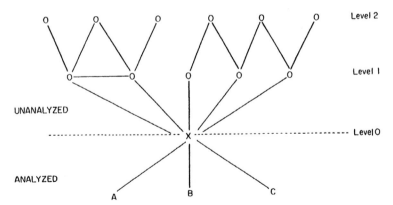

**Figure 3.6** *Node X is connected to some analyzed network structure and some unanalyzed structure. This figure is used to determine the effect of reverberation with the unanalyzed structure or patterns of activation in the analyzed structure.*

tions only to nodes in level $i - 1$, $i + 1$, and possibly $i$.[14] Let $s_1$ be the relative strength of all connections to level $i - 1$, $s_2$ the relative strength of all connections to level $i$, and $s_3$ the strength of all connections to level $i + 1$. $s_1 + s_2 + s_3 = 1$. It will be assumed that the same values for these parameters apply at all levels except 0.

For all levels except 0 and 1, the following equation describes the pattern of activation.

$$a_i = ps_1 a_{i-1} + ps_2 a_i + ps_3 a_{i+1} \qquad (3.11)$$

It can be shown that once again level of activation decays exponentially with distance such that

$$a_i = kr^i \qquad (3.12)$$

where

$$r = \frac{1 - ps_2 - \sqrt{(1 - ps_2)^2 - 4s_1 s_3 p^2}}{2ps_3} \qquad (3.13)$$

and

$$k = \frac{psV}{r(1 - ps_3 r - ps_2 - p^2 ss_3)} \qquad (3.14)$$

and

$$a_0 = \frac{V(1 - ps_3 r - ps_2)}{(1 - ps_3 r - ps_2 - p^2 ss_3)} \qquad (3.15)$$

where $V$ is the amount of activation input to $X$ from the analyzed structure. Assuming arbitrary but plausible values of $s = .67$, $s_1 = .6$, $s_2 = .1$, $s_3 = .3$, and $p = .8$, then $r = .623$, $k = 1.340V$, and $a_0 = 1.199V$.

The point of this analysis is to show that reverberation from the unanalyzed structure may just multiply by a constant the activation $V$ of $X$, calculated on the bases of the analyzed structure. This multiplicative constant might be called the correction factor. Hence calculations for the analyzed structure can be adjusted by introducing multiplicative constants to represent effects of reverberation through the unanalyzed structure, given values for $s$, $p$, $s_1$, $s_2$, and $s_3$. Thus the typical practice of analyzing part of the network need not lead to serious difficulties if the relationship between the analyzed and unanalyzed structure approximates that shown in Figure 3.6.

# 4 | Control of Cognition

H
UMAN COGNITION at all levels involves choosing
what to process. Alternatives present themselves, implicitly or explicitly, and our cognitive systems choose,
implicitly or explicitly, to pursue some and not others. We ori-
ent our senses to only part of the environment; we do not perceive everything we sense; what we do perceive we do not recognize in all possible patterns; only some of what we recognize
do we use for achieving our goals; we follow only some ways of
pursuing our goals; and we choose to achieve only some of the
possible goals.

In ACT* many of these choices are made by the conflict resolution principles. A theory of conflict resolution has an ambiguous status, given the current categories of cognitive psychology. In certain ways it is a theory of attention; in other ways it
is a theory of perception; in other ways it is a theory of problem
solving; in still other ways it is a theory of motor control. However, it is not really a schizophrenic theory, but a unified theory
facing a schizophrenic field. Unfortunately, the idea of conflict
resolution, as defined within production systems, is not familiar to cognitive psychology. While the term is more common in
artificial intelligence, it is still not that common. Therefore, in
this chapter I first set the stage and identify some of the relevant
issues and past work.

## Current Status of the Field

### Data-Driven versus Goal-Directed Processing

According to one of cognitive psychology's recurrent hypotheses, there are two modes of cognitive processing. One is automatic, less capacity-limited, possibly parallel, invoked directly

126

by stimulus input. The second requires conscious control, has severe capacity limitations, is possibly serial, and is invoked in response to internal goals. The idea was strongly emphasized by Neisser (1967) in his distinction between an early "preattentive" stage and a later controllable, serial stage. Lindsay and Norman (1977) made the distinction between data-driven and conceptually driven processing the cornerstone of their introductory psychology text. The idea is found in the distinction of Posner (1978) and Posner and Snyder (1976) between automatic pathway activation and conscious attention. They argue that the system can automatically facilitate the processing of some information without cost to the processing of other information. On the other hand, if attention is consciously focused on the processing of certain information, this processing will be facilitated but at a cost to the processing of what is not attended.[1]

Shiffrin and Schneider (1977) and Schneider and Shiffrin (1977) make a distinction between automatic and controlled processing of information and endorse the idea that automatic processing can progress without taking capacity away from other ongoing processing, whereas controlled processing consumes capacity. According to Shiffrin and Schneider, automatic processing can occur in parallel whereas controlled processing is serial. Only with a great deal of practice and only under certain circumstances can controlled information processing become automatic. LaBerge and Samuels (1974) argue for a similar conception of the development of automaticity. Recent work on problem solving (Larkin et al., 1980) has also found that a move from goal-directed to data-driven processing is associated with growing expertise.

A somewhat similar but not identical distinction, called bottom-up versus top-down processing, is frequent in computer science. Bottom-up processing starts with the data and tries to work up to the high level. Top-down processing tries to fit high-level structures to the data. The distinction is quite clear in parsers, where control can be in response to incoming words or to knowledge of a grammar. However, the distinction is also found in many models of perceptual processing. Interestingly, continued advances in architecture, as in the design of augmented transition networks (Woods, 1970) for parsing or the HARPY system for speech perception (Lowerre, 1976), have blurred this distinction. In such systems the processing occurs in response to goals and data jointly.

Whether one studies tasks that are basically perceptual (that is, they start at the bottom of the cognitive system) or basically problem-solving (that is, they start at the top of the system), one must address the issue of how top-down processing and bottom-up processing are mixed. There are numerous interesting psychological results concerning this mixing. Deliberately focusing one's attention on a perceptual task can facilitate its processing (LaBerge, 1973; Posner and Snyder, 1975). LaBerge shows, for instance, that subjects are faster to recognize letters they expect. Contextual factors have large effects on perceptual recognition, so an object that fits its context is better perceived. Goals and higher-order factors not only determine the speed and success of perception, they also determine what is perceived in a complex array.

The effects of the high level on the low level have been long known and are now well documented in the laboratory. A recent surprise has been how much low-level processes affect what is supposedly high-level processing. Some of the early evidence of this came from studies of chess and the game of go, in which it was found that what separated experts from novices was the ability to perceive relevant patterns on the gameboard (Chase and Simon, 1973; Reitman, 1976; Simon and Gilmartin, 1973). For an expert, the lines of development in the game are suggested directly by the patterns on the board, just as our perception of a dog is usually determined by the data, without any intent or plan to see a dog. The key to expertise in many problem-solving domains like physics (Larkin, 1981) or geometry (Anderson, 1982) is development of these data-driven rules. Such rules respond to configurations of data elements with recommendations for problem development, independent of any higher-level goals. In the problem shown in Figure 4.1, from our work on geometry, what distinguishes experienced from novice students is that experts very quickly perceive that $\Delta ACM \cong \Delta BDM$ even though they do not know how this fact will figure in the final proof.

## The HEARSAY System and Opportunistic Planning

Artificial intelligence has been greatly concerned with how to mix top-down and bottom-up processing in many domains. The HEARSAY architecture (Erman and Lesser, 1979; Reddy et al., 1973) was developed for speech perception but has proven quite influential in cognitive psychology (for example, Rumelhart, 1971). In particular, Hayes-Roth and Hayes-Roth (1979) have adapted it in their proposal for *opportunistic planning*. This type of architecture provides a set of comparisons and contrasts

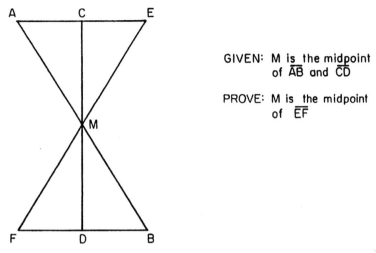

GIVEN: M is the midpoint
of $\overline{AB}$ and $\overline{CD}$

PROVE: M is the midpoint
of $\overline{EF}$

**Figure 4.1** *A geometry problem that serves to distinguish novice students from experienced. Experienced students immediately perceive that △ACM ≅ △BDM without knowing how the fact will fit into the final proof.*

that are useful for identifying what is significant about the ACT architecture.

Certain aspects of the HEARSAY architecture have much in common with production systems. For instance, there is a blackboard which, like working memory, contains a wide range of relevant data, organized generally according to level. In speech perception, HEARSAY's blackboard contained hypotheses about sounds, syllable structures, word structures, word sequences, syntax, semantics, and pragmatics. Numerous *knowledge sources*, which are like productions, respond to data at one level and introduce data at another level.

At any point in time the system must choose which source to apply, from a set of potentially relevant knowledge sources. This is the conflict-resolution problem, and it is in the solution to this problem that the HEARSAY architecture differs most fundamentally from ACT. In HEARSAY, conflict-resolution decisions are made dynamically and intelligently by considering any relevant information. Various knowledge sources are responsible for evaluating the state of knowledge and deciding what should be done next. This contrasts with the simple, compiled conflict-resolution schemes of production systems. The HEARSAY scheme has the potential for cognitive flexibility but at considerable computational cost. One of the potentials of HEARSAY is that it allows for a radical shift of attention when a new hypothesis seems promising.

The opportunistic system proposed by Hayes-Roth and Hayes-Roth is an interesting attempt to extend the flexible control structure of HEARSAY to planning. The dominant view of planning (Miller, Galanter, and Pribram, 1960; Newell and Simon, 1972; Sacerdoti, 1977) sees planning as a top-down, focused process that starts with high-level goals and refines them into achievable actions. This is sometimes referred to as *successive refinement* or *problem decomposition*. In contrast, Hayes-Roth and Hayes-Roth claim that multiple asynchronous processes develop the plan at a number of levels. The particular planning task studied by these researchers—subjects planning a series of errands through a town—supported their view. In this task subjects mixed low-level and high-level decision making. Sometimes they planned low-level sequences of errands in the absence or in violation of a prescriptive high-level plan. The researchers characterized this behavior as "opportunistically" jumping about in the planning space to develop the most promising aspects of the plan. This certainly seemed in violation of successive refinement and more compatible with HEARSAY's architecture, which can handle multiple focuses of attention at multiple levels.

To implement this opportunistic control structure, Hayes-Roth and Hayes-Roth proposed a complex blackboard structure that represents many aspects of the plan simultaneously. Again, knowledge sources respond to whatever aspect of the plan seems most promising. Figure 4.2 illustrates their blackboard structure and just a few of the knowledge sources (see Hayes-Roth and Hayes-Roth for an explanation). This structure, containing multiple planes, each with multiple levels, is even more complex than the original HEARSAY blackboard. This causes problems, because skipping among its many planes and levels makes unrealistic demands on working memory.[2] Human ability to maintain prior states of control in problem solving is severely limited (Chase, 1982; Greeno and Simon, 1974; Simon, 1975). Indeed, in some situations, phenomena that appear to violate hierarchical planning are actually simple failures of working memory. For instance, subjects may pursue details of a current plan that is inconsistent with their higher goals, simply because they have misremembered the higher goals.

Hayes-Roth and Hayes-Roth have made a clear contribution

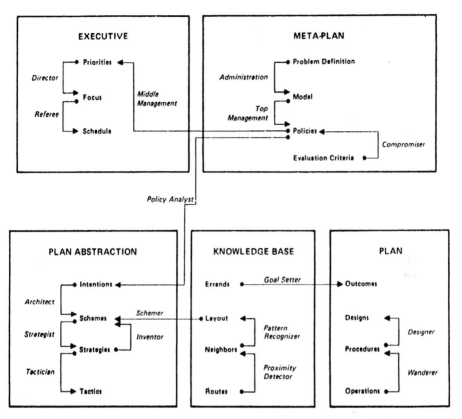

**Figure 4.2** *The blackboard structure for the opportunistic planner. (From Hayes-Roth and Hayes-Roth, 1979.)*

in noting that human behavior is not strictly top-down and that it can be distracted by opportunities. The earlier hierarchical models were ignoring something important. However, in making distractability the central purpose in a theory of cognitive control, they have lost the essential insight of the past theories, that human behavior acquires its organization through always being controlled by an organized structure of goals. The remainder of this chapter will set forth a psychologically more realistic theory of cognitive control, one that recognizes the two faces of cognition—its data-driven, bottom-up face, and its top-down, goal-directed face. This theory explains why we are at once single-minded and at the same time ready to respond to and process millions of possible events.

## The Principles of Conflict Resolution

The human production system probably consists of somewhere between tens of thousands of productions and tens of millions. For many reasons, we do not want to apply all the productions that could apply at any time. For instance, two productions that request the hand to move in conflicting directions should not apply simultaneously. Conflict resolution involves deciding which productions to apply. In the ACT theory there are five principles of conflict resolution: degree of match, production strength, data refractoriness, specificity, and goal-dominance. Each of these principles is achieved in ACT* through the operation of its pattern matcher for production conditions. In this, ACT* is unique; other production systems apply conflict resolution after pattern matching to choose a subset of the matched productions. In ACT*, conflict resolution is thus an integral part of information processing rather than something tacked on at the end to get adequate performance.

### DEGREE OF MATCH

In most production systems it is a necessary but not sufficient condition for production application that the condition of a production be fully matched by the contents of working memory. On computational grounds it might seem desirable to insist on full matching to avoid making errors. However, this constraint must be relaxed to have a psychologically valid model. Any number of phenomena point to the fact that productions can be evoked by partial matches.

Partial matching is essential because the world is full of partial data structures that must be matched. Faces change but still can be recognized. We can recognize partial lexical patterns, as the example in Figure 4.3 shows. It is also hard to explain why generally well-working human procedures occasionally make errors, unless one invokes the concept of partial match. Norman (1981) describes many such errors. For instance, there is the case of a person who threw a dirty shirt "by mistake" into the toilet rather than into the hamper. Apparently a "hamper-matching" pattern partially matched the toilet.

Looking at novices learning to program in LISP, we find

RⵔN Ɐⵏ RFⵔGⵏN

Figure 4.3    *An example of partial matching.*

many examples of errors that can be attributed to partial pattern matching. For instance, there is frequent confusion of the function CONS, which adds an element to the front of a list, and the function LIST, which takes two elements and makes a list out of them. Both functions create a new list with elements in it. While students appreciate the LIST-CONS difference, they will misapply these functions in the context of programming, particularly when they are holding other information in working memory. If students represented their goal as "I want to make a list with this element as its first element," both functions would have their description matched equally well and partially to the goal and there would be opportunity for error.

Partial matching notions can also explain how subjects can classify an instance as belonging to a category on the basis of its similarity to other instances (Franks and Bransford, 1971; Medin and Schaffer, 1978; Posner and Keele, 1970; Rosch and Mervis, 1975). For instance, it might be argued that some people in our culture possess the following "stereotyped" production:

IF a person is highly quantitative
   and the person is male
   and the person is conservative politically
   and the person tells poor jokes
   and the person has traditional values
   and the person is not creative or curious
   and the person is upper middle class
THEN the person is an engineer.

Such a production might be evoked if it was matched to the description of a person with just some of these attributes. In artificial prototype-formation experiments, we have found that the speed of such classifications varies with the closeness of match.

While a production system should accept partial matches sometimes, it should also prefer a full match to a partial match, and ACT's pattern matcher achieves this principle. It also responds more rapidly to more complete matches. The system should be tuned so that when a match is bad enough it is just not accepted (see Hayes-Roth, 1977, for a discussion of the desirable properties of partial matching).

PRODUCTION STRENGTH

In ACT the strength of a production reflects the frequency with which it has been successfully applied in the past. Stronger productions apply more rapidly and reliably. The principles for deciding when a production is successful and for accruing strength are part of the ACT learning theory (see Chapter 6). The strength factor is built into ACT's pattern-matching principles.

### DATA REFRACTORINESS

A third conflict-resolution principle is that the same data element cannot serve in two patterns simultaneously. Examples of this limitation can be found everywhere; one famous example is the Necker cube, in which it is impossible to see the same lines filling both interpretations. Another example is HE where we can see the shared bar as part of either the H or the E but not both simultaneously. This limitation is a major source of difficulty in geometry proofs, in which it is often necessary to see the same object in multiple roles. Figure 4.4 illustrates just three examples from our research. In (*a*) beginning students have difficulty seeing the line segments $\overline{AC}$, $\overline{BC}$, $\overline{DC}$, and $\overline{EC}$ simultaneously as parts of triangles and as parts of a vertical

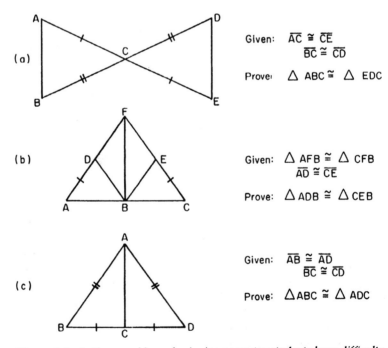

(a)    Given:  $\overline{AC} \cong \overline{CE}$
               $\overline{BC} \cong \overline{CD}$

       Prove:  $\triangle ABC \cong \triangle EDC$

(b)    Given:  $\triangle AFB \cong \triangle CFB$
               $\overline{AD} \cong \overline{CE}$

       Prove:  $\triangle ADB \cong \triangle CEB$

(c)    Given:  $\overline{AB} \cong \overline{AD}$
               $\overline{BC} \cong \overline{CD}$

       Prove:  $\triangle ABC \cong \triangle ADC$

**Figure 4.4**   *In these problems, beginning geometry students have difficulty in seeing that the same data element simultaneously serves two roles.*

angle configuration. In (b) it is difficult to see the angles and lines as belonging to two triangles, and in (c) they have difficulty in seeing the $\overline{AC}$ segment as part of two triangles. Indeed, one student spontaneously proposed a "construction" of splitting the $\overline{AC}$ segment into two.[3]

Examples involving perceptual pattern matching are more salient, but there are also abundant examples involving conceptual pattern matching. For instance, a person who commits suicide is not seen as a murderer, because the person (data object) fills the role of "dead person" (pattern) so he or she cannot also serve the other pattern role. In learning to program LISP, novices have great difficulty in keeping straight that the element NIL is at once the logical equivalent of false, the empty list, and an atom. In text editing, people have difficulty appreciating the dual role of blank as a character and a delimiter (fortunately they usually do not have to deal with the similar dual function of carriage return). The phenomenon of functional fixedness in problem solving (see Anderson, 1980b, chap. 9 for a review) depends on the inability to perceive a single object serving multiple functions.[4]

One consequence of data refractoriness is that the same production cannot match the same data more than once. This avoids getting into a loop in which the same production applies over and over. If data are matched to one production, they cannot be matched to another, including another instantiation of the same production. Most production systems have a principle of refractoriness whereby the same production cannot twice apply to the same data structure. In ACT* this is a consequence of the more general principle of data refractoriness.

SPECIFICITY

The specificity principle states that when two productions match the same data, preference is given to the production that has a more specific condition. Condition A is considered more specific than condition B if A matches in a proper subset of the situations where condition B would match. This principle proves important to the proper functioning of exceptions to rules, as illustrated by productions P1 and P2:

P1    IF the goal is to generate the plural of a noun
      THEN say the noun + *s*

P2    IF the goal is to generate the plural of *man*
      THEN say *men*

Production P1 gives the general rule for pluralizing a noun, while production P2 gives the exception for *men*. Specificity would enable the exception to take precedence over the general rule. There are two ways in which a production can be more specific than another. One, illustrated above, is when a production contains additional tests about a data structure. In the above case the more specific production contains a test for the identity of the noun. The other possibility is that the more specific production will contain additional clauses in its condition.

### GOAL-DOMINANCE

The principles that have been discussed have concerned data-driven selection of productions. Many of ACT*'s productions given in this book test for the current goal in their condition as well as for other factors. There can be only one current goal active in the system.[5] When a current goal is satisfied, attention shifts to the next goal in the goal stack. Productions that refer to the current goal take precedence over productions that might otherwise apply because of strength or specificity. A goal-directed production that matches the current goal applies more rapidly and reliably, but if it does not match the current goal, it will not apply no matter how well the rest of its condition matches. If a number of goal-directed productions match the current goal, the principles of strength, degree of match, and specificity select the one that will apply.

By appropriately setting a goal, the system can prepare itself to process a certain line of information with maximum speed. Because of data refractoriness it will also inhibit alternate lines of processing. The fact that the system can only seek a single goal puts a severe limit on how much can be done by goal-directed productions and makes this part of the system inherently serial. Thus, in its theory of goal management, ACT has a theory of focus of attention and an explanation of the seriality of higher-level cognition.[6]

It is interesting to speculate on why the system should be restricted to a single current goal and hence restricted to serial processing of what is most important. This may be a response to the limited capacity of system resources such as working memory and to the seriality of effectors, for example, hands. It is important that the system be able to assign as many resources as possible to the most important task. Given the number of resource breakdowns that occur in single-minded performance of tasks, there would be serious problems if resources had to be shared. In some situations it is essential that one task be done properly; it is seldom truly essential that two tasks be done simultaneously. It would have been an evolutionary disaster if humans, in using their hands to protect themselves, could have a competing production grab control of their hands to wipe the sweat from their brow.

ACT*'s use of goal structures to guide conflict resolution is a major departure from older versions of ACT and the neoclassical system of Newell. The basic philosophy of the neoclassical system was that any production could apply at any time. This made it difficult to guarantee a particular flow of control and resulted in many ad hoc conventions for using "control elements." Our use of goals provides a principled means for preventing application of any production that refers to a goal unless its goal condition is met. This idea for factoring a production set according to goals has also been suggested elsewhere (Greeno, 1976; Brown and Van Lehn, 1980).

### Activation-Based, Data-Flow Pattern Matching

All these conflict resolution principles are achieved by an activation-based pattern matcher. I should acknowledge my considerable debt to two sources in developing these ideas about pattern matching. One is the data-flow pattern matcher introduced by Forgy (1979) in his dissertation. The second is the interactive activation model proposed by McClelland and Rumelhart (1981) and Rumelhart and McClelland (1982). The McClelland and Rumelhart model provides a psychologically and physiologically plausible analysis of how pattern matching could occur in reading. However, their model is limited computationally and does not extend well to the more general pattern matching required for production systems. In contrast, Forgy's model is a wonder of computational efficiency and power, but like many pure computer-science efforts, it lacks psychological plausibility. However, the basic architectural principles of the two efforts are sufficiently similar that I was able to produce a synthesis that keeps the virtues of both and that also produces the five principles given earlier for conflict resolution.

In both systems small data structures come into working memory and are matched to primitive patterns. These small patterns are combined to form larger patterns, and combination continues until the full pattern is matched. Figure 4.5 illustrates one of the pattern networks implemented in ACT* for recognizing a small set of words. This figure, using the feature set for letters suggested in McClelland and Rumelhart, encodes some of the four-letter words that can be built from simply a horizon-

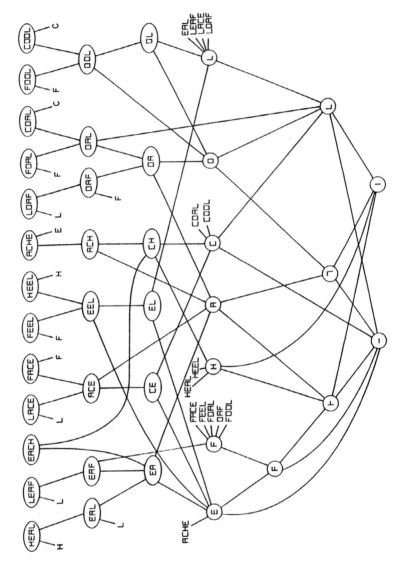

**Figure 4.5** A data-flow network for recognizing some four-letter words composed of horizontal and vertical bars.

tal bar with right and left articulation points and a vertical bar with bottom, middle, and top articulation points. This is a small subset of the four-letter words used by McClelland and Rumelhart, but it is sufficient for illustration.

Unlike McClelland and Rumelhart but like Forgy, patterns in ACT are put together by a binary piecing of subpatterns. Working from the top to the bottom, EACH is composed of the letter cluster patterns EA and CH; EA is formed from the latter patterns E and A; A is formed from the letter subpatterns ⊢ and ˥ ; ⊢ is formed by joining the left end of a horizontal bar to the middle of a vertical bar.

The exact combinations are somewhat arbitrary, and a goal of the project was that the pattern-matching principles would not depend on specifics of the network for their success. It is unlikely that experience is careful in how it "wires" the net, so we do not want brittle pattern-matching principles. In the Forgy data-flow scheme, simple data elements (in this case, vertical and horizontal bars) come in at the terminal nodes and flow through the various higher-order two-input pattern nodes. These pattern nodes perform tests for compatible combinations of the subpatterns. For instance, the A node performs two tests to determine if its two subpatterns join at the correct places. The EACH pattern performs a test to determine if the EA and CH patterns are adjacent. The Forgy data-flow scheme can be more efficient under one network organization than another but will function successfully under all.

A difference between my scheme in Figure 4.5 and the McClelland and Rumelhart network is the existence of intermediate units of letter clusters and feature clusters. McClelland and Rumelhart have only letter and word levels. The current proposal is not that there are specific new levels for word recognition, but that it is artificial to suppose the pattern network is neatly layered into a small number of levels.

DATA-FLOW MATCHING

*An example network.* A prerequisite to explaining the ACT pattern matcher is understanding some basics about data-flow matching. Data-flow matchers are not especially designed to recognize letter patterns and, as far as I know, mine is the only example of such a use. They are designed to match the more general class of patterns that appear in production conditions. If a word pattern is represented as a production condition, a data-flow matcher will handle letter recognition as a special case. However, before turning to letter patterns, let us consider how a data-flow matcher would be created for the following set of productions, which illustrate some important concepts about pattern matching. They are loosely adapted from our work on geometry proof generation:

P1      IF the goal is to prove LVstatement
           and LVstatement is about LVrelation
           and LVpostulate is about LVrelation
           and LVpostulate has not been tried
        THEN set as a subgoal to try LVpostulate
           and mark LVpostulate as tried.

P2      IF the goal is to prove LVstatement
           and LVstatement is about LVrelation
           and LVpostulate is about LVrelation
           and the teacher suggests LVpostulate
        THEN set as a subgoal to try LVpostulate
           and mark LVpostulate as tried.

P3      IF the goal is to prove LVstatement
           and LVstatement is about LVrelation
           and it is not the case that there is an LVpostulate
              about LVrelation where LVpostulate is not tried
        THEN give up.

To explain the data-flow matcher, these productions have been written with their local variables identified. The productions are relevant to using postulates in a proof system like geometry. P1 identifies untried postulates, so if the goal is to prove triangle congruence and the side-angle-side postulate has not been tried, it would recommend trying the postulate. P2 recommends a postulate even if it has been tried, if the teacher suggests it. P3 recognizes when there are no more untried postulates relevant to proving the current statement (for example, that two triangles are congruent).

Figure 4.6 illustrates a data-flow network that matches the conditions of these productions. Individual clauses of the productions correspond to terminal (bottom) nodes in the network. They are combined by two-input nodes that perform tests on the variable bindings of instantiations of the left and right nodes. Thus the two-input node F in Figure 4.6 tests whether LVstatement1 from terminal A is the same as LVstatement2 from terminal B. This amounts to building a pattern corresponding to the to-be-proven statement and its logical relation, LVrelation1. Node F feeds into nodes I, J, and K, which perform tests on the identity of LVrelation1.

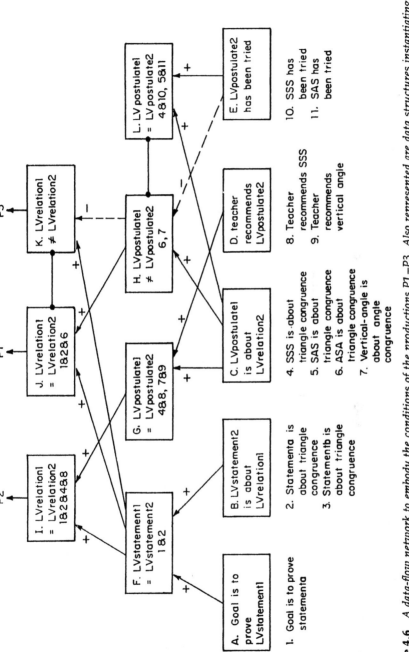

**Figure 4.6** A data-flow network to embody the conditions of the productions P1–P3. Also represented are data structures instantiating the various nodes.

Certain nodes look for a successful match to one subnode that is incompatible with any match to the other subnode. An example is node H, which looks for a postulate that matches subnode C such that there is no proposition at subnode E about that postulate being tried. A node such as H receives input and activation only from its positive node. It is called a *negative one-input* to contrast it with a *positive two-input* node. The negative test is performed implicitly. A positive two-input node is set up (Node L in Figure 4.6) that represents the positive conjunction of the two features. It competes by inhibitory links with the negative one-input node. If a positive conjunction is present, the positive two-input node will repress the negative one-input node. Otherwise, the negative one-input node will match. We already have seen this technique work in Figures 3.3 and 3.4. As I will explain later, this use of inhibition to perform absence tests is just a special case of the general use of inhibitory connections to force the pattern matcher to choose between alternative interpretations of a subpattern.

*An example.* Suppose the following information is active in working memory:

1. The goal is to prove statement*a*.
2. Statement*a* is about triangle congruence.
3. Statement*b* is about triangle congruence.
4. Side-side-side postulate is about triangle congruence.
5. Side-angle-side postulate is about triangle congruence.
6. Angle-side-angle postulate is about triangle congruence.
7. Vertical-angle postulate is about angle congruence.
8. The teacher recommends side-side-side postulate.
9. The teacher recommends vertical angle postulate.
10. Side-side-side has been tried.
11. Side-angle-side has been tried.

Figure 4.6 illustrates how these data would be matched to the pattern nodes. Fact 1 would be matched to node A; facts 2 and 3 to node B; facts 4–7 to node C; facts 8 and 9 to node D; and facts 10 and 11 to node E. These facts would then flow to the various first-level two-input nodes, and tests would be performed to ascertain the correct combinations. Combination 1 and 2 would pass the test at node F because both facts are about the same statement. Combination 1 and 3 would fail the test at node F because the two facts are about different statements. Combinations 4 and 8, 7 and 9, which reflect postulates the teacher recommends, would pass node G. Facts 6 and 7 would be stored as two instantiations of node H (these are instantiations of the left side incompatible with any instantiations of the right side). These first-level combinations would then flow to the next level to be combined. Combination 1, 2, 4, and 8 would be an instantiation of node I, which represents a postulate relevant to the current line recommended by the teacher. Combination 1, 2, and 6 would be an instantiation of node J, representing a postulate relevant to the current line that has not been tried. There are no instantiations of node K—that is, the current goal does not involve a statement to be proven with no untried methods.

The instantiation of node I means production P2 can apply, and the instantiation of node J means production P1 can apply. Both productions change the goal, so application of one will prevent application of the other. Whichever production applies first, as determined by the conflict resolution principles, will effectively block the other. Should P1 apply first, it will tag angle-side-angle as tried. Now, if the system returns to the goal of proving statement*a*, there will be no untried postulates relevant to triangle congruence, and production P3 can apply.

*Significant features of the example.* A number of features of this data-flow pattern matcher give it a computational advantage over other proposals for pattern matching. First, it capitalizes on the fact that multiple productions share the same clauses and the matcher performs the tests relevant to these clauses only once. This feature of data-flow networks is described as *spatial redundancy*. Second, if part of a pattern is in working memory, it can flow through the network to the relevant nodes, and the network can be effectively primed to receive the rest of the pattern. This feature is referred to as *temporal redundancy*.

In contrast to discrimination networks (Simon and Feigenbaum, 1964), a data-flow network does not expect features to appear in a certain order but will match the pattern no matter what order the features come in. This is particularly important in achieving a viable partial matcher. In a discrimination network, if the first tests fail, the pattern will never be matched. The data-flow scheme does not need to weigh any particular feature so heavily. Also, such a pattern matcher is at a considerable advantage over a discrimination network because it can take advantage of parallelism and perform many tests simultaneously.

Unlike the pattern matchers associated with early versions of ACT (Anderson, 1976), this one has a clear sense of time built into it. The time for a pattern to be matched will be the time for the tests to be performed at the two-input node that feeds into the production. Finally, the various pattern nodes (terminal and two-input) can process multiple instantiations, making this pattern-matching scheme more powerful than the Rumelhart and McClelland scheme. For instance, there were two distinct instantiations of node G in Figure 4.6, each one corresponding to a different set of terms instantiating the local variables in that pattern. Rumelhart and McClelland lack the power of this scheme because their patterns lack variables; all of their patterns are looking for specific combinations of specific data elements. One reason these researchers avoid multiple instantiations is that they cannot imagine how it would be implemented neurally (McClelland, personal communication). Considering our general ignorance of the nervous system, this reason is not totally convincing. Moreover, the capacity for multiple instantiations is critical for the successful functioning of production system pattern matching.

*Application to word recognition.* The EACH pattern in Figure 4.5 can be conceived of as implementing the condition of the following production:

> IF vertical bar V1 and horizontal bars H1, H2, and H3 are in position 1
> and the top of V1 is connected to the left of H1
> and the middle of V1 is connected to the left of H2
> and the bottom of V1 is connected to the left of H3
> and position 1 is before position 2
> and vertical bars V2 and V3 and horizontal bars H4 and H5 are in position 2
> and the top of V2 is connected to the left of H4
> and the top of V3 is connected to the right of H4
> and the middle of V2 is connected to the left of H5
> and the middle of V3 is connected to the right of H5
> and position 2 is before position 3
> and vertical bar V4 and horizontal bars H6 and H7 are in position 3
> and the top of V4 is connected to the left of H6
> and the bottom of V4 is connected to the left of H7
> and position 3 is before position 4
> and vertical bars V5 and V6 and horizontal bar H8 are in position 4
> and the middle of V5 is connected to the left of H8
> and the middle of V6 is connected to the right of H8
> THEN V1, H1, H2, and H3 form an E
> and V2, V3, H4, and H5 form an A
> and V4, H6, and H7 form a C
> and V5, V6, and H8 form an H
> and they all form the word EACH.

This production is testing for spatial code information as defined in Chapter 2. Specifically, tests are being performed for the location of various bars, the connections among them, and the juxtaposition of various feature clusters. The various nodes in the network perform tests of how well the spatial constraints specified in the condition are met. For instance, the ⊢ pattern tests whether a vertical and a horizontal bar come close to meeting the specification that the middle of the vertical bar is connected to the left of the horizontal.

The production above is quite complex relative to the other ones in this book. This is partly because the production is being represented so explicitly, but also because the condition contains more information than most productions. Such large condition productions can only be built with much practice (see Neves and Anderson, 1981, and Chapter 6).

Unlike Rumelhart and McClelland's scheme, the theory does not require separate pattern recognizers for separate positions. Rather, a single node represents the feature E in any position. As mentioned earlier, different instantiations are created of the E pattern for each instance.

USE OF ACTIVATION IN PATTERN MATCHING

As Forgy (1979) documents, time to match in his implementation is determined by factors such as size of working memory, number of patterns, and pattern complexity. The exact relationship of these factors to time is determined by constraints of the computer hardware, so no one proposes that the temporal properties of Forgy's system be taken in detail as a serious model of psychological processing time. In ACT* the pattern nodes in the data-flow network perform their tests at a rate determined by the level of activation. The level of activation of a node is determined by parallel excitatory and inhibitory interactions with other nodes in the network. Another important difference is that in McClelland and Rumelhart, activation determines whether the pattern matches, but in ACT, level of activation determines the rate of pattern matching. In both systems activation plays an important role in determining if a pattern will match, but in ACT there is also an important role for tests at the pattern nodes.

The level of activation at a particular pattern node is determined by four factors:

1.  The individual data elements that are matched to the terminal nodes have a level of activation. This activation is

divided among the various nodes as it flows up from the bottom through the pattern network.

2. Different pattern nodes that share the same subpattern compete with each other by means of lateral inhibitory effects. These effects can drive down the level of activation of a weak competitor to zero and so end its participation in the pattern matching.

3. To the extent that the superpattern of a pattern is active, it will increase the pattern's activation. This is a top-down facilitative effect.

4. The level of activation of a node can increase or decrease according to whether the tests being performed at the node are successful. These tests are performed gradually relative to the spread of activation through the network. Thus changes in the pattern of activation throughout the network are made largely in response to the growth of evidence, or lack of it, for the various pattern tests.

Partial matches can occur in this framework in one of two ways, as illustrated in Figure 4.7. First, tests at a two-input node may be only partially satisfied by its input as in (*a*). In this case the level of activation at the node should be adjusted to reflect the degree of match. Second, a critical feature may be simply absent from the input as in (*b*). The nodes that test for the combination of this feature, that is, ⊢, should have much lower activation.

An underlying assumption in this scheme is that activation is a limited resource. An interesting question is why the system should be limited in the amount of activation. There are two possible answers. First, imposing a limit on activation serves the computational function of forcing a choice among competing patterns. Second, although its exact neural analog is unclear, activation may well require the expenditure of finite metabolic resources. Unlimited activation would impose unacceptable high demands on the body—Geschwind (1980)

**Figure 4.7** *Examples of stimuli that partially match the CAT pattern.*

notes that the brain already requires fully 25 percent of the body's cardiac output.

In the ACT model activation spreads through the long-term declarative memory as well as through the production pattern network. Those elements that are active in long-term memory, plus input from the environment, constitute the working memory, and they are the input to the terminal nodes in the data-flow network. Declarative-memory activation is entirely facilitating or excitatory; that is, the activation of one element can only increase the level of activation of related elements. In contrast, activation in the pattern recognizer has both excitatory and inhibitory effects. The inhibitory effects in the pattern network are one of the important properties that distinguish procedural knowledge from declarative knowledge in ACT. These factors force selection of one pattern at the expense of another.

CALCULATION OF ACTIVATION LEVELS

A simulation of the pattern matcher has been implemented for ACT* that embodies the properties described. While I have a fair degree of faith in the general scheme for pattern matching, I do not have a great deal of faith in the precise mathematics of the simulation. Many aspects of it seem arbitrary. However, it is not the case that any plausible scheme for calculating excitation and inhibition will do. For instance, I tried to apply the mathematics described by McClelland and Rumelhart (1981) to the ACT* networks in Figure 4.5. The results were not totally satisfactory, and it is worth reviewing why. First, it was possible for a number of contradictory pattern nodes to reach maximum activation. For instance, running on the network in Figure 4.5, both the COOL and the FOOL nodes would reach maximum level, given the input in part (*a*) of Figure 4.8. Second, partial patterns could block the activation of more complete patterns. To take an example, consider the data structure in part (*b*) of Figure 4.8, which best matches EACH. Activation of ACHE, with ACH matching the last three letters, rises more

(a)  ⊢∏⊔∟

(b)  ⊢∏⊏⊢

**Figure 4.8** *Examples of test patterns that were presented to the network in Figure 4.5.*

rapidly and because of the inhibitory processes represses activation of EACH.

These difficulties do not arise in the McClelland and Rumelhart scheme because of the simplicity and special structure of the networks (for example, there are only letter, feature, and word nodes). All letter nodes for a position inhibit each other, and all word nodes inhibit each other. Given the network in Figure 4.5, it might be possible to come up with some values for excitatory and inhibitory links such that the McClelland and Rumelhart scheme would work. However, it is desirable to have a scheme that will work without a lot of trial and error in tinkering for the right parameters. Such a scheme can be achieved if it is endowed with the following two properties.

1. There is an initial rapid spread of excitatory influences representing the bottom-up evidence for a pattern. This is in keeping with existing ideas that excitatory influences can spread rapidly through the declarative network (as discussed in Chapter 3). This would permit large patterns to be identified before smaller patterns could repress their activation. Only after this initial wave would lateral inhibitory influences and top-down influences come into play. Moreover, these inhibitory influences would begin gradually. Their function would be both to sharpen initial differences based on bottom-up factors and to bring contextual factors and expectations to bear. Thus the important factor controlling the time course of activation turns out to be these second-order, inhibitory influences. This is achieved in the current framework by making inhibitory effects a function of the degree of evidence at local pattern tests. Initially, when there is no evidence, there is no inhibition. As the tests are performed and evidence builds up, so does the inhibition.

2. After the first wave of positive activation, the overall amount of activation in the network remains constant. This prevents a large number of contradictory patterns from receiving high activation and prevents all patterns from going to a zero level of activation. The lateral and top-down influences can only redistribute constant activation among competing pattern nodes. This scheme for activation calculation effectively forces a choice among competing patterns.

The appendix to this chapter describes in detail the mathematics used in both the excitatory and the inhibitory calculations. Here I would like to summarize the intent of that mathematics. The general character of these calculations may make a lasting contribution to our understanding of cognition, but the current means of achieving this character is a little arbitrary.

*Bottom-up excitation.* Excitation starts at the bottom (terminal) nodes in the network. Activation only flows upward. The level of activation of the bottom nodes is a function of the level of activation of the data that instantiate them. The activation flowing from a node to its superpatterns is divided among the superpatterns according to their strength, producing a "fan effect." Indeed, the process for upward spread of activation is very similar to the spread of activation in the declarative network.

The rules for calculating bottom-up spread of activation depend on whether the node is a positive two-input node or a negative one-input node. The activation of a positive two-input node is just the sum of the activation from the two inputs. If there are no data from one of the two subpatterns (for instance the horizontal bar is missing for the ⊢ subpattern in the letter A when the input is ∏ ), the activation is just that received from the one input.

Negative one-input nodes are competing with two-input nodes for their one input. For instance, the one-input node *L* in Figure 4.5 is competing with *C* and *O*. To compensate for the extra activation received by competing two-input nodes, the activation received from the one-input is multiplied by a scale factor. In the implementation of Figure 3.4 as well as of Figure 4.5, activation was simply doubled.

*Inhibition.* In ACT there is lateral inhibition among competing patterns involving the same subpattern. Figure 4.9 illustrates the basic inhibitory situation: pattern node *K* receives input from two subpatterns I and J. I is connected to nodes 1, 2, . . . , K, and node J is connected to nodes K, K + 1,

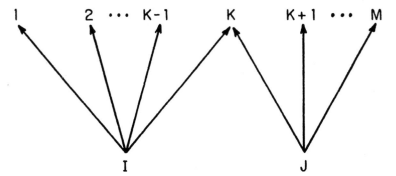

**Figure 4.9**   *A representation of the situation that leads to lateral inhibition. Node K receives input from I and J. It receives inhibition from all the nodes that receive input from I and J.*

. . . , M. Then 1 through K define one inhibitory set, and K through M another. Node K is in an inhibitory relation with all members of both sets except itself, that is, 1, 2, . . . , K − 1, K + 1, . . . , M.

If a pair of nodes is in an inhibitory relation, there is a net flow of activation from one node to the other. That is, activation is taken away from one node and added to the other. The direction of flow and amount of activation depend on the following factors:

1. The relative activations of the two nodes, which reflect the general evidence for each node.
2. The relative activations of the superpatterns involving each node. This is the means by which contextual, top-down factors are able to influence the pattern matching.
3. The current results of the tests being performed at each pattern node. This is the means by which the actual tests influence pattern matching. In the case of a positive two-input node, evidence increases or decreases as the pattern tests are performed. In the case of a negative one-input node, there are no explicit tests to perform, but evidence gradually accrues to mimic the two-input nodes with which it is competing.

It should be pointed out with respect to the third factor that activation controls the rate at which tests are performed at two-input nodes, so evidence will accrue more rapidly for more active two-input nodes. To mimic this, the rate at which evidence spontaneously accrues for negative one-input nodes is a function of their level of activation.

### TIME FOR A PRODUCTION TO EXECUTE

All the pattern nodes in the network are performing their tests asynchronously. The decision about whether to fire a production depends on its top pattern node, which represents the full condition. When this pattern node completes its tests and has a value that is above threshold, the production will execute. A number of factors influence the time, $T$, it takes for a production to fire:

1. The complexity, $C$, of the pattern being matched. The larger the structure, the longer it takes for activation to settle down on an interpretation of the data.
2. The strength, $S$, of the pattern. The excitatory component

gives greater activation to the stronger superpatterns of a pattern.

3. The level of activation, $A$, of the data elements that match the pattern.

4. The overall goodness of match, $G$, of the pattern to the data.

5. The goodness of match, $I$, of competing patterns that will inhibit the current pattern.

The exact interaction of $C$, $S$, $A$, $G$, and $I$ depends on the specifics of the data-flow network structure. It is almost impossible to decide on such specifics, and they probably vary from subject to subject. In fact the ACT theory does not prescribe a way to assign a numerical value to each factor. However, it is useful to have some general, if approximate, description of the relationship among these factors:

$$T = \frac{CI}{SAG} \qquad (4.1)$$

Thus time to match decreases with the strength of the pattern, level of data activation, and goodness of the match. It increases with the complexity of the pattern to be matched and the presence of competing patterns.

ACHIEVING CONFLICT RESOLUTION PRINCIPLES

The pattern-matching system as described achieves four of the five conflict-resolution principles set forth earlier (treatment of goals has not yet been discussed).

1. The scheme prefers larger partial matches for two reasons. A larger match will accumulate more activation from bottom-up sources and will have more evidence for it in the competition in the lateral inhibition.

2. This scheme prefers more specific patterns for the same reason it prefers larger partial matches. If they are more specific because they involve more data elements, they will receive greater bottom-up activation. If they are more specific because they perform more tests, they will have more evidence for the inhibitory competition.

3. Data refractoriness is produced by inhibition. Consider a set of data instantiating a pattern. The various superpatterns of the pattern instantiation are in inhibitory competition. Eventually one superpattern will win out and drive the activation of all the others to zero. This superpattern will then be the only

interpretation of that data instantiating the pattern. Thus the data can only participate in one production.

4. The strength of a pattern has a straightforward role in the distribution of activation: stronger patterns receive greater activation from their subpatterns.

WORD PERCEPTION

*The word superiority phenomenon.* McClelland and Rumelhart and Rumelhart and McClelland report many successful applications of their theory to predict results in the word recognition literature. They focused particularly on experimental studies related to the fact that letters are perceived better in the context of words or pseudo-words than alone or in the context of nonwords (Reicher, 1969; Wheeler, 1970). It is not clear whether the ACT* system can reproduce all of their predictive successes, because many of them depend on how the statistical properties of four-letter words interact with the properties of their model. We simply have not yet performed their admirable effort of incorporating thousands of words into the simulation. However, it is clear that ACT can at least produce some of the more basic results they address.

Consider first the basic word-superiority result. The ACT simulation was presented with stimuli (*a*)–(*c*) in Figure 4.10. Each stimulus is missing some features. Such partial stimuli would be the result of incomplete perception. In (*a*) and (*b*) we have information about all four letters of a word, whereas in (*c*) we have only a word fragment. The input for the first two letters is identical in all three cases. However, given the network in Figure 4.5, (*a*) can only be EACH, (*b*) can only be FOOL, but (*c*) is ambiguous.[7]

Figure 4.11 shows the growth of activation of the A and O interpretations of the second letter as well as the EACH and FOOL interpretations for each case. In (*a*) the EACH word interpretation and the A letter interpretation are chosen. In (*b*) the FOOL word interpretation and the O letter interpretation are chosen. In (*c*) the A letter interpretation is eventually chosen because it has a higher frequency in our network. No whole word interpretation was ever selected for this case. A star above the curve indicates when the pattern matching was complete. As can be seen, it took one cycle longer in the case of pattern (*c*).

Another result simulated by McClelland and Rumelhart is that letter perception is better for well-formed nonwords like COAF than for letters alone or completely random letter strings. They attribute this to support from similar words like COAL

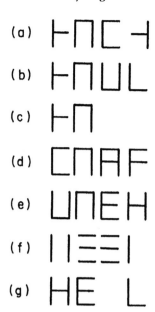

**Figure 4.10**    *Various test stimuli presented to the network in Figure 4.5.*

and LOAF. Our simulation also produces this result and for a similar reason. For instance, we contrasted recognition of the second letter in parts (*d*) and (*e*) of Figure 4.10. In (*d*) the second letter was recognized as O and the whole stimulus as LOAF. In (*e*) the second letter was recognized as A because of frequency, and the whole stimulus was not identified.

A third result reported by Rumelhart and McClelland is that context is more helpful if it precedes than if it follows the word. That is, subjects do better at perceiving O if they see F_OL context first and then O than vice versa. ACT predicts this because the system can be locked into the incorrect perception of a letter if it is presented too early. Once a pattern is decided, that interpretation will hold even in a contradictory context.

*Subpart bias.* One of the interesting phenomena of human perception is that it is easier to perceive a pattern when complete subparts of it are given than when the pattern is totally fragmented. For instance, consider the contrast between parts (*f*) and (*g*) of Figure 4.10. Both consist of nine letter strokes, but it is much easier to see (*g*), which has a complete subpart, as forming the word HEEL (or HELL). ACT reproduces this phenomenon of perception. The subpart forms a focus of high activation around which the whole pattern can be built and the missing subparts inferred. This is a phenomenon that cannot be easily explained by the Rumelhart and McClelland model because they do not represent subword fragments and because they do not need to perform tests of the appropriateness of various feature combinations. Palmer (1977) shows that connected subparts are more easily recognized in nonletter patterns.

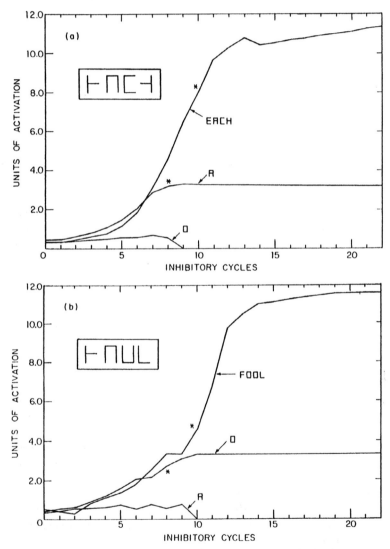

**Figure 4.11**     *The level of activation of various pattern nodes in the context of the stimuli in parts (a)–(c) of Figure 4.10.*

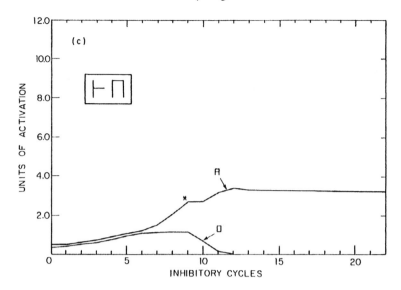

ACT's theory of pattern recognition is not to be justified solely in terms of its ability to deal with word recognition. Much of the motivation for the ACT scheme was to get a pattern matcher for production systems that would be able to function more generally. In addition to producing a scheme that works, a number of empirical phenomena support this pattern matcher. Much of this is discussed elsewhere in the book, but it is worth listing some of the considerations here:

1. Chapter 3 discussed the evidence that activation spreads rapidly in the declarative network and that processing time was a function of level of activation, not time to spread. The pattern matcher maps level of activation onto time because the level controls the rate at which the pattern tests are performed.
2. Chapter 3 discussed the interaction between pattern complexity and level of activation, which is predicted by the pattern matcher.
3. Chapter 3 discussed the evidence for inhibition by similar patterns with respect to fact retrieval and the Stroop phenomenon. Lawry and LaBerge (1981) have reported the same effect in word recognition.
4. As discussed earlier in this chapter, degree of match does have a strong effect on rate of pattern matching.

5. The section on data refractoriness in this chapter discussed the evidence for this principle of conceptual and perceptual pattern matching.
6. The model easily produces an effect of pattern frequency on rate of matching.
7. LaBerge (1974) has described some interactions between attention and perception that can be accounted for in this framework (to be discussed in the next section). More generally, this model produces the effects of goals on pattern matching.

## The Role of Goals

### Goals as Sources of Activation

So far, the role of goals has been ignored. Goal elements are treated in this system as sources of high and constant activation. Unlike other sources, goal elements do not spontaneously turn off. A goal element can only cease to be a source by explicitly being changed. To see how goal setting can interact with pattern matching, consider a simulation of an experiment by LaBerge (1973). In that experiment, he had subjects recognize familiar letters, such as P, or pseudo-letters, such as  Ν , in conditions where the subjects had either been primed to expect the letter or had not been so primed. Getting the subject to expect a letter amounts to having him set a goal to recognize the letter. To simulate primed recognition of unfamiliar letters, such as  Ν , productions were used of the form:

    IF the goal is to perceive pattern1
       and there is a vertical bar V1 and a right oblique bar R1
       and the top of V1 connects to the top of R1
    THEN an instance of pattern1 has been presented.

Such a production has an explicit goal to recognize the pattern. When the pattern was not primed, it was recognized by a production similar to the one above except that there was no goal test. The simulation involved other productions to recognize familiar patterns when primed and still other productions to recognize unfamiliar patterns when primed. The time was measured in terms of the number of inhibitory cycles before the production completed matching and fired. It took eight inhibitory cycles for the familiar pattern to fire with or without the goal setting. It took nine cycles for the unfamiliar pattern to fire with goal setting but thirteen cycles without goal setting. This corresponds to the pattern of data that LaBerge reports; namely, focusing attention has an advantage only in the case of unfamiliar patterns. In understanding the results of our simulation it is important to first understand why the unfamiliar pattern took much longer without the goal element. The production for recognition had in its condition only the vertical bar clause and the right oblique bar clause. When the elements that would be matched by these clauses were presented, most of the activation from them initially went to the pattern nodes for other familiar letters, such as K, which had stronger encodings. Therefore the rate of testing was much slower for the unfamiliar pattern. When the goal was set, however, it directed a great deal of additional activation to the pattern node and so increased its rate of matching. In the case of familiar patterns, the data elements contribute more activation to the pattern node, so the goal increment is less important. Also, the goal clause does require an additional test that means extra pattern matching. This can cancel out the advantage of the extra activation from the goal if a good deal of activation is coming from the data.

The rest of this section is not concerned with how goals are treated in pattern matching, but with other special provisions in the ACT* interpreter for handling goals. In this discussion, as often in other chapters, it will be assumed that the data are clear and unambiguous and that the pattern matcher will consequently function flawlessly to select the correct production. This is just a useful idealization. In production conditions with goals this idealization is more true than in the case of nongoal productions. The weighting given to goal activation increases the effort that goes into accurately matching the conditions of such productions.

HIERARCHICAL GOAL STRUCTURING

The ACT production system has a special facility for dealing with hierarchical goal structures. The Tower of Hanoi problem (see Figure 4.12) is a good illustration of how it is used. The first three productions in Table 4.1 are sufficient to handle an arbitrary Tower of Hanoi problem. They embody the goal-recursion strategy as described by Simon (1975).

Production P1, the work horse of the set, assumes in its operation the ability to build a new level in a hierarchical goal tree and to transfer control to the first new subgoal—namely, moving pyramid N-1 to peg Y. Figure 4.13 illustrates the goal structure these productions will generate for a five-disk problem.

**Table 4.1**   *Production rules for performing in the Tower of Hanoi problem*

---

P1   IF the goal is to transfer pyramid N to peg Z
    and pyramid N consists of disk N plus sub-pyramid N-1
    and pyramid N is on peg X
    and peg Y is not X or Z
  THEN set as subgoals to
      1.   Transfer pyramid N-1 to peg Y
      2.   Move disk N to peg Z
      3.   Transfer pyramid N-1 to peg Z.

P2   IF the goal is to transfer pyramid N to disk Z
    and pyramid N is a single disk
  THEN the goal is to move N to Z.

P3   IF the goal is to move disk N to peg Z
    and peg Z contains no disks smaller than N
  THEN move disk N to peg Z
    and the goal has been successfully satisfied.

P4   IF the top goal is to solve Tower of Hanoi
    and no next goal can be retrieved
    and disk N is the largest disk not on the goal peg
  THEN set as the next subgoal to move disk N
      to the goal peg.

P5   IF the goal is to move disk N to peg Z
    and there is no smaller disk on peg Z
    and the largest disk on N is M
    and disk N is on peg X
    and peg Y is not X or Z
  THEN set as subgoals to
      1.   Move disk M to peg Y
      2.   Move disk N to peg Z.

P6   IF the goal is to move disk N to peg Z
    and the largest disk on Z is M
    and N is larger than M
    and the largest disk on N is L
    and L is larger than M
    and N is on peg X
    and peg Y is not X or Z
  THEN set as subgoals to
      1.   Move disk L to peg Y
      2.   Move disk N to peg Z.

P7   IF the goal is to move disk N to peg Z
    and the largest disk on Z is M
    and N is larger than M
    and disk N is not covered
    and disk N is on peg X
    and peg Y is not X or Z

**Table 4.1** (*continued*)

| |
|---|
| THEN set as subgoals<br>  1.  To move disk M to peg Y<br>  2.  To move disk N to peg Z. |
| P8     IF the goal is to move disk N to peg Z<br>        and the largest disk on Z is M<br>        and N is larger than M<br>        and the largest disk on N is L<br>        and M is larger than L<br>        and N is on X<br>        and peg Y is not X or Z<br>THEN set as subgoals<br>  1.  To move disk M to peg Y<br>  2.  To move disk N to peg Z. |

Consider the state of its knowledge at the point where it makes its first move (starred in Figure 4.13). It must have stacked the following sequence of nine goals: move the 1 disk to peg C, the 2 disk to B, the 1 pyramid to B, the 3 disk to C, the 2 pyramid to C, the 4 disk to B, the 3 pyramid to B, the 5 disk to C, then the 4 pyramid to C. These goals are stored in ACT as a sequential structure. The data structure itself is nothing special—just a temporal string representation that the system uses for storing lists. The hierarchical goal structure at the point of the first move is given by the data structure above the dotted line in Figure 4.13. The data structure below the dotted line is provided by later expansions of goals.

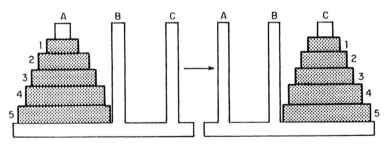

**Figure 4.12**   *The Tower of Hanoi problem. There are three pegs, A, B, and C, and five disks of different sizes, 1, 2, 3, 4, and 5, with holes in their centers so that they can be stacked on the pegs. Initially, the disks are all on peg A, stacked in a pyramid. The goal is to move all the disks to peg C. Only the top disk on a peg can be moved, and it can never be placed on top of a smaller disk.*

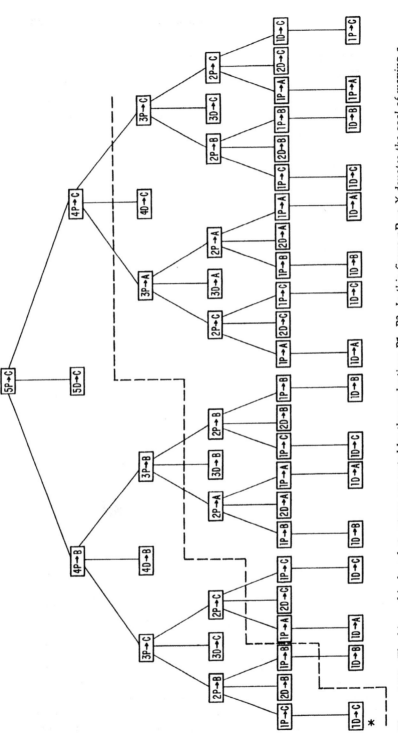

**Figure 4.13** The hierarchical goal structure generated by the productions P1–P3. In this figure nP → X denotes the goal of moving a pyramid of n disks to peg X, and nD → X denotes the goal of moving the nth smallest disk to pyramid X.

The system automatically moves around this goal structure. When a goal is satisfied, attention automatically goes to the next goal. When all the subgoals of a supergoal have been popped, the supergoal is popped. In many production systems the flow of control among goals would be implemented by separate productions,[8] but this clutters up conflict resolution and pattern matching with work that should be part of the production system interpreter. Goal handling in the interpreter rather than in the productions is much more efficient.

It is also necessary for the goal interpreter to treat goals in a special way to avoid the problem of data refractoriness. Recall earlier that a particular data structure could only match to one production. However, it may be necessary to use a goal statement repeatedly, as when we back up to it after one method has failed and try another. The assumption is that the goal interpreter reinstates the current goal after each use so that the goal statement will not be subject to data refractoriness.

MEMORY FOR GOAL STRUCTURES

This goal structure is a data structure in working memory, no different from other memory structures. Attention is focused on the current goal, which will be maintained in working memory. Activation spreading from the current goal will maintain in working memory the most closely linked goals. Consider, for instance, the state of memory at the point where the first move is made in the Tower of Hanoi problem. This involves moving disk 1 to peg C. It is reasonable to suppose that the intention to move disk 2 to peg B and then disk 1 to peg B are also in working memory. Perhaps, the future plans to move disk 3 to peg C and pyramid 2 to peg C are also in working memory. Thus it might be reasonable to assume that three to five goals are available. My own experience in running this algorithm is that I have access to about three to five. The rest of the goals, however, will have to be retrieved from long-term memory if they are to be had at all. Given the limitations of long-term memory, there will be many failures to retrieve goals. Certainly, I have never been able to execute a five-pyramid problem without hitting points where I was simply unable to remember what I had intended to do next. At such points, I use a set of rules like those in productions P4–P8 to reconstruct from the then-current configuration what move to make next. The productions in P4–P8 are special in that they could yield perfect performance from all configurations without temporary goal memory. That is, after every move, if the total goal sequence had been forgotten, it would be possible to calculate the next move from the configuration. These productions are similar to sophisticated perceptual strategy described in Simon (1975).

The effect of losing track of a hierarchical goal structure can be to make behavior seem less structured and more data-driven. One might describe as opportunistic the behavior of a subject who forgets his goals, analyzes the current state, and constructs some partial solution to it in response to its peculiar properties. While this might be an adequate description of the behavior, it need not imply that the architecture supporting this planning was nonhierarchical. The production system in Table 4.1 shows how such opportunistic behavior can be obtained from a hierarchical system subject to failures of working memory.

Behavior from the ACT architecture might appear to be opportunistic in character in that it responds to a complex, nonhierarchical control structure. It is quite possible in ACT for a data-driven production to produce a radical shift in the current goal—for instance:

> IF I suddenly feel extreme pain
> THEN set my goal to escape the pain.

This production illustrates that data can produce a shift of attention, but also that such a shift need not be evidence for control structure more sophisticated than ACT's mixture of hierarchical goal structure and flat data-driven structure.

THE LOGICAL STRUCTURE OF GOAL TREES

In a conjunctive goal tree like that in Figure 4.13, all the subgoals of a goal are necessary to satisfy the goal. If one subgoal fails, it is necessary to generate another conjunction of goals to achieve it. A search problem arises when one must consider a number of alternative decompositions (conjunctions) as ways to achieve a goal. As a simple example, consider the application of the following three productions to the problem in Figure 4.14($a$):

> IF the goal is to prove $\triangle XYZ \cong \triangle UVW$
> THEN try the method of angle-side-angle (ASA)
>     and set as subgoals to prove
>     1. $\angle ZXY \cong \angle WUV$
>     2. $\overline{XY} \cong \overline{UV}$
>     3. $\angle XYZ \cong \angle UVW$.

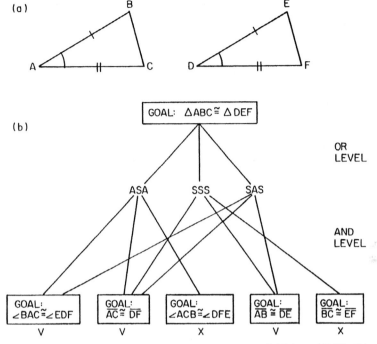

**Figure 4.14** (a) *A simple geometry problem: prove* △ABC ≅ △DEF. *(b) The goal structure that would be generated by the productions in the text. The* or-level *reflects different attempts by different productions to solve the problem. The* and-level *reflects the subgoals required for each attempt.*

IF the goal is to prove △*XYZ* ≅ △*UVW*
THEN try the method of side-side-side (SSS)
    and set as subgoals to prove
      1.  $\overline{XY} \cong \overline{UV}$
      2.  $\overline{YZ} \cong \overline{VW}$
      3.  $\overline{ZX} \cong \overline{WU}$.

IF the goal is to prove △*XYZ* ≅ △*UVW*
THEN try the method of side-angle-side (SAS)
    and set as subgoals to prove
      1.  $\overline{XY} \cong \overline{UV}$
      2.  ∠*XYZ* ≅ ∠*UVW*
      3.  $\overline{YZ} \cong \overline{VW}$.

Figure 4.14(*b*) illustrates the structure that would be generated if these productions applied in order to the goal of trying to prove that △*ABC* ≅ △*DEF*. First, ASA applies but fails because

$\angle ACB$ is not given as congruent to $\angle DFE$. Then SSS applies but fails because $\overline{BC}$ is not given as congruent to $\overline{EF}$. Finally, SAS successfully applies. As can be seen from Figure 4.14($b$), three productions produce an *or*-level in the graph structure where the system is searching through various methods to achieve its goal. This kind of blind search through methods is typical of novices in trying to generate a geometry proof (Anderson, 1982; Anderson et al., 1981). Chapter 6 discusses how experience can make students more judicious in their strategy selection. Finally, note that Figure 4.14($b$) illustrates the fact that separate productions provide the disjunctive component in ACT, while separate actions in a production provide the conjunctive component.

### PLANNING

The goal structures considered so far have at their termini goals that can be solved by direct actions. An important augmentation to cognitive control is to generate goal structures that do not produce action directly but rather serve as plans that will be transformed into executable action. For instance, when the chess player is considering various move sequences, he is not moving pieces on the board nor is he committing himself to the moves. He is generating a set of alternative plans from which he will select the best. The goal structures generated in each imagined scenario are data to be operated upon. The player may focus on a scenario, inspect it for flaws, and attempt to improve it.

Sacerdoti's book (1977) provides many examples that illustrate the computational character of planning. He describes a simple case in which the goal is to paint a ladder and paint a ceiling. It is critical that the system start by planning a solution and not executing one. The first step in solving the problem is produced by a rule that decomposes the conjoint goal into a sequence of two subgoals:

P1      IF the goal is to achieve A and B
    THEN try linear decomposition
        and set as subgoals
        1.  To achieve A
        2.  To achieve B.

For achieving the subgoal of painting the ladder, the following standard "paint" production applies:

P2        IF the goal is to paint X
          THEN apply the standard paint procedure
          and set as subgoals to
          1. Get the paint
          2. Apply the paint to X.

A somewhat more special-purpose production is evoked to plan painting the ceiling:

P3        IF the goal is to paint X
          and X is too high to reach
          THEN use the ladder method
          and set as subgoals to
          1. Get the paint
          2. Use the ladder
          3. Apply the paint to X.

Figure 4.15(a) shows the goal structure at this point. If a painter acted upon this structure there would be a serious impasse— the ladder would be painted first, which would make it useless for painting the ceiling. Therefore, it is important that the painter generate this structure as a plan to be operated upon rather than as an execution structure. If this were a data structure in memory, not acted upon, the following productions could apply:

P4        IF there is a goal2 to use X
          and an earlier goal1 will have just painted X
          THEN goal1 has clobbered goal2.

The repair for this situation would be proposed by the following general production:

P5        IF goal1 has clobbered goal2
          and goal1 is part of supergoal goal3
          and goal2 is part of supergoal goal4
          and goal3 and goal4 are brother goals
          THEN reorder goal3 and goal4.

This production transforms the goal structure.

The other nonoptimal feature of the goal structure in Figure 4.15(a) is that the paint is gotten twice. This nonoptimality is edited out by the following production:

(a)

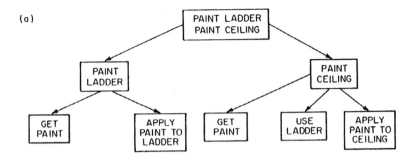

(b)

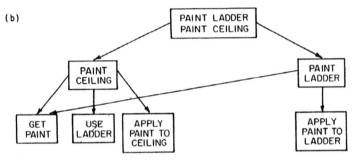

**Figure 4.15**    (a) *The goal structure underlying the paint problem after the decomposition productions have applied.* (b) *The goal structure after transformations to eliminate goal conflict and redundant goals.*

P6        IF the plan has subgoals goal1 and goal2
          and goal1 achieves X
          and goal2 achieves X
          and goal2 follows goal1
    THEN delete goal2
          and reinstate the goal to check the plan.

The resulting goal structure after applying these reordering and deletion transformations is given in Figure 4.15(*b*).

    There is reasonable evidence for at least modest goal-structured problem solving in infrahuman organisms such as the higher primates, but I know of no good evidence for planning in any creature but man. Indeed, when my son was nineteen months old, I did not see any evidence for planning. For example, in the various stacking games he played, the blocks or rings had to be stacked in a certain order. He tried to solve these problems in a largely random way, hit impasses, backed up, and started a new order. He did not spin out a mental plan and consider its consequences. Figure 4.15 illustrates a litmus test for planning: the system sets forth a sequence of intended actions, notes a conflict in the sequence, and reorganizes it. If it can be shown that a system reorders a preferred sequence of actions in anticipation of goal conflict, then that system is engaging in planning.

Planning structures underlie the transformational component of natural language. This will be expanded upon in Chapter 7, but the basic idea is that in generating a sentence, the speaker can first generate a sentence plan, transform it, then execute the plan. Because of the hierarchical character of goal structures, the sentence plan will have the phrase structures typical of natural language. The transformations are planning operations just like the reordering and deletion illustrated in Figure 4.15.

Transformations of goal structures in planning are another way in which observed problem-solving behavior might appear to deviate from strict and simple hierarchical decomposition. However, such transformations only reinforce evidence for the hierarchical structure of problem solving, because they are specified in terms of the hierarchical structure of the goal tree. For instance, in generating the question *Was the boy kicked?* it is reasonable to argue that a hierarchical verb phrase was generated as a unit and then transformed. Chomsky (1968) has stressed this point about transformations and phrase structure in natural language. Although transformations could logically apply with respect to the sequence of terminal elements independent of their hierarchical structure, all natural language transformations are formulated with respect to the hierarchical structure. Chomsky has taken this as evidence for the unique character of natural language. However, such transformations of hierarchical structure are characteristic of many nonlinguistic planning behaviors, such as the one illustrated in Figure 4.15.

Two demands are placed on the system to permit successful planning. First is the architectural feature of being able to spin forth a goal structure without acting upon it. Second, working memory has to be reliable enough to maintain the goal structure for operation. If these two preconditions are satisfied, it is possible to operate on the plan. In line with analyses that will be given in Chapter 5, probably one can maintain larger fragments of plans in domains where one has had extensive practice. This is perhaps one reason why linguistic transformations appear relatively late in children's language development.[9] It is also not atypical for people to have problems with nonlinguistic plans because of failures of working memory. We have all run into problems because we did not detect that an early goal would clobber a late goal. Chess players often have to rerun their plans because they have forgotten the planned sequence of moves.

## INTENTIONS

In performing a behavioral sequence under the control of a goal structure, one can hit points where insufficient information exists to achieve the next goal. If one is executing the goal structure as it is being generated, one has no choice but to "wing it" in such circumstances. For instance, if a person is packing and sets as a subgoal to get a suitcase and fill it, there is no choice but to select a suitcase of arbitrary size and hope it will be appropriate to the material he wants to put into it. However, in other situations one can postpone an action and set an intention to deal with it later. For instance, the following seems to model my son J. J.'s performance on the children's small jigsaw puzzles that he works with:

P1    IF the goal is to finish a puzzle
      and Y is an unplaced piece
   THEN set as subgoals to
      1. Place Y in the puzzle
      2. Finish the puzzle.

P2    IF the goal is to place Y in a puzzle
      and Y fits into an available location
   THEN place Y in the location
      and POP the goal.

P3    IF the goal is to place Y in a puzzle
      and Y does not fit into any available location
   THEN set an intention to later place Y in a location
      and POP the goal.

P4    IF there is an intention to place Y in a location
      and Y fits into an available location
   THEN place Y in the location.

These productions describe a puzzle-solving behavior in which he starts fitting pieces randomly into the periphery and fits center pieces when the periphery pieces have been placed. P1 is a production for randomly selecting pieces for placement. If the piece can be placed, P2 will place it; if not, P3 sets an intention to later place it. (The clause *Y fits into location* is meant to reflect recall of a memorized location—J. J. has the locations of the pieces memorized.) P4 is a data-driven "demon" which will place a suspended piece when the right prerequisite pieces are placed. J. J. does appear to return to suspended pieces when he can place them. Of course, this requires that he remember his intentions. If there were many interior pieces he would not be able to remember all his suspended intentions. Fortunately, his puzzles have at most two or three interior pieces.

### Appendix: Calculation of Pattern Node Activation

The following equations describe the behavior of the pattern matcher. For many reasons the simulation of the ACT* pattern matcher only approximates these equations. In part, this is because the simulation tries to create a discrete approximation of a continuous process. In part, this is because of optimizations associated with pruning the proliferation of pattern instantiations. The actual code can be obtained by writing to me.

As in the declarative network (see Chapter 3), the change in activation of the pattern node, $x$, is a positive function of the input and a negative function of a decay factor:

$$\frac{da_x(t)}{dt} = Bn_x(t) - p^*a_x(t) \qquad (4.2)$$

where $n_x(t)$ is the input to node $x$. It is the sum of excitatory bottom-up input, $e_x(t)$, and of inhibitory input, $i_x(t)$. Thus

$$n_x(t) = e_x(t) + i_x(t) \qquad (4.3)$$

The value of $e_x(t)$ is positive, but the value of $i_x(t)$ can be positive or negative.

The excitatory input depends on whether the node is a positive two-input node or a negative one-input node. If it is a positive two-input node, the excitatory factor is defined as the weighted sum of activation of its two subpatterns, $y$ and $z$:

$$e_x(t) = r_{yx} \cdot a_y(t) + r_{zx} \cdot a_z(t) \qquad (4.4)$$

where $r_{yx}$ is the strength of connection from $y$ to $x$. It is defined as:

$$r_{yx} = \frac{s_x}{\sum_i s_i} \qquad (4.5)$$

where the summation is over all patterns $i$ that include $y$ as a subpattern. The strength $s_i$ of a pattern $i$ is a function of its frequency and recency of exposure. In the case of a negative one-input node $x$, its excitatory input is a function of the activation of the one-input node $y$ that feeds into it:

$$e_x(t) = m \cdot r_{yx} \cdot a_y(t) \qquad (4.6)$$

where $m$ is a multiplicative factor greater than 1 to help $x$ compete with two-input nodes.

The inhibitory factor $i_x(t)$ in Eq. (4.3) is defined as the sum of all net inhibitory effects between $x$ and all of its competitors $y$:

$$i_x(t) = \sum_y i_{xy}(t) \qquad (4.7)$$

The net inhibitory effect between two nodes $x$ and $y$ is defined as

$$i_{xy}(t) = g_x(t)T_x(t) - g_y(t)T_y(t) \qquad (4.8)$$

where $g_x(t)$ is again a measure of the goodness of the tests, and $T_x(t)$ is the activation of the superpatterns of $x$ or the activation of $x$ if it has no superpatterns. The value of $g_x(t)$ can be positive or negative.

The assumption is that the tests performed at the pattern node are relatively slow and require some time to complete, and that evidence gradually accrues with time. The actual simulation emulates the result of this gradual accrual of evidence by the following equation

$$g_x(t) = \min[\text{Value}_x, g_x(t-1) + \text{increment}_x(t-1)] \qquad (4.9)$$

where

$$\text{increment}_x(t) = f \cdot a_x(t-1) \cdot \frac{\text{Value}_x}{\text{MAX}_x} \qquad (4.10)$$

where $\text{Value}_x$ is the total evidence for $x$ when the pattern matching completes, and $\text{MAX}_x$ is the value if there is a perfect match. In the case of a one-input node the increment is just $f \cdot a_x(t-1)$, and this increases until a maximum value is achieved.

The system described above is basically linear, with one important nonlinearity imposed on it. This is that the activation of a node is bounded below by zero. When it reaches this bound, it ceases to participate in the calculations.

# 5 | Memory for Facts

## Introduction

H UMAN MEMORY has been a major domain for testing the ACT theory. Although the theory is more
general than any particular memory paradigm, it is
important to show that its assumptions, when combined,
predict the results of specific paradigms. Every experimental
result that can be derived from existing assumptions is further evidence for the accuracy and generality of those assumptions. The first part of this chapter will discuss the
ACT assumptions about encoding, retention, and retrieval of
facts. The later sections will consider some of the major phenomena documented in the experimental literature on human
memory.

### ENCODING

Encoding in ACT refers to the process by which cognitive
units (in the sense of Chapter 2) become permanent long-term
memory traces. When a cognitive unit is created, to record either some external event or the result of some internal computation, it is placed in the active state. However, this active unit is
transient. There is a fixed probability that it will be made a permanent trace. The term *trace* is reserved for permanent units.
This encoding assumption is spectacularly simple. The probability is constant over many manipulations. It does not vary
with intention or motivation to learn, which is consistent with
the ample research indicating that intention and motivation are
irrelevant if processing is kept constant (Nelson, 1976; Postman, 1964). This is probably an adaptive feature, because it is
unlikely that our judgments about what we should remember
are very predictive of what will in fact be useful to remember.

171

The probability of forming a long-term memory trace also does not vary with the unit's duration of residence in working memory. This is consistent with research (Nelson, 1977; Woodward, Bjork, and Jongeward, 1973; Horowitz and Newman, 1969)[1] that finds uninterrupted presentation time is a poor predictor of ultimate recall probability. However, probability of recall is found to increase with two presentations, even if those presentations are back to back (Horowitz and Newman, 1969; Nelson, 1977). Similarly, Loftus (1972) found that duration of fixation on a picture part has no effect on the probability of recalling the part but that the number of fixations on that part does have an effect. One would suppose that a second presentation or fixation has some chance of creating a new working-memory copy. Every time an item is reentered into working memory it accrues an additional probability of being permanently encoded. In this assumption is a partial explanation of the spacing effect (see Crowder, 1976, for a review)—that two presentations of an item produce better memory the farther apart they are spaced. If two presentations are in close succession, the second may occur when a trace from the first is still in working memory, and a new working-memory trace might not be created. This is similar to Hintzman's (1974) habituation explanation of the spacing effect, or what Crowder more generally calls the inattention hypothesis. Consistent with this explanation is the evidence of Hintzman that at short intervals it is the second presentation that tends not to be remembered.[2]

Also consistent with this analysis is the evidence that memory is better when a difficult task intervenes between two studies (Bjork and Allen, 1970; Tzeng, 1973) than when an easy task intervenes. A difficult task is more likely to remove the original trace from working memory because it tends to interfere with the source nodes maintaining the trace. If the trace is removed from working memory, the second presentation will offer an independent opportunity for encoding the trace.

In most situations the length of uninterrupted study of an item has small but detectable effects on the probability of recall, so I would not want the above remarks to be interpreted as implying that duration of study has no effect. The duration of uninterrupted study might affect the probability of encoding in a number of ways. First, if the subject's attention wanders from the item, it may fall out of working memory, and when attention returns the item will get the benefit of a new entry into working memory. In some situations it is almost certain that traces exit from and reenter working memory—for instance, when a subject reads and then rereads a story that involves too many cognitive units to be all held simultaneously in working memory. In this situation the subject must shift his working memory over the material. The second effect of duration of study is that the subject may use the extra study time to engage in elaborative processing, which produces redundant traces. That is, while added duration of residence in working memory will not increase that trace's probability of being stored, the time may be used to create traces that are redundant with the target trace. For example, an image of a horse kicking a boy can be regarded as redundant with the paired associate horse-boy. This possibility will be discussed at great length later in the chapter.

This view is somewhat similar to the original depth-of-processing model (Craik and Lockhart, 1972; Craik and Watkins, 1973), which held that duration of rehearsal was not relevant to memory if the rehearsal simply maintained the trace in working memory. Rather, duration would have a positive impact only if the rehearsal involved elaborative processing. However, the current proposal differs from that in the claim that spaced repetition of an item will increase memory even if neither presentation leads to elaborative processing. The current proposal only claims that duration of uninterrupted residence in working memory is ineffective, which is more in keeping with Nelson's conclusions (1977) on the topic.

Additional presentations after a trace has been established increase the strength of the trace. All traces have an associated strength. The first successful trial establishes the trace with a strength of one unit, and each subsequent trial increases the strength by one unit. The strength of a trace determines its probability and speed of retrieval. Thus strength is the mechanism by which ACT predicts that overlearning increases the probability of retention and speed of retrieval.

RETENTION

According to the ACT theory, a trace once formed is not lost, but its strength may decay. Studies of long-term retention show gradual but continuous forgetting. Based on data summarized by Wickelgren (1976) and data of our own, trace strength, $S$, is a power function of time with the form

$$S = t^{-b} \qquad (5.1)$$

where the time $t$ is measured from the point at which the trace was created in working memory and the exponent $b$ has a value on the interval 0 to 1. The smaller the value of $b$ the slower the forgetting or loss of strength. It reflects the "retentiveness" of the system. The function has a strange value at $t = 0$, namely, infinity. However, the strength value is only relevant to performance at times $t > 0$. I regard this decay function as reflecting a fundamental fact about how the physical system stores memory in the brain (for example, see Eccles's discussion [1972] of neural effects of use and disuse). Such a power function is to be contrasted with an exponential function (for example, $S = a^t$ where $a < 1$), which would produce much more rapid forgetting than is empirically observed.

One interesting issue is what the retention function is like for a trace that has had multiple strengthenings. The ACT theory implies that its total strength is the sum of the strengths remaining from the individual strengthenings, that is,

$$S = \sum_i t_i^{-b} \tag{5.2}$$

where $t_i$ is the time since the $i$th strengthening. Evidence for this assumption will be given later, when the effects of extensive practice are discussed.

Traces are cognitive units that interconnect elements. Not only do the unit nodes have strength but so do the element nodes they connect. Every time a unit node acquires an increment in strength, there is also an increment in the strength of the elements. An element node can have more strength than a unit it participates in because it can participate in other units and gain strength when these are presented too. Thus all nodes in the declarative network have associated strengths, and all accumulate strength with practice.

The strength of a node affects its level of activation in two ways. First, the amount of activation spread to a node from associated nodes is a function of the relative strength, $r_{ij}$, of the link from node $i$ to node $j$, as developed in Chapter 3. Let $S_j$ be the strength of $j$. Then $r_{ij} = S_j / \Sigma_k S_k$ where the summation is over all nodes $k$ that are connected to element $i$. Second, every time a trace is strengthened there will be an increment in the activation capacity of its elements. This capacity determines how much activation the element can spread if it is presented as part of the probe (that is, the source activation capacity, in the terms of Chapter 3). This idea will be developed in the section on practice.

RETRIEVAL

The probability of retrieving a trace and the time taken to retrieve are functions of the trace's level of activation. Retrieval of a trace in the ACT framework requires that the trace be matched by a production or productions that generate the memory report. As developed in the last two chapters, the time to perform this matching will be an inverse function of the level of activation. Thus the time, $T(A)$, to generate a memory report of a trace with activation $A$ is:

$$T(A) = I + B/A \qquad (5.3)$$

In this equation, $I$ is an "intercept" parameter giving time to perform processes like initial encoding that are not affected by trace activation. As developed in Eq. (4.1), the parameter $B$ reflects factors such as pattern complexity $(C)$, pattern strength $(S)$, goodness of match $(G)$, and number of interfering patterns $(I)$. That is, $B = CI/SG$ from Eq. (4.1).

The memory trace will not be retrieved if the pattern matching fails or terminates before it is complete. Thus there is a race between some termination time and the time it takes to complete the pattern matching. For many reasons both the pattern-matching time and the cutoff time should be variable. The pattern matching can be variable because of variation either in activation or in the efficiency with which the pattern tests are performed. Different contexts can affect both the speed of pattern matching and the terminating conditions that determine the cutoff time. Without a detailed physiological model, it is foolish to make a strong claim about the form of this variability. However, in the past work on ACT (Anderson, 1974, 1976, 1981b; King and Anderson, 1976), we have assumed that the probability of a successful match before the cutoff was an exponential function of level of activation:

$$R(A) = 1 - e^{-K A/B} \qquad (5.4)$$

This is most naturally read as the probability of an exponentially variable matching process with mean $B/A$ completing before a fixed cutoff $K$. However, it is possible to read it as the probability of a fixed matching process completing before a variable cutoff.

The probabilistic retrieval process implies that if repeated memory tests are administered, the results should be a mixture of recall of an item and failure to recall it, and this is observed (Estes, 1960; Goss, 1965; Jones, 1962). It is also observed that an item successfully recalled on one trial has a greater probability of recall on a second trial. The above analysis would appear to imply that recall of each trial is independent, but there are a number of explanations for the observed nonindependence. First, the above analysis is only of retrieval and ignores the probability of encoding the trace. The all-or-none encoding process would produce nonindependence among successive recalls. Second, some nonindependence would result because the successful trial provides a strengthening experience and so increases the level of activation for the second test. Third, nonindependence could be produced by item selection effects if the items varied considerably in the level of activation they could achieve (Underwood and Keppel, 1962).

An implication of this analysis is that if enough time was put into trying to retrieve, every item that has had a long-term trace formed would be successfully recalled. If the subject repeats the retrieval process often enough he will eventually get lucky and retrieve the item. Indeed, it has been observed that there are slow increments in the ability to recall with increased opportunity for recall (Bushke, 1974).

In the rest of the chapter I will consider how ACT's general theory of memory applies to a number of the major memory phenomena. Of course, in motivating the preceding theoretical discussion we already reviewed some of the theory's most direct application to data.

## Judgments of Associative Relatedness

Chapter 2 mentioned that subjects can judge that concepts in memory are connected independent of the exact relationship and can make connectedness judgments more rapidly than judgments of exact relationship. This capacity is important to understanding memory performance in many situations. Therefore this chapter provides a more detailed analysis of two aspects of this phenomenon. One aspect concerns judging the thematic consistency of a fact rather than whether a fact has been studied. As Reder (1982) has argued, in many memory situations subjects are making consistency judgments rather than recognition judgments. The second aspect concerns selecting a subnode of a concept for focus of activation, which proves to be a way of avoiding the effects of interfering facts.

THEMATIC JUDGMENTS

The experiments of Reder and Anderson (1980) and Smith, Adams, and Schorr (1978) are examples of situations in which subjects can use this process of connectedness judgment to verify statements. These researchers had subjects study a set of facts about a person that all related to a single theme, such as running. So a subject might study:

Marty preferred to run on the inside lane.
Marty did sprints to improve his speed.
Marty bought a new pair of Adidas.

The subjects then had to recognize these facts about the individual and reject facts from different themes (for example, *Marty cheered the trapeze artist*). The number of such facts studied about a person was varied. Based on the research on the fan effect (see Chapter 3) one might expect recognition time to increase with the number of facts studied about the individual. However, this material is thematically integrated, unlike the material in the typical fan experiment. In these experiments, recognition time did not depend on how many facts a subject studied about the individual.

Reder and Anderson postulated, on the basis of data from Reder (1979), that subjects were actually judging whether a probe fact came from the theme and not carefully inspecting memory to see if they had studied that fact about the individual. To test this idea, we examined what happened when the foils involved predicates consistent with the theme of the facts that had been studied about the probed individual. So if the subject had studied *Marty preferred to run on the inside lane*, a foil might be *Marty ran five miles every day* (the subject would have studied *ran five miles every day* about someone other than Marty). In this situation subjects took much longer to make their verifications, and the fan effect reemerged.

We proposed that subjects set up a representation like that in Figure 5.1, in which the thematically related predicates are already associated with a theme node like *running*. A subnode has been created to connect the traces of that subset of the facts that were studied about the person. This subnode is associated with the theme and with the individual theme predicates. The subnode is basically a *token* of the theme node, which is the *type*. The figure shows two such theme nodes and two subnodes. Reder and Anderson proposed that in the presence of

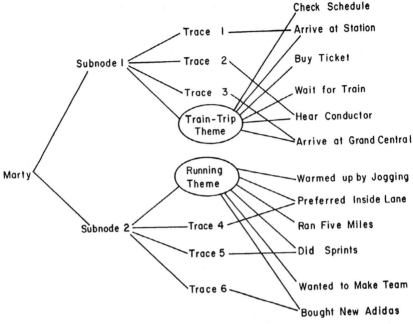

**Figure 5.1**   *Network representation for the Reder and Anderson experiments. Facts about Marty are organized into two subnodes according to theme.*

unrelated foils, subjects simply looked for a subnode attached to the theme of the predicate. In the current ACT framework, this would be done by retrieving a subnode on the constraint that it must be on a path connecting subject and predicate. If a subnode can be retrieved and if the foil is unrelated, subjects can respond positively without retrieving the fact. There would be no effect of fan out of the subnode. In the presence of a related foil, subjects would have to retrieve the fact from the subnode, and the fan effect should reemerge, as was observed.

As illustrated in Figure 5.1, Reder and Anderson had subjects learn two sets of facts about some of the individuals, for instance, some facts involving running and others involving a train trip. The structure in Figure 5.1 leads to a number of predictions about this manipulation. First, the number of themes studied about an individual should have an effect. A second theme should result in greater fan from the person and so should dissipate activation, and this effect of theme fan should be observed whether the foils are related or not. These predictions have been confirmed by Reder and Anderson (1980) and Reder and Ross (1983). Another prediction is that the number of facts learned about theme A should have no effect on the time to verify a fact from theme B (assuming at least one fact is studied about theme A). This is because the fan out of the subnode for theme A has no effect on the activation of theme B nor on the activation of any of the facts attached to that theme. Reder and Anderson and Reder and Ross verified this prediction that fan of the irrelevant theme has no effect on time to recognize a fact from the target theme.

*Calculation of activation patterns.* Activation patterns were calculated for a representation like that in Figure 5.1 by solving a set of simultaneous linear equations of the form of Eq. (3.7). In doing so, the amount of source activation from the predicate (which for simplicity is represented by a single node) was set at 10 and the activation from the person at 1, since more activation would come from the multiple familiar concepts of the predicate. All the links in Figure 5.1 were considered to be of equal relative strength. The conditions of the Anderson and Reder experiment can be classified according to the number of facts learned about the tested theme (one or three) and the number of facts about the untested theme (zero, one, or three). (The case of zero facts means there is not a second theme.) The pattern of activation was calculated in each of the six situations defined by the crossing of these two factors. For each of these conditions Table 5.1 reports the level of activation of the node corresponding to the trace in the presence of a target and also the level of activation of the subnode in the presence of a target, a related foil, and an unrelated foil.

Note that the activation of the target trace decreases with the number of facts in the same theme as the probe, decreases when there is a second theme, but shows very little variation between one and three facts in the nontested theme. This is precisely the fan effect reported by Reder and Anderson when related foils were used. Thus it appears, as hypothesized for the related-foil condition, that activation of the trace controls judgment time.

It was hypothesized that when the foils were unrelated, the level of activation of the subnode and not that of the trace would control judgment time. The subnode actually shows a reverse fan effect—greater activation for three facts—when a tar-

**Table 5.1**  *Level of activation of various nodes in Figure 5.1 under various conditions*

| Node and situation | Number of facts about other theme | 1 fact about tested theme | 3 facts about tested theme |
|---|---|---|---|
| TARGET TRACE IN PRESENCE OF TARGET | | | |
| | 0 | 7.78 | 6.83 |
| | 1 | 7.26 | 6.57 |
| | 3 | 7.24 | 6.56 |
| SUBNODE IN PRESENCE OF TARGET | | | |
| | 0 | 7.06 | 7.49 |
| | 1 | 5.59 | 6.29 |
| | 3 | 5.50 | 6.22 |
| SUBNODE IN PRESENCE OF RELATED FOIL | | | |
| | 0 | 5.30 | 5.94 |
| | 1 | 4.07 | 4.88 |
| | 3 | 4.00 | 4.81 |
| SUBNODE IN PRESENCE OF UNRELATED FOIL | | | |
| | 0 | 1.40 | 1.42 |
| | 1 | .70 | .75 |
| | 3 | .66 | .71 |

get is presented as a probe. This is because there are more paths converging on the subnode in the case of three facts. Although these additional paths may not be direct routes from sources of activation to the subnode, they are indirect routes. Thus, presented with *Marty arrived at the station*, activation can spread from *arrive at station* to train theme to *hear conductor* to subnode 1. Also note that the subnode has a high level of activation in the presence of a related foil. Although this level is not as high as for a target, it is sufficiently high to result in errors to such foils if the subject responds positively to any subnode on a highly active path.

If the time to identify the relevant subnode is affected just by its level of activation, there should be a reverse fan effect, as Table 5.1 indicates. However, Reder and Anderson (1980) and Smith and colleagues both report no fan effects in the presence of unrelated foils. Reder (1982) and Reder and Ross (1983) speculated that the subjects adopt a mixed strategy in this case, sometimes responding to subnode activations and sometimes to the trace. The direct and reverse fan effects would then tend to cancel each other out. Consistent with this hypothesis, Reder and Ross showed that when subjects are explicitly instructed to respond on a thematic basis (that is, accept both studied sentences and unstudied but related sentences), they do show a reverse fan effect. Reder and Ross also found subjects slower to accept unstudied related sentences than studied sentences in their thematic judgment conditions. This is to be expected from Table 5.1 because in the presence of related foils (which are the same as Reder and Ross's related, nonstudied targets) there is a lower level of activation of the subnode than in the presence of targets.

REFOCUSING ON SUBNODES

In the previous section the activation patterns were calculated on the assumption that the subject spreads activation from the person node, such as Marty in Figure 5.1. In these calculations the activation from Marty is broken up twice before getting to the target predicate, once between the two subnodes and then among the facts attached to the subnode. This implies that the activation level of the traces should be no different if six facts are attached to one subnode than if six facts are divided between two subnodes. In both cases, one-sixth of the activation reaches the subnode. In fact, however, there is evidence (McCloskey and Bigler, 1980; unpublished research in my lab) that subjects are faster in the two-subnode condition.

These and other results (Anderson, 1976; Anderson and Paulson, 1978) lead to the second aspect of the subnode model, the refocusing process. Even in cases where subjects must retrieve the specific fact, they can first identify the relevant subnode and then focus activation on it. This is a two-stage process: first the subnode is selected, then activation spreading from the subnode enables the target fact to be identified.

This subnode-plus-refocusing model explains the low estimate of the strength of prior associations that we have gotten in some previous experiments (Lewis and Anderson, 1976; Anderson, 1981). As suggested in Anderson (1976), subjects may create an experimental subnode and use contextual associations to focus on it, which would largely protect them from the interference of prior associations. This model offers an explanation for why people are faster at retrieving information about familiar concepts. Presumably such concepts have a well-developed and perhaps hierarchical subnode structure that can be used to focus the retrieval process on a relatively small subset of the facts known about that concept.

## Practice

People get better at remembering facts by practicing them, and it should come as no surprise that ACT predicts this. However, the serious issue is whether the ACT theory can predict the exact shape of the improvement function and how this varies with factors such as fan.

### ACCUMULATION OF STRENGTH WITH PRACTICE

ACT makes interesting predictions about the cumulative effects of extensive practice at wide intervals such as twenty-four hours. The reason for looking at such wide spacings is to avoid complications due to the diminished effects of presentations when they are massed together. In a number of studies I have done on this topic, we have given the subject multiple repetitions of an item on each day and repeated this for many days. In the analyses to follow, the cumulative impact of the multiple repetitions in a day will be scaled as one unit of strength.

Assume the material has been studied for a number of sessions, each one day apart. The total strength of a trace after the $p$th day and just before day $p + 1$ will be (by Eq. 5.2):

$$S = \sum_{i=1}^{p} si^{-b} \qquad (5.5)$$

It can be shown (Anderson, 1982) that this sum is closely approximated as:

$$S = D(P)^{+c} - a \qquad (5.6)$$

where $c = 1 - b$, $D = s/(1 - b)$, and $a = bs/(1 - b)$. Thus strength approximately increases as a power function of practice (that is, $P$ days). Note that not only will the unit nodes in these traces accrue strength with days of practice, but also the element nodes will accrue strength. As will be seen, this power function prediction corresponds to the data about practice.

### EFFECTS OF EXTENSIVE PRACTICE

A set of experiments was conducted to test the prediction that strength increases as a power function with extensive practice. In one experiment, after subjects studied subject-verb-object sentences of the form *The lawyer hated the doctor*, they had to discriminate these sentences from foil sentences consisting of the same words as the target sentence but in new combinations. There were twenty-five days of tests and hence practice. Each day subjects in one group were tested on each sentence twelve times, and in the other group, twenty-four times. There was no difference in the results for these two groups, which is consistent with earlier remarks about the ineffectiveness of massing of practice, so the two groups will be treated as one in the analysis.

There were two types of sentences—no-fan sentences, consisting of words that had appeared in only one sentence, and fan sentences, with words that had appeared in two sentences. Figure 5.2 shows the change in reaction time with practice. The functions that are fit to the data in the figure are of the form $T = I + BP^{-c}$, where $I$ is an intercept not affected by strengthening, $I + B$ is the time after one day's practice, $P$ is the amount of practice (measured in days), and the exponent $c$ is the rate of improvement. It turns out that these data can be fit, assuming different values of $B$ for the fan and no-fan sentences and keeping $I$ and $c$ constant. The equations are:

$$T = .36 + .77(P - \tfrac{1}{2})^{-.36} \qquad \text{for no fan} \qquad (5.7)$$

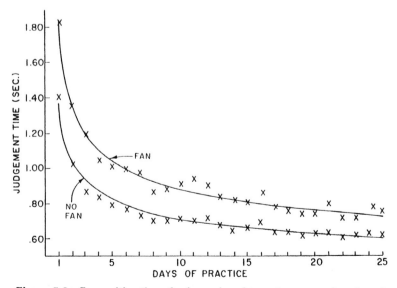

**Figure 5.2**  *Recognition times for fan and no-fan sentences as a function of practice. The solid lines represent the predictions of the model described in the text.*

$$T = .36 + 1.15(P - \tfrac{1}{2})^{-.36} \qquad \text{for fan} \qquad (5.8)$$

The value $P - \tfrac{1}{2}$ is the average practice on a day $P$. Note that one implication of Figure 5.2 and of these equations is that a practiced fan fact can be faster than a less practiced no-fan fact.

These equations imply that the fan effect diminishes with practice, but also that the fan effect never disappears. After $P$ days the fan effect is $.38(P - \tfrac{1}{2})^{-.36}$ according to these equations. Hayes-Roth (1977) reported data on practice from which she concluded that the fan effect disappeared after ten days and one hundred practice trials. However, this is not what these equations imply, and Figure 5.2 shows that there still is a fan effect after twenty-five days and six hundred trials. Perhaps the Hayes-Roth conclusion was a case of erroneously accepting the null hypothesis.

Equation (5.6) showed that strength increases as a power function of practice. As will now be shown, this implies that reaction time should decrease as a power function. Recall that the amount of activation sent to a trace from a concept is a product of the activation emitted from the concept and the strength of that trace relative to competing traces. The activation emitted by a concept is a function of its strength. If $R$ is the prior strength of a concept, then its strength after $P$ days of practice will be $S' + DP^c$ where $S' = R - a$ from Eq. (5.6). This assumes that the prior strength of $S$ is stable over the experiment.

The relative strength of one of $n$ experimental facts attached to a concept will be $1/n$ if we assume that subjects can completely filter out by a subnode structure any interference from preexperimental associations. This implies that the activation converging on the trace will be $3(S' + DP^{+c})/n$, with the 3 reflecting the fact that activation is converging from three concepts (subject, verb, object).

According to the earlier retrieval assumption, Eq. (5.3), recognition time will be a function of the inverse of this quantity:

$$RT(P) = I(P) + \frac{nB}{3(S' + DP^c)} = I(P) + \frac{nB'P^{-c}}{(S'/DP^c + 1)} \qquad (5.9)$$

where $B' = B/3D$ and $I(P)$ is the intercept after $P$ days of practice. To the extent that $S'$, the prior strength of the concept, is small relative to the impact of the massive experimental practice, this function becomes $nB'P^{-c}$, and total reaction time is predicted to be of the form

$$RT(P) = I(P) + nB'P^{-c} \qquad (5.10)$$

Some fraction of the intercept, $I(P)$, is speeding up, reflecting the strengthening of general procedures:

$$I(P) = I_1 + I_2 P^{-c} \qquad (5.11)$$

where $I_2$ reflects that part of the improvement due to general practice. It includes strengthening of the productions used in the task. It is assumed that the general speed-up is at the same rate (parameter $c$) as retrieval of the specific fact. So we can rewrite Eq. (5.10) as

$$RT(P) = I_1 + (I_2 + nB')P^{-c} \qquad (5.12)$$

Deviation of Eq. (5.12) required two approximating assumptions. The first is that prior strength $S'$ is zero and the second is that the general speed-up is at the same rate as speed-up in the retrieval of a specific fact. However, Eq. (5.12) will yield a good fit to data in many cases where these assumptions are not true. It is a more general form of Eqs. (5.7) and (5.8) that were fit to Figure 5.2. Equations (5.7) and (5.8) can be derived from Eq. (5.12) by setting $I_1 = .36$, $I_2 = .39$, $B' = .38$, and $c = .36$.

### INTERACTION BETWEEN PRACTICE AND PRIOR FAMILIARITY

One basic consequence of this increase in concept strength is that subjects can remember more facts about frequently used concepts and can more rapidly retrieve facts of similar relative strength about more frequently used concepts. Anderson (1976) reported that subjects can retrieve facts about familiar people— *Ted Kennedy is a senator*—more rapidly than facts about less familiar people—*Birch Bayh is a senator* (this experiment was done when he was still a senator). Anderson (1981b) noted that there are serious issues about whether pairs of facts like these are equated with each other in terms of other properties. In that research report, I had subjects learn new facts about familiar or unfamiliar people and tried to control such things as degree of learning for these new facts. Still subjects were at an advantage both in learning and in retrieving new facts about the more familiar person.

We recently performed an experiment in which we compared time to verify sentences studied in the experiment like *Ted Kennedy is in New York* with time to verify other studied sentences like *Bill Jones is in New Troy*. Subjects were initially more rapid at verifying the experimental facts about the familiar concepts, consistent with Anderson (1981). However, we also looked at the effects of fan and practice on these verification times. Figure

5.3 shows what happened to the effects of fan and familiarity over nine days of practice. As can be seen, the fan effects were largely maintained over the period, diminishing only from .30 sec to .20 sec, while the familiarity effects decreased from .30 sec to .12 sec. This is what would be predicted on the basis of Eq. (5.9). As practice $P$ increases, the effect of prior strength $S'$ diminishes.

The functions fit to the data in Figure 5.3 are of the form $I + B/(S + P^c)$ where $I$ is the asymptote, $B$ is the retrieval time parameter, $S$ is prior strength and strength accumulated in original learning, $P$ is the independent variable (number of days),

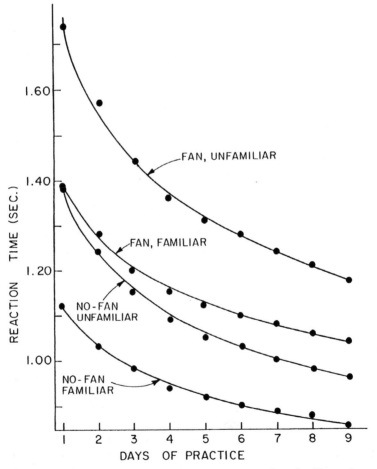

**Figure 5.3** *Recognition of fan and no-fan sentences about familiar and unfamiliar concepts as a function of practice.*

and $c$ is the exponent controlling growth of strength. The quantity $P^c$ reflects strength after $P$ days. The value of $I$ for all four conditions was estimated as .36 sec. Since the $B$ parameter reflects fan (that is, $B = I_2 + nB'$ from Eq. [5.12]), separate values of $B$ were estimated for the no-fan (1.42 sec) and fan conditions (1.94 sec). Since $S$ reflects prior strength, separate values of $S$ were estimated for the familiar material (.88) and the unfamiliar material (.39). Finally, a single parameter for $c$, .31, was estimated for all four conditions.

On day 10, subjects were asked to learn some new facts of a different form (*Bill Jones hated the doctor*) about the old people (those studied in the experiment) and about some new people not yet studied. Some of the new people were familiar famous names and others were unfamiliar. After learning these new facts, the subjects went through one session of verification for these. There was no difference in the time (.96 sec) they took to recognize the new facts about old familiar or new familiar people. They took longer to recognize new facts about the old unfamiliar people (1.00 sec), so the practice did not completely eliminate the differences between familiar and unfamiliar. However, they took longest to recognize facts about the new unfamiliar people (1.06 sec), so the practice increased the capacity of the unfamiliar nodes.

## OTHER RESULTS

The hypothesis that more frequent nodes have greater activation capacity is consistent with a number of results in the literature. For instance, Keenan and Baillet (1980) found that subjects are better able to remember material about more familiar people and locations. They used an incidental-learning paradigm in which subjects were asked an encoding question about these concepts (*Is your best friend kind?* versus *Is your teacher kind?* — where the second is about a less familiar person). Later, subjects were asked whether they had studied pairs like *teacher-kind*. Subjects were better able to remember such pairs when the people were more familiar. Keenan and Baillet also found that subjects answered the encoding questions more rapidly about familiar items, which is also what would be expected if familiarity affected level of activation.

A similar concept is needed to understand the marvelous performance of the subject SF, studied by Chase and Ericsson (1981), who was able to increase his memory span to over eighty digits after hundreds of hours of practice. He was able to commit these numbers to long-term memory with a rate of presentation typical of memory-span experiments and to reliably retrieve these items from long-term memory. Some of this performance depended on developing mnemonic encoding techniques, such as encoding three- and four-digit numbers into running times. He might encode 3492 as 3 minutes and 49.2 seconds, a near-record mile time. This allowed him to get his memory span up to more than twenty digits (for example, 7 running times × 4 digits = 28 digits). Presumably, SF's ability to remember these times reflects the fact that running times were more frequently used concepts for him than strings of four digits. He did not in fact have a prior concept of 3:49.2. However, the various elements that went into this concept were sufficiently familiar that they could be reliably retrieved.

Note that this mnemonic technique by itself left SF far short of the eighty-digit level. To achieve this, he developed an abstract retrieval structure for organizing the running times in a hierarchy. He stored these running times in long-term memory and then was able to reliably retrieve them back into working memory. Figure 5.4 illustrates the hierarchical structure proposed by Chase and Ericsson for SF's performance on an eighty-digit list. The numbers at the bottom refer to the size of the chunks he encoded mnemonically. If we ignore the last five numbers, which are in a rehearsal buffer, SF has a node-link structure that organizes twenty-one chunks in long-term memory. He had to practice with a particular hierarchy for a considerable time (months) before he became proficient with it. This practice was necessary to increase the capacity of the individual

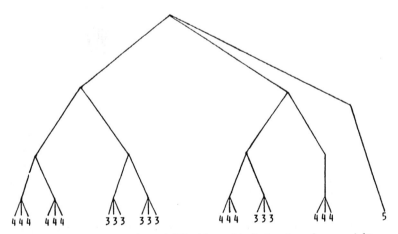

**Figure 5.4**  *Representation of SF's hierarchical structure for an eighty-digit list. (From Chase and Ericsson, 1981.)*

nodes in this hierarchy so that they could support accurate and rapid retrieval. This indicates that practice can increase the capacity of completely abstract nodes, such as the ones in this structure, as well as the capacity of more concrete nodes, such as people.

More generally, an important component of many mnemonic techniques is converting the task of associating unfamiliar, weak elements to the task of associating familiar, strong elements.[3] For instance, the critical step in the key-word method (Atkinson and Raugh, 1975) for foreign language acquisition is to convert the unfamiliar foreign word into a familiar word. When the foreign word becomes familiar through practice, the conversion step is no longer required for accurate recall of meaning.

## Recognition versus Recall

The difference between recognition and recall is straightforward under the ACT analysis. In a recognition paradigm, parts of a trace are presented and the subject is asked whether they were studied. In a recall paradigm, the subject is also asked to retrieve other components of the trace. In ACT, activation converges on the trace from all presented components. If there is sufficient activation, the trace becomes available. In a recognition test the subject simply announces that there is a trace. In a recall test the subject must also generate parts of the trace. More of the trace is usually presented in a recognition paradigm. For instance, in paired-associate recognition both stimulus and response are typically presented, but in paired-associate recall only the stimulus is presented. However, it is possible to test paired-associate recognition by simply presenting a stimulus. One would expect a high conditional probability between success at recognizing the stimulus and success at recalling the response, and indeed there is (Martin, 1967).

### PAIRED-ASSOCIATE RECOGNITION

In one interesting analysis of recognition versus recall, Wolford (1971) tried to relate recognition of a paired associate to the probability that the stimulus would lead to recall of the response and to the probability that the response would lead to recall of the stimulus. He showed that, correcting for guessing, recognition of a paired associate could be predicted by the probabilities of forward and backward recall. His model was basically that a paired associate could be recognized if the subject could retrieve the response from the stimulus or the stimulus from the response. Let $P_f$ and $P_b$ be these two probabilities of recall. On the assumption that the two directions are independent, Wolford derived the following equation for corrected recognition $P_r$:

$$P_r = P_f + (1 - P_f)P_b \qquad (5.13)$$

Under the ACT* theory the subject is viewed not as performing two independent retrievals in recognition but rather as converging activation from the two sources. This is an important way in which ACT* differs from the earlier ACT's (Anderson, 1976) and their predecessor HAM (Anderson and Bower, 1973). Nonetheless, ACT* can predict the relationship documented by Wolford. Let $A_S$ denote the amount of activation that comes from the stimulus and $A_R$ the amount from the response. The probability of retrieving the memory trace will be a function of the activation from the stimulus in the case of forward recall, of the activation from the response in the case of backward recall, and of the sum of these two activations in the case of recognition. The following equations specify probability of forward recall, backward recall, and recognition:

$$P_f = 1 - e^{-KA_S} \qquad (5.14)$$

$$P_b = 1 - e^{-KA_R} \qquad (5.15)$$

$$P_r = 1 - e^{-K(A_S+A_R)} \qquad (5.16a)$$

$$= 1 - (e^{-KA_S})(e^{-KA_R}) \qquad (5.16b)$$

$$= 1 - (1 - P_f)(1 - P_b) \qquad (5.16c)$$

$$= P_f + (1 - P_f)P_b \qquad (5.16d)$$

Thus, even though there are not two independent retrievals, ACT can predict that the probability of recognition is the probabilistic sum of forward and backward recall as found by Wolford.

The above analysis assumes that the probability of forming the trace is 1 and that all failures of recall derive from failures of retrieval. If there is some probability of failing to encode the trace, the ACT analysis predicts that probabilities of forward and backward recall would overpredict probability of recognition because forward and backward recall would no longer be independent. While Wolford found no evidence at all for non-independence, other researchers (for instance, Wollen, Allison, and Lowry, 1969) have found evidence for a weak nonindependence.

WORD RECOGNITION

Another major domain where recall and recognition have been contrasted is memory for single words. A subject is given a list of single words and then must either recall (typically, by free recall) or recognize them. Recognition performance can be much higher than recall performance in such experiments. According to the framework set forth in Anderson (1972) and Anderson and Bower (1972, 1974), it is assumed that the subject forms traces linking the words to the various contextual elements. Although the contextual elements are undoubtedly more complex, they are often represented as a single context node. This simplified situation is illustrated in Figure 5.5, where each line corresponds to a trace. With this model, recognition in-

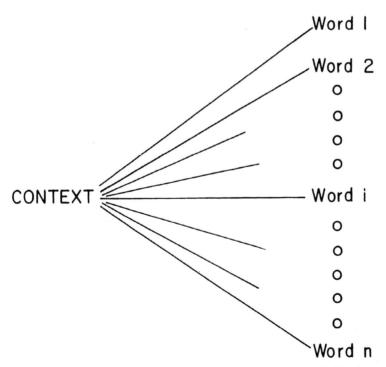

**Figure 5.5** *Network representation of the word-context associations for a single list.*

volves retrieving the context from the word and verifying that it is indeed a list context. Direct recall involves retrieving list words from the list context. However, because of the high fan from the context, the subject will have limited success at this. Thus the subject will use an auxiliary process, using various strategies to generate words that can then be tested for recognition. This has been called the *generate-test* model of recall. For a review of relevant positive evidence see Anderson and Bower (1972) or Kintsch (1970). The major challenge to this analysis has come from various experiments showing contextual effects. These results will be reviewed in the next sections.

The basic assumptions of the generate-test model are consistent with the current framework. The current framework makes it clear that recognition is better than recall because the fan from the word nodes is smaller than that from the context nodes. If the same word appears in multiple contexts the fan from the word node would be large, and this would hurt recognition. Anderson and Bower (1972, 1974) present evidence that recognition performance degrades if a word appears in multiple contexts.

### EFFECTS OF ENCODING CONTEXT

A large number of studies have displayed an effect of encoding context on both recognition and recall (for example, Flexser and Tulving, 1978; Tulving and Thomson, 1971; Watkins and Tulving, 1975). These experiments are said to illustrate the *encoding specificity principle*, that memory for an item is specific to the context in which it was studied. The experiment by Tulving and Thomson (1971) is a useful one to consider. Subjects studied items (for example, *black*) either in isolation, in the presence of a strongly associated encoding cue (*white*, say), or in the presence of a weakly associated encoding cue (*train*). The strong and weak cues were selected from association norms. Orthogonal to this variable, subjects were tested for recognition of the word in one of these three contexts. Recognition was best when the study context matched the test context.

We have explained this result in terms of selection of word senses (Reder, Anderson, and Bjork, 1974; Anderson and Bower, 1974) or in terms of elaborative encodings (Anderson, 1976). These explanations still hold in the current ACT* framework. Figure 5.6 illustrates the network structure that is assumed in this explanation for the case of study with a weak encoding cue—that is, the subject has studied the pair *train-black*. *Black*, the to-be-recalled word, has multiple senses. In this case

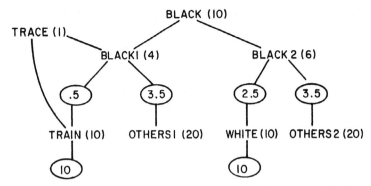

**Figure 5.6** *A representation of the relevant network structure in the encoding-specificity experiments. The numbers associated with the nodes are the strengths associated with the spreading activation analysis. This is the memory representation assumed when the subject has studied* train-black.

it is illustrated as having two senses, *black1*, to which is attached the weak associate *train*, and *black2*, to which is attached the strong associate *white*. The oval nodes in Figure 5.6 are the traces encoding these associations; the nodes leading to *others1* and *others2* represent other unidentified associations. Similarly, the nodes at the bottom attached to *train* and *white* represent other unidentified associations. For simplicity, only the multiple senses of *black* are represented.

At first, people often have the intuition that there is only one sense for a word like *black*. However, there are a number of distinct if similar senses. In the presence of *white*, one is likely to think of *black* as referring to a prototypical color or a race of people. In the presence of *train* one is likely to associate it with soot or the glistening color of a polished toy train.

The encoding context determines the sense of the word chosen, and a trace is formed involving that sense and, perhaps, the encoding context. When the subject is tested, context will again determine the sense chosen, and activation will spread from the chosen sense. The probability of recognition will be greater when the same sense is chosen, because activation will be spreading from a node directly attached to the trace.

It should be noted that a sense for the word can also be chosen by means of spreading activation. That is, the sense of *black* chosen in the context of *train-black* is the one that receives the greatest activation from *train* and *black*. In Figure 5.6 this will be *black1*, which lies at the intersection of *train* and *black*. Thus, there are two "waves" of activation. The first determines the senses of the words, and the second spreads activation from the chosen senses to retrieve the trace. This same double activation process is used in selecting a subnode.

EVIDENCE FOR MULTIPLE SENSE NODES

Although one can explain the encoding-specificity result by assuming multiple senses as in Figure 5.6, it is not necessary to assume multiple senses to explain why recognition is higher if the study context is presented at test. To see this, note in Figure 5.6 that the study context, *train*, is associated with the trace. This means that more activation will converge at the trace at test if *train* is presented again, independent of any sense selection.[4] However, a number of additional results indicate the need for the multiple-sense-node explanation. One is that recognition is worse in a test context that promotes selection of the wrong sense than in a neutral test context that simply fails to present any encoding word (Reder, Anderson, and Bjork, 1974; Tulving and Thomson, 1973; Watkins and Tulving, 1975). For instance, after studying *train-black*, subjects are worse at recognizing *black* in the context *white-black* than when *black* is presented alone. Thus, it is not just the absence of *train* that is hurting recognition, it is the presence of another context that actively selects against the original interpretation.

The multiple-sense representation is important for understanding the results of Light and Carter-Sobell (1970). They had subjects study a pair like *raspberry-jam*, with *jam* as the target word. At test, subjects were presented with *raspberry-jam* or *strawberry-jam*, which tapped the same sense of that word, or *log-jam*, which tapped a different sense. The identical pair produced the best recognition, and *log-jam*, which tapped a different sense, produced the worst. Figure 5.7 shows a schematic of the memory representation for their experiment. Simultaneous

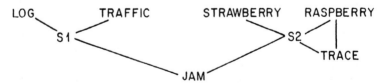

**Figure 5.7**  *A representation of the relevant memory structures for the Light and Carter-Sobell experiments. The subject has studied* raspberry-jam. *The nodes S1 and S2 identify the two senses.*

sets of linear equations in the mold of Eq. (3.7) were solved to derive the patterns of network activation when various cues were presented to serve as sources of activation. The predictions were derived under the assumption that all links have equal relative strength where multiple links emanate from a node. In these calculations it was assumed that the context word and the selected sense of the target word would serve as source nodes giving forth one unit of activation. When subjects were presented with *raspberry* and *jam*, there were 1.65 units of activation accumulating at the trace. When they were cued with *strawberry* and *jam*, 1.26 units accumulated at the trace. Finally, when cued with *log* and *jam*, .29 units accumulated at the trace. This corresponds to the ordering found by Light and Carter-Sobell. The difference between *raspberry-jam* and *strawberry-jam* results from the fact that *raspberry* is directly connected to the trace. The difference between *strawberry-jam* and *log-jam* results from the difference between the two senses selected.[5]

RECOGNITION FAILURE

Experiments such as those reported by Tulving and Thomson (1973) and by Watkins and Tulving (1975) are thought to be damaging for the generate-test models. In a typical example, subjects study a word with a weak associate, are then asked to recognize it in the context of a strong associate, and are then asked to recall it in the context of the old weak associate. In these cases it is often found that recall is superior to recognition and that many words are not recognizable but can be recalled. The phenomenon of recallable words not being recognized is called *recognition failure* and is sometimes interpreted as disproving generate-test models. Because recognition is one of the subprocesses in the generate-test model of recall, recognition of a word is a precondition for its recall. However, the activation patterns set up in ACT for the strong-associate recognition condition are very different from the patterns set up in the weak-associate recall condition. Therefore, there is no reason to assume that recognition should be predictive of recall unless it is in the same context. It makes no more sense to talk about recognition being conditional on recall when the contexts are different than it does to talk about a conditional measure when the target words are changed.[6]

Figure 5.6 was used to calculate how much activation should converge on the trace in the two conditions—recognition in the context of a strong associate and recall in the context of the studied weak associate. The calculations were performed under the assumption that an active node, representing a presented word, would be a source of one unit of activation. Thus, when the target and the strong cue are presented, *white* and *black2* would be active and send out one unit of activation each. In this case, .24 units of activation converge on the trace. When just *train* (the weak cue) is presented and is activated, .88 units of activation converge. So, the weak associate is a better prompt for the memory trace than is the target and strong cue. This is because *train* is directly connected to the trace, while *white* and *black2* are not. This analysis is consistent with the research and ideas of Bartling and Thompson (1977) and of Rabinowitz, Mandler, and Barsalou (1977), who have compared the cue in eliciting recall of the target with the target in eliciting recall of the cue in paired-associate tests. They showed that a considerable asymmetry existed between the forward recall condition (weak associate eliciting recall of the target word) versus the opposite backward recall condition (target eliciting recall of the cue); backward recall was much lower. Rabinowitz, Mandler, and Barsalou also noted that recognition failure was much reduced when recognition was conditionalized on backward rather than forward recall. Reder, Anderson, and Bjork (1974) suggested that such asymmetries might exist because the first word of a pair determines the encoding (sense selection) of the second word.

One phenomenon that has captured considerable attention (Flexser and Tulving, 1978; Wiseman and Tulving, 1975) is the relationship across experiments between probability of recognition conditionalized on recall, $P(Rn/Rc)$, and of unconditional recognition, $P(Rn)$. Flexser and Tulving claim that the relationship is characterized by the following equation:

$$P(Rn/Rc) = P(Rn) + c[P(Rn) - P(Rn)^2] \qquad (5.17)$$

where $c$ has been estimated to be .5. This indicates that the probability of recognition conditionalized on recall is only marginally superior to the probability of unconditional recognition. In the current framework, if the trace has been formed, the probability of retrieving the trace from the cue is independent of the probability of retrieving it from the target. The reason there is not complete independence is that if no trace was formed, there will be failure of recall in both cases. This is substantially the explanation of the function offered by Flexser and Tulving (1978).

## Elaborative Processing

One of the most potent manipulations for increasing a subject's memory for material is to have the subject elaborate on the to-be-remembered material (see Anderson and Reder, 1979; Anderson, 1980, for reviews). As Anderson and Reder argue, much of the research under the rubric of "depth of processing" (see Cermak and Craik, 1979, for a current survey) can be understood in terms of elaborative processing. That is, instructions that are said to promote deeper processing of the input can often be viewed as encouraging the subject to engage in more elaborative processing of the input. The phrase elaborative processing, though, is not much more technically precise than the much-lamented term depth of processing (Nelson, 1977).

The appendix to this chapter outlines a production system that will generate elaborations. It uses facts stored in memory to embellish on the to-be-studied material. These stored memory facts can describe specific events or can be abstractions. A subject given the paired associate *dog-chair* might recall a specific memory of his pet Spot tearing a chair, or he might recall general information about dogs frequently being forbidden to sleep on the furniture. While the retrieved declarative information may be general or specific, it is called a schema because of the similarity between the way it is used and the way schemata are used in other schema theories.

The to-be-studied material may include one or more facts or cognitive units, and the schema may similarly include one or more units. The elaborative process described in the appendix involves analogically mapping the schema onto the to-be-studied material in a way that maximizes compatibility and then inferring new information to correspond to what is in the schema but not in the material. So, given *dog-chair*, the subject will map *dog* onto Spot and *chair* onto the chair that Spot tore. Information about the tearing, a subsequent spanking, and so on, would be added as embellishments. The end product of this elaborative structure is a much more richly connected structure than what was specified in the to-be-studied material.

The interesting question is why an elaborated memory structure results in higher recall. This section discusses three ways in which elaborations can improve recall. The first, and weakest, improvement occurs when study elaborations redirect activation away from interfering paths and toward the target path. The second occurs when subjects spread activation at test from additional concepts not in the probe but which were part of the elaboration at study. This involves elaborating on the probe at test to try to generate additional concepts from which to spread activation. The third method involves inferring or reconstructing what the target trace must have been by using elaborations retrieved at test.

### REDIRECTING ACTIVATION

To illustrate the first possibility, consider an elaboration given in Anderson (1976). One subject, asked to memorize the paired associate *dog-chair*, generated the following elaboration:

> The dog loved his masters. He also loved to sit on the chairs. His masters had a beautiful black velvet chair. One day he climbed on it. He left his white hairs all over the chair. His masters were upset by this. They scolded him.

Figure 5.8 illustrates this elaboration in approximate network form. Note that it introduces multiple paths between *dog* and *chair*. There are two effects of this structure. First, it redirects activation that would have gone directly from *dog* to *chair* to other parts of the elaborative structure, so the activation will arrive at *chair* less directly and consequently will be somewhat dissipated. On the other hand, the activation from *dog* is also being taken away from the prior facts. For example, activation is taken away from the prior associates to spread to *master*, and some of the activation arriving at *master* spreads to *dog*. Thus the experimental fan from *dog* somewhat dissipates direct activation of *chair* but somewhat redirects activation toward *chair*. The network in Figure 5.8 was used to see what the overall effect would be. Equations such as Eq. (3.7) were solved to determine what the asymptotic patterns of activation would be. It was assumed that the total strength of the prior links attached to *dog* was 9, and the strength of all experimental links was 1. In

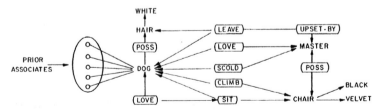

**Figure 5.8**  *Network representation of the elaborative structure generated to connect the pair* dog-chair.

this case, assuming *dog* was a source for 1 unit of activation, .19 units arrived at *chair*. In contrast, when there was a single experimental path from *dog* to *chair*, only .12 units arrived at *chair*. Clearly, whether the elaborated structure will be better depends on the specifics of the elaboration, but this example at least illustrates that an elaborated structure can result in greater activation of the target trace.

A question that naturally arises about such elaborations is how the subject discriminates between target traces and elaborations. For instance, how does the subject know he studied *dog-chair* and not *dog-master?* It is assumed that a trace includes a tag indicating whether it is an encoding of a study event or part of a subject elaboration. Reder (personal communication), who had subjects explicitly generate elaborations of text, found that her subjects were good at discriminating what they explicitly studied from what they generated as elaboration (see also Gould and Stephenson, 1967). However, to whatever extent subjects lose these tags and to whatever extent they are willing to venture guesses in their absence, there would be inferential and semantic intrusions and false alarms.

In some experiments (Bransford, Barclay, and Franks, 1972; Owens, Bower, and Black, 1979; Reder, 1982; Sulin and Dooling, 1974; Thorndyke, 1977), false acceptance of inferentially related foils is almost as high as acceptance of presented targets. Given the evidence that subjects are good at distinguishing elaborations from studied material, these high false alarm rates cannot be wholly attributed to loss of tags. A better explanation involves the notion of reconstructive recall, which will be discussed later in this section.

People have commented on the superficial contradiction between the fan analysis (which claims that the more experimental paths leading from a concept, the poorer the memory) and this elaborative analysis (which says that the more experimental paths, the better the memory). To help clarify the situation it is useful to distinguish between *irrelevant fan* and *relevant fan.* A typical fan experiment involves irrelevant fan in that the paths lead away from each other. In Figure 5.8 the fan is relevant in that the various paths leading from *dog* converge back on *chair*.

## ELABORATIVE SOURCES OF ACTIVATION

There are other, more powerful advantages of the structure in Figure 5.8 than its ability to direct more activation to the target. If the subject cannot directly retrieve the target, it may still be possible to retrieve an elaboration, focus on elements in the retrieved elaboration, and make them additional sources for activating the target. So if the subject recalls his elaboration *The dog loved his master*, he can use *master* as another point from which to spread activation to the target structure. That is, the subject need not confine himself to spreading activation from the presented word.

*Configural cuing.* The research on configural cuing of sentence memory can be understood in terms of this elaborative analysis. Anderson and Bower (1972) had subjects study sentences such as *The minister hit the landlord*, and then cued subjects for memory of the objects of the sentence with prompts such as

| | |
|---|---|
| The minister ____ the ____ | *S*-cue |
| The ____ hit the ____ | *V*-cue |
| The minister hit the ____ | *SV*-cue |

When the instructions were just to study the sentences, and when the subjects presumably studied the sentences passively (generated no elaborations), the experiments uncovered the following relationship among the probabilities of recall to the three cues:

$$P(SV) \leq P(S) + [1 - P(S)]P(V) \qquad (5.18)$$

On the other hand, when subjects were asked to generate meaningful continuations to the sentences, the following relationship was obtained:

$$P(SV) > P(S) + [1 - P(S)]P(V) \qquad (5.19)$$

Subsequent research by Anderson (1976), Foss and Harwood (1975), and Jones (1980) has confirmed that which relationship applies depends on the extent to which subjects process the meaning of these sentences. The research caused a minor flap about whether there are configural cues or not in memory, but the results can easily be explained in the current framework.

If subjects generate no elaborations, ACT predicts relationship (5.18) between the probability of recall to the configural *SV* cue and the single-word *S* or *V* cue. Subject and verb contribute independent and additive activations to the trace. As noted in the analysis of Wolford's recognition paradigm (see Eq. [5.16]), summing the activation from cues $C_1$ and $C_2$ produces a level of activation that gives us the following relation between probabilities of recall:

$$P(C_1 \& C_2) = P(C_1) + [1 - P(C_1)]P(C_2) \qquad (5.20)$$

One can get the inequality in Eq. (5.18) to the extent that a trace encoding the sentence is not formed. That is, let $P^*(C)$ be the probability of reviving the trace from cue $C$ conditional on the trace being formed, and let $P(C)$ be the unconditional probability of trace retrieval. Let $a$ be the probability of trace formation. Then,

$$P(C_1) = aP^*(C_1) \qquad (5.21)$$

$$P(C_2) = aP^*(C_2) \qquad (5.22)$$

$$P(C_1 \& C_2) = a\{P^*(C_1) + [1 - P^*(C_1)]P^*(C_2)\} \qquad (5.23a)$$

$$< aP^*(C_1) + [1 - aP^*(C_1)]aP^*(C_2) \qquad (5.23b)$$

$$= P(C_1) + [1 - P(C_1)]P(C_2) \qquad (5.23c)$$

The advantage of the subject and verb cue with meaningful processing instructions is explained if these instructions cause the subject to process the sentence elaboratively. A schematic memory structure for such a sentence showing the effect of elaborations is illustrated in Figure 5.9, in which a trace interconnects the subject (*minister*), the verb (*hit*), and the object (*landlord*). The assumption is that with meaningful processing instructions, the subject will retrieve one or more schemata for

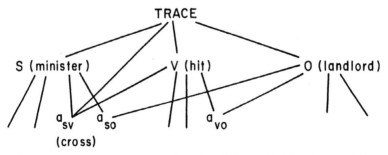

**Figure 5.9** *Network representation of a subject-verb-object trace and the overlapping network of associations among the concepts. One of the intersecting concepts has been included in the trace.*

elaboration. For instance, he might retrieve a general fact like *people hit people with hand-held objects*. This would lead to the elaboration that the minister hit the landlord with an object and that he held the object. This elaboration process can continue by retrieving another schema. If the subject recalls a movie in which a minister carried a wooden cross when confronting the devil, this would lead to elaborating that the hitting instrument was a wooden cross and that the landlord was the devil. (Actually, one subject did continue this sentence *with a cross*, but I have no idea about the exact elaborative processes that led her to this continuation.) Figure 5.9 indicates some of the impact of such elaborative activity by including *cross* in the trace for the sentence.

An important issue is why the subject chose these elaborations rather than others. Why didn't the subject retrieve *pens are hand-held objects for writing* and did retrieve an episode about an actress kissing an actor? From this she might generate the elaboration *The minister hit the landlord with a pen and kissed him*. The first schemata are more likely because they are more strongly associated with the elements in the sentence and will receive greater activation from them. Figure 5.9 indicates this with network paths connecting *minister* to *cross* and *hitting* to *cross*.

Such elaborative encoding by itself will not produce configural effects in terms of recall probabilities. If activation spreads from $S$, or from $V$, or from both, the same prediction in Eq. (5.18) holds for the structure in Figure 5.9, whether or not the subject adds embellishing elaborations. $S$ and $V$ make independent contributions to the overall pattern of activation. When presented together, their contributions are just summed.

A configural cue will have a special advantage if the subject also tries at test to elaborate with associates of the presented items. He might select the same schema, retrieve elaborations like *cross*, and spread activation from these. In the presence of $S$ or $V$ alone, the subject has a poor probability of regenerating the same elaborations as at study. However, if they are presented together, there is a good probability that the old schema will be at the intersection of activation of these two words, have the highest activation, and so be selected. Elaborating with this schema, a subject could generate an associate like *cross*, which is connected to the trace. In that case the subject could use this associate as an additional source of activation to converge on the trace and so boost his recall above what we would expect on the basis of the single-word cue.

If subjects can recreate at test the elaborative activities they engaged in at study, they can boost their recall. The probability of recalling the elaborations will vary with the number of terms in the test probe. This is basically the "semantic triangulation" explanation proposed by Anderson and Bower (1972) or the sense selection explanation proposed by Anderson (1976), where it is assumed that elaboration selects a particular word sense. Anderson and Bower (1973) showed that recall of an object was heightened if the subject could regenerate the old continuation, and Anderson (1976) showed heightened object recall conditional on ability to recognize the subject or verb.

*Configurally related sentence cues.* A similar analysis can be made of the experiment of Anderson and Ortony (1975), who had subjects study one of the following sentences:

A. Nurses are often beautiful.
B. Nurses have to be licensed.
C. Landscapes are often beautiful.

and cued subjects for recall with a term like *actress*. They point out that *nurse* has two interpretations—one as a female person and the other as a profession. Similarly, *beautiful* has two interpretations—one appropriate to women and one appropriate to landscapes. In the case of A, *actress* is appropriate to the selected senses of *nurse* and *beautiful*. This is not the case in B or C. They were interested in the relationship among the probability of *actress* evoking recall of sentence A, the probability of it evoking recall of sentence B, and the probability of it evoking recall of sentence C. Referring to these three probabilities as $t$, $s$, and $p$, respectively, they observed the following: $t > s + (1 - s)p$. This was interpreted as contrary to associative theory. The argument was that $s$ reflected the probability that *actress* could retrieve a sentence through *nurse*, and $p$ was the probability that *actress* could retrieve a sentence through *beautiful*. It was argued that according to associative theory, the probability of retrieving A, a sentence that involved both *nurse* and *beautiful*, should be no greater than the probabilistic sum of $s$ and $p$.

Figure 5.10 shows the network schematics for situations A, B, and C. In each case, concepts at the intersection of subject and predicate are chosen for inclusion in the trace elaboration. As an example, in case A *glamor* is at the intersection of *nurse* and *beautiful*. This is closely associated to *actress*, so *actress* is closely associated to the trace. In contrast, the elaborations at the intersection of subject and predicate in B and C are not closely asso-

(A)

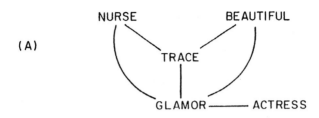

(B)

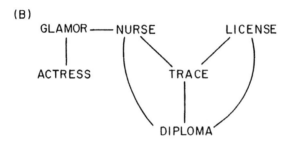

(C)

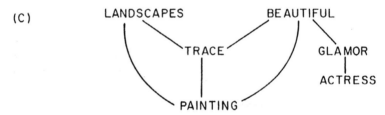

**Figure 5.10** *Network representation for the three conditions of the Anderson and Ortony experiment.*

ciated to *actress*, so *actress* is not closely associated to the trace. Thus this associative analysis predicts just what Anderson and Ortony found—much greater recall of the sentence with the *actress* cue in case A.

### INFERENTIAL RECONSTRUCTION

The elaboration productions in the appendix to this chapter lead to the prediction that if subjects engage in the same elaborative activities at test as at study, they may be able to regenerate the sentence they actually studied. To illustrate this, suppose a subject is asked to remember *The janitor chased the cat* and has in memory the following schema:

The janitor found the rat in the basement.
The janitor chased the rat.
The rat fled out the window.

This schema may be derived from actual events in the subject's life. The elaborative productions in the appendix would map this schema onto the to-be-studied sentence, generating the following elaboration:

The janitor found the cat in the basement.
The janitor chased the cat.
The cat fled out the window.

This elaboration is generated from the original memory by simple substitution of *cat* for *rat*.

Suppose the subject was not able to recall the target sentence but was able to recall two elaborations:

The janitor cornered the cat.
The cat fled out the window.

The subject can apply the same elaborative process to these sentences as was applied to the original studied sentence. If the same schema is retrieved for elaboration as at study, it could be used to generate, as an elaboration, the original study sentence *The janitor chased the cat*. The subject may be able to recognize the sentence as studied, even if he is unable to recall it. If the subject still could not recognize the sentence, there might be strong circumstantial evidence that this was the studied sentence. For instance, the sentence may embody the structure and concept choice that was typical of study sentences.

The above example illustrates the use of *inferential redundancy*. At recall, the subject will use those study elaborations he can recall to infer what schemata he must have been using at study. He can then use these to embellish the study elaborations. This is an important role for prior knowledge.

*Experimental evidence.* From this analysis of inferential reconstruction one can predict that manipulations which increase the use of elaborations should increase the level of both recall and intrusion. Experiments consistent with this prediction are reviewed by Anderson and Reder (1979) and Reder (1980). For instance, this prediction was nicely confirmed in the experiments of Owens, Bower, and Black (1979), who found that providing subjects with thematic information increased the level of both recall and intrusion. In one of their examples, subjects studied a story about a coed with or without the information that she had had an unwanted pregnancy. Presumably, this additional information would increase the likelihood of evoking pregnancy-related schemata. So when one of the target sentences read *The doctor said, "My expectations are confirmed,"* a subject could embellish this with a schema for a doctor telling a woman that she is pregnant. The effect of this embellishment would be to increase memory for the target sentence but also to increase the likelihood that subjects would intrude other elements from this schema, such as *The doctor told Nancy that she was pregnant.*

The influence of the Owens, Bower, and Black priming manipulation can be understood in terms of spreading activation. The schemata are data structures in memory that have to be retrieved themselves before they can be used for embellishments. Thus, the statement *The doctor said "My expectations are confirmed,"* would spread a little activation to *The doctor tells woman she's pregnant* schema, but also activation to many other compatible schemata such as *The doctor tells patient of cancer.* On the other hand, with the pregnancy concept already active, considerably more activation would converge on this schema, making it much more likely to be selected for elaboration.

Activation-based selection of schemata can explain the effect of pretest instructions such as those given by Sulin and Dooling (1974). They told subjects only at test that a passage they had read about "Carol Harris" was really about Helen Keller. This produced a large increase in subjects' willingness to accept foils like *She was deaf, dumb, and blind.* Identifying Carol Harris with Helen Keller should spread activation to the Helen Keller facts and thus strongly influence the elaborations that subjects generate at test. As a consequence, their elaborations will contain the foil sentence, which may then be falsely accepted.

This idea, that contextual information can influence the elaboration process, explains the powerful interaction we obtained in Schustack and Anderson (1979). We presented subjects with forty-two short historical passages for study, then tested their memory for sentences taken from these passages. We provided subjects with analogies for the referents of these passages at study or at test or both. For instance, it might be pointed out to the subject that the passage about Yoshida Ichiro had strong analogies to what they knew about Lyndon Johnson. Subjects' memory for the material was greatly improved with analogy information, but only if the analogy was presented both at study and at test. If subjects were given the analogy only at study or only at test, they were no better and in fact worse than if they had not been given the analogy at all. Thus it was important that subjects' study elaborations and their test elaborations both take advantage of information in the Lyndon Johnson schema.

The fact that schema availability fluctuates with activation level also helps to explain an interesting result reported by Bower, Black, and Turner (1979). They had subjects study one, two, or three stories that constituted variations on the same general theme. For instance, stories could be about visiting a doctor, a dentist, and a chiropractor. The greater the number of related stories the subject had studied, the greater the tendency was to intrude theme-related inferences in recall and to false alarm to such inferences in recognition. With each story studied, the subject would have another opportunity to rehearse and strengthen the elaborative schemata. He would also have in memory the earlier stories, which could themselves serve as elaborative schemata. Therefore, these schemata for making theme-related inferences would be more available the more stories had been studied.

If subjects recall by making various inferences from retrieved elaborations, they may be slower than if they were performing a direct fact retrieval. However, the use of these elaborations may allow the subject to recall additional information. Thus elaborations may prove more beneficial as measured by percentage of material recalled than as measured by reaction time (but see Reder, 1982, for an analysis of how elaborations might also improve reaction time measures). Bradshaw and Anderson (1982) recently put this prediction to experimental test by having subjects commit to memory facts about famous individuals in one of four conditions. These four conditions are illustrated in Table 5.2. In each condition there is a main fact that the subject was responsible for remembering. In the *cause* condition the subject learned two additional facts that are causes for the main fact. In the *effect* condition the subject learned two additional facts that are effects of this main fact. In these two conditions we were providing the subject with elaborative information that was inferentially redundant with the target information. In the *irrelevant* condition the subject studied two additional facts that were unrelated to the main fact. In the *alone* condition subjects just learned the main fact.

One week later subjects recalled 52 percent in the cause condition, 61 percent in the effect, 32 percent in the irrelevant, and

**Table 5.2** *Examples of materials used in the Bradshaw and Anderson (1982) experiment*

Condition *cause:* Mozart made a long journey from Munich to Paris.
  Two causes for this fact are:
  Mozart wanted to leave Munich to avoid a romantic entanglement.
  Mozart was intrigued by musical developments coming out of Paris.

Condition *effect:* Newton became emotionally unstable and insecure as
  a child.
  Two consequences of this fact are:
  Newton became irrationally paranoid when challenged by col-
  leagues.
  Newton had a nervous breakdown when his mother died.

Condition *irrelevant:* Locke was unhappy as a student at Westminster.
  Two unrelated facts about this person are:
  Locke felt fruits were unwholesome for children.
  Locke had a long history of back trouble.

Condition *alone:* Kipling matured at an early age.

38 percent in the alone. Thus, consistent with our hypothesis about the benefit of inferential redundancy on accuracy, subjects were best in the caused-by and resulted-in conditions.

This recall test was followed with a speeded recognition test. Here the mean reaction times were 2.14 seconds in the cause condition, 2.22 in the effect condition, 2.16 in the irrelevant, and 2.12 in the alone condition. The effects are neither dramatic nor significant. However, if anything, reaction times were longer in the conditions of inferential redundancy than in the alone condition. (The irrelevant condition is just the traditional fan condition.) Thus, as predicted, inferential redundancy does not improve reaction time as it does percentage of recall.

## Conclusions

The theory of memory that has been developed here is quite basic. Information is encoded probabilistically into a network of cognitive units. The nodes of this network vary in strength with practice and with the passage of time. The strength of a node controls the amount of activation it can emit and the amount of activation it will receive. Although the theory is relatively simple, it can account for a broad range of phenomena from the memory literature. The fact that such a wide variety of phenomena can be understood in terms of this spreading activation mechanism is evidence for that mechanism.

A large part of the current research in memory concerns the encoding, retention, and retrieval of stories and discourse. A frequent question is whether these phenomena can be explained by the same principles that apply to more traditional memory paradigms. The answer of the ACT theory should be apparent from the way results from the two domains are mixed in this chapter. Processing of discourse differs only in that the material is richer and more complex. For instance, there might be more elaborative processing, and it might be more predictable. However, there is no reason to believe that the embellishment of a story is different in kind from the embellishment of the lowly paired associate.

### Appendix: A Production Set for Generating Elaborations

Table 5.3 provides a production set for generating elaborations. Besides providing a concrete model for elaboration generation, this production set has relevance to the issue discussed in Chapter 1, whether the basic architecture consists of production systems or schema systems. This production set will illustrate how the effect of a schema system can be achieved in a production system architecture.

The knowledge attributed to schemata is stored in knowledge structures in declarative memory. The productions in Table 5.3 serve to *interpret* these declarative structures and to create elaborations by analogically mapping the schema onto the to-be-studied material. The declarative knowledge structures will be sets of one or more propositions describing specific or general events. Each proposition will involve a relation or set of arguments. The fact that these schemata describe events and involve propositions makes them rather like the scripts of Schank and Abelson (1977). A wider set of schemata (to include things like descriptions of spatial objects) could have been handled by augmenting the set of productions in Table 5.3. However, what is provided is enough to get the general idea across.

Figure 5.11 illustrates the flow of control among the productions in Table 5.3. Suppose a subject studies:

1. Fred christened the *Tia Maria*.
2. Fred broke the bottle.
3. The *Tia Maria* went to Vancouver.
4. Fred did not delay the trip.

**Table 5.3**  *Some of the productions that would be needed to embellish studied material with stored schemata*

| | |
|---|---|
| P1 | IF the goal is to embellish the studied material<br>and LVschema is a connected knowledge structure<br>THEN set as a subgoal to embellish the material with LVschema. |
| P2 | IF the goal is to embellish the studied material with LVschema<br>and LVschema-unit is an unused unit in LVschema<br>THEN set as a subgoal to embellish the studied material with LVschema-unit. |
| P3 | IF the goal is to embellish the studied material with LVschema<br>and there are no unused units in LVschema<br>THEN POP. |
| P4 | IF the goal is to embellish the studied material with LVschema-unit<br>and LVschema-unit involves LVrelation<br>and LVfact from the studied material involves LVrelation<br>THEN set as a subgoal to make a correspondence between LVschema-unit and LVfact. |
| P5 | IF the goal is to embellish the studied material with LVschema-unit<br>and LVschema-unit involves LVrelation<br>and there is no fact from the studied material that involves LVrelation<br>THEN infer LVfact for the studied material involving LVrelation<br>and set as a subgoal to make a correspondence between LVschema-unit and LVfact. |
| P6 | IF the goal is to make a correspondence between LVschema-unit and LVfact<br>and LVschema-unit involves LVargument1 in LVrole which has not been mapped<br>and LVfact involves LVargument2 in LVrole<br>THEN set as a subgoal to check the correspondence between LVargument1 and LVargument2. |
| P7 | IF the goal is to make a correspondence between LVschema-unit and LVfact<br>and LVschema-unit involves LVargument1 in LVrole which has not been mapped<br>and LVfact has no argument in LVrole<br>THEN set as a subgoal to infer the correspondence for LVargument1. |
| P8 | IF the goal is to make a correspondence between LVschema-unit and LVfact<br>and there are no unmapped arguments in LVschema-unit<br>THEN POP. |

P9       IF the goal is to check the correspondence between LVargument1 and LVargument2
         and LVargument1 has no assignment
THEN set as a subgoal to check the compatibility of LVargument1 and LVargument2
         and if compatible assign LVargument2 to LVargument1 and then POP.

P10      IF the goal is to check the correspondence between LVargument1 and LVargument2
         and LVargument2 has been assigned to LVargument1
THEN POP.

P11      IF the goal is to check the correspondence between LVargument1 and LVargument2
         and LVargument3 has been assigned to LVargument1
         and LVargument2 ≠ LVargument3
THEN set as a subgoal to resolve the conflict between LVargument2 and LVargument3.

P12      IF the goal is to infer the correspondence of LVargument1 for LVrole in LVfact
         and LVargument2 has been assigned to LVargument1
THEN assign LVargument2 to LVrole in LVfact and POP.

P13      IF the goal is to infer the correspondence of LVargument1 for LVrole in LVfact
         and nothing has been assigned to LVargument1
         and LVargument2 from the studied material is connected to LVargument1
THEN set as a subgoal to check the compatibility of LVargument1 and LVargument2
         and if compatible assign LVargument2 to LVrole in LVfact
         and assign LVargument2 to LVargument1 and POP.

P14      IF the goal is to infer the correspondence of LVargument1
         and no corresponding argument can be found
THEN POP with failure.

P15      IF the goal is to make a correspondence between LVschema-unit and LVfact
         and there has been a failure to find a correspondence for LVargument1 in LVrole in LVschema-unit
THEN assign LVdummy to LVrole in LVfact
         and note that LVdummy is like LVargument1
         and set as an intention to find the correspondence for LVdummy.

P16      IF there is an intention to find the correspondence for LVdummy
         and LVdummy is like LVargument1
         and LVargument2 has been assigned to LVargument1
THEN infer that LVdummy is really LVargument2.

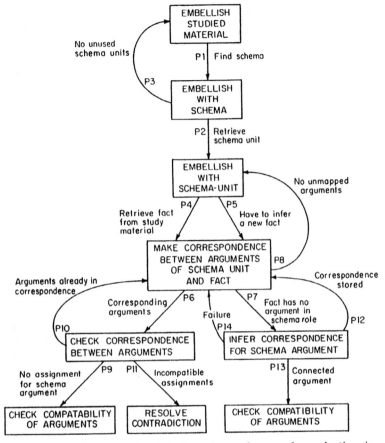

**Figure 5.11**   *An illustration of the flow of control among the productions in Table 5.3.*

and has in memory the following schema:

5. Person christens ship.
6. Person breaks bottle against ship.
7. Ship leaves port.
8. Ship goes to location as a trip.

This is stated in general terms, but the production set in Table 5.3 would work if *person, ship, port,* and *location* were replaced by specific terms from a single experience.

Production P1, which is responsible for selecting a schema for embellishment, selects a knowledge structure that is connected to the terms in the story. Undoubtedly, there will be more than one such knowledge structure. P1 selects the most active and sets the goal to use it. It is reasonable to suppose that, given sentences 1–4, the christening schema is the most active and so is selected. Production P2 iterates through the facts in the schema, setting as a subgoal to put each in correspondence with the story.

Suppose that the first schema fact chosen is *Person christens ship*. Productions P4 and P5 determine whether there is a structure in the studied material involving the relationship *christening*. In this case there is—*Fred christened the Tia Maria*—and P4 applies and sets the goal of putting the schema fact into correspondence with the studied fact. This amounts to putting the arguments of the two facts into correspondence. In this case, it will attempt to find correspondences for *person* and *ship*. P6 will identify that *person* is in the agent role in the schema fact and that *Fred* is in the agent role in the studied fact. It sets the subgoal of checking whether these two arguments correspond. P9 will apply in a case like this where the schema argument, *person*, has not yet been given an assignment. It checks first to see if this schema argument is compatible with the argument in the study fact. Although the productions to model it are not included in this case, the fact that *Fred* is a person's name would be retrieved and used as a basis for deciding positively about compatibility. Thus, *Fred* would be assigned the role of *person* in the schema. A similar process of P6 followed by P9 would assign *Tia Maria* to the role of *ship*. This would exhaust the arguments of the schema fact, P8 would apply, and control would go back to the goal of embellishing the story with schema facts.

The second schema fact is *person breaks bottle against ship*. The corresponding study fact would be *Fred broke the bottle*. Production P6 and then P10 would note that *Fred* was already assigned to the person role. P6 and P9 would assign *bottle* from the story to *bottle* from the schema. However, the schema involves an additional argument, *ship*, that is not in the story. P7 would set the subgoal of inferring a correspondence for that role, and P12 would retrieve *Tia Maria* from the association through the first sentence. Thus an inference has been made that helps connect the first two sentences in the story.

The third schema fact would be *ship leaves port*. P5 would have to create a new story fact. P3 and P12 would assign *Tia Maria* to the subject of this fact. There is no correspondence for *port*, so P7 would be followed by P14, which would report failure in the attempt to assign a correspondence for *port*. Production P15 would then apply and assign a dummy node to the *port* role.

The last schema fact is *Ship goes to location as a trip*. This will be matched against sentence 3, *The Tia Maria goes to Vancouver*. The story fact has no assignment for *trip*. However, P13 will select the related *trip* from story sentence 4 and assign it to the *trip* slot. Thus, sentences 3 and 4 in the story become integrated.

The embellished story is:

1'.   Fred christened the *Tia Maria*.
2'.   Fred broke the bottle against the *Tia Maria*.
7'.   The *Tia Maria* leaves some port.
3'.   The *Tia Maria* goes to Vancouver as a trip.
4'.   Fred did not delay the trip.

At this point, control returns to the top-level goal of embellishing the story. Another schema might be retrieved—for instance, one about breaking a bottle against a metal object or about taking a trip on a ship. The eventual product can be represented much more richly than the original material. For purposes of understanding memory, two features should be noted. First, the final memory structure is more densely interconnected. Second, the resulting knowledge structure will overlap with the schemata that generated it. This means that if only fragments of the structure remain at recall, the schemata can be reinvoked to replace the forgotten fragments.

This shows that production systems are capable of the kind of inferential embellishment associated with a schema system. The fact that one does not need a special architecture to achieve this embellishment is an argument of a sort against schema systems as a primitive architecture. ACT brings to this problem one element that is not well handled by schema systems. This is the spreading activation mechanism, which handles the initial selection of a schema and the problem of identifying possible correspondences among the arguments (producton P13).

# 6 | Procedural Learning

## Introduction

IF THERE IS ONE TERM that is most central to the ACT theory, it is "production." Productions provide the connection between declarative knowledge and behavior. They solve the dilemma of Tolman's rat that was lost, buried in thought and inaction (Guthrie, 1952, p. 143). The productions themselves are not part of the fixed architecture of the system; rather, they are a second kind of knowledge that complements the declarative knowledge contained in long-term memory. The productions constitute the procedural knowledge of ACT, that is, knowledge about how to do things. The phrase "how to do things" first brings to mind motor skills because these are the most concrete examples of procedural knowledge. Motor skills like riding a bike or typing are certainly instances of procedural knowledge, but they have not been the focus of the ACT theory. Its focus has been on cognitive skills such as decision making, mathematical problem solving, computer programming, and language generation.

The acquisition of productions is unlike the acquisition of facts or cognitive units in the declarative component. It is not possible to simply add a production in the way it is possible to simply encode a cognitive unit. Rather, procedural learning occurs only in executing a skill; one learns by doing. This is one of the reasons why procedural learning is a much more gradual process than declarative learning.

### DECLARATIVE VERSUS PROCEDURAL EMBODIMENTS OF SKILL

That productions cannot be directly acquired is not a perversity of the cognitive system. Rather, it is an adaptive design fea-

215

ture. Productions, unlike declarative units, have control over behavior, and the system must be circumspect in creating them. Suppose, as a gross example, a gullible child were told, "If you want something, then you can assume it has happened." Translated into a production, this would take the following form:

IF the goal is to achieve X
THEN POP with X achieved.

This would lead to a perhaps blissful but deluded child who never bothered to try to achieve anything because he believed it was already achieved. Once locked into this production, the child would have no feedback that would register that this production was leading to problems. As a useful cognitive system the child would come to an immediate halt.

It is only when a procedure has been tried out and has proven itself that one wants to give it irrevocable control. This seems to create a paradox. If productions to perform a procedure are not created until the procedure proves itself, and if productions are required to execute a procedure, how can the procedure ever be tried out to prove itself? How can new productions ever be acquired? How can instruction ever be effective in getting a person to do something new?

Declarative facts can influence behavior. For instance, a declarative encoding of a recipe can be used to guide cooking behavior by a general recipe-following production set. In this case the declarative information is being used as a set of instructions. Subsequent sections of this chapter will discuss examples in which the declarative information is not a set of instructions, but nonetheless exerts as strong an influence on behavior.

When an existing set of productions uses declarative knowledge to guide new behavior, it is said to be applying the knowledge *interpretively*. In certain senses the production set is using this knowledge the way a computer interpreter uses the statements in a program. After the knowledge has been applied interpretively a number of times, a set of productions can be compiled that applies the knowledge directly. .

### STAGES OF SKILL ACQUISITION

In ACT, acquisition of a skill first begins with an interpretive stage in which skill-independent productions use declarative representations relevant to the skill to guide behavior. Then skill-specific productions are compiled. This sequence corresponds to the sequence that Fitts (1964) claimed generally characterized the development of a skill. In Fitts's first stage, which he called the cognitive stage, the learner acquires an initial, often verbal, characterization of the skill, which is sufficient to generate the desired behavior to at least some crude approximation. In this stage it is common to observe verbal mediation, in which the learner rehearses the information required to execute the skill. In the second stage, called the associative stage, the skill performance is "smoothed out." Errors in the initial understanding of the skill are gradually detected and eliminated. Concomitant with this is the drop-out of verbal mediation. It is natural to identify Fitts's cognitive stage with the interpretive application of knowledge in ACT. The verbal rehearsal serves the function of holding in working memory declarative information relevant to the skill. Fitts's associative stage corresponds to the period of knowledge compilation during which a procedural embodiment is being created for the skill.

Fitts noted that improvement in the skill did not end with the termination of the associative stage. In his analysis there was a third stage, called the autonomous stage, which consisted of gradual continued improvement in the skill. In ACT there are further gradual learning processes that can only apply to productions and so will apply to the skill only when it has a procedural embodiment. Specifically, there are strengthening processes, which can speed up the rate of production application, and tuning processes, which make productions more judicious in terms of the situations in which they will apply.

This chapter is organized into three sections in accord with Fitts's analysis. The section on the declarative stage argues that initial learning of a skill involves just acquiring facts, and it illustrates how general-purpose productions can interpret these facts to generate performance of the skill. The next section discusses the evidence for and nature of the knowledge compilation process. The final section discusses the continued improvement of a skill after it has achieved a procedural embodiment.

### The Declarative Stage: Interpretive Procedures

Depending on the nature of the declarative information, there are a number of ways people can use it to guide behavior. When the information is in the form of direct instructions, as in the case of a recipe, people can follow the instructions step by step. However, in many instructional situations the information is not nearly so direct. This section will consider two other ways in which a student can use declarative information. One way is to use it to provide the data required by general problem-solving operators. The second is to use analogy-forming procedures to map a declarative representation of a worked-out behavior onto new behavior.

### APPLICATION OF GENERAL PROBLEM-SOLVING METHODS

Figures 6.1 and 6.2, from our work on geometry, illustrate a situation in which most students resort to some sort of general problem-solving strategy. Figure 6.1, taken from the text of Jur-

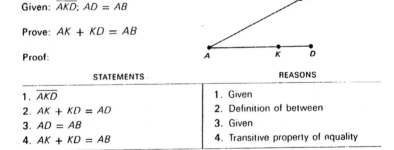

**1-7** *Proofs in Two-Column Form*

You prove a statement in geometry by using deductive reasoning to show that the statement follows from the hypothesis and other accepted material. Often the assertions made in a proof are listed in one column, and reasons which support the assertions are listed in an adjacent column.

**EXAMPLE.** A proof in two-column form.

Given: $\overline{AKD}$; $AD = AB$

Prove: $AK + KD = AB$

Proof:

| STATEMENTS | REASONS |
|---|---|
| 1. $\overline{AKD}$ | 1. Given |
| 2. $AK + KD = AD$ | 2. Definition of between |
| 3. $AD = AB$ | 3. Given |
| 4. $AK + KD = AB$ | 4. Transitive property of equality |

Some people prefer to support Statement 4, above, with the reason *The Substitution Principle.* Both reasons are correct.

The reasons used in the example are of three types: *Given* (Steps 1 and 3), *Definition* (Step 2), and *Postulate* (Step 4). Just one other kind of reason, *Theorem,* can be used in a mathematical proof. Postulates and theorems from both algebra and geometry can be used.

---

**Reasons Used in Proofs**

Given (Facts provided for a particular problem)
Definitions
Postulates
Theorems that have already been proved.

---

**Figure 6.1**   *The text instruction on two-column proofs in a geometry textbook. AKD means the points A, K, and D are collinear. (From Jurgenson et al., 1975.)*

**Written Exercises** Copy everything shown. Complete the proof by writing reasons.

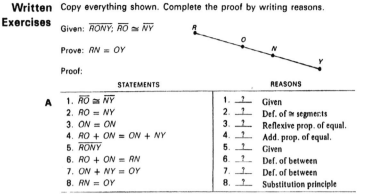

Given: $\overline{RONY}$; $\overline{RO} \cong \overline{NY}$

Prove: $RN = OY$

Proof:

| | STATEMENTS | | REASONS |
|---|---|---|---|
| A | 1. $\overline{RO} \cong \overline{NY}$ | 1. _?_ | Given |
| | 2. $RO = NY$ | 2. _?_ | Def. of $\cong$ segments |
| | 3. $ON = ON$ | 3. _?_ | Reflexive prop. of equal. |
| | 4. $RO + ON = ON + NY$ | 4. _?_ | Add. prop. of equal. |
| | 5. $\overline{RONY}$ | 5. _?_ | Given |
| | 6. $RO + ON = RN$ | 6. _?_ | Def. of between |
| | 7. $ON + NY = OY$ | 7. _?_ | Def. of between |
| | 8. $RN = OY$ | 8. _?_ | Substitution principle |

**Figure 6.2** *A reason-giving task from a geometry textbook. This is the first problem the student encounters that requires use of the knowledge about two-column proofs. This figure, showing the correct reasons, is taken from the instructor's copy of the text. These reasons are not given in the students' text. (From Jurgenson et al., 1975.)*

gensen et al. (1975), represents the total of that text's instruction on two-column proofs. We observed four students attempting to give reasons for two-column proof problems immediately after reading the instructions in the figure. The first such proof problem is illustrated in Figure 6.2, which all four students were able to solve with some success. Even though Figure 6.1 does not specify anything like a procedure for performing the reason-giving task, the instructions must somehow make it possible to perform the task.

General problem-solving procedures can take the declarative information in Figure 6.1 and interpret it to produce coherent and domain-appropriate behavior. On first consideration, it was not obvious to many people, including myself, how it was possible to model novice behavior in a task like Figure 6.2 in a purely interpretive system. However, because the theory presented here claims that knowledge in a new domain always starts out in declarative form and is used interpretively, it is absolutely essential that there be an interpretive system in ACT that accurately describes the behavior of a novice. Therefore I took it as a critical test case to develop a detailed explanation of how a student, extracting only declarative information from Figure 6.1, could generate task-appropriate behavior in Figure 6.2. The explanation below, which captures important aspects of the behavior of our four high-school students on this problem, assumes that the students possess some general-purpose problem-solving techniques.

*The production set.* Even though the student coming upon the instruction in Figure 6.1 has no procedures specific to doing two-column proof problems, he has procedures for solving problems in general, for doing mathematics-like exercises, and perhaps even for performing certain types of deductive reasoning. These problem-solving procedures can use instructions such as those in Figure 6.1 as data to generate task-appropriate behavior when faced with a problem like that in Figure 6.2. They serve as the procedures for interpreting the task-specific information. Table 6.1 lists the productions that embody the needed problem-solving procedures, and Figure 6.3 illustrates their hierarchical flow of control when applied to problems such as this.

Consider the application of this production set to the problem of finding a reason for the first two lines in Figure 6.2. It is assumed that the student encodes (declaratively) the exercise in the figure as a list of subproblems, each of which is to write a reason for a line of the proof. Production P1 from Table 6.1 matches this list encoding of the problems. Therefore P1 applies first and focuses attention on the first subproblem—that is, it sets as the subgoal to write a reason for $\overline{RO} \cong \overline{NY}$ (that the two line segments are congruent). Next production P4 applies. P4's condition, "the goal is to write the name of a relation," matches the current subgoal "to write the name of the reason for $\overline{RO} \cong \overline{NY}$." P4 creates the subgoal of finding a reason for the line. It is quite general and reflects the existence of a prior procedure for writing statements that satisfy a constraint.

The student presumably has encoded the boxed information in Figure 6.1 as a set of methods for providing a reason for a line. If so, production P8 applies next and sets as a subgoal to try givens, the first method in the boxed reason list, to justify the current line. Note this is one point where a fragment of the instruction (the boxed information) is used by a general problem-solving procedure (in this case, for searching a list of methods) to determine the course of behavior. Two of our students in fact went back and reviewed the methods when they started this problem.

The students we studied had extracted from the instruction in Figure 6.1 that the *givens* reason is used when the line to be justified is among the givens of the problem. (Note that this fact is not explicitly stated in the instruction but is strongly implied.) Thus it is assumed that the student has encoded the

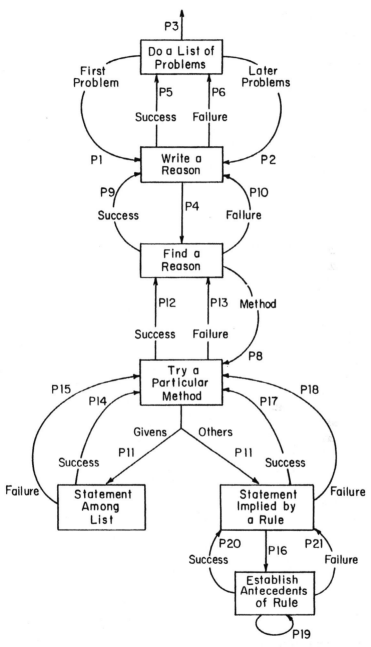

**Figure 6.3** *A representation of the flow of control in Table 6.1 among various goals. The boxes correspond to goal states and the arrows to productions that can change these states. Control starts with the top goal.*

**Table 6.1** *Interpretive productions evoked in performing the reason-giving task*

| | |
|---|---|
| P1 | IF the goal is to do a list of problems<br>THEN set as a subgoal to do the first problem in the list. |
| P2 | IF the goal is to do a list of problems<br>and a problem has just been finished<br>THEN set as a subgoal to do the next problem. |
| P3 | IF the goal is to do a list of problems<br>and there are no unfinished problems on the list<br>THEN POP the goal with success. |
| P4 | IF the goal is to write the name of a relation<br>and the relation is not yet known<br>THEN set as a subgoal to find the relation. |
| P5 | IF the goal is to write the name of a relation<br>and a relation has been found<br>THEN write the name of the relation<br>and POP the goal with success. |
| P6 | IF the goal is to write the name of a relation<br>and no relation has been found<br>THEN POP the goal with failure. |
| P8 | IF the goal is to find a relation<br>and there is a set of methods for achieving the relation<br>and there is an untried method in that set<br>THEN set as a subgoal to try that method. |
| P9 | IF the goal is to find a relation<br>and there is a list of methods for achieving the relation<br>and a method has been successfully tried<br>THEN POP the goal with success. |
| P10 | IF the goal is to find a relation<br>and there is a list of methods for achieving the relation<br>and they have all proven unsuccessful<br>THEN POP the goal with failure. |
| P11 | IF the goal is to try a method<br>and that method involves establishing a relationship<br>THEN set as a subgoal to establish the relationship. |
| P12 | IF the goal is to try a method<br>and the method was a success<br>THEN POP the goal with success. |
| P13 | IF the goal is to try a method<br>and the method was a failure<br>THEN POP the goal with failure. |
| P14 | IF the goal is to establish that a structure is among a list of structures<br>and the list contains the structure<br>THEN POP the goal with success. |

**Table 6.1**  (*continued*)

| | |
|---|---|
| P15 | IF the goal is to establish that a structure is among a list of structures<br>and the list does not contain the structure<br>THEN POP the goal with failure. |
| P16 | IF the goal is to establish that a statement is implied by a rule in a set<br>and the set contains a rule of the form *consequent if antecedents*<br>and the consequent matches the statement<br>THEN set as a subgoal to determine if the antecedents correspond to established statements<br>and tag the rule as tried. |
| P17 | IF the goal is to establish that a statement is implied by a rule in a set<br>and the set contains a rule of the form *consequent if antecedents*<br>and the consequent matches the statement<br>and the antecedents have been established<br>THEN POP the goal with success. |
| P18 | IF the goal is to establish that a statement is implied by a rule in a set<br>and there is no untried rule in the set which matches the statement<br>THEN POP the goal with failure. |
| P19 | IF the goal is to determine if antecedents correspond to established statements<br>and there is an unestablished antecedent clause<br>and the clause matches an established statement<br>THEN tag the clause as established. |
| P20 | IF the goal is to determine if antecedents correspond to established statements<br>and there are no unestablished antecedent clauses<br>THEN POP the goal with success. |
| P21 | IF the goal is to determine if antecedents correspond to established statements<br>and there is an unestablished antecedent clause<br>and it matches no established statement<br>THEN POP the goal with failure. |

fact that "the givens method involves establishing that the statement is among the givens." Production P11 will match this fact in its condition and so will set as a subgoal to establish that $\overline{RO} \cong \overline{NY}$ is among the givens of the problem. P14 models the successful recognition that $\overline{RO} \cong \overline{NY}$ is among the givens and returns a success from the subgoal. Scanning lists to find matches to symbol structures is something students have had ample experience with (for example, searching a class list for their name). P12 and P9 then pop success back up to the next-to-top-level goal of writing a reason for the line. Then production P5 applies to write "given" as a reason and pops back to the top-level goal. In fact, three of our four students scanned the given list and had no difficulty with the first line of this proof. The other student had to go back to the example in the instruction (Figure 6.1) to induce what was meant by the givens method.

At this point P2 applies to set the subgoal of writing a reason for the second line, $RO = NY$ (the length of $\overline{RO}$ is equal to the length of $\overline{NY}$). Then P4, P7, and P11 apply in that order, setting the subgoal of seeing whether $RO = NY$ was among the givens of the problem. Production P15 recognizes this as a failed goal, then P13 returns control to the level of choosing methods to establish a reason.

The instruction in Figure 6.1 does not explain how a definition should be applied. However, the text assumes that the student knows that a definition should imply the statement and knows how to determine whether a logical implication holds. Some earlier exercises in the text on conditional and biconditional statements make this assumption at least conceivable. All four students knew that some inference-like activity was required, but three had a faulty understanding of how to apply inference to this task. (For a discussion of some of the problems encountered by those three, see Anderson, 1982b.) The other subject performed the inferential reasoning modeled in Table 6.1 almost flawlessly. In any case, assuming that the student knows as a *fact* (in contrast to a procedure) that use of definitions involves inferential reasoning, production P11 will match in its condition the fact that "definitions involve establishing that the statement is implied by a definition," and P11 will set the subgoal of proving that $RO = NY$ was implied by a definition.

Productions P16–P21 constitute a general inference-testing procedure for checking the applications of logical implications. These productions apply to postulates and theorems as well as to definitions. Production P16 selects a conditional rule that matches the current line (the exact details of the match are not unpacked in Table 6.1). It is assumed that a biconditional definition is encoded as two implications each of the form *conse-*

*quent if antecedent.* The definition relevant to the current line 2 is that two line segments are congruent if and only if they are of equal measure, which is encoded as "$XZ = UV$ if $\overline{XZ} \cong \overline{UV}$" and "$\overline{XZ} \cong \overline{UV}$ if $XZ = UV$." The first implication is selected, and the subgoal is set to establish the antecedent $\overline{XZ} \cong \overline{UV}$ (or $\overline{RO} \cong \overline{NY}$, in the current instantiation). The production set P19–P21 describes a procedure for matching zero or more clauses in the antecedent of a rule. In this case P19 finds a match to the one condition, $\overline{XZ} \cong \overline{UV}$, with $\overline{RO} \cong \overline{NY}$ in the first line. Then P20 pops with success, followed by successful popping of P17, then P12, and then P9, which returns the system to the goal of writing out a reason for the line.

*Significant features of the example.* The flow of control in Figure 6.3 is not fixed ahead of time but rather emerges in response to the instruction and the problem statement. The top-level goal in Figure 6.3, of iterating through a list of problems, is provided by the problem statement. This goal is unpacked into a set of subgoals to write statements indicating the reasons for each line. This top-level procedure reflects a general strategy the student has for decomposing problems into linearly ordered subproblems. Then another prior routine sets as subgoals to find the reasons. At this point the instruction about the list of acceptable relationships is called into play (through yet another prior problem-solving procedure) and is used to set a series of subgoals to try out the various possible relationships. So the unpacking of subgoals in Figure 6.3 from "do a list of problems" to "find a reason" is in response to the problem statement; the further unpacking into the methods of givens, postulates, definition, and theorems is in response to the instruction. The instruction identifies that the method of givens involves searching the given list and that the other methods involve applying inferential reasoning. The text assumes, reasonably enough, that the student has as a prior procedure the ability to search a list for a match. The ability to apply inferential reasoning is also assumed as a prior procedure, but in this case the assumption is often mistaken.

In summary, then, the separate problem-solving procedures in Figure 6.3 are joined in a novel combination by the declarative information in the problem statement and instruction. In this sense, the student's general problem-solving procedures are interpreting the problem statement and instruction. Note that the problem statement and the instruction are brought into play by being matched as data in the conditions of the productions of Table 6.1.

## Use of Analogy

The preceding example illustrated how general problem-solving procedures are used to interpret declarative knowledge. This is only one type of interpretive use of declarative knowledge. Analogy is another way of using knowledge interpretively (see also Gentner, in press; Rumelhart and Norman, 1981). Anderson (1981d) discusses in detail the role of analogy in many geometry problem-solving procedures. For instance, students will try to transform a solution worked out for one problem into a solution for another problem. A somewhat different possibility is that students will transform the solution of a similar nongeometry problem into a solution for the current geometry problem.

To illustrate the variety of uses of analogy, this chapter will consider an example drawn from the language-generation domain, concerning how students can use their knowledge of English plus translation rules to speak a foreign language. Table 6.2 provides the relevant production rules, and Figure 6.4 gives a hierarchical trace of the process of translation. Production P1 sets the basic plan for generating the French sentence: first an English sentence will be planned, then the translation to French will be planned, and then the French sentence will be generated. Productions P2–P4 give three of the many productions that would be involved in generating English sentences. Figure 6.4(*a*) illustrates how they would apply to generate the sentence *The smart banker is robbing the poor widow.*

Productions P5–P13 model some of the procedural knowledge actually involved in the sentence translation. Note that these productions are not specific to French. They attempt to model a person's general ability to apply textbook rules to map sentences from the native language onto a foreign language. They are the interpretive productions. The declarative knowledge they are using is the sentence representation and the textbook translation rules for French.

Production P5 is a default decomposition rule. It maps the goal of translating a clause onto the goal of translating the elements of the clause. Applied to Figure 6.4, it decomposes the sentence generation into generation of subject, verb, and object; applied a second time, it decomposes the subject generation into the subgoals of generating article, adjective, and noun.

In this example, it is at the point of the individual word translation that nondefault rules apply. For instance, P7 applies to the translation of *the* and retrieves that *le* is an appropriate

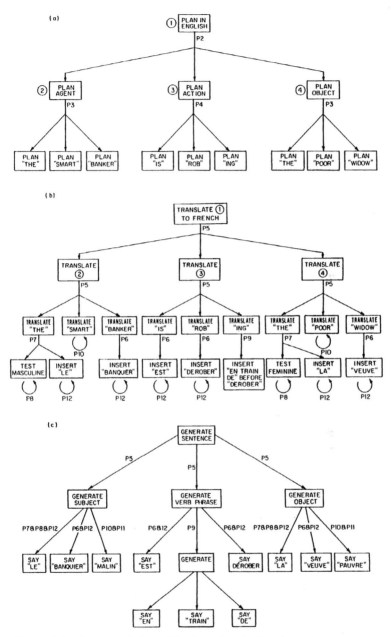

**Figure 6.4** *A representation of the flow of control by the sentence-genera-
tion productions in Table 6.2. Part (a) illustrates the generation
of the original English sentence; (b) illustrates its translation to
French; and (c) illustrates the French execution plan that is the
result of the translation.*

**Table 6.2**  *Productions for generation and translation of English sentences*

P1    IF the goal is to describe a fact in LVforeign-language
      THEN set as subgoals to plan a description of the fact in English
            and then to plan the translation of the English sentence
                into LVforeign-language
            and then to generate the plan in LVforeign-language.

P2    IF the goal is to describe (LVrelation LVagent LVobject) in
            English
      THEN set as subgoals to describe LVagent
            and then to describe LVrelation
            and then to describe LVobject.

P3    IF the goal is to describe LVobject
            and LVobject is known to the listener
            and LV object has a property named LVadjective
            and LVobject is a member of a category named LVnoun
      THEN set as subgoals to say *the*
            and then to say LVadjective
            and then to say LVnoun.

P4    IF the goal is to describe LVrelation
            and the agent of LVrelation is singular
            and LVrelation is describing ongoing LVaction
      THEN set as subgoals to say *is*
            and then to say LVaction
            and then to say *ing*.

P5    IF the goal is to translate LVstructure into LVlanguage
      THEN the subgoals are to translate the elements of LVstructure.

P6    IF the goal is to translate LVword into LVlanguage
            and LVword1 is the vocabulary equivalent of LVword in
                LVlanguage
      THEN the subgoal is to insert LVword1.

P7    IF the goal is to translate LVword into LVlanguage
            and LVword1 is the vocabulary equivalent of LVword in
                LVlanguage
            and LVcondition is a constraint of the use of LVword1
      THEN the subgoals are to test LVcondition
            and if successful to insert LVword1.

P8    IF the goal is to test if LVtype has LVproperty
            and LVword in the current phrase is an LVtype
            and LVword1 is the translation of LVword
            and LVword1 has LVproperty
      THEN POP with success.

P9    IF the goal is to translate LVword into LVlanguage
            and LVword1 is the vocabulary equivalent of LVword in
                LVlanguage
            and LVword1 is an LVtype1

**Table 6.2**   (*continued*)

|  |  |
|---|---|
|  | and LVtype1 occurs in LVrelation to LVtype2 in LVlanguage |
|  | and LVword2 is a translated instance of LVtype2 |
|  | THEN insert LVword1 in LVrelation to LVword2 |
|  | and POP. |
| P10 | IF the goal is to translate LVword into LVlanguage |
|  | and LVword1 is the vocabulary equivalent of LVword in LVlanguage |
|  | and LVword1 is an LVtype1 |
|  | and LVtype1 occurs in LVrelation to LVtype2 in LVlanguage |
|  | THEN set the intention to insert LVword1 in LVrelation to an instance of LVtype2 |
|  | and POP. |
| P11 | IF the intention is to insert LVword in LVrelation to LVtype |
|  | and LVword1 is an instance of LVtype |
|  | and LVword1 has been translated |
|  | THEN insert LVword in LVrelation to LVword1. |
| P12 | IF the goal is to insert LVword |
|  | THEN insert LVword next |
|  | and POP. |

translation but also retrieves that *le* requires that the noun be masculine. Therefore P7 sets as subgoals to perform this test and will only insert *le* if the test confirms that *banquier* (the translation of *banker*) is masculine. Similarly, P10 retrieves that the translation of *smart* is *malin* but also that the adjective has a different position in French; *malin* is the type of adjective that occurs after the noun. Since the noun has not yet been translated, it sets an intention to insert *malin* after the noun. P6 simply translates *banker* as *banquier* and then the demon P11 (see discussion of intentions in Chapter 4) can insert *malin*.

The output of these productions is a plan for executing *le banquier malin* as illustrated in Figure 6.4(*c*). Other productions in P5–P13 apply to generate the rest of the plan in the figure. With the plan completed, control will switch to execution of the plan.

Generation of the French sentence depends on tacit knowledge in the English sentence generation productions. Knowledge about definite articles, present tense, and progressive aspect all derive from tests buried in the English productions. For instance, the English P3 contains the knowledge that *the* is used to refer to known referents. This is not contained in the translation production nor in the knowledge of French grammer.

This translation example illustrates some features of analogy. Problem solution by analogy is powerful because it borrows knowledge from the source domain. However, for analogy to be successful, it cannot be a mindless mapping of the source onto the new domain. Rules of the new domain (in this case, vocabulary and translation rules) have to be called in to permit a correct mapping. These rules have declarative representations. To the extent that these domain constraints are applied, analogy will be successful. To the extent that they are ignored, performance will be less than perfect; for instance, the verb phrase in the example is a somewhat awkward construction.

With experience it is possible for the learner to short-circuit the path through the explicit English sentence and the word-by-word translation. This is accomplished by the compilation process to be described. However, the compilation process preserves the original mappings of the translation, so any inadequacies of grammar, vocabulary, and style that arise because of word-for-word translation will remain after compilation. It is only with later tuning that the learner can begin to develop rules that capture the subtleties of the foreign language.

### THE NEED FOR AN INITIAL DECLARATIVE ENCODING

This section has shown how students can generate behavior in a new domain when they do not have specific procedures for acting in that domain. Their knowledge of the domain is declarative and is interpreted by general procedures. This is an adaptive way for a learning system to start out. New productions have to be integrated with the general flow of control in the system. Most people do not adequately understand their cognitive flow of control to form such productions directly. One of the reasons why instruction is so inadequate is that the teacher likewise has a poor conception of the student's flow of control. Attempts to directly encode new procedures, as in the Instructible Production System (Rychener, 1981; Rychener and Newell, 1978), have run into trouble because of this problem of integrating new elements into a complex existing flow of control.

As an example of the problem of creating new procedures out of whole cloth, consider how the definition of congruence by the production set in Table 6.1 is used to provide a reason for the second line in Figure 6.2. One could build a production that would directly recognize the application of the definition to this situation rather than going through the interpretive rigamarole of Figure 6.3 (Table 6.1). This production would have the form:

IF the goal is to give a reason for $XY = UV$
   and a previous line has $\overline{XY} \cong \overline{UV}$
THEN POP with success
   and the reason is definition of segment congruence.

However, it is implausible that the subject could know that this knowledge was needed in this procedural form before he stumbled on its use to solve line two in Figure 6.2. Thus ACT should not be expected to encode its knowledge into procedures until it has seen examples of how the knowledge is to be used.

Although new productions must be created at some time, forming them is potentially dangerous. Because productions have direct control over behavior, there is an ever-present danger that a new production may wreak great havoc in a system. Anyone who incrementally augments computer programs will be aware of this problem. A single erroneous statement can destroy the behavior of a previously fine program. In computer programming the cost is slight—one simply has to edit out the bugs introduced by the new procedure. For humans, however, the cost can be much higher. Consider, for instance, what would happen if a child could compile a procedure for crossing the street without looking from a single instance of this behavior. The next section describes a highly conservative and adaptive way of entering new procedures.

### Knowledge Compilation

Interpreting knowledge in declarative form has the advantage of flexibility, but it also has serious costs in terms of time and working-memory space. The process is slow because interpretation requires retrieving declarative information from long-term memory and because an interpreter's individual production steps are small in order to achieve generality. (For instance, the steps of problem refinement in Figure 6.3 and of translation in Figure 6.4 were painfully small.) The interpretive productions require that the declarative information be represented in working memory, and this can place a heavy burden on working-memory capacity. Many of the subjects' errors and much of their slowness seem attributable to working-memory errors. Students keep repeating the same information over and over again as they lose critical intermediate results and have to recompute them. This section describes the compilation processes by which the system goes from this interpretive application of declarative knowledge to procedures (productions) that

**POSTULATE 14** If two sides and the included angle of one
(SAS POSTULATE) triangle are congruent to the corresponding
parts of another triangle, the triangles are congruent.

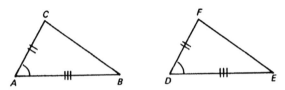

According to Postulate 14:

If $\overline{AB} \cong \overline{DE}$, $\overline{AC} \cong \overline{DF}$, and $\angle A \cong \angle D$,
then $\triangle ABC \cong \triangle DEF$.

**Figure 6.5** *Statement of the side-angle-side postulate. (From Jurgenson et al., 1975.)*

apply the knowledge directly. By building up procedures to
perform specific tasks like reason giving in geometry, a great
deal of efficiency is achieved in terms of both time and working-memory demands.

The Phenomenon of Compilation

One process in geometry involves matching postulates
against problem statements. Consider the side-angle-side
(SAS) postulate from the text by Jorgensen et al. (1975), given in
Figure 6.5. We followed a student through the exercises in the
text involving this postulate and the side-side-side (SSS) postulate. The first problem that required the use of SAS is illustrated
in Figure 6.6. The following is the portion of the student's protocol in which he actually called up this postulate and managed
to put it in correspondence to the problem:

If you looked at the side-angle-side postulate [long pause] well, *RK*
and *RJ* could almost be [long pause] what the missing [long pause]
the missing side. I think somehow the side-angle-side postulate
works its way into here. [long pause] Let's see what it says: "two
sides and the included angle." What would I have to have to have
two sides. *JS* and *KS* are one of them. Then you could go back to
*RS* = *RS*. So that would bring up the side-angle-side postulate.
[long pause] But where would ∠1 and ∠2 are right angles fit in

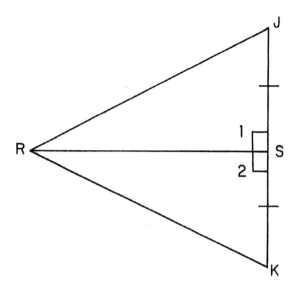

Given: ∠ 1 and ∠ 2 are right angles   JS = KS

Prove: △RSJ = △RSK

**Figure 6.6**   *The first proof-generation problem a student encounters that requires application of the SAS postulate.*

[long pause]—wait, I see how they work. [long pause] *JS* is congruent to *KS* [long pause] and with angle 1 and angle 2 are right angles that's a little problem. [long pause] OK, what does it say— check it one more time. "If two sides and the included angle of one triangle are congruent to the corresponding parts." So I have got to find the two sides and the included angle. With the included angle you get angle 1 and angle 2. I suppose [long pause] they are both right angles, which means they are congruent to each other. My first side is *JS* is to *KS*. And the next one is *RS* to *RS*. So these are the two sides. Yes, I think it is the side-angle-side postulate.

After reaching this point the student still had to go through a long process of writing out the proof, but this is the relevant portion for assessing what goes into recognizing the application of SAS.

After a series of four more problems (two were solved by SAS and two by SSS), the student came to the problem illustrated in

Figure 6.7. The method recognition portion of his protocol follows:

> Right off the top of my head I am going to take a guess at what I am supposed to do— ∠DCK ≅ ∠ABK. There is only one of two, and the side-angle-side postulate is what they are getting to.

The contrast between these two protocols is striking in a number of ways. First, the application of the postulate has been speeded up. Second, the student did not verbally rehearse the statement of the postulate in the protocol associated with Figure 6.7. This is evidence that the student is no longer calling a declarative representation of the problem into working memory. Note also that in the first protocol there are a number of failures of working memory, points where the student had to recompute information he had forgotten. Third, the piecemeal appli-

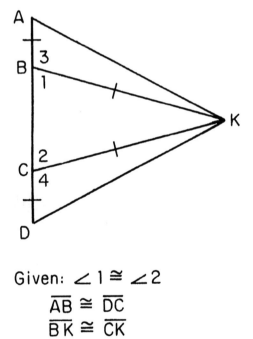

Given: ∠1 ≅ ∠2

$\overline{AB} \cong \overline{DC}$

$\overline{BK} \cong \overline{CK}$

Prove: △ABK ≅ △DCK

**Figure 6.7** *The fourth proof-generation problem that requires application of the SAS postulate. This problem, like many in geometry texts, does not explicitly state the collinearity of the points A, B, C, and D; rather, the diagram implies it.*

cation of the postulate is eliminated. In the first protocol the student separately identified every element of the postulate. In the second protocol he apparently matches the postulate in a single step.

### THE MECHANISMS OF COMPILATION

The knowledge compilation processes in ACT can be divided into two subprocesses. One, called *composition*, takes a sequence of productions that follow each other in solving a particular problem and collapses them into a single production that has the effect of the sequence. The idea of composition as applied to productions was first developed by Lewis (1978). Composition speeds up the process considerably by creating new operators that embody the sequences of steps used in a particular problem domain. The second process, *proceduralization*, builds versions of the productions that no longer require the domain-specific declarative information to be retrieved into working memory. Rather, the essential products of these retrieval operations are built into the new productions.

The basic processes of compilation can be illustrated with telephone numbers. It has been noted (Anderson, 1976) that with a frequently dialed telephone number, one develops a special procedure for dialing it; sometimes declarative access to the number is lost, and the only access one has to the number is through the procedure for dialing it.

Consider the following two productions that might serve to dial a telephone number:

P1     IF the goal is to dial LVtelephone-number
          and LVdigit1 is the first digit of LVtelephone-number
   THEN dial LVdigit1.

P2     IF the goal is to dial LVtelephone-number
          and LVdigit1 has just been dialed
          and LVdigit2 is after LVdigit1 in LVtelephone-number
   THEN dial LVdigit2.

Composition creates "macroproductions" that do the operation of a pair of productions that occurred in sequence. Applied to the sequence of P1 followed by P2, composition would create

P1&P2     IF the goal is to dial LVtelephone-number
          and LVdigit1 is the first digit of
            LVtelephone-number
          and LVdigit2 is after LVdigit1
   THEN dial LVdigit1 and then LVdigit2.

Compositions like this will reduce the number of production applications to perform the task.

A composed production like P1&P2 still requires that the information (in this case, the phone number) be retrieved from long-term memory, held in working memory, and matched to the second and third clauses in P1&P2. Proceduralization eliminates clauses in the condition of a production that require information to be retrieved from long-term memory and held in working memory. In P1&P2, the second and third condition clauses would be eliminated. The local variables that would have been bound in matching these clauses are replaced by the values they are bound to in the special case. If this production is repeatedly applied in dialing Mary's telephone number, which is 432-2815, the local variables in P1&P2 would be bound as follows:

LVtelephone-number = Mary's number
        LVdigit1 = 4
        LVdigit2 = 3

Substituting these values for the variables and eliminating the second and third condition clauses transforms the production into:

P1&P2*      IF the goal is to dial Mary's telephone number
        THEN dial 4 and then 3.

By continued composition and proceduralization, a production can be built that dials the full number:

P*      IF the goal is to dial Mary's number
        THEN dial 4-3-2-2-8-1-5.

It should be emphasized that forming this production does not necessarily imply the loss of the declarative representation of the knowledge. In the few instances reported of loss of declarative access to a telephone number, the declarative knowledge has probably ceased to be used and has simply been forgotten.

Proceduralization reduces the load on working memory because long-term information need no longer be held there. This makes it easier for the system to simultaneously perform a second concurrent task that does make working-memory demands. This is achieved by creating a knowledge-specific procedure. The original productions P1 and P2 could dial any telephone number; P* can only dial Mary's number. As with all of ACT's learning mechanisms, composition and proceduralization do not replace old productions with new ones. Rather they augment the existing production set with the new productions. In this way the old productions are still around to deal with situations not captured by the new ones. Also, if the new productions are faulty they may be weakened (as will be explained in the section on tuning), and then the old productions can return to full control of behavior.

This example illustrates how knowledge compilation produces the three phenomena noted in the geometry protocols at the beginning of this section. The composition of multiple steps into one produces the speed-up and leads to unitary rather than piecemeal application. Verbal rehearsal drops out because proceduralization eliminates the need to hold long-term memory information in working memory.

In addition to these general phenomena, a fair amount of empirical data can be explained by the mechanisms of knowledge compilation. Some of this is reviewed in Anderson (1982b), where it was shown that proceduralization mechanisms can produce some of the phenomena associated with the automatization of behavior. In particular, proceduralization reduces the set-size effect in the Sternberg task with repeated practice on a constant set (Briggs and Blaha, 1969). Repeated practice compiles specific productions to recognize specific set members and thus eliminates a search of a working-memory set. By a similar process ACT reduces the effect of display size (Shiffrin and Schneider, 1977). Proceduralization does seem to have many of the characteristics of automatization as described in Shiffrin and Schneider (1977) and Shiffrin and Dumais (1981). Composition was also shown to be responsible for a combination of speedup and rigidity in behavior. In particular, it was shown to produce the Einstellung phenomenon (Luchins, 1942). That is, specific productions are composed that embody a particular problem solution, and these specific productions can prevent more general productions from detecting a simpler solution.

THE ISSUE OF WHEN TO COMPOSE PRODUCTIONS

An important issue is what productions to compose together. In the original development by Neves and Anderson (1981), we composed pairs of productions that applied one after the other. However, many pairs of productions follow each other accidentally and would thus be spuriously composed. Such spurious composition might not have disastrous consequences, but it would be wasteful. Also, unrelated productions might inter-

vene between the application of productions that belonged together. For instance, suppose the following three productions
happened to apply in sequence:

P5       IF the subgoal is to add in a digit in a column
         THEN set as a subgoal to add the digit to the running total.

P6       IF I hear footsteps in the aisle
         THEN the teacher is coming my way.

P7       IF the goal is to add two digits
             and a sum is the sum of the two digits
         THEN the result is the sum
             and POP.

This sequence might apply, for instance, as a child is doing
arithmetic exercises in a class. The first and third are set to process subgoals in solving the problem. The first sets up the subgoal that is met by the third. The second production is not related to the other two and is merely an inference production
that interprets the sound of the teacher approaching. It just
happens to intervene between the other two. Composition as
described by Neves and Anderson would produce the following pairs:

P5&P6    IF the subgoal is to add in a digit in a column
             and I hear footsteps in the aisle
         THEN set as a subgoal to add the digit to the running total
             and the teacher is coming my way.

P6&P7    IF I hear footsteps in the aisle
             and the goal is to add two digits
             and a sum is the sum of the two digits
         THEN the teacher is coming my way
             and the result is the sum
             and POP.

These productions are harmless but basically useless. They also
have prevented formation of the following useful composition:

P5&P7    IF the subgoal is to add in a digit in a column
             and the sum is the sum of the digit and the
                 running total
         THEN the result is the sum.

Anderson (1982b) proposed that composition should apply to
productions that are logically contiguous in terms of the goal
structure rather than temporally contiguous.[1] This would avoid

wasteful compositions as in the above example and enable the desired composition to take place. In this way the learning mechanisms can profitably exploit the goal structuring of production systems. The appendix to this chapter reviews the ideas developed so far on how to use goal structures to direct composition.

## THE RATE OF KNOWLEDGE COMPILATION

*Rate of composition.* Compositions will occur whenever there is an opportunity. As discussed in Anderson (1982b), in some empirical situations, such as the Einstellung phenomenon (Luchins, 1942), compositions do appear to occur rapidly. Also in our protocol studies of learning to do proofs in geometry or to write programs in LISP, we have seen numerous episodes of what appears to be rapid composition of operators. However, a number of factors slow down the rate of composition.

1. Since composition must inspect the goal structure in order to decide what productions to put together, composition requires that all the relevant goal structures are available in working memory. Since there are probabilistic limits on the amount of goal structure that can be maintained in working memory, there will be failures to act upon potentially composable productions.

2. Even though there are often redundant condition and action elements that can be pruned when forming a composition, productions still tend to get larger as composition progresses. In particular, the condition sides of productions tend to increase in size. A production whose condition specifies more information than can be held in working memory will not be matched and so will not execute. So composition will not progress further once such too-large productions are created.

3. There are breaks in many information-processing tasks beyond which composition cannot go. For instance, in the Sternberg task one cannot compose productions beyond the single trial, since one cannot know ahead of time what the probe will be for the next trial.

4. Newly composed productions are weak and may require multiple creations before they gain enough strength to compete successfully with the productions from which they were created.[2] Composition does not replace productions; rather, it supplements the production set. Thus a composition may be created on the first opportunity but may be masked by stronger productions for a number of subsequent opportunities until it has built up sufficient strength.

5. It is not the case that productions always apply in the same sequence. The longer the sequence, the less likely it is to be repeated. This means that opportunities for learning large compositions occur less frequently. Suppose productions 1, 2, 3, 4, 5, 6, 7, and 8 can apply in that order. There are many occasions when a pair (say 1 and 2) will be repeated, giving an opportunity to form a pair composition; there are considerably fewer occasions when a quadruple (1, 2, 3, and 4) will repeat, giving an opportunity to compose two pair compositions; and still less frequently will all eight be repeated, giving an opportunity to compose two quadruple productions into a production covering the whole sequence. (This idea is developed at great length by Newell and Rosenbloom, 1981.)

*Rate of proceduralization.* In the implementation of Neves and Anderson, proceduralization occurred as rapidly as composition. In one pass, all condition clauses that matched long-term memory elements were deleted and all variables bound in these clauses were replaced by constants from the long-term memory structures. However, proceduralization should be made to occur less rapidly. Verbal rehearsal of information in protocols does not disappear after one application. In an automatization task like that in Schneider and Shiffrin (1977), it takes much practice before the effects of retrieving memory set disappear. It seems reasonable to propose that proceduralization only occurs when long-term memory knowledge has achieved some threshold of strength and has been used some criterion number of times.

## THE ADAPTIVE VALUE OF KNOWLEDGE COMPILATION

In contrast to computer compilation, human compilation is gradual and occurs as a result of practice. The computer is told what is program, what is data, and how to apply one to the other. Thus, it can decide once and for all what the flow of control will be. The human does not know which are going to be the procedural components in instructions before using the knowledge in the instructions. Another reason for gradual compilation is to provide some protection against the errors that occur in a compiled procedure because of the omission of conditional tests. For instance, if an ACT-like system is interpreting a series of steps that includes pulling a lever, it can first reflect on the lever-pulling step to see if it involves any unwanted consequences in the current situation. (An error-checking production that performs such tests can be made more specific so that it will take precedence over the normal course of action.)

When the procedure is totally compiled, the lever pulling will be part of a prepackaged sequence of actions with many conditional tests eliminated. If the procedure moves gradually between the interpretive and compiled stages, it is possible to detect the erroneous compiling out of a test at a stage where the behavior is still being partially monitored interpretively and can be corrected. It is interesting to note here the folk wisdom that most grave errors in acquiring a skill, like airplane flying, are made neither at the novice nor at the expert stage, but at intermediate stages of development. This is presumably where the conversion from procedural to declarative is occurring and is the point where unmonitored mistakes may slip into the performance.

## Tuning Productions

Much learning still goes on after a skill has been compiled into a task-specific procedure, and this learning cannot just be attributed to further speedup through more composition. One type of learning involves an improvement in the choice of method for performing the task. One can characterize all tasks as having an associated search although in some cases the search is trivial. The subject must choose among various alternate paths of steps for tackling the problem. Some of these paths lead to no solution, and some lead to nonoptimal solutions. With high levels of expertise in a task domain, the problem solver becomes more judicious about choosing a path and may fundamentally alter the method of search (see Larkin et al., 1980). In terms of traditional learning theory, the issue is similar, though by no means identical to, the issue of trial and error versus insight in problem solving. A novice's search of a problem space is largely a matter of trial-and-error exploration. With experience the search becomes more selective and more likely to lead to rapid success. The learning underlying this selectivity is called *tuning*. This use of the term is close to that of Rumelhart and Norman (1978).

Anderson, Kline, and Beasley (1977, 1980) proposed a set of three learning mechanisms that still serve as the basis for much of our work on the tuning of search for the correct solution. There is a generalization process by which production rules become broader in their range of applicability, a discrimination process by which the rules become narrower, and a strengthening process by which better rules are strengthened and poorer rules weakened. These ideas are related to concepts in the traditional learning literature, but they have been somewhat modified to be computationally more adequate. One can think of production rules as implementing a search in which productions correspond to individual operators for searching the problem space. Generalization and discrimination produce a "meta-search" over the production rules, looking for the right features to constrain the application of these productions. Strengthening evaluates the various changes produced by the other two processes.

## GENERALIZATION

The ability to perform successfully in novel situations is an important component of human intelligence. For example, *productivity* has often been identified as a critical feature of natural language, referring to the speaker's ability to generate and comprehend utterances never before encountered. Traditional learning theories have been criticized (McNeill, 1968) because of their inability to account for this productivity, and one of our goals in designing the generalization mechanism for ACT was to avoid this sort of problem.

Good examples of generalization occur in first language acquisition, as will be discussed in the next chapter. Here I will illustrate generalization by a couple of examples from the game of bridge. Many bridge players learn the rules of play from a text or through expert instruction, in which case the rules are already quite general. However, these examples assume that the person has compiled rather more special-case production rules from experience. Suppose the following two rules have been created:[3]

P1      IF I am playing no trump
              and my dummy has a long suit
        THEN try to establish that suit
              and then run that suit.

P2      IF I am playing spades
              and my dummy has a long suit
        THEN try to establish that suit
              and then run that suit.

ACT will create a generalization of these two productions:

P3      IF my dummy has a long suit
        THEN try to establish that suit
              and then run that suit.

This is created by deleting a condition clause that was different in the two original productions.

As another example of generalization, consider the following pair of productions:

P4      IF I am playing no trump
        and I have a king in a suit
        and I have a queen in that suit
        and my opponent leads a lower card in that suit
      THEN I can play the queen.

P5      IF I am playing no trump
        and I have a queen in a suit
        and I have a jack in the suit
        and my opponent leads a lower card in that suit
      THEN I can play the jack.

The generalization of these two productions cannot be captured by deleting clauses in the condition, but it can be captured by replacing constants with variables. As stated in earlier papers (Anderson, Kline, and Beasley, 1977, 1980), one variable would replace king in the first production and queen in the second, while another variable would replace queen in the first production and jack in the second. This would lead to the following production:

P6      IF I am playing no trump
        and I have LVcard1 in a suit
        and I have LVcard2 in the suit
     ·  and my opponent leads a lower card in that suit
      THEN play LVcard2.

Here the variable replacement has been made explicit with the terms prefixed with LV.

The above generalized production has lost the important structure of the original production; thus, it makes the point that one does not want to just replace constants with variables. One wants to find constraints that are true of the variables in both of the to-be-generalized productions and add these constraints to the generalized production. Relevant facts are that the cards are honors and that they follow each other. Adding these constraints produces the following, more satisfactory generalization:

P7      IF I am playing no trump
        and I have LVcard1 in a suit
        and LVcard1 is an honor
        and I have LVcard2 in the suit
        and LVcard2 is an honor

and LVcard1 follows LVcard2
and my opponent leads a lower card in that suit
THEN I can play LVcard2.

This is the rule for playing touching honors in bridge. Generalization by variable replacement should not take place unless additional constraints like these can be uncovered. This is an advance over the earlier version of generalization in ACT. Similar ideas about constraining generalization have been proposed by Langley (1980) and Vere (1977).

*Discipline for forming generalizations.* In our simulations (Anderson, 1981c; Anderson, Kline, and Beasley, 1979), we have had successful performance by forming generalizations whenever possible. That is, whenever a production is formed, an attempt is made to compare it to other existing productions to see if a potential generalization exists. If one does exist, it will be created but with a low level of strength.

An interesting question is how similar productions are identified for possible generalization. One intriguing possibility (one instantiation of which has been developed by Kline, 1981) is that generalizations are detected by the same partial-matching mechanisms that match production conditions. When a new production is created, its condition can be entered as data into the data-flow network representing the conditions of existing productions. The data-flow matching process would identify the condition that best matches the condition of this production. The overlap between the two conditions would identify the clauses that the productions have in common. The points where the constant values of the two productions differed would be identified as points for variable replacement. When such a partial match is found, a test can be made to see whether the production actions can be generalized and whether appropriate constraints can be found to permit variable replacement.

### DISCRIMINATION

Just as it is necessary to generalize overly specific procedures, it is also necessary to restrict their range of application. A production may become overly general either because the generalization process deleted critical information or because the critical information was not encoded in the first place. The possibility of encoding failure is particularly likely with textbook instruction that provides information about general rules but does not discuss when those rules should be evoked. The discrimination process tries to restrict the range of application of a production to just the appropriate circumstances. This process requires that ACT have examples of both correct and incorrect applications of the production. The algorithm remembers and compares the values of the variables in the correct and incorrect applications. It randomly chooses a variable for discrimination from among those that have different values in the two applications. Having selected a variable, it looks for some attribute that the variable has in only one of the situations. A test is added to the condition of the production for the presence of this attribute.

*An example.* An example from geometry will illustrate discrimination. Suppose ACT starts out with the following productions:

P1      IF the goal is to prove that $\triangle UVW \cong \triangle XYZ$
      THEN try the method of side-side-side and set as subgoals
         1.  To prove that $\overline{UV} \cong \overline{XY}$
         2.  To prove that $\overline{VW} \cong \overline{YZ}$
         3.  To prove that $\overline{WU} \cong \overline{ZX}$.

P2      IF the goal is to prove that $\triangle UVW \cong \triangle XYZ$
      THEN try the method of side-angle-side and set as subgoals
         1.  To prove that $\overline{UV} \cong \overline{XY}$
         2.  To prove that $\angle UVW \cong \angle XYZ$
         3.  To prove that $\overline{VW} \cong \overline{YZ}$.

These two productions could be compiled from study and practice of the side-side-side (SSS) and the side-angle-side (SAS) postulates. They are general rules without any strategic component. There are no tests for suitability of the SSS or the SAS postulate, so a student would be at a loss in trying to decide which production to apply.

These productions seem a reasonable model of the competence of one high-school student we studied at the point where he was just learning about triangle-congruence proofs. At this point SSS and SAS were the only two rules he possessed for proving triangle congruence. Part (*a*) of Figure 6.8 illustrates a critical problem, and part (*b*) illustrates the goal tree of his attempt to solve it (as inferred from his verbal protocol). First he tried SSS, the method that had worked on the previous problem and that perhaps had a recency advantage. However, he was not able to prove $\overline{RK}$ and $\overline{RJ}$ congruent. Then he turned to SAS and focused on proving that the included angles were congruent. Interestingly, it was only in the context of this goal that he recognized that right angles were congruent. After he finished this problem, he made a post-problem review in which he announced that a critical feature was that angles were mentioned in the givens of the problem.

The goal tree of Figure 6.8 provides most of the information ACT requires to be able to form discriminations. That is, there is a trace of a production P1 (the one recommending SSS) applying and failing, and there is feedback as to what the correct action (SAS) would be. In addition, ACT needs a circumstance in which SSS had worked successfully, which the previous problem provided. It was identical to the current problem except that instead of ∠1 and ∠2 are right angles, it had $\overline{RK} \cong \overline{RJ}$. The discrimination mechanism looks for some feature of the current situation that is different from the situation in which SSS had worked successfully. This has to be a feature that is true of the variables in the condition of the misapplied production. The variables in the SSS production are the points $U$, $V$, $W$, $X$, $Y$, and $Z$. One possible feature for discrimination is the fact that in the SAS problem angles are mentioned in the givens involving these points. Since the two problems are so similar, there is virtually nothing else that is different.

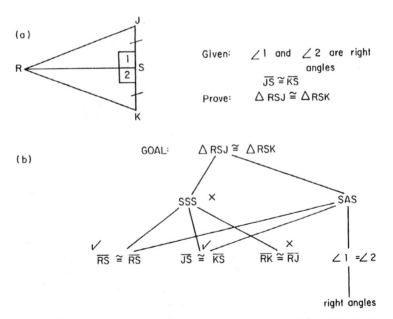

**Figure 6.8**  *A geometry problem and the structure of its solution. This leads ACT to form both condition and action discriminations.*

With this information ACT can form two types of discriminations of P1 (SSS). It could formulate a production for the current situation that recommends the correct SAS action:

P3    IF the goal is to prove $\triangle UVW \cong \triangle XYZ$
        and the angles $\angle UVW$ and $\angle XYZ$ are mentioned in
        the condition
    THEN try the SAS method and set as subgoals
        1.  To prove $\overline{UV} \cong \overline{XY}$
        2.  To prove $\angle UVW \cong \angle XYZ$
        3.  To prove $\overline{VW} \cong \overline{YZ}$.

This is created by *both* adding the discriminating information to the condition of the SSS production and changing the action. Also ACT can produce a production that would restrict the SSS to the previous successful situation:

P4    IF the goal is to prove $\triangle UVW \cong \triangle XYZ$
        and nothing is mentioned about their angles
    THEN try the SSS method and set as subgoals
        1.  To prove $\overline{UV} \cong \overline{XY}$
        2.  To prove $\overline{VW} \cong \overline{YZ}$
        3.  To prove $\overline{WU} \cong \overline{ZX}$.

The first discrimination, P3, is called an *action discrimination* because it involves learning a new action, while the second, P4, is called a *condition discrimination* because it restricts the condition for the old action.[4] Because of specificity ordering, the action discrimination will block misapplication of the overly general P1. The condition discrimination, P3, is an attempt to reformulate P1 to make it more restrictive. These discriminations do not replace the original production; rather, they coexist with it.

*Principles for forming discriminations.* ACT does not always form both types of discriminations. It can form an action discrimination only when it obtains feedback about the correct action for the situation. If the feedback is only that the old action is incorrect, it can only form a condition discrimination. However, ACT will only form a condition discrimination if the old rule (P1 in the above example) has achieved a level of strength to indicate that it has some history of success. The reason for this restriction is that if a rule is formulated that is simply wrong, it can perseverate forever by a process of endlessly proposing new condition discriminations.

The feature selected for discrimination is determined by comparing the variable bindings in the successful and unsuccessful production applications. A variable is selected on which they differ, and features are selected to restrict the bindings. It is possible for this discrimination mechanism to choose the wrong variables or features. In the case of condition discriminations, such mistakes have no negative impact on the behavior of the system. The discriminated production produces the same behavior as the original in the restricted situation, so it cannot lead to worse behavior. If an incorrect action discrimination is produced, its greater specificity may block the correct application of the original production in other situations. However, even here the system can recover by producing the correct discrimination and then giving the correct discrimination a specificity or strength advantage over the incorrect discrimination.

The probability of choosing the right feature to discriminate upon depends on the similarity of the successful and unsuccessful situations. The more similar they are, the fewer the distracting possibilities, and the easier it is to identify the critical feature. This is the idea of near-misses (Winston, 1970).

The current discrimination mechanism also attempts to speed up the process of finding useful discriminations by its method of selecting propositions from the data base as constraints. Though it still uses a random process to guarantee that any appropriate propositions in the data will eventually be found, this random choice is biased to increase the likelihood of a correct discrimination. That is, the discrimination mechanism chooses propositions with probabilities that vary with their activation levels. The greater the amount of activation that has spread to a proposition, the more likely it is that the proposition will be relevant to the current situation.

*The issue of feedback.* A prerequisite for discrimination is that the system have feedback indicating that a particular production has misapplied and, in the case of an action discrimination, feedback indicating what the correct action should have been. In principle, a production application could be characterized as being in one of three states—known to be incorrect, known to be correct, or correctness unknown. However, the mechanisms we have implemented for ACT do not distinguish between the second and third states. If a production applies and there is no comment on its success, it is treated as if it were a successful application.

There are two basic ways in which ACT can identify that a production application is in error and determine the correct action. One is through external feedback, and the other is through internal computation. In the external feedback situation the learner may be directly told that his behavior is in error or he may infer this by comparing his behavior to an external referent (such as a model or a textbook answer). In the internal computation case the learner must identify that a fact is contradictory, that a goal has failed, or that there is some other failure to meet internal norms. In either case the feedback is only indirectly about the production. It is directly about the action of the production that entered into working memory.

A goal structure, like that in Figure 6.8, can be critical for internally identifying failed and successful production applications. The goal tree in Figure 6.8 records the search for a successful proof. Productions that led to creation of unsuccessful portions of the search tree are regarded as incorrect and are subject to discrimination. To see that these are not all of the unsuccessful productions, consider this example. Suppose the top-level goal is to prove two angles congruent. A subgoal is set to prove this by showing that they are corresponding parts of congruent triangles. Suppose all methods for proving the triangles congruent fail, but the top-level goal is eventually proven by showing that the angles are supplementary to congruent angles. The mistake was not in the unsuccessful productions that proposed methods for proving the triangles congruent, but in the production that set the subgoal of triangle congruence. This is the production that would be selected for discrimination.

This example shows again the importance of goal structures for directing learning mechanisms. For the goal structures to serve this function in directing discrimination, they must be available in working memory at the time of discrimination. Thus capacity limitations on maintaining goal structures will impose limitations on the rate of discrimination. This predicts that the delay between a production's application and feedback would have considerable impact on the ability to make a discrimination. This prediction has been supported (Lewis and Anderson, unpublished) in that delay of feedback has been shown to have a fairly substantial effect on the rate of learning of successful operators in an artificial search task.

STRENGTHENING

The generalization and discrimination mechanisms are the inductive components in the learning system in that they try to extract from examples of success and failure the features that characterize when a particular production rule is applicable. These two processes produce multiple variants on the conditions controlling the same action. At any point in time the system is entertaining as its hypothesis not just a single production but a set of different productions with different conditions to control the action. Having multiple productions, differing in their conditions, for the same action provides advantages in expressive power. Since the features in a production condition are treated conjunctively, but separate productions are treated disjunctively, one can express the condition for an action as a disjunction of conjunctions of conditions. Many real-world categories have the need for this rather powerful expressive logic. Also, because of specificity ordering, productions can enter into even more complex logical relations.

However, because they are inductive processes, generalization and discrimination will sometimes err and produce incorrect productions. There are possibilities for overgeneralization and useless discrimination. The phenomenon of overgeneralization is well documented in the language-acquisition literature occurring in learning both syntactic rules and natural language concepts. The phenomenon of pseudodiscrimination is less well documented in language because it does not lead to incorrect behavior, just unnecessarily restrictive behavior. However, there are some documented cases in careful analyses of language development (Maratsos and Chaikley, 1981). One reason a strength mechanism is needed is because of these inductive failures. It is also the case that the system may simply create productions that are incorrect—either because of misinformation or because of mistakes in its computations. ACT uses its strength mechanism to eliminate wrong productions, whatever their source.

Other examples of incorrect production rules can be drawn from domains that are more clearly problem solving in character. For instance, beginners in bridge often start with a rule that they should always play the highest card in the suit led—a disastrously overgeneral rule. As another example, high-school geometry students often make their proof rules specific to a particular orientation of a problem. In this case the rule is too restrictive. Again, ACT's strengthening mechanism can serve to identify the best problem-solving rules.

The strength of a production determines the amount of activation it receives in competition with other productions during pattern matching. Thus, all other things being equal, the condition of a stronger production will be matched more rapidly and so repress the matching of a weaker production. Chapter 4 specified the algebra by which strength determined the rate of pattern matching. Here I will specify the algebra by which experience determines the strength of productions. When first created, a production has a strength of 1. Each time it applies, its strength increases by 1. However, when a production applies and receives negative feedback, its strength is reduced by 25 percent. Because a multiplicative adjustment produces a greater change in strength than an additive adjustment, this "punishment" has much more impact than a reinforcement. The exact strengthening values encoded into the ACT system are somewhat arbitrary. The general relationships among the values are certainly important, but the exact relationships are probably not.

There are further principles to deal with the strength values of new general productions. Because these new productions are introduced with low strength, they would seem to be victims of a vicious cycle: they cannot apply unless they are strong, and they are not strong unless they have applied. What is required to break out of this cycle is a way to strengthen a production that does not rely on its actual application. This is achieved by taking all of the strength adjustments (increases or decreases) that are made to a production that does apply and making these adjustments to all of its generalizations as well. Since a general production will be strengthened every time any one of its possibly numerous specializations applies, new generalizations can amass enough strength to extend the range of situations in which ACT performs successfully. Also, because a general production applies more widely, a successful general production will gather more strength than its specific variants.[5]

It is possible for the learning mechanisms of proceduralization, composition, generalization, and discrimination to create productions that are identical to ones already in the system. In this case, rather than creating a copy, the old production receives a strength increment of 1, and so do all of its generalizations.

Except for the decrement rule in the case of negative feedback, ACT's strengthening mechanism for productions is the same as the strengthening rule for declarative memory. It is also part of the ACT theory that there is a power-law decay in production strength with disuse, just as there is a power-law decay in the strength of declarative units. It might be argued from these identical strengthening principles that declarative and procedural memory are really the same. However, there are so many differences between them, including the learning principles discussed in this chapter, that one common feature does not provide much evidence for a common base. The similarity of the strengthening principles probably exists because the systems are implemented in the same kind of neural tissue, and that neural tissue has certain basic retentiveness characteristics.

*Comparison with Thorndike's laws of effect and exercise.* It is interesting to contrast the ACT theory with Thorndike's (1932, 1935) ideas about learning. Thorndike concluded that pure practice produced no improvement in performance and that punishment also had no effect. Only rewarding the behavior led to improvement. ACT has almost the opposite system: exercise leads to increased production strength when the system has no reason to judge its performance a failure. On the other hand, negative feedback (not necessarily punishment) leads to a weakening of production strength.

Thorndike's evidence for the ineffectiveness of pure practice consisted of observations of behavior such as repeated attempts to draw a line exactly three inches long while blindfolded. Without feedback there was no improvement in accuracy, no matter how frequent the repetitions. ACT would produce the same result, though it would produce a system that would draw the line more rapidly. That is, without feedback there would be no discrimination to change the production, but the repeated practices would strengthen it. There are numerous problem-solving and game-playing situations where it can be shown that repeated practice without external feedback leads to more rapid performance, as ACT's strengthening mechanism would predict (see Newell and Rosenbloom's [1981] discussion of the card game Stair). Whether the accuracy of the performance improves depends on whether the system can make reliable internal judgments about correctness and so inform the discrimination mechanism. Internal or external feedback is necessary for discrimination, but not for strengthening. Both discrimination and strengthening are necessary for improving accuracy; only strengthening is necessary for improving speed.

Again, punishment does not lead to improved performance unless there is feedback about what the correct behavior is in that situation. This is just what Thorndike failed to provide in his experiments that manipulated punishment. Again, ACT's strengthening mechanism will not improve accuracy in the absence of information that can be used by the discrimination mechanisms. Only when there are competing tendencies, one correct and the other not, can punishment repress the incorrect tendency. Punishment without the opportunity to identify the correct response will lead to slower performance but will not affect the accuracy.

*Power-law speedup.* Because production strength decays by a power law, it can be shown that it will increase as a power function of spaced practice, just as declarative memory strength increases as a power function. This strengthening mechanism can be shown to be responsible for the ubiquitous log-linear law about the effect of practice on the speed of the performance of a skill (Anderson, 1982b). Figure 6.9 illustrates data from Neves and Anderson (1981) on the effect of practice on the rate of giving reasons for lines of a geometry proof.

It is not immediately obvious that the ACT learning mechanism should predict the power-law relationship. Even if it is true that strengthening does obey a power law, one might think that other learning mechanisms like composition would produce more rapid learning—for instance, making processing time an exponential function of practice. That is, rather than having the power relation $T = A + BP^{-C}$, where $T$ is time and $P$ is practice, one might propose $T = A + BC^{-P}$. In both equations $A + B$ is the initial speed (in the first case when $P = 1$, and in the second when $P = 0$), $A$ is the final asymptotic speed, and $C$ ($<1$) determines rate of speedup. However, Anderson (1982b) showed that the strengthening factor would dominate the other learning processes such as composition, generalization, and discrimination. These processes can require a great

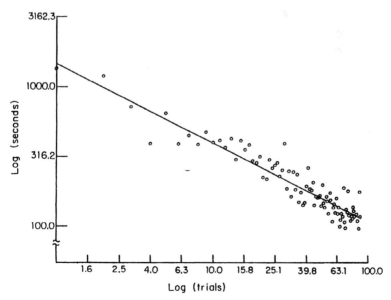

**Figure 6.9** *The effect of practice on time to perform a reason-giving task.*

deal of information to be available in working memory, so the stronger the encoding in declarative memory of the relevant information, the more that can be kept active. The stronger the relevant productions, the more likely that they will complete matching while the information is still available. Thus the increase of strength in declarative and production memory generally proves to be the rate-limiting factor controlling speed of improvement.

### General Comments on the ACT Tuning Mechanisms

This section has described separately generalization, discrimination, and strengthening. The question naturally arises as to how well the mechanisms function in concert. The next chapter will review how these mechanisms in combination result in some relatively impressive performance in the domain of language acquisition.

It is difficult to assess the psychological accuracy of the simulations in these areas. Because of the scale of the phenomena, there are not the careful empirical characterizations of the type an experimental psychologist likes to work with. For the same reason it is not possible to get reliable statistics about the performance of the simulation programs. In addition, the simulations require rather major simplifying assumptions. To check the empirical accuracy of the tuning mechanisms, ACT was applied to simulating the various schema-abstraction or prototype-formation tasks (Franks and Bransford, 1971; Hayes-Roth and Hayes-Roth, 1977; and Medin and Schaeffer, 1978). These learning phenomena are on a much smaller scale and hence more tractable experimentally. Subjects are presented with instances of ill-defined categories and must implicitly or explicitly develop a characterization of that category. Anderson, Kline, and Beasley (1979) showed that ACT's mechanisms were capable of simulating many of the established schema-abstraction phenomena. Elio and Anderson (1981) were able to confirm predictions from ACT's generalization mechanism that served to discriminate it from other theories.

In ACT, recognition of category memberships is modeled by productions that specify features of the category member. For instance:

IF a person is a Baptist
    and has a high-school education
    and is married to a nurse
THEN he is a member of the Koala club.

ACT's generalization and discrimination processes can do a search over these features (Baptist, high-school education, and so on), looking for combinations that identify a category member. ACT's learning mechanisms were shown to be superior to mechanisms that store correlations between single features and categories (rather than correlations between combinations of features and categories), mechanisms that form a single category prototype (rather than multiple productions describing different types of category members), or mechanisms that store just individual instances (rather than generalizations summarizing multiple instances).

## Summary

Skill development, according to the ACT learning theory, starts out as the interpretive application of declarative knowledge; this is compiled into a procedural form; and this procedural form undergoes a process of continual refinement of conditions and raw increase in speed. In a sense this is a stage analysis of human learning. Much like other such analyses of behavior, this stage analysis of ACT is offered as an approximation of a rather complex system of interactions. Any interesting behavior is produced by a set of elementary components, with different components at different stages. For instance, part of a task can be performed interpretively while another part is performed compiled.

The claim is that the configuration of learning mechanisms described is involved in the full range of skill acquisition, from language acquisition to problem solving to schema abstraction. Another strong claim is that the mechanisms of skill acquisition function within the mold provided by the basic problem-solving nature of skills. Moreover, to function successfully, these learning mechanisms require goal structures and planning structures. As skills develop they are compiled and better tuned; consequently, the original search of the problem space may drop out as a significant aspect.

## Appendix: Production Composition

We are still experimenting with various principles for composing productions. However, the following principles reflect the ideas we have developed so far in our GRAPES simulation (Anderson, Farrell, and Sauers, 1982) of the acquisition of LISP programming skills.

Brother Productions

On some occasions two productions apply in sequence as steps to a common goal. An example is the telephone productions (P1 and P2) discussed earlier in the chapter. Two productions of this sort can be composed simply, as were the telephone productions.

Subgoal Setting and Return

A second case, illustrated by the addition productions (P5 and P7), occurs when one production sets a subgoal, and a second production returns success from that subgoal. Then a composite can be formed, for example, P5&P7, that omits the subgoal setting and return. The composition directly produces the effect of the subgoal.

An elaboration of this circumstance occurs when a series of subgoals is set that fails, followed by a subgoal that succeeds. As an example, consider the following productions that search a set to see if any member begins with a letter (for instance, find a month that begins with A).

P8　　　IF the goal is to find a member of LVset that begins
　　　　　with LVletter
　　　　and LVitem is a member of LVset
　　THEN set as a subgoal to test if LVitem begins with
　　　　　LVletter.

P9　　　IF the goal is to test if LVitem begins with LVletter
　　　　and LVletter is the first letter in the spelling of
　　　　　LVitem
　　THEN POP with success
　　　　and LVitem is the answer.

P10　　IF the goal is to test if LVitem begins with LVletter
　　　　and LVletter is not the first letter in the spelling of
　　　　　LVitem
　　THEN POP with failure.

Production P8 might choose some incorrect months, for instance January and September, before selecting a correct month, such as August.[6] Thus the sequence might be P8, P10, P8, P10, P8, and then P9. Composition in this case would ignore the failed attempts (P8, P10, P8, P10) and simply produce a composition of P8 and P9:

P8&P9　　IF the goal is to find a member of LVset that begins
　　　　　　with LVletter

and LVitem is a member of LVset
and LVletter is the first letter in the spelling of
LVitem
THEN LVitem is the answer.

In this example it was critical that the correct instantiation of P8 and P10 did not depend on the failed instantiations. Suppose the desired answer was the *first* member of a set that began with the specified letter. Then P8 would be replaced by

P8a    IF the goal is to find the first member of LVset that
begins with LVletter
and LVitem is the first member of LVset
THEN set as a subgoal to test if LVitem begins with
LVletter.

P8b    IF the goal is to find the first member of LVset that
begins with LVletter
and LVitem1 has just been tried
and LVitem2 comes after LVitem1
THEN set as a subgoal to test if LVitem2 begins with
LVletter.

In forming the composition, the value of LVitem2 chosen in the successful instantiation of P8b will depend on past instantiations of P8a and P8b. In this case, all of the previous instantiations have to be preserved in the composition. If April is retrieved as the first month beginning with A, we would have to form the following composition:

IF the goal is to find the first member of LVset that begins
with LVletter
and LVitem1 is the first member of LVset
and LVletter is not the first letter in the spelling of
LVitem1
and LVitem2 comes after LVitem1
and LVletter is not the first letter in the spelling of
LVitem2
and LVitem3 comes after LVitem2
and LVletter is not the first letter in the spelling of
LVitem3
and LVitem4 comes after LVitem3
and LVletter is the first letter in the spelling of LVitem4
THEN the answer is LVitem4.

This production will retrieve the answer when the fourth item in the set is the first one that begins with the specified letter.

This is a highly specific and complex production. It may well be too complex to be actually formed, because of working-memory limitations. It is presented here principally for contrast with the earlier P8&P9.

Composition does not need to "understand" the semantics of *first* and *member* to behave differently in composing new productions for these two types of problems. Its behavior is totally determined by the semantics of goal structures and by examining how the variables are instantiated in the case of the successful production. In the *member* case the instantiation did not depend on the prior failed productions; in the *first* case each failed production was relevant.

An Illustration

The ideas considered so far can be combined to produce a relatively interesting composition involving the production set in Table 6.1. Figure 6.10 illustrates the application of that production set to the justification of $RO = ON$. First givens was attempted, then definitions. In attempting definitions, the definition of congruence was selected, and $\overline{RO} \cong \overline{ON}$ was found among the established statements. Note that P16 followed by P19 followed by P20 constitute a successful call to and return

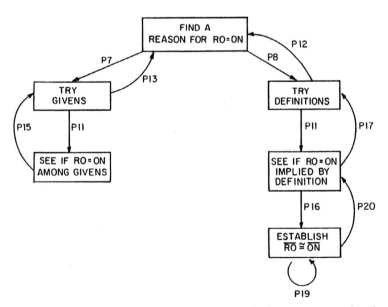

**Figure 6.10**   *The structure of the subroutine calls that are composed and proceduralized in the example in the text.*

from a subgoal. Therefore, they can be composed to form the following production:

P16&P19&P20
 IF the goal is to establish that a statement is implied by a rule
  in a set
 and the set contains a rule of the form *consequent if*
  *antecedent*
 and the consequent matches the statement
 and the antecedent matches an established statement
THEN consider the statement established by the rule.

This production now eliminates the need to achieve the specific goal in the case of a single antecedent rule.

P11 followed by this rule and then by P17 again constitute a successful call to and return from a goal. So now they can be composed:

P11&P16&P19&P20&P17
 IF the goal is to try a method
 and the method involves establishing that a statement is
  implied by a rule in a set
 and the set contains a rule of the form *consequent if*
  *antecedent*
 and the consequent matches the statement
 and the antecedent matches an established statement
THEN the method leads to a success with the rule.

Again P8 followed by this rule followed by P12 constitute a successful call to and return from a goal. The unsuccessful call to the givens method is ignored, and the following rule is formed:

P8&P11&P16&P19&P20&P17&P12
 IF the goal is to find a relation (1)
 and there is a set of methods for achieving the relation (2)
 and the method involves establishing that a statement is
  implied by a rule in a set (3)
 and the set contains a rule of the form *consequent if*
  *antecedent* (4)
 and the consequent matches the statement (5)
 and the antecedent matches an established statement (6)
THEN the method has been successfully tried with the rule. (7)

Such products of composition can be improved considerably if they are also proceduralized. Applying proceduralization to this composed production would eliminate clauses 2, 3, and 4, which retrieve from memory the definitions method for giving a reason and the congruence rule. They would replace the terms *relation, consequent, antecedent, method,* and *rule* in the remaining clauses with the specific information retrieved from long-term memory. The production resulting from proceduralization would be:

P*      IF the goal is to find a reason for the current statement (1)
         and $UV = XY$ matches the statement (5)
         and $\overline{UV} \cong \overline{XY}$ matches an established statement (6)
THEN the definitions method has successfully been tried with
         the definition of segment congruence (7).

The instantiated clauses in P* have been numbered to indicate the clauses they originated from in P8&P11&P16&P19&P20& P17&P12. This production successfully applies the definition of congruence in the context of the reason-giving task.

COMPOSITION OF PLANS

Another interesting composition case occurs when subject behavior is being governed by a planning process in advance of execution. An example of this is the translation of English to French in Figure 6.4. Planning involves iterating through a series of hierarchical plan structures until a final structure is achieved for execution. These intermediate planning structures are only important as steps to the final structure. It is not essential that they be computed if the final structure is computed. The goal for composition here is to produce a set of productions that will directly generate the execution structure without transformations from the planning structure.

The end product of applying composition and proceduralization to eliminate the planning productions would be a production that directly generates the desired French phrase. Such a production would be:

IF the goal is to describe LVobject in French
   and LVobject is known to the listener
   and LVobject has property named LVadjective in French
   and LVobject is in a category named LVnoun in French
   and LVadjective follows the noun
   and LVnoun is masculine
THEN say "Le LVnoun LVadjective."

# 7 | Language Acquisition

A MAJOR ISSUE in the field of cognitive science is whether
language is cut from the same cloth as the other cognitive processes. The basic premise in this book is that
all higher-level cognitive functions are achieved by the same
underlying architecture. This chapter will show that some features of language can be explained by the architectural assumptions presented earlier. Here I am concerned with the acquisition of syntax as it is manifest in children's generations.[1] I have
chosen this domain because the strongest claims for the
uniqueness of language have concerned syntax. It has been argued that children need language-specific knowledge to figure
out the syntax of their native language. Generation provides the
clearest evidence about a child's syntactic knowledge, and most
of the data on children's syntax have come from analyses of their
generations. I will argue here that the syntax of natural language mirrors the structure of procedural control. Thus, a concern with syntax dictates a focus on the procedural component
of ACT. Therefore, this chapter will mainly use ideas from
Chapters 4 and 6 about skill organization and acquisition.[2]

## Language Performance

In ACT, language is produced by a set of productions that approaches generation of a sentence as a problem-solving task.
The speaker begins with a meaning to convey, decomposes this
meaning into a set of components, and then turns to the subproblems of generating each component. Each subproblem is
similarly decomposed until the speaker gets down to meaning
units, which correspond to words or to phrase-structure patterns. The ability to generate syntactically correct utterances
amounts to having problem-solving operators that specify how

**Table 7.1**   *A set of productions for generating a fragment of English*

| | |
|---|---|
| G1 | IF the goal is to communicate a meaning structure<br>of the form (LVrelation LVagent LVobject)<br>THEN set as subgoals<br>  1.  To describe LVagent<br>  2.  To describe LVrelation<br>  3.  To describe LVobject. |
| G2 | IF the goal is to describe LVtopic<br>and it is supposed that (LVrelation LVtopic LVobject)<br>THEN set as subgoals<br>  1.  To describe LVtopic<br>  2.  To generate *who*<br>  3.  To describe LVrelation<br>  4.  To describe LVobject. |
| G3 | IF the goal is to describe LVtopic<br>and the listener knows of LVtopic<br>THEN set as subgoals<br>  1.  To generate *the*<br>  2.  To describe LVtopic. |
| G4 | IF the goal is to describe LVtopic<br>and the listener does not know of LVtopic<br>THEN set as subgoals<br>  1.  To generate *a*<br>  2.  To describe LVtopic. |
| G5 | IF the goal is to describe LVtopic<br>and LVtopic has LVproperty that is to be described<br>THEN set as subgoals<br>  1.  To generate the name for LVproperty<br>  2.  To describe LVtopic. |
| G6 | IF the goal is to describe LVtopic<br>THEN set as a subgoal to generate the name for LVtopic. |
| G7 | IF the goal is to describe LVrelation<br>and LVrelation describes ongoing LVaction<br>and LVaction is currently happening<br>THEN set as subgoals<br>  1.  To generate *is*<br>  2.  To generate the name for LVaction<br>  3.  To generate *ing*. |
| G8 | IF the goal is to describe LVrelation<br>and LVrelation describes ongoing LVaction<br>and LVaction has finished<br>THEN set as subgoals<br>  1.  To generate *was*<br>  2.  To generate the name for LVaction<br>  3.  To generate *ing*. |

**Table 7.1**   (*continued*)

| | |
|---|---|
| G9 | IF the goal is to describe LVrelation<br>and LVrelation describes completed LVaction<br>and LVaction has just completed<br>THEN set as subgoals<br>  1.  To generate *has*<br>  2.  To generate the name for LVaction<br>  3.  To generate *ed*. |
| G10 | IF the goal is to describe LVrelation<br>and LVrelation describes completed LVaction<br>and LVaction has been completed for some time<br>THEN set as subgoals<br>  1.  To generate *had*<br>  2.  To generate the name for LVaction<br>  3.  To generate *ed*. |

to decompose the problem and what phrase-structure patterns to use. These problem-solving operators are realized as goal-structured productions in ACT. The phrase structure that is ubiquitous in natural languages derives from hierarchical goal structures.

GENERATION PRODUCTIONS: AN EXAMPLE

Table 7.1 provides a set of productions that will generate a small fragment of English. Production G1 generates the main clause of a subject-verb-object structure, productions G2–G6 generate noun phrases (by expanding on various attributes of the topic of the noun phrase), and productions G7–G10 generate verb-auxiliary structures. There are many simplifications in this production set, such as the fact that the verb productions do not test for number or that G3 and G4 capture only two of a complex constellation of principles for using definite and indefinite articles. But these simplifications are inessential to the points being made here. Also, for purposes of readability, linguistically mnemonic labels like LVagent have been used. However, the reader should not be deceived by these labels into thinking that there is anything language-specific in the way the production-system interpreter processes these productions.

The noun-phrase rules are ordered according to specificity. The first rule that would apply if legal is G2, since this contains the most specific information in its condition. Then G3 and G4, which test for a specific property, would be ordered next before

G5, which tests for any property. Finally, G6 simply retrieves the category for the object. Because of its specificity rules, ACT will generate a noun-phrase matrix with the most complex and specific attributions most external and the simplest attributions internal, ending with the category information about category membership (that is, the noun). Thus ACT's conflict-resolution principles predict the "nouniness" ordering that has been observed of natural languages (Vendler, 1968), that the more nounlike descriptions tend to occur closest to the noun. The basic claim is that the less nounlike descriptors require a more complex pattern specification in the productions that retrieve them, and therefore their selection will be favored in conflict resolution. Because they are selected first they will be inserted more externally in the noun phrase.

Figure 7.1 illustrates the hierarchical goal structure that would underlie generation of the sentence *The smart lawyer who has sued the rich doctor is buying an expensive car*. The meaning structure underlying the generation of this sentence is illustrated in Figure 7.2. The generation began with production G1 matching the goal to communicate proposition P3. This was unpacked into the subgoals of describing the agent X, the buying relation, and the object Y. Any of productions G2–G6 could match the goal of describing X, but G2 was the most specific and so applied first. It set the subgoals of again describing X, of generating *who*, of describing the suing relation, and of describing Z. The production set would continue to unpack the goals in a left-to-right, depth-first manner and so turn to describe X. This time G2 could not apply because of data refractoriness, so G3 would apply to generate the subgoals of saying *the*, followed once again by describing X. The rest of the goal tree in Figure 7.1 was similarly generated.

### COMPILATION AND TRANSFORMATION

While the production set in Table 7.1 is relatively elegant in that it reduces the knowledge to a minimal set of general rules, the rules underlying language generation probably are often more specific. For instance, it is reasonable to propose that composition forms rules like:

IF the goal is to describe LVobject
    and LVobject is known to the listener
    and LVobject has LVproperty that is to be described
THEN set as subgoals
    1.  To generate *the*
    2.  To generate the name for LVproperty
    3.  To generate the name for LVobject.

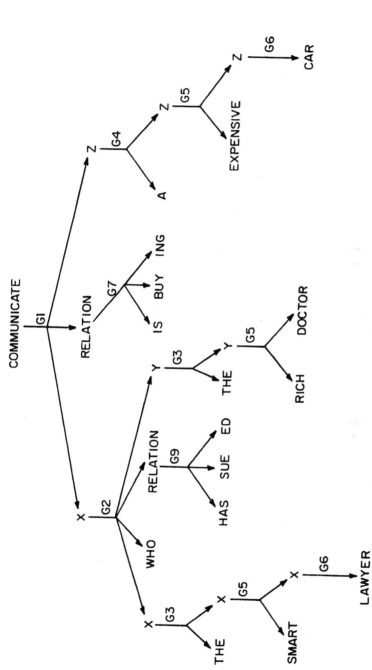

**Figure 7.1** *The flow of control in the hierarchical goal structure underlying generation of the sentence* The smart lawyer who has sued the rich doctor is buying an expensive car.

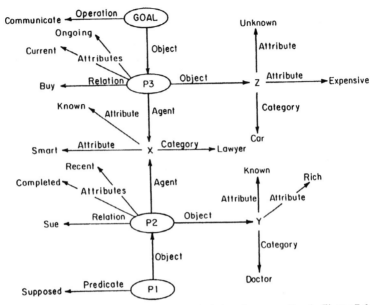

**Figure 7.2**   *The meaning structure underlying the generation in Figure 7.1.*

This one production would be able to generate the phrase *The rich doctor*, which required three productions in Figure 7.1. This production speeds up generation considerably and greatly reduces the demand on working memory for retrieving information about goal structure. The original productions that gave rise to compiled productions like this would still be around but would only apply in unusual circumstances where none of the compiled productions would.

These hierarchical goal structures permit the computation of transformations.[3] For instance, consider the question transformation in English that converts *The lawyer is buying the car* into *Is the lawyer buying the car?* The following production generates this transformation, starting with a queried meaning structure.

> IF the goal is to question whether the proposition (LVrelation LVagent LVobject) is true
> THEN set as subgoals
>     1.   to plan the communication (LVrelation LVagent LVobject)
>     2.   to move the first word in the description of LVrelation to the beginning
>     3.   to execute the plan.

This production would generate the declarative sentence, transform it to question form, then say the transformed sentence. Thus ACT's planning and transformation processes (see Chapter 4) underlie the transformational component of English.[4] The compilation process can apply to this goal structure too, and it could create the following production, which compiles out the planning:

> IF the goal is to question whether the proposition (LVrelation
>    LVagent LVobject) is true
> and LVrelation describes ongoing LVaction
> and LVaction is currently happening
> THEN set as subgoals
>    1. To generate *is*
>    2. To describe LVagent
>    3. To generate the name for LVrelation
>    4. To generate *ing*
>    5. To describe LVobject.

In this case, information controlling generation of the auxiliary verb *is* has migrated to the main generation production. The previous production planned a sentence, transformed it, and then executed it; the current production directly generates the question. Such a compiled production would lead to more automatic and less resource-demanding sentence generation.

## SIGNIFICANT PROPERTIES OF LANGUAGE GENERATION

This example illustrates some of the properties of language generation as developed in the ACT* framework. Language generation is similar in character to other cognitive activities, and its structure is basically a problem-solving one. Sentences are generated by decomposing goals successively until achievable goals are reached. This produces the hierarchical structure of language. Transformations can apply to generation plans just as to other problem-solving plans. We tend to associate slow, conscious, and effortful processing with problem solving and automatic processing with language generation. However, there are many problem-solving situations where behavior is automatic (for example, expert computer text editing—Card, Moran, and Newell, 1980) and situations where language generation is effortful, as in speaking a foreign language. The issue of conscious effort versus automaticity is one of practice, not one of problem solving versus language.

It is useful to consider how the ACT theory handles the insertion of lexical items into the sentence. Insertion of function words (such as *the*) and inflections (such as *-ed*) is specified, like word order, by templates in the action sides of productions for generation. Content words are retrieved from long-term memory through their meaning and inserted into the variable slots of these templates.[5] This implies that the semantic features controlling the insertion of a morpheme like *the* are implicit, hidden in the productions that generate *the*. Thus the speaker will not be able to tell us what *the* means. On the other hand, the speaker should have conscious and declarative access to the meaning of a content term like *doctor*.[6] The separation between function words and content words is consistent with the neurological evidence that word order and function words are affected by lesions to Broca's area and that content words are affected by lesions to Wernicke's area (Goodglass and Geschwind, 1976). There are, of course, always other interpretations of lesion results, but this evidence is at least suggestive. ACT is a considerable advance over our earlier work on language acquisition (LAS—Anderson, 1977) because it treats word order and function words together as parts of language templates. The earlier LAS found it much easier to learn languages that relied heavily on word order and did not deal well with highly inflected languages that relied less on word order. This is not a problem for the current system.

In ACT syntactic knowledge is encoded separately for generation and for comprehension. Productions for the two behaviors may have striking similarities, but they are distinct. This is an unavoidable consequence of the production system architecture. Knowledge is applied efficiently only by compiling specific versions of the knowledge for specific applications.

It is *possible* that at some past time common rules underlay the generation and comprehension of language. These would be declarative rules that would be applied interpretively as discussed in the previous chapter. For instance, it is not unreasonable to suppose that initial generation and comprehension of a class-taught foreign language refer often to a common set of declarative rules of syntax. However, as discussed in the previous chapter, such interpretive application of knowledge is inefficient. Efficiency comes when productions are compiled that are specific to the intended use of the language.

It is unlikely that in *first* language acquisition the representation of syntax for generation is ever the same as that for comprehension. Some studies (Fraser, Bellugi, and Brown, 1963; Petretic and Tweney, 1977) show that young children have access to a syntactic rule in receptive circumstances, but not in generative circumstances, and vice versa. Moreover, it is not just a case of comprehension being ahead of generation or vice versa. Some studies (Schustack, 1979) have shown that the child has access to some rules in comprehension and different rules in generation.

While generation and comprehension productions are distinct, some declarative knowledge is used in common by the two processes. For instance, the productions modeled in Table 7.1 referred to declarative facts about word-meaning connections. These same facts can be used in comprehension. My young son seems to have no vocabulary items in generation that he does not have in comprehension (excluding nonreferential terms like *the*, *by*, and so on). Comprehension may lay the groundwork for generation by building in many of the word-concept links that will be used.

There are probably other examples of structures shared by generation and comprehension. Semantic properties such as animateness may be declaratively represented and used by both. Word-class information is another candidate for common knowledge. However, all syntactic knowledge that has production embodiment is specific to use, and this is the major fraction of syntax.

The fact that adults are quite consistent in their syntactic rules in comprehension and generation might seem to contradict ACT*'s separation between comprehension and generation. Even for children inconsistency is probably the exception. However, this is not inconsistent with ACT since both abilities must deal with the same language. Indeed, generation and comprehension productions can be generated from the same learning experience. That they agree is only testimony that the acquisition mechanisms are successful in both cases. In addition, it is certainly possible that generation can be used to train comprehension and vice versa. For instance, comprehension productions can be acquired by using generated sentences. Also, failures of the comprehension productions to process self-generations can be used as evidence that these generations are in error.

The rest of this chapter is concerned with acquisition. There are four major sections in the discussion to follow. First, I will state some general assumptions about language learning, then I will report on two simulations of the acquisition of English.[7] The first simulation concerns how acquisition would proceed if it were not burdened by capacity limitations. This work has been reported elsewhere (Anderson, 1981c), but the current simulation is more advanced. In this effort, the concern is only with reproducing some of the most salient aspects of language-learning phenomena. The second simulation incorporates limitations one might assume for a child between the ages of one and three. Here the goal is to have the simulation produce sentences that correspond to those of the child. Finally, the chapter will discuss more generally ACT's language-acquisition facility, focusing on how it might account for the purported universals in the syntax of natural languages.

## Assumptions about Language Learning

### Meaning-Utterance Pairings

One basic assumption of this simulation is that the learner has access to pairings of an utterance and its meaning. This assumption underlies most formal analyses of language acquisition (Anderson, 1977; Langley, 1981; MacWhinney, 1980; Pinker and Lebeaux, in press; Selfridge, 1981; Wexler and Culicover, 1980). Such pairings can occur in several ways. The speaker may generate an utterance and the learner may figure out its meaning from the context. Or the learner may generate an utterance and get a correct expansion of that sentence. It is also possible for the learner to have memorized complete strings and to use these as targets against which to compare and correct his generations (MacWhinney, 1980). For instance, if the learner generates *goed* but recalls having heard *went* to communicate past tense, he has a basis for correcting his generation.

In the first simulation the program is always given correct pairings of meaning and sentence. This is an idealization in many ways. The learner will encounter many sentences that do not have their meanings identified, and he will have many to-be-expressed meanings without getting feedback as to the correct sentence. However, ACT would not learn on these trials, so the idealization avoids wasted cycles. A more serious problem is that in a realistic situation the learner would receive mispairings of sentence and meaning. The first simulation ignores this difficulty, but the second one will consider how a program can cope with as much as 50 percent mispairings. This is an idealization also in that the learner may be able to determine the meaning only of individual phrases, not whole sentences. However, the same learning mechanisms will work for phrase-meaning correlations, as will be seen in the child-language simulation.

Another assumption of this first learning simulation is that the program knows the meaning of a substantial number of the referential words before learning of syntax begins. There is evidence that children accomplish their initial lexicalization by having individual words paired directly with their referents (MacWhinney, 1980). (Certainly this was very much the case for my son.) This assumption allows us to focus on the learning of syntax; it is not essential to the working of the program. Again, the child-language simulation will consider what happens when the child starts without knowing the meanings of any words. In that simulation most of the initial learning is devoted to inducing word meaning; only later does the program pick up any interesting syntax. A function of the one-word stage in children's language acquisition may be to permit this initial lexicalization.

IDENTIFYING THE PHRASE STRUCTURE

Before ACT can learn from a paired sentence and meaning, it must identify the sentence's hierarchical phrase structure. For a number of reasons, inducing the syntax of language becomes easier once the phrase structure has been identified:

1. Much of syntax is concerned with placing phrase units within other phrase units.
2. Much of the creative capacity for generating natural-language sentences depends on recursion through phrase-structure units.
3. Syntactic contingencies that have to be inferred are often localized to phrase units, bounding the size of the induction problem by the size of the phrase unit.
4. Natural-language transformations are best characterized according to phrase units, as the transformational school has argued.
5. Finally, many of the syntactic contingencies are defined by phrase-unit arrangements. For instance, the verb is inflected to reflect the number of the surface-structure subject.

The ACT theory predicts that natural language will have a phrase structure. Given ACT's use of hierarchical goal structures, it has no choice but to organize sentence generation into phrases. The learning problem for the child is to identify the adult's hierarchical organization and make the hierarchical control of his behavior match that. Seen this way, language acquisition is just a particularly clear instance of acquiring a society-defined skill.

Also, even before it knows the language, ACT* cannot help but impose a hierarchical structure on a long string of words that it hears. That is, long temporal strings can only be encoded hierarchically, as was discussed in Chapter 2. ACT has a set of perceptual principles for chunking a string of words as it comes in. I will specify these principles in a language-specific manner, but it is an open question to what degree these principles are language-specific and to what degree they reflect general principles for perceptually chunking a temporal string. A production system has been created that will actually apply these principles to segment an incoming string. However, to ease the burden of detail in exposition and to get to the point, I will not present this production system but rather describe the principles it implements and their effect.[8] One simplification is that the system receives sentences segmented into morphemes, so this work completely ignores the issues of how the speech stream is segmented or how morphemes are discovered. This is also an assumption of other efforts (Langley, 1981; Pinker and Lebeaux, in press; Selfridge, 1981; Wexler and Culicover, 1980), and I do not feel that it distorts the essential character of syntax acquisition. As it turns out, this simplification can create problems that a child does not have. In breaking *kicked* into *kick* plus *ed*, we solved the segmentation problem for the program but create the problem of how to decide that *kick* and *ed* are closely related.

*The graph-deformation principle.* Natural-language sentences usually satisfy the graph-deformation condition (Anderson, 1977), which claims that the hierarchical structure of the sentence preserves the structure of the semantic referent. The graph-deformation condition is illustrated in Figure 7.3. Part (*a*) is a semantic-network representation for a set of propositions, and part (*b*) is a sentence that communicates this information. The network structure in (*a*) has been *deformed* in (*b*) so that it sits above the sentence, but all the node-to-node linkages have been preserved. As can be seen, this captures part of the sentence's surface structure. At the top level is the subject clause (node X in the graph), *gave*, *book*, and the recipient (node Y) identified as a unit. The noun phrases for X and Y are segmented into phrases according to the graph structure. For instance, the graph structure identifies that *lives* and *house* belong together in a phrase and that *big*, *girl*, *lives*, and *house* belong together in a larger phrase.

Because sentences usually satisfy the graph-deformation condition, one can use the semantic referent of a sentence to infer its surface structure. For instance, the graph deformation in (*b*)

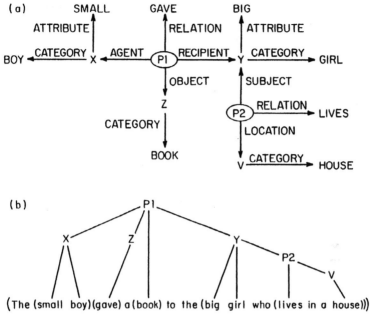

**Figure 7.3** *An illustration of the application of the graph-deformation condition.*

identifies the location of the terms for which there are meanings in the surface structure of the sentence. However, a term like *the* before *big girl* remains ambiguous in its placement. It could either be part of the noun phrase or directly part of the main clause. Thus, some ambiguity about surface structure remains and will have to be resolved on other bases. In LAS the remaining morphemes were inserted by a set of ad hoc heuristics that worked in some cases and completely failed in others. One of the goals in the current enterprise is to come up with a better set of principles for determining phrase boundaries.

Research on acquisition of artificial grammars provides empirical evidence for the use of the graph-deformation condition. Moeser and Bregman (1972, 1973) have shown that possession of a semantic referent is critical to induction of syntax, as would be predicted by the graph-deformation condition. Morgan and Newport (1981) show that the critical feature of the semantic referent is that it provides evidence for the chunking of elements, as predicted by the graph-deformation condition. Anderson (1975) demonstrated that languages with referents that systematically violated the graph-deformation condition are at least as difficult to learn as languages with no semantic referent.

The graph-deformation condition is violated by certain sentences that have undergone structure-modifying transformations that create discontinuous elements. Examples in English are: *The news surprised Fred that Mary was pregnant*, and *John and Bill borrowed and returned, respectively, the lawnmower*. Transformations that create discontinuous elements are more common in languages in which word order is less important than it is in English. However, the graph-deformation condition is a correct characterization of the basic tendency of all languages. The general phenomenon has been frequently commented upon and has been called Behaghel's First Law (see Clark and Clark, 1977).

Sentences that violate the graph-deformation condition cause two problems. First, such a sentence cannot be hierarchically organized by using the semantic referent, as was done in Figure 7.3. Fortunately, ACT has other principles for chunking. Second, it is necessary to learn the transformations underlying these sentences. As will be seen, ACT can learn such transformations but with difficulty.

*Other principles for phrase-structure identification.* The existence of nonreferential morphemes means that the graph-deformation condition in itself cannot provide an adequate basis for the phrase structuring of sentences. For instance, consider the placement of the article *a* between *gave* and *book* in Figure 7.3(*b*). Given that *a* has no meaning association, there is no basis for deciding whether it is part of the verb phrase or the noun phrase. To assign such morphemes to the appropriate phrases, the simulation will have to use nonsemantic cues.

A number of other cues can be used for chunking a string into phrases. First, there may be pauses after certain morphemes and not after others. Normal speech does not always have such pauses in the correct places and sometimes has pauses in the wrong places; however, pausing is a fairly reliable indicant of phrase structure (Cooper and Paccia-Cooper, 1980). Also, as Cooper and Paccia-Cooper discuss, there is information in the intonational contour as to the correct segmentation of a string. It is argued that parent speech to children is much better segmented than adult speech to adults (see de Villiers and de Villiers, 1978). Furthermore, ACT does have the facility to recover from the occasional missegmentation. Children also occasionally missegment (MacWhinney, 1980) and, of course, they recover eventually.

Another basis for segmentation relies on the use of statistics about morpheme-to-morpheme transitions. For instance, in

Latin the segment *ae* will more frequently follow *agricol,* with which it is associated, than it will precede *laud,* with which it is not associated. The differences in transitional frequencies would be sharper in Latin, which has a free word order, but they also exist in English. Thus, ACT can associate *ae* with *agricol* if *ae* has followed *agricol* more frequently than it has preceded *laud.* It strikes some as implausible to suppose that people could keep the necessary statistical information about morpheme-to-morpheme transitions. However, Hayes and Clark (1970) have shown that in listening to nonsense sound streams subjects can use differential transition probabilities as a basis for segmentation. Such information has also proven useful in computational models of speech recognition (Lesser et al., 1977).

The foregoing analysis has assumed that the learner has no grammatical rules for chunking the sentence string. However, in many situations the learner will have rules that can analyze a subchunk of the sentence, for example, a noun phrase. In that case, the grammatical analysis can be used to help anchor the chunking of the remainder.

*Application of segmentation rules.* In various simulations I have either used these segmentation rules to chunk the strings, or I have skipped their application and provided the learning program with chunked strings. Anderson (1981c) compares these two methods. Learning proves to be slower by almost an order of magnitude when the program must induce the segmentation, for two reasons. First, certain sentences come in without adequate basis for segmentation, particularly early in the learning history when clear-cut transition frequencies have not been compiled and there are no syntactic rules available to anchor the sentence chunking. Second, misparsings can occur, and these have to be overcome. The existence of misparsings in children's language is evidence that they have similar difficulties.

In the two simulations reported on here, the program was provided with prechunked strings. The rate of learning was slow enough to make another order of magnitude intolerable. All our simulations have worked with less than 10,000 utterance-meaning pairings, while a child probably encounters many more than that in a single month. Therefore in many ways our learning simulations are forced to be unrealistically fast.

## FORMATION OF INITIAL RULES

The initial chunking analyzes the sentence into chunks and assigns meaning to each chunk. These provide the necessary ingredients for the formation of language-generation rules. That is, the learner can form the rule that he should generate the structure associated with the chunk to communicate the meaning associated with the chunk. So, for instance, suppose ACT encounters the pairing of the meaning ((*carry*) (*horse X*) (*farmer Y*)) and the chunked string ((*equ + i*) (*agricol + as*) (*port + ant*)). Further, assume ACT knows that the meaning of *equ* is *horse*, the meaning of *agricol* is *farmer*, and the meaning of *port* is *carry*. Then, it would form the following rules:[9]

> IF the goal is to communicate ((carry) agent object)
> THEN set as subgoals
> > 1.  to describe the agent
> > 2.  to describe the object
> > 3.  to describe (carry).
>
> IF the goal is to describe (horse X)
> THEN generate (*equ + i*).
>
> IF the goal is to describe (farmer Y)
> THEN generate (*agricol + as*).
>
> IF the goal is to describe (carry)
> THEN generate (*port + ant*).

As a shorthand, these rules are denoted:

> (relation agent object) → "agent object relation" if relation
> > involves *carry*
> > (horse X) → *equ + i*
> > (farmer Y) → *agricol + as*
> > (carry) → *port + ant*.

As discussed in Chapter 6, the claim is not really that the learner forms such production rules from a single experience. Rather, a single experience would only create a declarative structure that could be interpreted analogically to guide later generations.[10] Production rules such as those above would eventually be compiled from the analogical application. However, again to speed up the rate of learning, the program creates these rules in production form right away.

In general, the simulation will learn in the following way. The program starts out not knowing any of the syntactic rules of the language. In this situation the program can either not generate anything or can fall back on some default order based on structure and salience in the meaning referent. There is some evidence that children use default word orders; that is, they generate word orders not found in adult speech (Clark, 1975; de Villiers and de Villiers, 1978; MacWhinney, 1980). In any case, the program will start to acquire rules like those above. These will require generalization and discrimination, which much of the learning history will be concerned with. Also, the program will encounter sentences that violate the graph-deformation condition and require learning transformations.

My simulations of child language acquisition have focused on the acquisition of rules for phrase structures and transformations and on the discrimination, generalization, and strengthening of these rules. The learning mechanisms involved are those of the previous chapter, but they have distinctive applications in the context of language acquisition. The next section, on the acquisition of a rather demanding fragment of English, illustrates this application.

## A Competence Example

The first simulation involved learning a fragment of English that had a heavy weighting of the verb-auxiliary system and question transformations. The sentences could contain the modals *can* (able), *could* (able), *should* (obligation), *would* (intention), *will* (future), *did* (emphatic), *do* (emphatic), *does* (emphatic), and *may* (possibility), with the corresponding meaning components in parentheses. These meaning components were not assigned to the terms, but rather had to be induced from the context. The sentences were also marked for tense and, optionally, for perfect, progressive, and stative. There were sets of four adjectives, eight nouns, six transitive verbs, and four intransitive verbs. Among the words were *man*, *hit*, *shoot*, and *run*, all of which have irregular inflections. Therefore another problem for the simulation was to learn the special inflections associated with these terms. Finally, the training set involved yes-no questions and wh-questions.

The learning history involved 850 pairings of target sentences with meaning structures. For each sentence the program generated a candidate sentence and then tried to learn by comparing its generation to the feedback provided by the target sentence. Table 7.2, later in the chapter, illustrates some of the sentences in that learning history along with the sentences generated by the program. The peculiar semantic character of the sentences derives from the fact that they were generated randomly within the syntactic constraints. By adjusting the random generation parameters, we made the sentences more complex on the average with time. However, this gradual increase in syntactic complexity is not particularly critical to performance of the simulation. See Anderson (1981c) for a rather similar record of success on a rather similar subset without gradually increasing syntactic complexity.

### THE FIRST SENTENCE

The first target sentence presented to the program was *The boys are tall;* its meaning structure is illustrated in Figure 7.4. All the relevant semantic information controlling this syntactic structure is present in this figure, including the subject's definite and plural features and the predicate's present and stative features. However, it is unreasonable to suppose that the learner actually knows that all these features are relevant to the communication. Suppose *stative* and *definite* are thought to be relevant, but not *present* or *plural*. Then we should represent the hierarchical structure imposed by the to-be-communicated structure as ((stative (*tall*)) (definite (*boy y*))).[11] In all meaning structures used in the simulation, the relational descriptors are embedded around the core relation (for example, *tall*) of the communication and similarly around the core nouns. This will produce a "nouniness" ordering on words in the noun matrix and a "verbiness" ordering on verbs in the verb matrix. As discussed earlier in the chapter, the same effect can be achieved by a data-specificity principle of production selection. However, this simulation did not have that conflict-resolution principle built into it in a way that reflected the specificity of the meaning structure. Therefore one might think of noun-phrase and verb-phrase embedding as implementing this aspect of the specificity principle.

The program had no syntactic rules at this point, so it fell back on the default rule of generating the terms it knew in the order they occurred in the semantic referent (generally ordered as

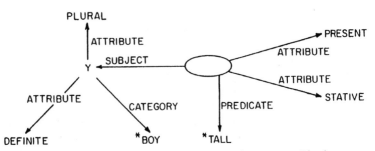

**Figure 7.4** *The meaning structure underlying the sentence* The boys are tall.

predicate-object or relation-agent-object). Since it knew the words for *tall* and *boy*, it generated *tall boy*. The target sentence it received as feedback after chunking was ((*the* (*boy* + *s*)) (*are* (*tall*))). Comparing the target sentence and the meaning led to creation of generation rules. From the noun phrase it formed the rules:

1. (Definite object) → "*the* object."
2. (*Boy* term) → "*boy* + *s*."

From the main clause, the following rule was learned:

3. (Predicate object) → "object predicate" if predicate ascribes *tall*.

and from the predicate it formed the rule

4. (Stative attribute) → "*are* attribute."
5. (*Tall*) → "*tall*."

Each of these rules[12] was entered with one unit of strength. These strength measures increased or decreased as the rules proved successful or not.

THE SECOND SENTENCE

The next pairing involved the target sentence ((*the* (*boy*)) (*shoot* + *s*) (*a* (*lawyer*))) and was paired with the meaning structure ((*shoot*) (definite (*boy* W)) (indefinite (*lawyer* V))). The program generated *shoot the boy* + *s lawyer*. The verb-agent-object ordering is just the default ordering. The noun phrase *the boys* was generated by application of rules 1 and 2 learned for the previous sentence.

The program formed rules to handle the cases for which there were only default orderings:

6. (Relation agent object) → "agent relation object" if the relation is about *shoot*.
7. (*Shoot*) → "*shoot* + *s*."
8. (Indefinite object) → "*a* object."
9. (*Lawyer*) → "*lawyer*."

Rule 1, which was learned from the first sentence and which generated *the* in this context, was correct and so was strengthened by one unit. Rule 2, which inflected the noun with *s*, was incorrect and so was weakened to zero strength and disappeared.[13] An action discrimination was formed. A search was made for a feature that was true of the current context and not true of the previous use of *boy* + *s*. Although this was not the only difference, a random search retrieved the fact that the term was singular in the current context. So the following rule is formed:

10.   (*Boy* term) → "*boy*" if term is singular.

### THE FIRST TWENTY-FIVE SENTENCES

Some of the more interesting of the first twenty-five sentences are illustrated in Table 7.2. Note that sentence 9 is the first one in which ACT's generation matched the target sentence. It acquired the rule for *the* from the first sentence. From the sixth sentence it learned the agent-action ordering for *jump* and the *ed* inflection. From sentence 7 it learned the *s* inflection for *lawyer*. At this point all of the grammatical rules are specific to single concepts.

ACT's performance on the tenth sentence reveals that its performance on the ninth was luck. Here it uses the *s* inflection for *lawyer* when the noun is singular. It also incorrectly uses the *ed* inflection for *dance* (acquired from the third sentence). This leads to a set of three discriminations. The *s* inflection for *lawyer* is strong enough to justify a condition discrimination as well as an action discrimination:

11.   (*Lawyer* term) → "*lawyer* + *s*" if term is plural.
12.   (*Lawyer* term) → "*lawyer*" if term is singular.

It also makes an action discrimination to give the *s* inflection for *dance*. Contrasting sentence 3 with sentence 10, it selects the tense feature:

13.   (*Dance*) → "*dance* + *s*" if the tense is present.

In these discriminations ACT is just looking for some feature in the semantic or syntactic context where the correct and the incorrect applications differ. ACT is biased to detect differences closer to the discriminated term (for example, *dances* in rule 13) before more distant differences. So ACT will use the number of the subject noun to constrain the subject-noun inflection before it will consider the number of the object noun for that purpose. This reflects the principle of selecting discriminations according to level of activation, which was discussed in Chapter 6.

**Table 7.2** *Sample sentences generated by ACT and the feedback provided*

| Sentence number | Sentence generated by ACT | Feedback from target sentence |
|---|---|---|
| 1 | TALL BOY | THE BOY S ARE TALL |
| 2 | SHOOT THE BOY S LAWYER | THE BOY SHOOT S A LAWYER |
| 3 | DANCE THE LADY | THE LADY DANCE ED |
| 6 | JUMP THE FARMER | THE FARMER S JUMP ED |
| 7 | GOOD THE LAWYER | THE LAWYER S ARE GOOD |
| 9 | THE LAWYER S JUMP ED | THE LAWYER S JUMP ED |
| 10 | THE LAWYER S DANCE ED | THE LAWYER DANCE S |
| 14 | KISS THE FARMER A BOY | THE FARMER S ARE KISS ING THE BOY S |
| 117 | THE TALL LAWYER HAS IS JUMP ING | THE TALL LAWYER HAS BEEN JUMP ING |
| 170 | SOME FARMER S HIT ED THE LADY | SOME FARMER S HIT THE LADY |
| 208 | THE DOCTOR MAY TICKLE ED THE FUNNY FARMER | THE DOCTOR MAY TICKLE THE FUNNY FARMER |
| 358 | THE SAILOR S MAY ARE BEING BAD | THE SAILOR S MAY BE BEING BAD |
| 472 | WHO WAS THE FUNNY LAWYER BEING HIT ED BY | WHO WAS THE FUNNY LAWYER BEING HIT BY |
| 632 | THE FUNNY SAILOR S IS KISSED BY THE BAD BOY | THE FUNNY SAILOR S ARE KISS ED BY THE BAD BOY |
| 751 | WHO HAVE RUN ED | WHO HAVE RUN |
| 770 | THE GIRL HAS RUN ED | THE GIRL HAS RUN |
| 790 | ARE SOME DOCTOR S BEING HIT ED BY SOME LADY S | ARE SOME DOCTOR S BEING HIT BY SOME LADY S |
| 806 | HAS A SAILOR RUN ED | HAS A SAILOR RUN |
| 811 | WHO MAY BE SHOOT ED BY ˙SOME GOOD LAWYER S | WHO MAY BE SHOT BY SOME GOOD LAWYER S |
| 815 | THE ANGRY BOY CAN BEING BAD | THE ANGRY BOY CAN BE BAD |
| 824 | THE SMART LADY S MAY RUN ED | THE SMART LADY S MAY RUN |
| 835 | SOME MEN DANCE | SOME MEN DANCE ED |
| 838 | SOME TALL GIRL S MAY SHOOT ED THE ANGRY SAILOR | SOME TALL GIRL S MAY SHOOT THE ANGRY SAILOR |
| 843 | WOULD THE BOY S HAVE RUN ED | WOULD THE BOY S HAVE RUN |

ACT will also consider elements in the semantic structure before it considers the syntactic structure (goal structure). Other than that, it chooses randomly from among the possible features. Therefore, the fact that all three discriminations were correct in the above example was somewhat a matter of luck.

Sentence 14 is a good illustration of an erroneous discrimination. Note that ACT had generated the term *a* where the target used *some*. In response to this difference ACT formed an action discrimination. This time, by chance, ACT noted that the successful use of *a* had not been in the context of *\*kiss*. Therefore it built the following erroneous rule:

19.  (Indefinite object) → "*some* object" in the context of *\*kiss*.

This rule later died when it led to an incorrect generation.

GENERALIZATION

The first generalizations occurred after sentence 25. At this point ACT had the following rules, among others:

20.  (Relation agent) → "agent relation" if relation involves *\*dance*.
13.  (*\*Dance*) → "dance + s" if present tense.
21.  (*\*Dance*) → "dance + ed."
22.  (*\*Dance*) → "dance + s" if present and singular agent.
23.  (*\*Dance*) → "dance" if present and plural agent.
24.  (Relation agent) → "agent relation" if relation involves *\*jump*.
25.  (*\*Jump*) → "jump + s" if present.
26.  (*\*Jump*) → "jump + ed."
27.  (*\*Jump*) → "jump + ing" if there is the context of progressive.
28.  (Relation agent) → "agent relation" if relation involves *\*play*.
29.  (*\*Play*) → "play + ed."

These rules are not a particularly parsimonious (let alone accurate) characterization of the language structure. Because of specificity ordering, they work better than might seem possible. For instance, rules 22 and 23 take precedence over 13, which does not test for number, so 13 will not cause trouble. Similarly, rules 13, 22, and 23 all take precedence over rule 21. Thus rule 21 will not be able to generate an *ed* inflection when the tense is present, even though 21 does not explicitly test for past tense.

ACT's generalization mechanism would like to generalize rules 20, 24, and 28 together. This would involve replacing the concepts *\*dance*, *\*jump*, and *\*play* by a variable. However, as discussed in the previous chapter, there must be a constraint on what fills the variable slot. Similarly, ACT wants to generalize rules 21, 26, and 29 by replacing the concepts *\*dance*, *\*jump*, and *\*play* by a variable and the words *dance*, *jump*, and *play* by a variable. However, to make such generalizations, it again needs a constraint on what may be substituted for these variables. ACT does not have any appropriate constraint stored in memory for any of these potential generalizations.

When faced with a number of potential generalizations, all of which require a variable constraint, ACT decides to create a word class. It created a class, which I will call verb, and stored in long-term memory the facts that *\*dance*, *\*jump*, and *\*play* (or, equivalently, *dance, jump, play*) are instances of this class. Having done so, it was in a position to create the following rules:

30. (Relation agent) → "agent relation" if relation involves a verb.
31. (*Verb) → "verb + *s*" if present tense.
32. (*Verb) → "verb + *ed.*"
33. (*Verb) → "verb + *s*" if present and singular.
34. (*Verb) → "verb" if present and plural.
35. (*Verb) → "verb + *ing*" if in the context of progressive.

In these rules verb refers to a word in the verb class, and *verb refers to its meaning.

The development of the verb word class does not stop after the first twenty-five sentences. As evidence builds up about the syntactic properties of other words, ACT will want to add additional words to the class. A major issue is when words should be added to the same class. It is not the case that this occurs whenever two rules can be merged, as above. The existence of overlapping declensions and overlapping conjugations in many languages would result in disastrous overgeneralizations. ACT considers the set of rules that individual words appear in. It will put two words into a single class when

1. The total strength of the rule for both words exceeds a threshold indicating a satisfactory amount of experience. Thus, one does not form class generalizations until a sufficient data base has been created.
2. A certain fraction (currently two-thirds) of the rules that have been formed for one word (as measured by strength) has been formed for the other word.

When such a class is formed, the rules for the individual words can be generalized to it. Also, any new rules acquired for one word will generalize to others in that class. Once a class is formed, new words can be added according to criteria (1) and (2). Further, two classes can be merged, again according to the same criteria. Thus, it is possible to gradually build up large classes, such as the first declension in Latin (see Anderson, 1981c).

The word-specific rules are not lost when the class generalizations appear. Furthermore, one form of discrimination is to create a rule that is special for a word. For instance, if the general rule for pluralization does not apply for *man*, one action discrimination would be to propose that *men* is the special plural form for *man*. Because of the specificity ordering in production selection, these word-specific rules will be favored when applicable. This means that the system can live with a particular word (such as *dive*) that is in a general class but has some exceptional features.

The creation of word classes could be a language-specific operation, but it is possible that there are other cases of class formation in nonlinguistic skill acquisition. Most constraints on variables involve use of properties that are already stored with the objects. In the bridge generalization discussed in the preceding chapter, the variable cards were constrained by the fact that they were touching honors. Rules for acting on general (variabilized) objects (for example, *throwing*) make reference to the objects' physical properties (say, size and weight). Word classes are arbitrary. The only features their members have in common is that the same set of syntactic rules apply to them. It is tempting to think that adjectives and verbs have distinctive semantic properties, but this may not be so (see Maratsos and Chaikley, 1981; MacWhinney, in press, for discussion). For instance, why should *active* be an adjective and *think* a verb? The arbitrariness of word classes is even clearer in other languages, where nouns are almost randomly divided among declensions and verbs among conjugations.[14]

Robert Frederking (personal communication) has argued that arbitrary nonlinguistic classes do occur in game playing. There are arbitrary classes of pieces determined only by their function in the game. In the game of Hi-Q he induced the existence of four classes of pieces. Having those four classes was essential to his being able to win the game.

### THE FINAL PHRASE-STRUCTURE RULES

It is useful to examine some of the sets of rules that ACT possessed after 850 sentences. Among the word classes it formed was the noun class, which included all the nouns. The final rules for this class were:

34. (*Noun term) → "noun + s." (11)
35. (*Noun term) → "noun" if singular. (511)
36. (*Noun term) → "noun + s" if plural. (385)
37. (*Noun term) → *"men"* if plural and *noun = *man.* (71)

To the right of each rule is its eventual strength. Rule 34 is a residual rule that will always be blocked by the others according to specificity. Rules 35 and 36 are the standard rules for plural and singular inflection. Rule 37 is an exception that was formed by an action discrimination from 36.

In contrast to the noun word class, which had a relatively parsimonious structure, the rules for inflection of the perfect aspect as *has, had,* or *have* had a relatively complex structure. Figure 7.5 is an attempt to illustrate the structure of these rules. Each terminus in the discrimination tree represents a single production; the number beside it is its strength. The paths through the network reflect the operation of conflict resolution in choosing a production. The tests involving class 4750 and class 3795 are tests of whether perfect occurs in the context of a modal. By the

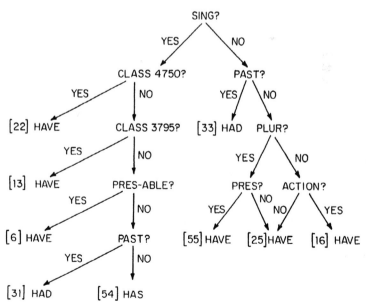

**Figure 7.5**  *A discrimination network specifying the various rules learned for inflecting perfect tense.*

same generalization process that led to formation of word classes, ACT has formed classes of modal contexts. Class 4750 contains the modals *would, should,* and *may.* Class 3795 contains the modals *do, did, will,* and *could.* Eventually, they would have been collapsed into a single class, but that had not yet occurred by sentence 850. Also present–able *(can)* appears in Figure 7.5 as a separate test because it has not been merged into a modal class. The nine rules in the figure lead to nearly perfect performance on the perfect. However, they could have been replaced by the following three rules:

(Perfect action) → *had* action if past tense.
(Perfect action) → *has* action if present and singular.
(Perfect action) → *have* action.

Because of specificity, the last rule would apply only if the first two did not. Given its learning history, ACT has worked its way to a more complex characterization. In general, rules derived from language learning are not likely to be the most parsimonious, nonredundant characterization of the language. This is an important way in which the conception of language based on ACT differs from the conception promoted in linguistics. Parsimony has been applied in linguistics to a too narrow range of phenomena, and the result is a seriously misleading characterization of language (see Chapter 1).

### Syntactic versus Semantic Discrimination

The production set for perfect in Figure 7.5 is in error in that it tests the semantic subject (agent) of the sentence for number rather than the syntactic subject. This means the simulation would generate *The boy + s has been hug + ed by the girl,* where the number of the verb agrees with the number of the syntactic object.[15] There are a number of places where ACT has a similar error for other verbal constructions. This derives from the assumption that the semantic structure is more active than syntactic structure and consequently ACT would consider a discrimination involving the semantic structure first. Situations where the number of the semantic and of the syntactic subject is different are sufficiently rare that it takes a long time for ACT to form the right discrimination. Eventually it would, but it failed to achieve this for the perfect construction in the first 850 sentences.

This is somewhat distressing, because I know of no cases in the child-language-acquisition literature where children made this particular error. Perhaps the assumption about precedence of semantic features is incorrect. It is also possible that children generate such errors covertly, as will be discussed more fully in the section on the child simulation.

### ACQUISITION OF TRANSFORMATIONS

ACT needs to get its syntactic rules clear before it is ready to deal with question transformations. Actually, the subject question does not involve learning a transformation. Given the meaning structure ((progressive (*hit*)) (query X) (definite (*boy* Y))), ACT would generate by its subject-verb-object rule *? was hitting the boys*. The question mark indicates that it failed to have a lexical item for query. Comparing this with the feedback *Who was hitting the boys?*, ACT would infer that query is realized as *who*. However, the other two constructions are more difficult: *Was the girl hitting the boys?* and *Who was the girl hitting?* In both cases the graph-deformation condition is violated in moving the participle *was* from the verb matrix to the front of the sentence. Early in the learning history, ACT typically refused to try to learn from a sentence that violated the graph-deformation condition because it could not formulate any phrase-structure rule to accommodate it and could not see a way to transform the output of existing phrase-structure rules. However, as its phrase-structure rules became more adequate, it was eventually able to propose a transformation.

Figure 7.6, showing ACT's first postulation of a question

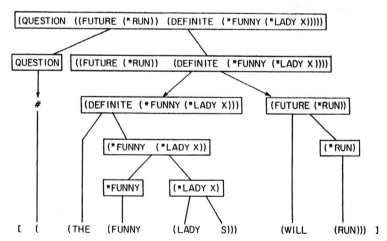

**Figure 7.6**  *The goal structure generated for the sentence that led to the first question transformation.*

transformation, illustrates the decomposition of the meaning structure into components according to the rules ACT possessed at this time. Not knowing how to realize the question element, ACT simply tried to generate the embedded proposition that was questioned. This was realized as *The funny ladies will run*. The target sentence came in chunked as (*Will* (*the* (*funny* (*lady* *s*))) (*run*)). ACT noticed that it could achieve the target sentence by simply rearranging the structure of its generation. This is one of the circumstances for learning a transformation. Therefore it formed the following planning rule:

> IF the goal is to communicate (question assertion)
> THEN plan the generation of assertion
>     and move the first morpheme in the relation matrix to the
>       front
>     and then generate the sentence.

As discussed at the beginning of this chapter, this planning rule might eventually be replaced by a compiled rule of the form:

> IF the goal is to communicate (question (relation agent))
>     and the tense is future
> THEN set as subgoals
>     1.  to generate *will*
>     2.  to describe agent
>     3.  to describe relation.

A separate compiled rule would be learned for all frequent sentence structures. The planning rule above would remain for these infrequent constructions that had not been compiled.

ACT offers an explanation for an interesting aspect of the question transformation. Note that the general transformation rule does not apply to the simplest verb constructions. For example, applied to the sentence *The boy kicked the sailor*, this rule would produce the ungrammatical *Kicked the boy the sailor?* Rather, the best way to create a question is to propose a *do*-insertion: *Did the boy kick the sailor?* The acquisition of this rule can be explained by supposing that the general planning rule was applied (probably covertly) and led to this incorrect question form. Then the discrimination process would be evoked to produce the right action, as shown by the following planning production:

> IF the goal is to communicate (question ((*verb) agent object))
>     and the tense is past
>     and there is no modal, perfect, or progressive aspect
> THEN plan the generation of ((*verb) agent object)
>     and then insert *did* at the front
>     and replace verb + *ed* by verb
>     and then generate the sentence.

Compiled, this becomes

> IF the goal is to communicate (question ((*verb) agent object))
>     and the tense is past
>     and there is no modal, perfect, or progressive
> THEN set as subgoals
>     1.  to say *did*
>     2.  then to describe agent
>     3.  then to say verb
>     4.  then to describe object.

Thus our compiled rule for *did* insertion is no different from any of the other compiled rules for the question transformation. The same learning principles can deal with *did* insertion without any special-case heuristics.

### SUMMARY OF ACT's PERFORMANCE

Figure 7.7 summarizes ACT's progress. The number of syntactic errors per sentence are plotted against the number of sentences studied. Since the complexity of sentences tends to increase through the learning history (because of a bias in the random sentence generator), there are more opportunities for errors on later sentences. Thus the rate of learning is actually faster than the graph implies. The sentences in Table 7.2 are a sample biased to represent errors, because these are the more interesting cases. The table lists all the errors made in the last hundred sentences. As can be seen, the final errors almost exclusively involve irregular verbs in less frequent constructions. With time ACT would learn these too, but it has not yet had enough opportunities to learn them. Children also have a long history of residual trouble with irregular constructions.

One type of error produced by the program seems unlike the errors made by children. This is illustrated in sentence 117, where the program generated the verb matrix *has is jumping* rather than *has been jumping*. It had learned from previous sentences that *is* plus *ing* communicates the progressive in the con-

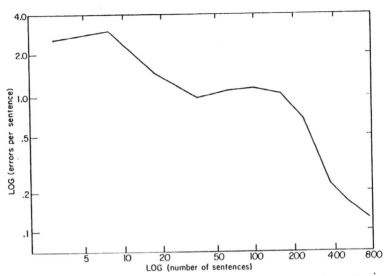

**Figure 7.7** *The mean number of errors per sentence generated as a function of the number of sentence-meaning pairings.*

text of present singular. The program has not yet learned that the element *is* becomes *been* in the context of perfect. Thus, it is a perfectly (pun intended) reasonable generalization. Perhaps children remember word-to-word transitions and are unwilling to venture an infrequent transition (such as *has is*) except in the context of a strong rule. This idea will be employed in the section on child language.

In summary, this example simulation should make a fairly convincing case for the power of ACT's language-acquisition system. Except for limitations of time and computer memory, it is unclear whether there are any aspects of a natural language that this program cannot acquire. The full import of this claim is a little uncertain, however. The success of the learning program depends on properties of the semantic referent, and it is difficult to know whether I have built in solutions to critical problems in the structure of the semantic referent. This question can be resolved by using the same semantic referent to learn very different languages, but that project will require a great deal of effort.

## Child Language

The performance generated by the previous simulation is definitely unchildlike in ways other than its vocabulary choice. Its rate of initial progress is rapid, and its length of utterance is unbounded from the start. Every sentence it generates is a serious attempt to reproduce a full-length English sentence and, as we see in sentence 9, it can hit the target early. In contrast, utterances generated by children are one word in length for a long while, then two words for quite a while; only after considerable experience do longer utterances start to appear. The first multiword combinations are clearly not English sentences. (My son's first noted two-word utterance was "more gish"—translated "I want more cheese.")

### Constraints on Child Language Acquisition

It would be easy to conclude that children are simply less capable than ACT, but this would fail to understand what is going on. The preceding simulation has numerous unrealistic aspects, and the child's behavior is largely in response to the reality of his situation.

*Vocabulary learning and rule learning.* Unlike the previous simulation, the child starts out knowing neither the pronunciation of the words nor their meaning. Therefore, a lot of the initial learning is drill and practice, setting in place the prerequisites to syntax acquisition. Also the child cannot immediately create compiled productions for generation. It will take some time to compile the rules, and in the meantime executing them will impose extra short-term memory burdens. Indeed, generating a single word is probably not a single compiled unit for a child. For instance, I noted for my son that the quality of generation of a word deteriorates when it is preceded by a word, and the more syllables there are in that first word, the more the quality deteriorates.

*Rate of learning.* In addition to slow compilation, there are limitations on the amount of information the child can learn from a meaning-utterance pairing. In the preceding simulation, the program acquired six rules from sentence 14. Acquiring each rule requires holding and inspecting a trace of the meaning, the sentence generation, and the target sentence. A child would be lucky if he could hold enough information to enable one rule to be formed.

*Quality of training data.* Because of cognitive limitations (short-term memory) and because of noisy data (ungrammatical utterances, sentences that do not correspond to the assumed meaning), the process of identifying the meaning-utterance correspondences is much more precarious for a child and there will be many erroneous correspondences. Therefore, the child must proceed with a lot more caution.

*Short-term memory limitations and conceptual limitations.* There are severe limitations on the intake and analysis of a meaning-sentence pairing in the absence of comprehension of the sentence. According to traditional assertions and the discussion in Chapter 3, a child can hold five or fewer chunks in memory. Early in language these chunks may be a morpheme or less; later they may be as large as a word; still later they will be the length of comprehended phrases. Moreover, when a child's short-term memory is overloaded, it will be selective in what it retains. Anderson (1975) proposed the *telegraphic-perception hypothesis* that children tend to retain the words they know and the semantically important words. The child presented with *The dog is catching the ball* might record *doggy catch ball*. Small wonder, then, that his utterances have the same telegraphic quality.

In addition to a limitation on the strings he encodes, there is a limitation on the meaning structures the child can pair with these utterances. These are limitations of memory capacity but also of conceptual development. If the child is not perceiving possession in the world he can hardly acquire the syntactic structures that communicate it. Slobin (1973) has argued that much of the timing of the child's syntactic development is determined by his conceptual development.

*Understanding the nature of language.* The child's appreciation of the function of linguistic communication is probably also developing as he acquires language. In the preceding simulation, and indeed in the forthcoming one, it is assumed that the learner is always operating with the motivation to learn the full communicative structure of language. However, a child may well start out with more limited goals, and restrictions on his utterances may reflect only his aspiration level.

*Impact of the constraints.* It is important to determine what happens to the performance of the ACT language-learning program when the child's situation is better approximated. The character of its generations should better approximate the character of the child's generations. And it should still eventually learn a natural language just as a child does. This second point is not trivial. The child initially produces (and presumably learns) a language which is not the target language. His rules are not simply a subset of the adult grammar, they are different from the adult grammar. Therefore, in acquiring the correct rules, the child must overcome his initial formulations.

Are initial rules hindrances, neutral, or stepping stones to acquiring the correct rules? For instance, where the adult will model *Mommy kisses Daddy*, the child might generate *Mommy kiss* or *Daddy kiss*. In ACT these initial rules can either be replaced by stronger and more specific rules, or transformations can be acquired to convert their output into more adequate expressions.

### SIMULATION OF J.J.

ACT was applied to simulating the early linguistic development of my son, J.J., who began to use words at twelve months and was beginning the two-word stage at eighteen months. When the final draft of this book was written, J.J. was twenty-four months and was producing some fairly interesting three-word and some occasional four- or five-word utterances (*I need more water, Daddy; Mommy coming back in a minute*).[16] To this point the simulation did a fair job of keeping up with his development and reproducing the character of his generations (as well as reproducing some of the generations themselves).

At the time of writing, the simulation had been exposed to 6,000 sentences, which is presumably what J.J. would encounter in several days. Given that the program has reproduced a great deal of the syntactic development from twelve to twenty-four months, there are still some unrealistic idealizations left in it. However, this is a more realistic simulation than the first in a number of ways.

*Vocabulary learning and rule learning.* The simulation does not start out knowing the meanings of words; it must infer these from the sentence-meaning pairings. Furthermore, a word is not considered a chunk until it has achieved a criterion frequency of exposure (frequency divided by number of syllables must be 10 in the current simulation). The consequence of trying to generate a nonchunk word is that the rest of the generation plan is destroyed. Many times the program started to produce *Bye-bye Daddy*, but had its capacity used up in generating *Bye-bye*. The program much sooner learned to generate *Hi Daddy*, because *Hi* has a single syllable. Interestingly, this was the ordering observed in J.J.'s learning, even though we said *bye-bye* to him (I regret to report) at least as often as *hi*.

Also, the program will not make a transition between two words unless it has encountered that transition a criterion frequency (five times in the current simulation) or the rule that calls for the transition has achieved a criterion strength (ten units in the current simulation). Thus, the simulation edits generations from weak rules according to its memory of correct utterances and so avoids expressions like *has is jumping* (see the discussion in the previous section). Consequently, the program's initial utterances are repeats of sequences in the adult model; only later does it come up with novel utterances. The same was observed of J.J. His first uses of *more* were utterances like *more gish* (*I want more cheese*) and *more nana* (*I want more banana*), and only later did he produce novel generations that had not been modeled. An example of a novel combination is *more high*, by which he asked to be lifted high again. (Please note that *high* does not refer to drug use.) Interestingly, when he had wanted to be lifted high before this point, he simply would say *more* or *high*.

An interesting consequence of these assumptions can be illustrated with utterances like *Russ bark* or *Mommy bark*. For a while, the simulation was not capable of these two-word transitions, nor was J.J. This simply reflected the weakness of the rule authorizing this two-word transition. Thus J.J. and the program would generate only one of these two words. If the simulation generated this plan and went through it left to right, it would generate *Russ* or *Mommy*. However, J.J.'s one-word utterance in this situation was *bark*, although he knew the words *Mommy* and *Russ*, and we had modeled the two-word transitions many times. Therefore, the program has a "subgoal omitter"; if it came upon a subgoal that was going to exhaust its resources and a more important part of the utterance remained, it simply omitted that subgoal and went on to the more important part. Similar ideas have been proposed by Bloom (1970). Thus, in our program, as in J.J., the first generations were *bark* and only later did they become agent + *bark*. The program regarded the relational term as most important, then the object, and finally the agent. This reproduced J.J.'s ordering, although it is reported (MacWhinney, 1980) that many children prefer the agent. In the case of J.J.—an only child—it was usually obvious from context who the agent was, and this perhaps accounts for his preference. MacWhinney (1980) reports that some children will move the most important term forward out of its correct position, but we did not observe any clear cases of this with J.J.

Another interesting consequence of the assumptions concerns the frequency of generations of the structure operator + object versus object + operator. Braine (1963) has characterized early child speech as being formed by these two structures, and indeed early on the J.J. simulation did create two word classes, one consisting of first-position operators and one consisting of all second-position operators. However, in the early speech of J.J. and the program, the operator + object construction was more frequent because the operators were more frequently used and compiled more rapidly. Thus the first word in the operator + object sequence was less likely to exhaust capacity than the first word in the object + operator sequence.

*Rate of learning.* In line with the earlier discussion on rate of learning, the program was limited to learning one rule per meaning-string presentation. Because the utterances it worked with were so short, there was often just a single rule to learn. However, when there were multiple rules to learn, the program chose the left-most rule with the smallest span. For instance, if given the generation *Doggy chases kitty* and it did not know the meaning for *doggy*, it would learn this lexical item in preference to learning the sequence agent-action-object. This ordering was produced by a program that scanned the sentence in a left-to-right depth-first manner looking for the first to-be-learned structure. It seemed reasonable that the program should focus on the pieces before learning how to put the pieces together. One consequence was that the utterances first produced tended to be short and fragmentary.

*Quality of training data.* When the program failed to generate any utterance or when it failed to match the target utterance, 50 percent of the time it received incorrect feedback as to the correct utterance. (When incorrect feedback is given, another random utterance is chosen from the model's repertoire.) Even when its generations matched the target utterance, it was given incorrect feedback 20 percent of the time. The smaller percentage in this second situation reflects the idea that learner and model are often not in correspondence when the learner cannot express himself, but are more often in correspondence when the learner does express himself correctly. One consequence of this is that when the program does hit upon the correct rule, that rule is generally reinforced.

The program takes various measures to protect itself from noisy data. When it detects too great a disparity between its generation and the model's, it just refuses to learn. More important, it does not weaken the rules that led to generation of the mismatched sentences.

Incorrect feedback creates the greatest problems for acquisition of word-meaning pairings. Almost 50 percent of the program's hypotheses as to a word's meaning are incorrect. Therefore, a word-meaning correspondence is encoded only after a certain number—currently three—of consistent reinforcements. So set, there was one occasion when a wrong hypothesis was formed, but the program kept accumulating information about word-meaning pairings and eventually the correct hypothesis acquired greater frequency and replaced the wrong one.

*Short-term memory limitations and conceptual limitations.* This simulation's limitations on sentence complexity and conceptual complexity were relatively unsystematic. Whenever we could identify a conceptualization that was part of J.J.'s repertoire and that we found ourselves communicating in our utterances, I added it to the array of sentence-meaning pairings that were presented to the program. For instance, at the 1,500th pairing (I equate this pairing with J.J.'s development at about seventeen months), we had evidence that J.J. could understand the construction involving a relation between people and their body parts, and we were practicing constructions like *J.J.'s nose, Mommy's ear, Russ's eye, Daddy's hand*. Therefore "possesser bodypart" constructions were included in the presentation set along with an appropriate semantics after the 1,500th pairing.

*Understanding the nature of language.* There was no attempt to model J.J.'s growing appreciation of the function of language, solely for lack of relevant ideas. However, there is evidence that he did not start out appreciating the full communicative power of language. There was a curious early stage (around thirteen–fourteen months) when J.J. would only use his utterances descriptively to name objects and not to request them. He had the concept of nonverbal request, as he was a very effective pointer. It was frustrating to us as parents that our son could want something, be crying for it, have the name in descriptive mode, and "refuse" to tell us what he wanted. It was a joyous day for us all when he pointed to a banana he wanted and said *nana*. Negation and question-asking came in even later, although J.J. understood both much earlier. His increase in appreciation of the communicative function of language is reflected (but not explained) in the growth in the type of constructions provided in the training sequence for the program.

PERFORMANCE OF THE J.J. SIMULATION

*Training data.* The total set of constructions presented to the simulation is described by the following pairings:

1. (Describe/request (*object/*property)) → "object/property" (such as "cookie," "up").
2. (Point out (*object)) → "this."
3. (Request (*more (*object X))) → "more object" ("more cheese").

4. (Request (*up/down* (*JJ* X))) → *"up/down JJ."*
5. (Describe (*see (*person X))) → *"hi person"* (*"hi Russ"*).
6. (Describe (*depart (*person X))) → *"bye-bye person"* (*bye-bye Daddy"*).
7. (Request/describe (*action (*person X))) → *"person action"* (*"Mommy jump"*).
8. (Describe (*property (*object X))) → *"property object"* (*"hot bagel"*).
9. (Negative conceptualization) → *"no conceptualization"* (*"no more Sally"*).
10. (Describe (bodypart (*person X)) → *"person part"* (*"Mommy nose"*).
11. (Describe (associate (*object 1 X)(*object 2 X))) → *"object 1 object 2"* (*"baby book"*).
12. (Describe/request (*verb (*agent X)(*object Y))) → *"agent verb object"* (*"daddy feed Russ"*).
13. (Describe/request (*direction (*agent X))) → *"agent go direction"* (*"JJ go down"*).
14. (Describe/request (*back (*agent X)(*object Y))) → *"agent put back object"* (*"Daddy put back blocks"*).
15. (Describe/request (*off (*agent X)(*object Y))) → *"agent turn off object"* (*"Sarah turn off Sally"*).
16. (Describe (*open/*close/*broken (*object X))) → *"object open/close/broken"* (*"door open"*).
17. (Question (location (object X))) → *"where's object"* (*"where's balloon"*).
18. (Describe/request (*up (agent X)(object Y)(location Z))) → *"agent put object up on location"* (*"Ernie put duck up on bed"*)
19. Delete agent in all requests.
20. Optional transformations: *put back* object → *put* object *back* *turn off* object → *turn* object *off.*
21. Optional transformation: replace inanimate object by *it.*
22. (Proposition location) → proposition *in* location (*"Mommy read book in playroom"*).

These constructions are given in the order they were introduced into the training sequence. As can be seen, there is an increase in complexity of both meaning and utterance. The first nine were introduced by the 1,500th pairing, which I equate with J.J.'s development at seventeen months. The next eight were introduced by the 3,000th pairing, which I equate with nineteen months. The last five pairings were introduced by the 4,000th pairing.

The system started out just learning single word pairings (construction 1). This is intended to model a true one-word stage in ability when the child is given or records only a single word and selects a single object as its referent. Construction 2 was introduced to account for our child's early tendency to present objects to us with the utterance *dis.* Construction 3 received a lot of modeling at the kitchen table: "Does J.J. want more cheese?" Sometimes we modeled just the two-word pairing "More apple juice?" and sometimes full sentences, but again the assumption was that J.J. extracted the critical two words from the longer utterances. The expression "up JJ" derives from our idiosyncratic use of "up with J.J." and "down with J.J." Although we did frequently use the more normal order "Does J.J. want down?" our son latched onto the other order.

Rules 12, 14, and 15 all describe agent-verb-object sequences that we started modeling with fairly high frequency. Until the twenty-first month, we heard only verb-object utterances from J.J. There are multiple hypotheses for the omission of the agent. He may have been modeling the command form, which omits the agent. Or he may have been omitting the most obvious term because of capacity limitations and to avoid blocking the critical verb.

Initially, the simulation was trained on requests with sentences that contained the agent. This corresponds to forms we sometimes used to J.J.—"Russ, drop the ball" or "Will J.J. give me the ball?" However, I decided at the 3,000th pairing that it was more appropriate to provide the simulation with the deleted-agent version of requests (rule 19). Whatever the justification for this midstream change, it demonstrated the learning program's ability to recover from mistraining. Rules 20 and 21 reflect optional transformations and so tap the program's ability to deal with constructions in free variation. In this case, if the program generated the equivalent expression (*Daddy put back ball* for *Daddy put ball back*), the program was not given feedback that it was incorrect, but was presented with the alternative form as another construction.

Note that function morphemes (*a, the -ed, -s,* and so on) are not part of the input to the program. This reflects the belief that J.J. did not initially record these items (the telegraphic-perception hypothesis). When he began echoing our phrases at the twenty-first month he often succeeded in echoing constructions and words he was not producing spontaneously. However, usually he omitted the function words. So for instance, "Russ is a good dog" would become "Russ good dog," and "Nicky goes to the doctor" would become (approximately) "Nicka go docka." The first function word he began to use productively was *it* (rule 21), at about twenty-two months. The articles (*a, the*) and *s* for pluralization and possessive only appeared in the

**Table 7.3** *Growth in the linguistic competence of the simulation*

| Number of pairings | Vocabulary size | Mean length of utterance |
|---|---|---|
| 1–500 | 12 | 1.00 |
| 501–1,000 | 31 | 1.00 |
| 1,001–1,500 | 39 | 1.09 |
| 1,501–2,000 | 44 | 1.13 |
| 2,001–2,500 | 54 | 1.16 |
| 2,501–3,000 | 65 | 1.26 |
| 3,001–3,500 | 77 | 1.24 |
| 3,501–4,000 | 97 | 1.26 |
| 4,001–4,500 | 110 | 1.23 |
| 4,501–5,000 | 122 | 1.41 |
| 5,001–5,500 | 136 | 1.50 |
| 5,501–6,000 | 142 | 1.58 |

twenty-fourth month.[17] In addition to slowly increasing the complexity of the training constructions, we increased the training vocabulary as J.J. appeared to understand more words. Undoubtedly the simulation's training vocabulary seriously underestimated the pool of words J.J. was working with. J.J.'s vocabulary is increasing so rapidly that it is impossible to keep an up-to-date inventory of all the words he understands. At seventeen months his vocabulary was approximately a hundred words. By sampling every tenth page of *Webster's Collegiate Dictionary* and adding 20 percent for items not included (*Grover, Milkbones,* and so on), we estimated that he had a 750-word vocabulary at twenty-four months.

RESULTS

Table 7.3 provides a summary of the J.J. simulation through the first 6,000 pairings (twenty-fourth month) in terms of vocabulary size and mean length of utterance. Compared to the previous simulations, the growth of linguistic competence was spectacularly slow. The mean length of utterance was calculated, omitting those cases where the program failed to generate anything. So, as in measures of mean length of utterance for children, this measure is bounded below at 1.0. As can be inferred, the first multiword utterances only began appearing after the 1,000th pairing. The following list gives some of the program's notable multiword utterances in the order generated during the first 6,000 pairings:

MORE BOTTLE                MOMMY READ
HI MOMMY                   WANNA GRAPES

| | |
|---|---|
| BYE DADDY | PLEASE MORE |
| DOWN JJ | DADDY GO DOWN |
| UP JJ | DADDY EAT COOKIE |
| RUSS WALK | DOOR CLOSED |
| MOMMY BARK | SARAH READ BOOK |
| NO MORE | MOMMY CHIN |
| NO MORE APPLE JUICE | ROGERS EAT ORANGE |
| NO MOMMY WALK | WHERE'S IT |
| GOOD FOOD | JJ GO DOWN, DADDY |
| NICE RUSS | ERNIE GO BY CAR |
| MOMMY TALK | WANNA IT |
| JJ COOK | READ BOOK |
| HOT FIRE | PLEASE MOMMY READ BOOK |
| DADDY GO UP | DADDY EAT BIG CRACKER |
| GO WALK | |

It is of interest that the program generates *No Mommy walk.* This is a generalization of the construction *No more apple juice* which has the form negation followed by conceptualization.

By the 3,000th utterance the simulation had merged *more, hi,* and *bye* into a single word class of prefix operators; *walk, bark, talk,* and *cook* into a class of postfix operators; and *down* and *up* into a third class. By the 4,000th utterance it had formed a class of transitive verbs. It is worth noting that the program's generations underestimate its grammatical competence. For instance, the program has agent-verb-object rules like *Mommy turn off Sally* or *Daddy put back blocks.* However, the rules and words have not been sufficiently practiced to appear in the generations. This is one advantage of a computer simulation over a child. That is, one can peer below the surface performance to see what the system really knows. (It also doesn't spit up in restaurants.)

It is interesting that the J.J. simulation has been run to the limit of the current implementation; there is just not any more memory in the SUMEX INTERLISP system the simulation is run on. Any further simulation will have to use a new system, and the implementation will have to be optimized for space efficiency. To do a realistic simulation requires storing a great many rules and information about many past sentences.

## SUMMARY

This simulation establishes that the same learning mechanisms that gave superhuman learning in the previous simulation can result in much better approximations of early child language when these mechanisms are constrained by the limitations believed to constrain the child. It was able to reproduce J.J.'s early two- and three-word utterances. However, the system is still at a very early stage of development, and much remains to be determined.

## Adequacy

This chapter has reported two simulation efforts to assess the adequacy of the ACT learning mechanisms for natural language. The first simulation showed that it was capable of acquiring a reasonable subset of natural language. The second showed that when constrained by reasonable information-processing limitations, it provides a good approximation to child language acquisition. These two demonstrations are in lieu of the impractical demonstration, that is, that the program can learn any natural language in a humanlike manner.

Wexler and Culicover (1980) have attempted an approximation of this goal for a rather different learning system. They showed that a set of learning mechanisms could acquire any transformational grammar that satisfied a good number of constraints. Their formal proof of this did not say anything about whether the course of language acquisition would approximate child language acquisition. Nonetheless, if natural languages satisfy these constraints, then they at least have a sufficiency proof for their learning scheme. Coming at the problem from this point of view, they actually are more interested in the constraints than the learning scheme. Although some of the constraints seem purely technical for purposes of achieving a successful proof, others are important claims about the universal properties of natural language.

While the Wexler and Culicover endeavor makes sense if one accepts their framework, it does not if one comes at the problem from the ACT point of view. If ACT is the right kind of model for language acquisition, there is no elegant characterization of what constitutes a natural language. A natural language is anything that the learning mechanisms can acquire, given meaning-sentence pairings. This is unlikely to be a member of some pristine formal class satisfying just a small number of elegant formal constraints.[18] Thus, while it is certainly worthwhile to identify the formal properties of languages that ACT can and cannot learn, a proof in the mold of Wexler and Culicover does not make much sense.

### LINGUISTIC UNIVERSALS

Wexler and Culicover propose that their constraints on natural language are linguistic universals. Chomsky popularized the idea that the syntax of all natural languages satisfies certain universal constraints and that natural languages are learnable only because of these constraints. There have been numerous proposals for what might be universal features of natural languages. If it could be established that such universals exist, it is often thought that they would be evidence for a language-specific acquisition device. This is because the universal properties are only meaningful in the context of acquiring language and would not have relevance in other learning situations.

An interesting question is whether the purported universals of natural language can be accounted for in the ACT scheme. This would provide another way of determining whether ACT is adequate to the properties of natural language. A number of general syntactic properties are often considered to be universals of natural languages. These include the facts that all languages have nouns and verbs, phrase structure, and transformations, and that transformations are cast with respect to phrase structure rather than word strings. All these features are also true of the languages learned by ACT. The fact that all languages have elements like noun and verb derives from the relation-argument structure of propositional units. The fact of phrase structures and transformations on these phrase structures derives from ACT's goal structure and planning structure.

However, some rather specific constraints have been suggested on the types of transformations that might apply. One of the more discussed constraints started out with some observations by Chomsky (1973) of what he called the A-over-A constraint. For instance, sentence 1 below seems acceptable while sentence 2 is not:

1. Which woman did John meet who knows the senator?
2. *Which senator did John meet the woman who knows?

These would be derived transformationally from 3 and 4, respectively:

3. John did meet (which woman) who knows the senator.
4. John did meet the woman who knows (which senator).

The constraint appeared to be that one could not extract a noun phrase for wh-fronting that was itself embedded within a noun phrase. Chomsky proposed in general that any extraction transformation must apply to the highest constituent that satisfies the structural description of that transformation. It is worth noting that wh-fronting can extract a term many levels deep if there are not intervening relative clauses:

5. Which woman does Mary believe that Bill said that John likes?

but that the identical semantic content becomes unacceptable if a relative clause is inserted:

6. *Which woman does Mary believe the fact that Bill said that John likes?

Ross (1967) noted that a similar restriction appears to hold for movement of adjectives. Contrast

7. Stupid though Mary believes John said Fido is, everyone likes the dog.
8. *Stupid though Fido bit a man who was, everyone blames the dog.

Ross proposed the complex NP constraint—the term *complex NP* refers to noun phrases that contain relative clauses—that no transformation can extract a constituent from a complex NP.

Ross also noted that it is impossible to extract a constituent from a coordinate structure, as in

9. *Who does Mary like John and?

Therefore he proposed a coordinate-structure constraint that nothing can be moved out of a coordinate structure. In total, he enumerated a fair number of apparent distinct constraints on transformations in English.

These constraints may derive from ambiguities in applying transformational specifications. Consider a production for wh-movement:

> IF the goal is question LVobject in (LVrelation LVagent LVobject)
> and this occurs as part of LVstructure
> THEN set as subgoals
> 1. to plan the communication of LVstructure
> 2. to move the first morpheme in the main verb structure to the front
> 3. to move the object after the main verb structure to the front.

There is an ambiguity in this transformation if more than one object follows a verb. Assuming the pattern matcher selects the highest object, this transformation would successfully generate

1 and 5 but not 2, 6, or 9. (A similar statement of the transformation for 7 and 8 would produce that phenomenon.)

There is nothing language-specific about this analysis. Such ambiguities in specification about in computer text editors, where one has the same problem of retrieving multiple elements that meet the same description. In various problem-solving situations, one is likely to find that an optimization transformation selects the first object that satisfies its description. Consider a plan to paint three objects, with the structure of the plan specified as:

1a.    Fill bucket with enough paint for object A.
1b.    Paint A.
2a.    Fill bucket with enough paint for object B.
2b.    Paint B.
3a.    Fill bucket with enough paint for object C.
3b.    Paint C.

If the bucket can hold enough paint for any two objects, a likely transformation of this plan is

1a'.    Fill bucket with enough paint for A + B.
1b'.    Paint A.
1c'.    Paint B.
2a'.    Fill bucket with enough paint for C.
2b'.    Paint C.

The optimization transformation has applied to the first two objects in the sequence but not the last two.

If this discussion is correct, this constraint is not a fundamental limitation on natural language. There is no reason why, if the learner received appropriate training, he could not learn a fuller description that could select the appropriate object. This would require more complex training data and make learning somewhat more difficult. However, it would just be a matter of degree. Thus, this analysis predicts that if English had constructions like 2, 6, and 9, it would still be learnable, if more difficult.

There has been a considerable constellation of research around the A-over-A constraint and its related manifestations. It may well be that the exact idea offered here will not extend to all of this constellation. However, a general point about such "constraints on transformations" is that given finite bounds on pattern descriptions, it is always possible to come up with data structures sufficiently complex that the pattern descriptions will fail to extract a desired object. This will be true for linguistic pattern descriptions, other "human" pattern descriptions, and nonhuman pattern descriptions such as those one gives to a text editor. Any system that learns finite pattern descriptions is going to face ambiguities in their range of application.

Therefore the mere observation that our adult system seems unable to extract certain patterns says nothing about the language specificity of that system nor of its acquisition. In order to show that the system is language-specific, it must be shown that in nonlinguistic systems the human pattern extractor functions differently. This has never been attempted. Similarly, the mere observation of such a limitation says nothing about whether there is a fundamental limitation on pattern extraction or whether the experience just has not been sufficiently complex to force sufficiently refined pattern specifications. Unless one can establish a fundamental limitation, the observation of constraints says little about whether or not the learning mechanism is language-specific.

# Notes

## 1. Production Systems and ACT

1. Relevant to this interpretation is the fact that children who suffer damage to their language areas are nonetheless capable of acquiring a language—presumably using other areas to store the linguistic programs (Lenneberg, 1967).

2. It might be argued that models that go down to the neural level (for example, Hinton and Anderson, 1981) are more precise. However, these models have been applied in such a small range of tasks that they are totally vague on the issue of control of cognition (see Chapter 4) in which the precision of production systems is most exact. This is not to say it would not be possible to construct a neural model more precise than production systems.

3. In Table 1.1 and elsewhere productions are presented in an English-like syntax for readability. In the actual computer implementations the syntax tends to be much more technical and much less comprehensible. Readers can obtain the actual production code by writing to me.

4. Unlike this version, earlier versions of ACT had a construct of a *global variable* whose value could be passed from one production to the next.

5. The typical formal definition of *computationally universal* is that the system is capable of mimicking a Turing Machine. The things computable by a Turing Machine have been shown to be identical to the things computable by a number of formalisms, including the modern computer (Minsky, 1967). A frequently accepted conjecture, known as Church's thesis, is that any behavior capable of being precisely specified will be in the class of things computable by a Turing Machine.

6. This follows from the fact that there are always different ways to specify the solution of the task, and each of these specifications can be implemented. However, the phenomenon of multiple ways to perform the same task is not unique to computationally universal

systems. For instance, this ambiguity occurs with finite-state machines.

7. Others may prove more successful at uncovering negative evidence because it is difficult for the theorist to recognize the weakest points of his theory. In the past the majority of negative evidence has come from the research and theoretical analyses of others.

8. It should be noted that a limit on the size of cognitive units is quite different from a limit on the capacity of working memory. An interesting question is whether there is a connection between these two limits. ACT* does not contain in its assumptions an answer to this question.

9. Chunking assumptions do not really help. Many tasks require having simultaneously available a lot of information that cannot reasonably be assumed to be part of the same chunk. For instance, in parsing a sentence one needs to simultaneously hold information about a novel string of words, about the state in each level of parsing, about the semantics of words, about the speaker's knowledge and intentions, about references introduced earlier in the conversation, about analogous past experiences, and more.

## 2. Knowledge Representation

1. A similar set of codes was proposed by Wallach and Averbach (1955).

2. It should be noted that temporal strings are not tied to the verbal modality, nor spatial images to the visual modality. For instance, a temporal string can encode the place of people in a queue, and a spatial image can encode the position of sounds in space.

3. Burrows and Okada (1974) present evidence that a pause is treated like an item in a Sternberg task.

4. It is an entirely open question how to represent music, in which some interval properties do seem to be represented. One possibility is that blank time is represented by pauses as elements of the string (as it explicitly is on sheet music). It is also possible that music has its own code or is an instance of a motor-kinesthetic code.

5. This is not to deny that there are strong *statistical* correlations among objects in an image. For instance, it is improbable to have a fire hydrant in a scene of a room (Biederman, Glass, and Stacy, 1973). However, statistical probability is not the same as logical necessity, given the semantics of the relational terms, and it is possible to have a fire hydrant in a room. On the other hand, it is not possible to have the proposition *John decided the fire hydrant* (except as in *John decided to buy the fire hydrant*, where the object is an embedded proposition, not *fire hydrant*).

6. As will be discussed with respect to tangled hierarchies, a unit may be an element of more than one larger structure. In this case there is an ambiguity in going up as to which larger structure to retrieve. The subject must use features such as other elements of the structure or contextual tags to select the correct structure.

7. Galambos and Rips (1974) document that a script involves temporal string structures organized hierarchically. That is, they show effects associated both with hierarchical structure (an advantage for information high in the hierarchy) and with temporal structure (distance effects for order judgments).

## 3.  Spread of Activation

1. As this example illustrates, I do not intend to correlate active memory with what one is currently conscious of.

2. While the units in Figure 3.1 are all propositions, the same analysis would apply if the units were strings or images.

3. If the source node is an encoding of an external stimulus, its source activation reflects sensory stimulation. If it is the result of a production execution, its source activation is a result of activation pumped into the network from the production. If it is linked to the goal, its activation comes from the goal.

4. This assumes that there is a set of activation sources that stay constant for a long period of time relative to the decay rate and the delay of transmission. In many situations this can be a useful idealization.

5. In contrast to productions like P1 that exist before the experiment, it is assumed that productions P2–P6 in Table 3.2 are created specifically to perform in the experiment and that they are compiled (see Chapter 6) during the first few trials.

6. This implies that subjects go through a stage of processing in which a nonword is identified with a word. There is no need to assume that subjects are conscious of this at the level of being able to make a verbal report, but I can report that in piloting such experiments I am aware of identifying a nonword with a similar word on the majority of the trials.

7. It should be noted that this analysis predicts particularly large Stroop interference when the word is itself a color name. In this case the response code for the word is being primed by the task and the color to be named. Also, new partial instantiations of productions will compete with the correct one.

8. For simplification the first goal clause is ignored since it is constant across the productions.

9. I thank Robert Frederking for pointing out to me the analysis of foil judgments reported here.

10. As noted earlier, for this model to work S1&~S2 must receive more activation from S1 than S1&S2 does.

11. There are, of course, limits on this prediction, related to limits on the number of items that can be maintained as sources of activation.

12. It is important to note that these judgments cannot be done by deciding if the probe belongs to a category. That is, *plane, mountain, crash, clouds,* and *wind* do not belong to any category that would exclude the foils.

13. For instance, no node in the unanalyzed structure for $X$ can be connected to node $C$.

14. If the node had any connections to nodes of lower level than $i - 1$, its minimum link distance from node $X$ would not be $i$. The node cannot have connections to nodes higher than $i + 1$ because they are only one link removed from a level-$i$ node.

## 4. Control of Cognition

1. One example of the distinction was developed in the preceding chapter in the distinction between conscious and automatic priming in the lexical decision task. We saw that automatic priming occurred when information was made especially active in the network, and conscious priming occurred when the subject set his goal to allow a potentially more efficient production to apply. In general, conscious attention or controlled processing corresponds in ACT to setting goals to favor a special mode of processing.

2. In the last chapter I argued that the *momentary* capacity of working memory is high. However, opportunistic planning requires a large *sustained* capacity.

3. It appears that students get around these difficulties by building larger patterns that encompass both uses of the data. Thus, rather than seeing two triangle patterns sharing the same segment, they see one "adjacent triangles" pattern that involves a single shared segment. Associated with the pattern is the information that the one segment can be used with the reflexive rule of congruence.

4. Later in the chapter I discuss how goal structures have special mechanisms to deal with data refractoriness.

5. As will be discussed later, "goal" in ACT refers to immediate goals of current behavior, such as generating a sentence. Only one such goal can be active. This is not to deny that a person may have many "high-level" goals like "making money." Such goals are better called policies because they do not have direct control over current behavior. Again, under this analysis hunger, fear, attraction, and the like are not goals but states that can lead to the setting of goals.

6. It should be noted that this seriality is a property of the goal productions only. Productions that do not involve the goal element and match disjoint sets of data can apply in parallel. A particularly important class of such productions consists of those for automatic pattern matching. Thus multiple letters on a page can be matched simultaneously.

7. Many people's introspective reports do not agree with this particular simulation. Some people fail to see either (*a*) or (*b*) as a word. A number of people have reported seeing (*b*) as FOUL, which is not represented in Figure 4.5. Such examples are only meant to illustrate how the word-superiority effect is obtained. Until we actually implement a reasonable approximation to a human lexicon, the perceptions of our simulation are unlikely to correspond exactly to human perceptions.

8. For instance, rather than simply executing a pop, other production languages might have many special-case production rules like:

IF the current goal is to be POPped
  and the current goal has a supergoal
  and the supergoal has another subgoal
  and that subgoal is ordered after the current goal
THEN make that subgoal the current goal.

IF the current goal is to be POPped
  and the current goal has a supergoal
  and the supergoal has no subgoals after the current goal
THEN set the supergoal as the current goal
  and this supergoal is to be POPped.

9. Wexler and Culicover (1980) note that linguistic transformations tend to apply only to two levels of a linguistic phrase structure at a time. Perhaps the reason for this restriction is that this is all the goal structure that can be kept active in working memory at one time.

## 5. Memory for Facts

1. Although Woodward et al. found that presentation time had no effect on probability of recall, they found that it did have an effect on recognition time. Crowder (1976) and Glenberg, Smith, and Green (1977) have proposed that this is because of formation of contextual tags. One might argue that context changes with time and that this creates new units encoding the associations between the item and the new contexts. Thus time does not increase the probability of encoding a contextual unit but rather increases the probability of forming a new contextual unit.

2. It is unlikely that this is the sole explanation of the spacing effect, particularly at long intervals (Glenberg, 1974; Bahrick, 1979). It is improbable that the spacing effect has a single explanation. Other factors probably include change in context (Glenberg) and some general fatiguing of the capacity of nodes to form and strengthen associations (see the section on practice later in this chapter).

3. This is not to deny that there are other important components to some mnemonic techniques, such as chunking multiple units into a single unit or imposing an orderly retrieval structure on recall.

4. Past versions of the generate-test model assumed that the context word made no contribution to the retrieval of the trace except in terms of sense selection. However, in this model the context word can be just as important a source of activation as the target word. In fact, some results suggest it might be a more important source (Bartling and Thompson, 1977; Rabinowitz, Mandler, and Barsalou, 1977). To the extent that the context word is the more important

source, encoding-specificity results should occur even with those words that truly have a single sense (Tulving and Watkins, 1977).

5. Underwood and Humphreys (1977) have basically replicated the results of Light and Carter-Sobell, but they argue that the magnitude of the results does not justify the multiple-sense interpretation. It is hard to make clear predictions about the magnitude of the effect.

6. It is interesting to ask to what extent the difference in activation patterns set up in ACT instantiates what Tulving means by encoding specificity.

## 6. Procedural Learning

1. This assertion does not imply that composition can only apply to productions that involve goals. However, goal structures provide one important means for determining which productions belong together and for producing certain optimizations in the products of composition.

2. Each time an attempt is made to recreate an existing production (for instance, through composition), the existing production gains an increment of strength rather than a copy being created.

3. No claim is made for the appropriateness of these rules for actually playing bridge.

4. These terms are slight misnomers. A condition discrimination just changes the condition of the incorrect production. However, an action discrimination makes a change in both condition and action.

5. Recall, however, from Chapter 4, that an exception to a strong general production can still take precedence because of a specificity advantage. This requires that the exception have a modest amount of strength. This has some interesting implications for exceptions to inflectional rules for words (for example, the plural of *man* is *men*). For an exception production to take precedence over the regular rule, the word must occur with at least moderate frequency. The exceptions to general inflectional rules do appear to occur for more frequent words.

6. Data refractoriness (see Chapter 4) will prevent the selection of January or September a second time.

## 7. Language Acquisition

1. It is somewhat unfortunate that the term "generation" is used throughout this chapter, since it has a different technical meaning in linguistics. However, the other obvious choice, "production," is even more contaminated in the current context.

2. The earlier set of ideas about declarative knowledge representation and spreading activation defined on that knowledge representation are no doubt also applicable to language processing, as indeed the priming studies indicate (Swinney, 1979). However, these mechanisms are more important to the semantics of language than to the syntax.

3. Recently, it has been argued in linguistics (for example, Bresnan, 1981) that there are no transformations. While earlier linguistic theories may have overemphasized their use, it seems improbable that there are no transformations. For instance, constructions like *respectively* and *vice versa* remain for me consciously transformational.

4. Later I will discuss what to do about verb phrases that do not have auxiliaries for pre-posing.

5. As discussed later in the chapter, content words in ACT are those that have an associated concept.

6. Of course, at certain points in the processing of content words, implicit, production-based knowledge comes in. Thus it is very reasonable to propose that our knowledge of what a dog looks like is embedded in dog-recognition productions. However, in generating the word *dog*, the speaker calls on a declarative link between the lexical item and its meaning representation.

7. Some work has been done with Latin and French; see Anderson (1981c).

8. A description of this production system will be provided upon request.

9. It would also be possible to form analogous comprehension rules from this experience. Thus, the acquisition of comprehension and generation rules need not be independent, even if the rules are.

10. See the discussion in Chapter 6 of analogy as a basis for using declarative rules.

11. Asterisks are being used to denote the concept corresponding to content words.

12. Each of these rules is specific to a particular concept. For instance, (1) is specific to *definite* and (2) is specific to *boy*.

13. Unlike the weakening principles set forth in the last chapter, which involved a multiplicative change, this simulation simply subtracts one unit of strength. The success of the current simulation illustrates the arbitrariness of the exact strengthening principles.

14. If MacWhinney is right in this debate and there are distinguishing semantic features, the ACT learning mechanisms described in Chapter 6 will apply without this modification to incorporate arbitrary classes.

15. As it turns out, ACT learns the passive as a separate phrase-structure rule rather than as a transformation. Unlike the question transformations to be discussed, the passive does not violate the graph-deformation condition.

16. How one should measure the length of these utterances is an interesting question. We are fairly certain that *I need, coming back,* and *in a minute* are fixed phrases for J.J.

17. It is of some interest to consider J.J.'s use of the fourteen morphemes discussed by Brown (1973). He used the *ing* inflection to describe actions, but he most definitely did not have the present progressive auxiliary (*is, are,* and so on). He used *in* and *on* quite

successfully (thank you, *Sesame Street*). He occasionally used articles, plural inflections, and possessives. Except for *ing*, all verb auxiliaries and inflections were missing.

18. However, it is not the case that any language is learnable in an ACTlike framework. Given an input, ACT will entertain certain possible hypotheses, and not others, about the structure of that input. It is logically impossible for any inductive system to identify all possible languages, given finite input. ACT is no exception. It is an open question whether ACT's preferences about language hypotheses always correspond to human choice. The chapter has shown that it does in the case of the two subsets of English.

# References

ABELSON, R. P. 1981. Psychological status of the script concept. *American Psychologist* 36, 715–729.

ANDERSON, J. A. 1973. A theory for the recognition of items from short memorized lists. *Psychological Review* 80, 417–438.

ANDERSON, J. A., and HINTON, G. E. 1981. Models of information processing in the brain. In G. E. Hinton and J. A. Anderson, eds., *Parallel Models of Associative Memory*. Hillsdale, N.J.: Erlbaum Associates.

ANDERSON, J. R. 1972. FRAN: A simulation model of free recall. In G. H. Bower, ed., *The Psychology of Learning and Motivation*, vol. 5. New York: Academic Press.

———— 1974. Retrieval of propositional information from long-term memory. *Cognitive Psychology* 6, 451–474.

———— 1975. Computer simulation of a language acquisition system: a first report. In R. L. Solso, ed., *Information Processing and Cognition: The Loyola Symposium*. Hillsdale, N.J.: Erlbaum Associates.

———— 1976. *Language, Memory, and Thought*. Hillsdale, N.J.: Erlbaum Associates.

———— 1977. Induction of augmented transition networks. *Cognitive Science* 1, 125–157.

———— 1978. Arguments concerning representations for mental imagery. *Psychological Review* 85, 249–277.

———— 1979. Further arguments concerning representations for mental imagery: a response to Hayes-Roth and Pylyshyn. *Psychological Review* 86, 395–406.

———— 1980a. Concepts, propositions, and schemata: what are the cognitive units? *Nebraska Symposium of Motivation* 28, 121–162.

———— 1980b. *Cognitive Psychology and Its Implications*. San Francisco: Freeman.

———— 1981a. Tuning of search of the problem space for geometry proofs. *Proceedings of the Seventh International Joint Conference on Artificial Intelligence*.

———— 1981b. Effects of prior knowledge on memory for new information. *Memory and Cognition* 9, 237–246.

———— 1981c. A theory of language acquisition based on general learning mechanisms. *Proceedings of the Seventh International Joint Conference on Artificial Intelligence.*

———— 1981d. Acquisition of cognitive skill. ONR Technical Report, 81–1.

———— 1981e. Interference: The relationship between response latency and response accuracy. *Journal of Experimental Psychology: Human Learning and Memory 7*, 311–325.

———— 1982a. A proposal for the evolution of the human cognitive architecture. Unpublished manuscript, Carnegie-Mellon University.

———— 1982b. Acquisition of cognitive skill. *Psychological Review 89*, 369–406.

———— 1982c. Acquisition of proof skills in geometry. In J. G. Carbonell, R. Michalski, and T. Mitchell, eds., *Machine Learning, An Artificial Intelligence Approach.* San Francisco: Tioga Press.

———— 1982d. Representational Types: A Tricode Proposal. Technical Report #ONR-82-1, Carnegie-Mellon University.

ANDERSON, J. R., and BOWER, G. H. 1972a. Recognition and retrieval processes in free recall. *Psychological Review 79*, 97–123.

———— 1972b. Configural properties in sentence memory. *Journal of Verbal Learning and Verbal Behavior 11*, 594–605.

———— 1973. *Human Associative Memory.* Washington: Winston and Sons.

———— 1974a. A propositional theory of recognition memory. *Memory and Cognition 2*, 406–412.

———— 1974b. Interference in memory for multiple contexts. *Memory and Cognition 2*, 509–514.

ANDERSON, J. R., FARRELL, R., and SAUERS, R. 1982. Learning to plan in LISP. Technical Report #ONR-82-2, Carnegie-Mellon University.

ANDERSON, J. R., GREENO, J. G., KLINE, P. J., and NEVES, D. M. 1981. Acquisition of problem-solving skill. In J. R. Anderson, ed., *Cognitive Skills and Their Acquisition.* Hillsdale, N.J.: Erlbaum Associates.

ANDERSON, J. R., KLINE, P. J., and BEASLEY, C. M. 1977. A theory of the acquisition of cognitive skills. ONR Technical Report 77-1, Yale University.

———— 1979. A general learning theory and its application to schema abstraction. In G. H. Bower, ed., *The Psychology of Learning and Motivation*, vol. 13, 277–318. New York: Academic Press.

———— 1980. Complex learning processes. In R. E. Snow, P. A. Federico, and W. E. Montague, eds., *Aptitude, Learning, and Instruction*, vol. 2. Hillsdale, N.J.: Erlbaum Associates.

ANDERSON, J. R., KLINE, P., and LEWIS, C. 1977. A production system model for language processing. In P. Carpenter and M. Just, eds., *Cognitive Processes in Comprehension.* Hillsdale, N.J.: Erlbaum Associates.

ANDERSON, J. R., and PAULSON, R. 1977. Representation and retention of verbatim information. *Journal of Verbal Learning and Verbal Behavior 16*, 439–451.

—— 1978. Interference in memory for pictorial information. *Cognitive Psychology* 10, 178–202.

ANDERSON, J. R., and REDER, L. M. 1979. An elaborative processing explanation of depth of processing. In L. S. Cermak and F. I. M. Craik, eds., *Levels of Processing in Human Memory*. Hillsdale, N.J.: Erlbaum Associates.

ANDERSON, J. R., and ROSS, B. H. 1980. Evidence against a semantic-episodic distinction. *Journal of Experimental Psychology: Human Learning and Memory* 6, 441–478.

ANDERSON, R. C. 1974. Substance recall of sentences. *Quarterly Journal of Experimental Psychology* 26, 530–541.

ANDERSON, R. C., and ORTONY, A. 1975. On putting apples into bottles—a problem of polysemy. *Cognitive Psychology* 7, 167–180.

ANDERSON, R. E. 1976. Short-term retention of the where and when of pictures and words. *Journal of Experimental Psychology: General* 105, 378–402.

ANGIOLILLIO-BENT, J. S., and RIPS, L. J. 1982. Order information in multiple element comparison. *Journal of Experimental Psychology: Human Perception and Performance* 8, 392–406.

ATKINSON, R., and SHIFFRIN, R. 1968. Human memory: a proposed system and its control processes. In K. Spence and J. Spence, eds., *The Psychology of Learning and Motivation*, vol. 2. New York: Academic Press.

ATKINSON, R. C., and RAUGH, M. R. 1975. An application of the mnemonic keyword method to the acquisition of Russian vocabulary. *Journal of Experimental Psychology: Human Learning and Human Memory* 104, 126–133.

BADDELEY, A. D. 1976. *The Psychology of Memory*. New York: Basic Books.

BADDELEY, A. D., and ECOB, J. R. 1973. Reaction-time and short-term memory: implications of repetition for the high-speed exhaustive scan hypothesis. *Quarterly Journal of Experimental Psychology* 25, 229–240.

BADDELEY, A. D., THOMSON, N., and BUCHANAN, M. 1975. Word length and the structure of short-term memory. *Journal of Verbal Learning and Verbal Behavior* 14, 575–589.

BAGGETT, P. 1975. Memory for explicit and implicit information in picture stories. *Journal of Verbal Learning and Verbal Behavior* 14, 538–548.

BAHRICK, H. P. 1979. Maintenance of knowledge: questions about memory we forgot to ask. *Journal of Experimental Psychology: General* 108, 296–308.

BARTLING, C. A., and THOMPSON, C. P. 1977. Encoding specificity: retrieval asymmetry in the recognition failure paradigm. *Journal of Experimental Psychology: Human Learning and Human Memory* 3, 690–700.

BECKER, C. A. 1980. Semantic context effects in visual word recognition: an analysis of semantic strategies. *Memory and Cognition* 8, 493–512.

BEGG, I. 1971. Recognition memory for sentence meaning and wording. *Journal of Verbal Learning and Verbal Behavior* 10, 176–181.

BEGG, I., and PAIVIO, A. 1969. Concreteness and imagery in sentence memory. *Journal of Verbal Learning and Verbal Behavior* 8, 821–827.

BIEDERMAN, I., GLASS, A. L., and STACY, E. W. 1973. Searching for aspects in real world scenes. *Journal of Experimental Psychology* 97, 22–27.

BJORK, R. A., and ALLEN, T. W. 1970. The spacing effect: consolidation or differential encoding? *Journal of Verbal Learning and Verbal Behavior* 9, 567–572.

BLOOM, L. M. 1970. *Language Development: Form and Function in Emerging Grammars.* Cambridge, Mass.: MIT Press.

BOBROW, D. G., and WINOGRAD, T. 1977. An overview of KRL, a knowledge representation language. *Cognitive Science* 1, 3–46.

BORING, E. G. 1950. *A History of Experimental Psychology.* New York: Appleton Century.

BOWER, G. H. 1972. Mental imagery and associative learning. In L. Gregg, ed., *Cognition in Learning and Memory.* New York: Wiley.

—— 1977. Contacts of cognitive psychology with social learning theory. Address to the convention of American Association of Behavior Therapists, Atlanta, Georgia, Dec. 9.

BOWER, G. H., BLACK, J. B., and TURNER, T. J. 1979. Scripts in memory for text. *Cognitive Psychology* 11, 177–220.

BOWER, G. H., KARLIN, M. B., and DUECK, A. 1975. Comprehension and memory for pictures. *Memory and Cognition* 3, 216–220.

BOWER, G. H., and SPRINGSTON, F. 1970. Pauses as recoding points in letter series. *Journal of Experimental Psychology* 83, 421–430.

BRADSHAW, G. L., and ANDERSON, J. R. 1982. Elaborative encoding as an explanation of levels of processing. *Journal of Verbal Learning and Verbal Behavior* 21, 165–174.

BRAINE, M. D. S. 1963. The ontogeny of English phrase structure: the first phase. *Language* 39, 1–13a.

BRANSFORD, J. D., BARCLAY, J. R., and FRANKS, J. J. 1972. Sentence memory: a constructive versus interpretive approach. *Cognitive Psychology* 3, 193–209.

BRANSFORD, J. D., and FRANKS, J. J. 1971. The abstraction of linguistic ideas. *Cognitive Psychology* 2, 331–350.

BRESNAN, J. W. 1981. *The Mental Representation of Grammatical Relations.* Cambridge, Mass.: MIT Press.

BRIGGS, G. E. 1974. On the predictor variable for choice reaction time. *Memory and Cognition* 2, 575–580.

BRIGGS, G. E., and BLAHA, J. 1969. Memory retrieval and central comparison times in information-processing. *Journal of Experimental Psychology* 79, 395–402.

BROADBENT, D. E. 1975. The magical number seven after fifteen years. In R. A. Kennedy and A. Wilkes, eds., *Studies in Long-term Memory.* New York: Wiley.

BROWN, J. S., and VAN LEHN, K. 1980. Repair theory: a generative theory of bugs in procedural skills. *Cognitive Science* 4, 379–426.

BROWN, R. 1973. *A First Language*. Cambridge, Mass.: Harvard University Press.

BURROWS, D., and OKADA, R. 1974. Scanning temporally structured lists: evidence for dual retrieval processes. *Memory and Cognition* 2, 441–446.

BUSCHKE, H. 1974. Spontaneous remembering after recall failure. *Science* 184, 579–581.

CARD, S. K., MORAN, T. P., and NEWELL, A. 1980. Computer text-editing: an information-processing analysis of a routine cognitive skill. *Cognitive Psychology* 12, 32–74.

CARPENTER, P. A., and JUST, M. A. 1978. Eye fixations during mental rotation. In J. W. Senders, D. F. Fisher, and R. A. Monty, eds., *Eye Movements and the Higher Psychological Functions*. Hillsdale, N.J.: Erlbaum Associates.

CERMAK, L. S., and CRAIK, F. I. M. 1979. *Levels of Processing in Human Memory*. Hillsdale, N.J.: Erlbaum Associates.

CHASE, W. G., and CLARK, H. H. 1972. Mental operations in the comparison of sentences and pictures. In L. Gregg, ed., *Cognition in Learning and Memory*. New York: Wiley.

CHASE, W. G., and ERICSSON, K. A. 1981. Skilled memory. In J. R. Anderson, ed., *Cognitive Skills and Their Acquisition*. Hillsdale, N.J.: Erlbaum Associates.

———— 1982. Skill and working memory. In G. H. Bower, ed., *The Psychology of Learning and Motivation*, vol. 16. New York: Academic Press.

CHASE, W. G., and SIMON, H. A. 1973. The mind's eye in chess. In W. G. Chase, ed., *Visual Information Processing*. New York: Academic Press.

CHOMSKY, N. 1965. *Aspects of the Theory of Syntax*. Cambridge, Mass.: MIT Press.

———— 1968. *Language and Mind*. New York: Harcourt, Brace and World.

———— 1973. Conditions on transformations. In S. Anderson and P. Kiparsky, eds., *Festschrift for Morris Halle*. New York: Holt, Rinehart and Winston.

———— 1980. Rules and representations. *Behavioral and Brain Sciences* 3, 1–61.

CLARK, E. V. 1975. First language acquisition. Unpublished manuscript, Stanford University.

CLARK, H. H., and CLARK, E. V. 1977. *Psychology and Language: An Introduction to Psycholinguistics*. New York: Harcourt, Brace, Jovanovich.

COLLINS, A. M. 1977. Processes in acquiring knowledge. In R. C. Anderson, R. J. Spiro, and W. E. Montague, eds., *Schooling and the Acquisition of Knowledge*. Hillsdale, N.J.: Erlbaum Associates.

COLLINS, A. M., and QUILLIAN, M. R. 1969. Retrieval time from semantic memory. *Journal of Verbal Learning and Verbal Behavior* 8, 240–247.

———— 1972. Experiments on semantic memory and language comprehension. In L. Gregg, ed., *Cognition and Learning*. New York: Wiley.

COOPER, L. A., and PODGORNY, P. 1976. Mental transformation and visual comparison processes: effects of complexity and similarity. *Journal of Experimental Psychology: Human Perception and Performance* 2, 503–514.

COOPER, W. E., and PACCIA-COOPER, J. 1980. *Syntax and Speech*. Cambridge, Mass.: Harvard University Press.

CRAIK, F. I. M., and LOCKHART, R. S. 1972. Levels of processing: a framework for memory research. *Journal of Verbal Learning and Verbal Behavior* 11, 671–684.

CRAIK, F. I. M., and WATKINS, M. J. 1973. The role of rehearsal in short-term memory. *Journal of Verbal Learning and Verbal Behavior* 12, 599–607.

CROWDER, R. G. 1976. *Principles of Learning and Memory*. Hillsdale, N.J.: Erlbaum Associates.

DE VILLIERS, J. G., and DE VILLIERS, P. A. *Language Acquisition*. Cambridge, Mass.: Harvard University Press.

DOSHER, B. A. 1976. The retrieval of sentences from memory: a speed-accuracy study. *Cognitive Psychology* 8, 291–310.

DYER, F. N. 1973. The Stroop phenomenon and its use in the study of perceptual, cognitive, and response processes. *Memory and Cognition* 1, 106–120.

ECCLES, J. C. 1972. Possible synaptic mechanisms subserving learning. In A. G. Karyman and J. C. Eccles, eds., *Brain and Human Behavior*. New York: Springer-Verlag.

ELIO, R., and ANDERSON, J. R. 1981. Effects of category generalizations and instance similarity on schema abstraction. *Journal of Experimental Psychology: Human Learning and Memory* 7, 397–417.

ERMAN, L. D., and LESSER, V. R. 1979. The HEARSAY-II speech understanding system. In W. A. Lea, ed., *Trends in Speech Recognition*. Englewood Cliffs, N.J.: Prentice-Hall.

ESTES, W. K. 1960. Learning theory and the new "mental chemistry." *Psychological Review* 67, 207–223.

FAHLMAN, S. E. 1981. Representing implicit knowledge. In G. E. Hinton and J. A. Anderson, eds., *Parallel Models of Associative Memory*. Hillsdale, N.J.: Erlbaum Associates.

FIKES, R. E., and NILSSON, N. 1971. STRIPS: A new approach to the application of theorem proving to problem solving. *Artificial Intelligence* 2.

FISCHLER, I. 1977. Semantic facilitation without association in a lexical decision task. *Memory and Cognition* 5, 335–339.

FISCHLER, I., and BLOOM, P. A. 1979. Automatic and attentional processes in the effects of sentence context on word recognition. *Journal of Verbal Learning and Verbal Behavior* 8, 1–20.

FISCHLER, I., BRYANT, K., and QUERNS, E. n.d. Rapid priming of episodic and semantic word recognition. Unpublished manuscript.

FISCHLER, I., and GOODMAN, G. O. 1978. Latency of associative activation in memory. *Journal of Experimental Psychology: Human Perception and Performance* 4, 455–470.

FITTS, P. M. Perceptual-motor skill learning. In A. W. Melton, ed., *Categories of Human Learning*. New York: Academic Press.

FITTS, P. M., and POSNER, M. I. 1967. *Human Performance*. Belmont, Calif.: Brooks Cole.

FLEXSER, A. J., and TULVING, E. 1978. Retrieval independence in recognition and recall. *Psychological Review* 85, 153–172.

FORGY, C. L. 1979. On the efficient implementation of production systems. Ph.D. dissertation, computer science department, Carnegie-Mellon University.

FORGY, C., and McDERMOTT, J. 1977. OPS, a domain-independent production system. *Proceedings of the Fifth International Joint Conference on Artificial Intelligence* 933–939.

FOSS, D. J., and HARWOOD, D. A. 1975. Memory for sentences: implications for human associative memory. *Journal of Verbal Learning and Verbal Behavior* 14, 1–16.

FRANKS, J. J., and BRANSFORD, J. D. 1971. Abstraction of visual patterns. *Journal of Experimental Psychology* 90, 65–74.

FRAZER, C., BELLUGI, U., and BROWN, R. 1963. Control of grammar in imitation, comprehension, and production. *Journal of Verbal Learning and Verbal Behavior* 2, 121–135.

GALAMBOS, J. A., and RIPS, L. J. 1982. Memory for routines. *Journal of Verbal Learning and Verbal Behavior* 21, 260–281.

GENTNER, D. 1982. Flowing water or teeming crowds: mental models of electronic circuits. In D. Gentner and A. L. Stevens, eds., *Mental Models*. Hillsdale, N.J.: Erlbaum Associates.

GESCHWIND, N. 1980. Neurological knowledge and complex behaviors. *Cognitive Science* 4, 185–194.

GILL, G., GOLDMAN, H., REDDY, R., and YEGNANARAYANA, B. 1978. A recursive segmentation procedure for continuous speech. Technical report, department of computer science, Carnegie-Mellon University.

GLASS, A. L., and HOLYOAK, K. 1974. The effect of *some* and *all* on reaction time for semantic decisions. *Memory and Cognition* 2, 436–440.

GLENBERG, A. M. 1976. Monotonic and nonmonotonic lag effects in paired-associate and recognition memory paradigms. *Journal of Verbal Learning and Verbal Behavior* 7, 311–325.

GLENBERG, A., SMITH, S. M., and GREEN, C. 1977. Type I rehearsal: maintenance and more. *Journal of Verbal Learning and Verbal Behavior* 16, 339–352.

GLUCKSBERG, S., and McCLOSKEY, M. 1981. Decisions about ignorance: knowing that you don't know. *Journal of Experimental Psychology: Human Learning and Memory* 7, 311–325.

GLUCKSBERG, S., GILDEA, P., and BOOKIN, H. B. 1982. On understanding nonliteral speech: can people ignore metaphors? *Journal of Verbal Learning and Verbal Behavior* 21, 85–98.

GOETZ, E. T., ANDERSON, R. C., and SCHALLERT, D. L. 1981. The representation of sentences in memory. *Journal of Verbal Learning and Verbal Behavior* 20, 369–385.

GOSS, A. E. 1965. Manifest strengthening of correct responses of paired-associates under postcriterion zero percent occurrence of response members. *Journal of General Psychology* 72, 135–144.

GOULD, A., and STEPHENSON, G. M. 1967. Some experiments relating to Bartlett's theory of remembering. *British Journal of Psychology* 58, 39–50.

GRAESSER, A., and MANDLER, G. 1975. Recognition memory for the meaning and surface structure of sentences. *Journal of Experimental Psychology: Human Learning and Memory* 104, 238–248.

GREEN, C., and RAPHAEL, B. 1968. Research on intelligent question answering systems. In *Proceedings of the ACM*, 169–181. Princeton: Brandon Systems Press.

GREENO, J. G. 1976. Indefinite goals in well-structured problems. *Psychological Review* 83, 479–491.

GREENO, J. G., and SIMON, H. A. 1974. Processes for sequence production. *Psychological Review* 81, 187–198.

GUTHRIE, E. R. 1952. *The Psychology of Learning*. New York: Harper and Row.

HAYES, J. R. 1965. Memory, goals, and problem solving. In B. Kleinmuntz, ed., *Problem Solving: Research, Method, and Theory*. New York: Wiley.

HAYES, J. R., and CLARK, H. H. 1970. Experiments in the segmentation of an artificial speech analogue. In J. R. Hayes, ed., *Cognition and the Development of Language*. New York: Wiley.

HAYES-ROTH, B. 1977. Evolution of cognitive structures and processes. *Psychological Review* 84, 260–278.

HAYES-ROTH, B., and HAYES-ROTH, F. 1975. Plasticity in memorial networks. *Journal of Verbal Learning and Verbal Behavior* 14, 506–522.

——— 1977. The prominence of lexical information in memory representations of meaning. *Journal of Verbal Learning and Verbal Behavior* 16, 119–136.

——— 1979. A cognitive model of planning. *Cognitive Science* 3, 275–310.

HAYES-ROTH, F. 1977. The role of partial and best matches in knowledge systems. Rand Corporation, P-5802.

HEALY, A. F. 1975. Coding of temporal-spatial patterns in short-term memory. *Journal of Verbal Learning and Verbal Behavior* 14, 481–495.

——— 1977. Pattern coding of spatial order information in short-term memory. *Journal of Verbal Learning and Verbal Behavior* 16, 419–437.

HEBB, D. O. 1949. *The Organization of Behavior*. New York: Wiley.

HINTON, G. E. 1979. Some demonstrations of the effects of structural descriptions in mental imagery. *Cognitive Science* 3, 231–250.

HINTON, G. E., and ANDERSON, J. A. 1981. *Parallel Models of Associative Memory*. Hillsdale, N.J.: Erlbaum Associates.

HINTZMAN, D. L. 1974. Theoretical implications of the spacing effect. In R. L. Solso, ed., *Theories in Cognitive Psychology: The Loyola Symposium*. Potomac, Md.: Erlbaum Associates.

HITCH, G. J. 1974. Short-term memory for spatial and temporal information. *Quarterly Journal of Experimental Psychology* 26, 503–513.

HOCHBERG, J., and GELMAN, L. 1977. The effect of landmark features on mental rotation times. *Memory and Cognition* 5, 23–26.

HOCK, H. S., and EGETH, H. E. 1970. Verbal interference with encoding in a perceptual classification task. *Journal of Experimental Psychology* 83, 299–303.

HOLYOAK, K. J., and PATTERSON, K. K. 1981. A positional discriminability model of linear-order judgments. *Journal of Experimental Psychology: Human Perception and Performance* 7, 1283–1302.

HOROWITZ, L. M., and NEWMAN, W. 1969. An interrupted stimulus can facilitate PA learning. *Journal of Verbal Learning and Verbal Behavior* 8, 219–224.

HOROWITZ, L. M., WHITE, W. A., and ATWOOD, D. W. 1968. Word fragments as aids to recall: the organization of a word. *Journal of Experimental Psychology* 76, 219–226.

HULL, C. L. 1943. *Principles of Behavior*. New York: Appleton-Century-Crofts.

HUNT, E. B. 1978. Mechanics of verbal ability. *Psychological Review* 85, 109–130.

HUNT, E. B., and POLTRACK, S. E. 1974. The mechanics of thought. In B. H. Kantowitz, ed., *Human Information Processing: Tutorials in Performance and Cognition*. Hillsdale, N.J.: Erlbaum Associates.

JAMES, C. T. 1975. The role of semantic information in lexical decisions. *Journal of Experimental Psychology: Human Perception and Performance* 1, 130–136.

JEFFRIES, R., TURNER, A. A., POLSON, P. G., and ATWOOD, M. E. 1981. The processes involved in designing software. In J. R. Anderson, ed., *Cognitive Skills and Their Acquisition*. Hillsdale, N.J.: Erlbaum Associates.

JOHNSON, N. F. 1970. The role of chunking and organization in the process of recall. In G. H. Bower, ed., *Psychology of Language and Motivation*, vol. 4, 172–247. New York: Academic Press.

JONES, G. V. 1978. Tests of a structural theory of the memory trace. *British Journal of Psychology* 69, 351–367.

——— 1980. Interaction of intrinsic and extrinsic knowledge in sentence recall. *Attention and Performance VIII*. Hillsdale, N.J.: Erlbaum Associates.

JONES, J. E. 1962. All-or-none versus incremental learning. *Psychological Review* 69, 156–160.

JONES, W. P. 1982. The effects of information load and relatedness on memory retrieval. Doctoral dissertation, Carnegie-Mellon University.

JONES, W. P., and ANDERSON, J. R. 1982. Semantic categorization and high-speed scanning. *Journal of Experimental Psychology: Learning, Memory, and Cognition* 8, 237–242.

JURGENSEN, R. C., DONNELLY, A. J., MAIER, J. E., and RISING, G. R. 1975. *Geometry*. Boston: Houghton Mifflin.

JUST, M. A., and CARPENTER, P. A. 1976. Eye fixations and cognitive processes. *Cognitive Psychology* 8, 441–480.

KEENAN, J. M., and BAILLET, S. D. 1980. Memory for personally and socially significant events. *Attention and Performance VIII*. Hillsdale, N.J.: Erlbaum Associates.

KIERAS, D. E., and BOVAIR, S. 1981. Strategies for abstracting main ideas from simple technical prose. Technical report no. UARZ/DP/TR-81/9, University of Arizona.

KING, D. R. W., and ANDERSON, J. R. 1976. Long-term memory search: an intersecting activation process. *Journal of Verbal Learning and Verbal Behavior* 15, 587–606.

KINTSCH, W. 1970. Models for free recall and recognition. In D. A. Norman, ed., *Models of Human Memory*, 307–373. New York: Academic Press.

———— 1974. *The Representation of Meaning in Memory*. Hillsdale, N.J.: Erlbaum Associates.

KLAHR, D., CHASE, W. G., and LOVELACE, E. A. 1983. Structure and process in alphabetic retrieval. *Journal of Experimental Psychology: Learning, Memory, and Cognition*. In press.

KLAHR, D., LANGLEY, P., NECHES, D., eds. 1983. *Self-modifying Production System Models of Learning and Development*. Cambridge, Mass.: Bradford Books/MIT Press. In press.

KLINE, P. J. 1981. The superiority of relative criteria in partial matching and generalization. *Proceedings of the Seventh International Joint Conference on Artificial Intelligence*.

KOLERS, P. A. 1978. A pattern-analyzing basis of recognition. In L. S. Cermak and F. I. M. Craik, eds. *Levels of Processing in Human Memory*. Hillsdale, N.J.: Erlbaum Associates.

KOSSLYN, S. M. 1980. *Image and Mind*. Cambridge, Mass.: Harvard University Press.

KOSSLYN, S. M., and POMERANTZ, J. R. 1977. Imagery, propositions, and the form of internal representations. *Cognitive Psychology* 9, 52–76.

KUBOVY, M., and PODGORNY, P. 1981. Does pattern matching require the normalization of size and orientation? *Perception and Psychophysics* 30, 24–28.

LABERGE, D. 1973. Attention and the measurement of perceptual learning. *Memory and Cognition* 1, 268–276.

LABERGE, D., and SAMUELS, S. J. 1974. Toward a theory of automatic information processing in reading. *Cognitive Psychology* 6, 293–323.

LANGLEY, P. 1980. Finding common paths as a learning mechanism. *Proceedings of the Third National Conference of the Canadian Society for Computational Studies of Intelligence*, 12–18.

———— 1981. Language acquisition through error recovery. Paper presented at the AISB Workshop on Production Systems in Psychology, Sheffield, England.

LARKIN, J. H. 1981. Enriching formal knowledge: a model for learning to solve textbook problems. In J. R. Anderson, ed., *Cognitive Skills and Their Acquisition*. Hillsdale, N.J.: Erlbaum Associates.

LARKIN, J. H., McDERMOTT, J., SIMON, D. P., and SIMON, H. A. 1980a. Models of competence in solving physics problems. *Cognitive Science* 4, 317–345.

——— 1980b. Expert and novice performance in solving physics problems. *Science* 208, 1335–1342.

LAWRY, J. A., and LABERGE, D. 1981. Letter and word code interactions elicited by normally displayed words. *Perception and Psychophysics* 30, 71–82.

LEE, C. L., and ESTES, W. K. 1981. Item and order information in short-term memory: evidence for multilevel perturbation processes. *Journal of Experimental Psychology: Human Learning and Memory 7*, 149–169.

LENAT, D. B., and HARRIS, G. 1978. Designing a rule system that searches for scientific discoveries. In D. A. Waterman and F. Hayes-Roth, eds., *Pattern-Directed Inference Systems*. New York: Academic Press.

LENNEBERG, E. 1967. *Biological Foundations of Language*. New York: Wiley.

LESGOLD, A. M. 1972. Pronominalizations: a device for unifying sentences in memory. *Journal of Verbal Learning and Verbal Behavior 11*, 316–323.

LESSER, V. R., HAYES-ROTH, F., BIRNBAUM, M., and CRONK, R. 1977. Selection of word islands in the Hearsay-II speech understanding system. *Proceedings 1977 IEEE Inter. Conference on ASSP*. Hartford, Conn.

LEWIS, C. H. 1978. Production system models of practice effects. Dissertation, University of Michigan at Ann Arbor.

LEWIS, C. H., and ANDERSON, J. R. 1976. Interference with real world knowledge. *Cognitive Psychology 8*, 311–335.

LEWIS, M., and ANDERSON, J. R. n.d. The role of feedback in discriminating problem-solving operators. Unpublished manuscript.

LIGHT, L. L., and CARTER-SOBELL, L. 1970. Effects of changed semantic context on recognition memory. *Journal of Verbal Learning and Verbal Behavior 9*, 1–11.

LINDSAY, P. H., and NORMAN, D. A. 1977. *Human Information Processing: An Introduction to Psychology*. New York: Academic Press.

LOFTUS, G. R. 1972. Eye fixations and recognition memory for pictures. *Cognitive Psychology 3*, 525–551.

LOWERRE, B. T. 1976. The HARPY speech recognition system. Doctoral dissertation, Carnegie-Mellon University.

LUCHINS, A. S. 1942. Mechanization in problem solving. *Psychological Monographs 54*, no. 248.

MACWHINNEY, B. 1980. Basic syntactic processes. In S. Kuczaj, ed., *Language Development: Syntax and Semantics*. Hillsdale, N.J.: Erlbaum Associates.

——— 1983. Hungarian language acquisition as an exemplification of a general model of grammatical development. In D. I. Slobin, ed., *The Crosslinguistic Study of Language Acquisition*. Hillsdale, N.J.: Erlbaum Associates. In press.

MAKI, R. H. 1981. Categorization and distance effects with spatial linear orders. *Journal of Experimental Psychology 7*, 15–32.

MAKI, R. H., MAKI, W. S., and MARSH, L. G. 1977. Processing locational and orientational information. *Memory and Cognition* 5, 602–612.

MANDLER, G. 1967. Organization and memory. In K. W. Spence and J. A. Spence, eds., *The Psychology of Learning and Motivation*, vol. 1, 328–372. New York: Academic Press.

MANDLER, G., and ANDERSON, R. E. 1971. Temporal and spatial cues in seriation. *Journal of Experimental Psychology* 90, 128–135.

MANDLER, J. M., and RITCHEY, G. H. 1977. Long-term memory for pictures. *Journal of Experimental Psychology: Human Learning and Memory* 3, 386–396.

MARATSOS, M. P., and CHALKLEY, M. A. 1981. The internal language of children's syntax: the ontogenesis and representation of syntactic categories. In K. Nelson, ed., *Children's Language*, vol. 1. New York: Gardner Press.

MARR, D., and NISHIHARA, H. K. 1978. Representation and recognition of the spatial organization of three-dimensional shapes. *Proceedings of the Royal Society B* 200, 269–294.

MARTIN, E. 1967. Relation between stimulus recognition and paired-associate learning. *Journal of Experimental Psychology* 74, 500–505.

McCLELLAND, J. L. 1979. On the time relations of mental processes: an examination of systems of processes in cascade. *Psychological Review* 86, 287–330.

McCLELLAND, J. L., and RUMELHART, D. E. 1981. An interactive model of context effects in letter perception: pt. I. An account of basic findings. *Psychological Review* 88, 375–407.

McCLOSKEY, M., and BIGLER, K. 1980. Focused memory search in fact retrieval. *Memory and Cognition* 8, 253–264.

McDERMOTT, D., and DOYLE, J. 1980. Non-monotonic logic I. *Artificial Intelligence* 13, 41–72.

McDERMOTT, J. 1981. R1: The formative years. *AI Magazine* 2, 21–29.

McKOON, G., and RATCLIFF, R. 1979. Priming in episodic and semantic memory. *Journal of Verbal Learning and Verbal Behavior* 18, 463–480.

——— 1980. Priming in item recognition: the organization of propositions in memory for text. *Journal of Verbal Learning and Verbal Behavior* 19, 369–386.

McNEILL, D. 1968. On theories of language acquisition. In T. R. Dixon and D. L. Horton, eds., *Verbal Behavior and General Behavior Theory*. Englewood Cliffs, N.J.: Prentice-Hall.

MEDIN, D. L., and SCHAFFER, M. M. 1978. A context theory of classification learning. *Psychological Review* 85, 207–238.

MEYER, D. E. 1970. On the representation and retrieval of stored semantic information. *Cognitive Psychology* 1, 242–300.

MEYER, D. E., and SCHVANEVELDT, R. W. 1971. Facilitation in recognizing pairs of words: evidence of a dependence between retrieval operations. *Journal of Experimental Psychology* 90, 227–234.

MEYER, D. E., SCHVANEVELDT, R. W., and RUDDY, M. G. 1972. Activation of lexical memory. Paper presented at meeting of the Psychonomic Society, St. Louis, November.

MILLER, G. A. 1956. The magical number seven, plus or minus two: some limits on our capacity for processing information. *Psychological Review* 63, 81–97.

MILLER, G. A., GALANTER, E., and PRIBRAM, K. H. 1960. *Plans and the Structure of Behavior.* Holt, Rinehart and Winston.

MINSKY, M. L. 1967. *Computation: Finite and Infinite Machines.* Englewood Cliffs, N.J.: Prentice-Hall.

———— 1975. A framework for representing knowledge. In P. H. Winston, ed., *The Psychology of Computer Vision.* New York: McGraw-Hill.

MOESER, S. D., and BREGMAN, A. S. 1972. The role of reference in the acquisition of a miniature artificial language. *Journal of Verbal Learning and Verbal Behavior* 11, 759–769.

———— 1973. Imagery and language acquisition. *Journal of Verbal Learning and Verbal Behavior* 12, 91–98.

MORGAN, J. L., and NEWPORT, E. L. 1981. The role of constituent structure in the induction of an artificial language. *Journal of Verbal Learning and Verbal Behavior* 20, 67–85.

MORTON, J. 1969. Categories of interference: verbal mediation and conflict in card sorting. *British Journal of Psychology* 60, 329–346.

MURDOCK, B. B., Jr. 1974. *Human Memory: Theory and Data.* Hillsdale, N.J.: Erlbaum Associates.

NAVON, D. 1977. Forest before trees: the precedence of global features in visual perception. *Cognitive Psychology* 9, 353–383.

NEELY, J. H. 1977. Semantic priming and retrieval from lexical memory: roles of inhibitionless spreading activation and limited-capacity attention: *Journal of Experimental Psychology: General* 106, 226–254.

NEISSER, U. 1967. *Cognitive Psychology.* New York: Appleton.

NELSON, T. O. 1976. Reinforcement and human memory. In W. K. Estes, ed., *Handbook of Learning and Cognitive Processes,* vol. 3. Hillsdale, N.J.: Erlbaum Associates.

———— 1977. Repetition and depth of processing. *Journal of Verbal Learning and Verbal Behavior* 16, 151–172.

NEVES, D. M., and ANDERSON, J. R. 1981. Knowledge compilation: mechanisms for the automatization of cognitive skills. In J. R. Anderson, ed., *Cognitive Skills and Their Acquisition.* Hillsdale, N.J.: Erlbaum Associates.

NEWELL, A. 1972. A theoretical exploration of mechanisms for coding the stimulus. In A. W. Melton and E. Martin, eds., *Coding Processes in Human Memory.* Washington: Winston.

———— 1973. Production systems: models of control structures. In W. G. Chase, ed., *Visual Information Processing.* New York: Academic Press.

———— 1980a. HARPY, production systems, and human cognition. In R. A. Cole, ed., *Perception and Production of Fluent Speech.* Hillsdale, N.J.: Erlbaum Associates.

———— 1980b. Reasoning, problem-solving, and decision processes: the problem space as a fundamental category. In R. Nickerson, ed., *Attention and Performance VIII.* Hillsdale, N.J.: Erlbaum Associates.

NEWELL, A., and MCDERMOTT, J. 1975. *The PSG Manual.* Department of computer science, Carnegie-Mellon University.

NEWELL, A., and ROSENBLOOM, P. 1981. Mechanisms of skill acquisition and the law of practice. In J. R. Anderson, ed., *Cognitive Skills and Their Acquisition.* Hillsdale, N.J.: Erlbaum Associates.

NEWELL, A., and SIMON, H. A. 1972. *Human Problem Solving.* Englewood Cliffs, N.J.: Prentice-Hall.

NORMAN, D. A. 1981. Categorization of action slips. *Psychological Review* 88, 1–15.

NORMAN, D. A., and RUMELHART, D. E. 1975. *Explorations in Cognition.* San Francisco: Freeman.

OHLSSON, S. 1977. Production system reconstruction of theories for the solving of three-term series problems. *Umea Psychological Reports,* no. 133, department of psychology, University of Umea.

——— 1980. A possible path to expertise in the three-term series problem. Working paper from the cognitive seminar, no. 10, University of Stockholm.

ORNSTEIN, R. E. 1969. *On the Experience of Time.* Baltimore: Penguin Books.

OWENS, J., BOWER, G. H., and BLACK, J. B. 1979. The "soap opera" effect in story recall. *Memory and Cognition* 7, 185–191.

PAIVIO, A. 1971. *Imagery and Verbal Processes.* New York: Holt, Rinehart and Winston.

——— 1975. Perceptual comparisons through the mind's eye. *Memory and Cognition* 3, 635–647.

PALMER, S. E. 1975. Visual perception and world knowledge: notes on a model of sensory-cognitive interaction. In D. A. Norman and D. E. Rumelhart, eds., *Explorations in Cognition.* San Francisco: Freeman.

——— 1977. Hierarchical structure in perceptual representation. *Cognitive Psychology* 9, 441–474.

PETRETIC, P. A., and TWENEY, R. D. 1977. Does comprehension precede production? The development of children's responses to telegraphic sentences of varying grammatical adequacy. *Journal of Child Language* 4, 201–209.

PINKER, S., and LEBEAUX, D. n.d. A learnability-theoretic approach to children's language. Cambridge, Mass.: Harvard University Press. Forthcoming.

POSNER, M. I. 1967. Characteristics of visual and kinesthetic codes. *Journal of Experimental Psychology* 75, 103–107.

——— 1973. *Cognition: An Introduction.* Glenview, Ill.: Scott, Foresman.

——— 1978. *Chronometric Explorations of Mind.* Hillsdale, N.J.: Erlbaum Associates.

POSNER, M. I., and KEELE, S. W. 1970. Retention of abstract ideas. *Journal of Experimental Psychology* 83, 304–308.

POSNER, M. I., and SNYDER, C. R. R. 1975. Attention and cognitive control. In R. L. Solso, ed., *Information Processing and Cognition.* Hillsdale, N.J.: Erlbaum Associates.

POST, E. L. 1943. Formal reductions of the general combinatorial decision problem. *American Journal of Mathematics* 65, 197–268.

POSTMAN, L. 1964. Short-term memory and incidental learning. In A. W. Melton, ed., *Categories of Human Learning*. New York: Academic Press.

POTTS, G. R. 1972. Information processing strategies used in the encoding of linear orderings. *Journal of Verbal Learning and Verbal Behavior* 11, 727–740.

———— 1975. Bringing order to cognitive structures. In F. Restle, R. M. Shiffrin, N. J. Castellan, H. R. Lindman, and D. B. Pisoni, eds., *Cognitive Theory*, vol. 1. Hillsdale, N.J.: Erlbaum Associates.

PYLYSHYN, Z. W. 1973. What the mind's eye tells the mind's brain: a critique of mental imagery. *Psychological Bulletin* 80, 1–24.

———— 1979. The rate of "mental rotation" of images: a test of a holistic analogue hypothesis. *Memory and Cognition* 7, 19–28.

QUILLIAN, M. R. 1969. The teachable language comprehender. *Communications of the ACM* 12, 459–476.

RABINOWITZ, J. C., MANDLER, G., and BARSALOW, L. W. 1977. Recognition failure: another case of retrieval failure. *Journal of Verbal Learning and Verbal Behavior* 16, 639–663.

RATCLIFF, R. 1978. A theory of memory retrieval. *Psychological Review* 85, 59–108.

RATCLIFF, R., and MCKOON, G. 1981. Does activation really spread? *Psychological Review* 88, 454–457.

REDDY, D. R., ERMAN, L. D., FENNEL, R. D., and NEELY, R. B. 1973. The HEARSAY-II speech understanding system: An example of the recognition process. *Proceedings of the International Joint Conference on Artificial Intelligence*, Stanford: 185–194.

REDER, L. M. 1979. The role of elaborations in memory for prose. *Cognitive Psychology* 11, 221–234.

———— 1980. The role of elaboration in the comprehension and retention of prose. *Review of Educational Research* 50, 5–53.

———— 1982. Plausibility judgment versus fact retrieval: alternative strategies for sentence verification. *Psychological Review* 89, 250–280.

———— 1983. What kind of pitcher can a catcher fill? Effects of priming in sentence comprehension. *Journal of Verbal Learning and Verbal Behavior*. In press.

REDER, L. M., and ANDERSON, J. R. 1980a. A comparison of texts and their summaries: memorial consequences. *Journal of Verbal Learning and Verbal Behavior* 19, 121–134.

———— 1980b. A partial resolution of the paradox of interference: the role of integrating knowledge. *Cognitive Psychology* 12, 447–472.

REDER, L. M., ANDERSON, J. R., and BJORK, R. A. 1974. A semantic interpretation of encoding specificity. *Journal of Experimental Psychology* 102, 648–656.

REDER, L. M., and ROSS, B. H. 1983. Integrated knowledge in different tasks: positive and negative fan effects. *Journal of Experimental Psychology: Human Learning, Memory, and Cognition* 9, 55–72.

REED, S. K. 1974. Structural descriptions and the limitations of visual images. *Memory and Cognition* 2, 329–336.

REICHER, G. 1969. Perceptual recognition as a function of meaningfulness of stimulus material. *Journal of Experimental Psychology* 81, 275–280.

REITMAN, J. S. 1971. Mechanisms of forgetting in short-term memory. *Cognitive Psychology* 2, 185–195.

———— 1974. Without surreptitious rehearsal, information in short-term memory decays. *Journal of Verbal Learning and Verbal Behavior* 13, 365–377.

———— 1976. Skilled perception in GO: deducing memory structures from inter-response times. *Cognitive Psychology* 8, 336–356.

RIPS, L. J. 1975. Quantification and semantic memory. *Cognitive Psychology* 7, 307–340.

ROBINSON, J. A. 1965. A machine-oriented logic based on the resolution principle. *Journal of the ACM* 12, 23–41.

ROSCH, E., and MERVIS, C. B. 1975. Family resemblances: studies in the internal structure of categories. *Cognitive Psychology* 7, 573–605.

ROSENBLOOM, P. S., and NEWELL, A. 1983. Learning by chunking: a production-system model of practice. In D. Klahr, P. Langley, and D. Neches, eds., *Self-modifying Production System Models of Learning and Development*. Cambridge, Mass.: Bradford Books/MIT Press. In press.

ROSS, J. R. 1967. Constraints on variables in syntax. Doctoral dissertation, Massachusetts Institute of Technology.

RUMELHART, D. E. 1977. *An Introduction to Human Information Processing*. New York: Wiley.

———— 1978. Understanding and summarizing brief stories. In D. LaBerge and J. Samuels, eds., *Basic Processes in Reading: Perception and Comprehension*. Hillsdale, N.J.: Erlbaum Associates.

RUMELHART, D. E., LINDSAY, P., and NORMAN, D. A. 1972. A process model for long-term memory. In E. Tulving and W. Donaldson, eds., *Organization of Memory*. New York: Academic Press.

RUMELHART, D. E., and MCCLELLAND, J. L. 1982. An interactive activation model of context effects in letter perception: pt. 2. The contextual enhancement effect and some tests and extensions of the model. *Psychological Review* 89, 60–94.

RUMELHART, D. E., and NORMAN, D. A. 1978. Accretion, tuning, and restructuring: three modes of learning. In J. W. Cotton and R. Klatzky, eds., *Semantic Factors in Cognition*. Hillsdale, N.J.: Erlbaum Associates.

———— 1981. Analogical processes in learning. In J. R. Anderson, ed., *Cognitive Skills and Their Acquisition*. Hillsdale, N.J.: Erlbaum Associates.

———— 1982. Simulating a skilled typist: a study of skilled cognitive-motor performance. *Cognitive Science* 6, 1–36.

RUMELHART, D. E., and ORTONY, A. 1976. The representation of knowledge in memory. In R. C. Anderson, R. J. Spiro, and W. E.

Montague, eds., *Schooling and the Acquisition of Knowledge*. Hillsdale, N.J.: Erlbaum Associates.

RYCHENER, M. D. 1981. Approaches to knowledge acquisition: the instructible production system project. Unpublished manuscript, Carnegie-Mellon University.

RYCHENER, M. D., and NEWELL, A. 1978. An instructible production system: basic design issues. In D. A. Waterman and F. Hayes-Roth, eds., *Pattern-Directed Inference Systems*. New York: Academic Press.

SACERDOTI, E. D. 1977. *A Structure for Plans and Behavior*. New York: Elsevier North-Holland.

SACHS, J. 1967. Recognition memory for syntactic and semantic aspects of connected discourse. *Perception and Psychophysics* 2, 437–442.

SANTA, J. L. 1977. Spatial transformations of words and pictures. *Journal of Experimental Psychology: Human Learning and Memory* 3, 418–427.

SCHANK, R. C. 1972. Conceptual dependency: a theory of natural language understanding. *Cognitive Psychology* 3, 552–631.

———— 1980. Language and memory. *Cognitive Science* 4, 243–284.

SCHANK, R. C., and ABELSON, R. P. 1977. *Scripts, Plans, Goals, and Understanding: An Inquiry into Human Knowledge Structures*. Hillsdale, N.J.: Erlbaum Associates.

SCHANK, R. C., and BIRNBAUM, L. Memory, meaning and syntax. In J. Carroll and L. Miller, eds., *Talking Minds: The Study of Language and Cognitive Sciences*. MIT Press. In Press.

SCHNEIDER, W., and SHIFFRIN, R. M. 1977. Controlled and automatic human information processing. I. Detection, search, and attention. *Psychological Review* 84, 1–66.

SCHUSTACK, M. W. 1979. Task-dependency in children's use of linguistic rules. Paper presented at the annual meeting of the Psychonomic Society, Phoenix, Ariz.

———— 1981. Word-meaning comprehension: syntactic and associative effects of sentential context. Doctoral dissertation, Carnegie-Mellon University.

SCHUSTACK, M. W., and ANDERSON, J. R. 1979. Effects of analogy to prior knowledge on memory for new information. *Journal of Verbal Learning and Verbal Behavior* 18, 565–583.

SEJNOWSKI, T. J. 1981. Skeleton filters in the brain. In G. E. Hinton and J. A. Anderson, eds., *Parallel Models of Associative Memory*. Hillsdale, N.J.: Erlbaum Associates.

SELFRIDGE, M. 1981. A computer model of child language acquisition. *Proceedings of International Joint Conference on Artificial Intelligence* 92–96.

SEYMOUR, P. H. K. 1977. Conceptual encoding and locus of the Stroop effect. *Quarterly Journal of Experimental Psychology* 29, 245–268.

SHEPARD, R. N., and METZLER, J. 1971. Mental rotation of three-dimensional objects. *Science* 171, 701–703.

SHIFFRIN, R. M. 1973. Information persistence in short-term memory. *Journal of Experimental Psychology* 100, 39–49.

——— 1975. Short-term store: the basis for a memory system. In F. Restle, R. M. Shiffrin, N. J. Castellan, H. R. Lindman, and D. B. Pisoni, eds., *Cognitive Theory*, vol. 1. Hillsdale, N.J.: Erlbaum Associates.

SHIFFRIN, R. M., and DUMAIS, S. T. 1981. The development of automatism. In J. R. Anderson, ed., *Cognitive Skills and Their Acquisition*. Hillsdale, N.J.: Erlbaum Associates.

SHIFFRIN, R. M., and SCHNEIDER, W. 1977. Controlled and automatic human information processing. II. Perceptual learning, automatic attending, and a general theory. *Psychological Review* 84, 127–190.

SHORTLIFFE, E. H. 1976. *Computer-Based Medical Consultations: MYCIN*. New York: Elsevier North-Holland.

SHWARTZ, S. P. 1980. Mental image size and rotation speed: evidence for quasi-pictorial visual images. Unpublished manuscript.

SIMON, H. A. 1974. How big is a chunk? *Science* 83, 482–488.

——— 1975. The functional equivalence of problem solving skills. *Cognitive Psychology* 7, 268–288.

——— 1978. On forms of mental representation. In C. Wade Savage, ed., *Perception and Cognition: Issues in the Foundation of Psychology*, vol. 9. Minnesota Studies on the Philosophy of Science. Minneapolis: University of Minnesota Press.

SIMON, H. A., and FEIGENBAUM, E. A. 1964. An information-processing theory of some effects of similarity, familiarity, and meaningfulness in verbal learning. *Journal of Verbal Learning and Verbal Behavior* 3, 385–396.

SIMON, H. A., and GILMARTIN, K. 1973. A simulation of memory for chess positions. *Cognitive Psychology* 5, 29–46.

SLOBIN, D. I. 1973. Cognitive prerequisites for the development of grammar. In C. A. Ferguson and D. I. Slobin, eds., *Studies of Child Language Development*, 175–208. New York: Holt, Rinehart and Winston.

SMITH, E. E., ADAMS, N., and SCHORR, D. 1978. Fact retrieval and the paradox of interference. *Cognitive Psychology* 10, 438–464.

STERNBERG, S. 1969. Memory scanning: mental processes revealed by reaction time experiments. *American Scientist* 57, 421–457.

STEVENS, A., and COUPE, P. 1978. Distortions in judged spatial relations. *Cognitive Psychology* 10, 422–437.

STIRLING, N. 1979. Stroop interference: an input and an output phenomenon. *Quarterly Journal of Experimental Psychology* 31, 121–132.

SULIN, R. A., and DOOLING, D. J. 1974. Intrusion of a thematic idea in retention of prose. *Journal of Experimental Psychology* 103, 255–262.

SWINNEY, D. A. 1979. Lexical access during sentence comprehension: (re)consideration of context effects. *Journal of Verbal Learning and Verbal Behavior* 18, 645–659.

TEITLEMAN, W. 1976. *INTERLISP reference manual*. Xerox Palo Alto Research Center.

THORNDIKE, E. L. 1932. *The Fundamentals of Learning*. New York: Teachers College.

———— 1935. *The Psychology of Wants, Interests, and Attitudes.* New York: Appleton-Century-Crofts.

THORNDYKE, P. W. 1977. Cognitive structures in comprehension and memory of narrative discourse. *Cognitive Psychology* 9, 77–110.

THORNDYKE, P. W., and BOWER, G. H. 1974. Storage and retrieval processes in sentence memory. *Cognitive Psychology* 6, 515–543.

TOWNSEND, J. T. 1974. Issues and models concerning the processing of a finite number of inputs. In G. H. Kantowitz, ed., *Human Information Processing: Tutorials in Performance and Cognition.* Hillsdale, N.J.: Erlbaum Associates.

TRABASSO, T., and RILEY, C. A. 1975. The construction and use of representations involving linear order. In R. L. Solso, ed., *Information Processing and Cognition.* Hillsdale, N.J.: Erlbaum Associates.

TULVING, E., and THOMPSON, D. M. 1971. Retrieval processes in recognition memory: effects of associative context. *Journal of Experimental Psychology* 87, 116–124.

TULVING, E., and WATKINS, O. C. 1977. Recognition failure of words with a single meaning. *Memory and Cognition* 5, 513–522.

TZENG, O. J. L. 1973. Stimulus meaningfulness, encoding variability, and the spacing effect. *Journal of Experimental Psychology* 99, 162–166.

UNDERWOOD, B. J., and HUMPHREYS, M. 1979. Content change and the role of meaning in word recognition. *American Journal of Psychology* 92, 577–609.

UNDERWOOD, B. J., and KEPPEL, G. 1962. One-trial learning. *Journal of Verbal Learning and Verbal Behavior* 1, 1–13.

VENDLER, Z. 1968. *Adjectives and Nominalizations.* The Hague: Mouton.

VERE, S. A. 1977. Induction of relational productions in the presence of background information. *Proceedings of the Fifth International Joint Conference on Artificial Intelligence*, 349–355. Boston.

WALLACH, H., and AVERBACH, E. 1955. On memory modalities. *American Journal of Psychology* 68, 249–257.

WANNER, H. E. 1968. On remembering, forgetting, and understanding sentences: a study of the deep structure hypothesis. Doctoral dissertation, Harvard University.

WARREN, R. E. 1974. Association, direction, and stimulus encoding. *Journal of Experimental Psychology* 102, 151–158.

———— 1977. Time and the spread of activation in memory. *Journal of Experimental Psychology: Learning and Memory* 3, 458–466.

WATERMAN, D. A. 1970. Generalization learning techniques for automating the learning of heuristics. *Artificial Intelligence* 1, 121–170.

———— 1974. Adaptive production systems. CIP working paper no. 285, psychology department, Carnegie-Mellon University.

———— 1975. Serial pattern acquisition: a production system approach. CIP working paper no. 286, psychology department, Carnegie-Mellon University.

WATERMAN, D. A., and HAYES-ROTH, F. 1978. *Pattern-Directed Inference Systems.* New York: Academic Press.

WATKINS, M. J., and TULVING, E. 1975. Episodic memory: when recognition fails. *Journal of Experimental Psychology: General* 104, 5–29.

WEXLER, K., and CULICOVER, P. 1980. *Formal Principles of Language Acquisition.* Cambridge, Mass.: MIT Press.

WHEELER, D. D. 1970. Processes in word recognition. *Cognitive Psychology* 1, 59–85.

WICKELGREN, W. A. 1976a. Network strength theory of storage and retrieval dynamics. *Psychological Review* 83, 466–478.

———— 1976b. Memory storage dynamics. In W. K. Estes, ed., *Handbook of Learning and Cognitive Processes*, vol. 4. Hillsdale, N.J.: Erlbaum Associates.

———— 1979. Chunking and consolidation: a theoretical synthesis of semantic networks, configuring in conditioning, S-R versus cognitive learning, normal forgetting, the amnesic syndrome, and the hippocampal arousal system. *Psychological Review* 86, 44–60.

WINSTON, P. H. 1970. Learning structural descriptions from examples. MIT Artificial Intelligence Laboratory Project AI-TR-231.

WISEMAN, S., and TULVING, E. 1976. Encoding specificity: relation between recall superiority and recognition failure. *Journal of Experimental Psychology: Human Learning and Memory* 2, 349–361.

WOLFORD, G. 1971. Function of distinct associations for paired-associate performance. *Psychological Review* 73, 303–313.

WOLLEN, K., ALLISON, T., and LOWRY, D. 1969. Associative symmetry versus independent association. *Journal of Verbal Learning and Verbal Behavior* 8, 283–288.

WOOCHER, F. D., GLASS, A. L., and HOLYOAK, K. J. 1978. Positional discriminability in linear orderings. *Memory and Cognition* 6, 165–174.

WOODS, W. A. 1970. Transition network grammars for natural language analysis. *Communications of the ACM* 13, 591–606.

WOODWARD, A. E., BJORK, R. A., and JONGEWARD, R. H. 1973. Recall and recognition as a function of primary rehearsal. *Journal of Verbal Learning and Verbal Behavior* 12, 608–617.

YOUNG, R. K. 1968. Serial learning. In T. R. Dixon and D. L. Horton, eds., *Verbal Learning and General Behavior Theory.* Englewood Cliffs, N.J.: Prentice-Hall.

# Index of Authors

Abelson, R. P., 2, 36, 37, 38, 79, 209
Adams, N., 177
Allen, T. W., 172
Allison, T., 191
Anderson, J. A., 15, 27, 35, 36, 119
Anderson, J. R., 6, 13, 15, 17, 18, 23, 27, 38, 39, 45, 46, 49, 52, 59, 70, 71, 72, 74, 76, 78, 79, 80, 86, 87, 96, 107, 111, 112, 113, 114, 116, 120, 128, 135, 143, 145, 164, 175, 177–180, 181, 185, 190, 191–192, 194, 196, 197, 198–199, 200, 203, 205, 206, 207, 224, 226, 235, 237, 238–239, 241, 243, 244, 249, 253, 254, 255, 268, 269, 270, 272, 273, 275, 278, 284, 292
Anderson, R. C., 72, 78
Anderson, R. E., 51
Angiolillio-Bent, J. S., 52–53
Atkinson, R. C., 14, 189
Atwood, D. W., 52
Atwood, M. E., 7

Baddeley, A. D., 23–25, 29, 119, 120
Baillet, S. D., 187
Barclay, J. R., 199
Barsalou, L. W., 196

Bartling, C. A., 196
Beasley, C. M., 17, 38, 241, 243, 244, 254
Becker, C. A., 96, 104
Begg, I., 70, 75
Bellugi, U., 268
Bigler, K., 181
Birnbaum, L., 5
Birnbaum, M., 275
Bjork, R. A., 172, 192, 194, 196
Black, J. B., 78, 199, 205–206, 207
Blaha, J., 237
Bloom, L. M., 294
Bloom, P. A., 96, 102, 104
Bobrow, D. G., 2, 36
Bookin, H. B., 113
Boring, E. G., 2
Bovair, S., 7
Bower, G. H., 7, 18, 23, 46, 49, 59, 70, 71, 72, 76, 78, 79, 87, 107, 120, 190, 191–192, 199, 200, 203–204, 205–206, 207
Bradshaw, G. L., 207
Braine, M. D. S., 294
Bransford, J. D., 38, 70, 133, 199, 254
Bregman, A. S., 273
Briggs, G. E., 120, 237
Broadbent, D. E., 25, 49, 76–77, 119
Brown, J. S., 7, 12, 137
Brown, R., 268

335

# General Index

Abstract propositions: construction, 75; encoding process, 69–71; function, 75–76; pattern matching, 73–75; storage and retrieval, 72–73, 76; versus string representations, 49–51. *See also* Connectedness judgments; Representational types

Acquisition of productions, *see* Learning

ACT: as a framework, 19–20; assumptions of ACT*, 20–35; assumptions of ACTE, 24; history, 17–19; overview, 17. *See also* Production systems

Activation, 26–27, 86–125; decay, 28, 29, 104; in priming paradigm, 96–106; interaction with pattern matching, 105, 111, 116–117, 150–151, 155; source nodes, 28–29, 89–90, 93–95, 114–116, 156, 157; spread, 28, 92–96, 121–125. *See also* Fact retrieval paradigm; Goal structures; Memory; Pattern matching; Working memory

Analogy, 209–214, 226–230

A-over-A constraint, 302–305

Associations, *see* Abstract propositions; Activation; Knowledge representation; Network

Associative relatedness, *see* connectedness judgments

Attention, 156–157. *See also* Automatization; Goal structures; Priming paradigm

Automaticity, *see* Automatization; Priming paradigm

Automatization, 34, 127, 237, 267

Bottom-up processing, *see* Topdown processing versus bottom-up processing

Cognitive units, 23, 76–78, 91–92, 171–176. *See also* Knowledge representation

Compilation, *see* Knowledge representation

Composition, *see* Knowledge compilation

Computer programming, 4–5. *See also* LISP programming

Concept formation, *see* Prototype formation

Conflict resolution, 21, 126–170; data refractoriness, 134–135, 151–152; degree of match, 132–133, 151; goal dominance, 136–137, 156–157; in neoclassical system, 15–16; production strength, 133–134; speci-